Dy... Alone!

W/D

'*Ma, He Sold Me for a Few Cigarettes*, by Martha Long, is without question the most harrowing tale I have ever read. Even Charles Dickens, whom we appreciate for being the voice of so many abused children, is left in the dust. Why? Because Dickens was writing about abused children, while Martha Long was herself abused, horribly, unbelievably, by her mother's "man" and by her own mother. Managing to stay alive, only just, by her own wits, in a world determined to erase her life and to make her believe, in her very soul, that she is nothing. It is a hair-raising read.

'That it is a bestseller in Ireland and England gives me hope. Martha Long is not being abandoned again. Still, it is so difficult to read one might ask: Why should we bother? We must bother because it begins to show us the deeper, perhaps most elemental source of our world's despair: the chronic, horrific, sustained abuse of children. Especially those children who, unwittingly, inherit the brutalities of colonialism, whether in Ireland, where this story is set, or the rest of the globe. I was amazed to feel some of the English, Irish, Scottish ancestors of both enslaved Africans and indentured Europeans (in the Americas) showing up in the characters of the Dubliners Martha Long depicts. There they are, in a Dublin slum in the 1950s, yes (Martha Long's childhood city), but recognisable as the same twisted beings who made life hell on earth for millions of people over the course of numerous centuries. And who, some of them, unfortunately, still walk among us.

'As I read this book I thought: This is exactly why they've kept women ignorant for so long; why they haven't wanted us to learn to read and write. "They" (you can fill this in) knew that we would tell our stories from our point of view and that all the terrible things done to us against our will would be exposed, and that we would free ourselves from controlling pretensions, half-truths and lies.

'The destruction of our common humanity through the manipulation of imposed poverty, misogyny, alcoholism and drug abuse is a major source of our misery, worldwide, and has been for a long time. Reading this startling testament to one child's valiant attempts to live until the age of sixteen (four years to go!) is a worthy reminder that we can do better as adults if we turn to embrace the children who are suffering, anywhere on earth, who are coming towards us, their numbers increasing daily, for help.'

Ma, Jackser's Dyin Alone

MARTHA LONG

MAINSTREAM
PUBLISHING

EDINBURGH AND LONDON

Copyright © Martha Long, 2013

First published in Great Britain in 2013 by
MAINSTREAM PUBLISHING COMPANY
(EDINBURGH) LTD
7 Albany Street
Edinburgh EH1 3UG

ISBN 9781780576770

A catalogue record for this book is available
from the British Library

Printed in Great Britain by
CPI Group (UK) Ltd, Croydon, CR0 4YY

1 3 5 7 9 10 8 6 4 2

To my children, every breath I take is for you.

Kathleen O'Donoghue, there is me, and so many, many others greatly indebted to you.

Fidelma, Mary, Rita, Teresa, Victoria (Vicki)
    Gone, but you are not forgotten.
    May you rest in peace.

Ronan O'Neill, a great friend and 'A Man For All Seasons'.

Donal L. A man who will look kindly and reach you a helping hand. He's simply built that way and put on this earth just so we know life is worth living.

Victor! We need you, the working man's hero! Get thee to the Dail! I'm right behind you!

Finally, I hope T.G. will find the way back.
    The night is drawing in; it is almost the closing of the day.
    Soon, there will be no more tomorrows.
    Until then, I will be waiting.

Also by Martha Long

Ma, He Sold Me for a Few Cigarettes
Ma, I'm Gettin Meself a New Mammy
Ma, It's a Cold Aul Night an I'm Lookin for a Bed
Ma, Now I'm Goin Up in the World
Ma, I've Got Meself Locked Up in the Mad House
Ma, I've Reached for the Moon an I'm Hittin the Stars

ACKNOWLEDGEMENTS

To Bill Campbell and Peter MacKenzie. Their name legendary, their success only a publisher's dream, but they made it! Oh, they did! They had vision when everyone else was blind. Sure, ask me! Well! . . . *Ma, He Sold Me?* For a short while that book was doing the rounds and publishers were probably using it for arse paper! Oh! They went mad when it dawned on them they had been shitting on a gold mine.

Yes, Mainstream were the best. No wonder Random House had to step in – oh, they did! And put a stop to their gallop by making them an offer they couldn't refuse. Mainstream? They were putting too much of a dent in their share of the market! Bestsellers! Bestsellers and more bestsellers! Sure, didn't they make my books a bestseller over and over again?! Now the 'Ma' series is getting read in deepest Africa, finding its way out into the Australian outback . . . the bush! Only Mainstream, them two geniuses, Bill and Peter, could do that.

Now they're bowing out and taking that old world of all that was good and great in the publishing world. Their like will never be seen again. Oh, it scalds my heart! God, I will miss them!

I will miss too all at Mainstream. Bill and Peter had the incredible knack of getting only the most competent, the most gifted to work with them. Once in, there they stayed. It was a tight little community . . . family. No one wanted to leave.

Fiona Brownlee, their 'right-arm' woman. Nothing she couldn't do! Sell rights, sell you! Sell your books! PR second to none! Sure, why wouldn't she be so successful?! Wasn't she steeped in charm, charisma, stunning good looks?!

Jaysus, the angels must have been drunk, having a party, when she was born. They showered her with all the gifts a body could want to make women hate her . . . Funnily enough they don't! No!! And men kill just to have her favour. It's the sapphire-blue eyes! Yeah, that and the killer smile, but then the eye travels to the hair! Gorgeous blonde! Anyway, if David Cameron was bright enough, and lucky, she could be making her way there now, to become his next spin doctor!

Ailsa Bathgate! My wonderful Ailsa. My editor! Look! She is the kind of editor Hemmingway, Joyce, O'Casey, G.B. Shaw would demand and get because they were the best, and only the best can demand that calibre of editor. Ailsa is the best! There is no one to match her the length and breadth of the British Isles. We authors, I, was so lucky to have her.

Graeme Blaikie, editorial coordinator, quietly and calmly he goes about his Trojan work, but he gets it done. His gentle words of kindness and encouragement when all around me was losing their head. He kept me going.

Seonaid MacLeod in contracts, that girl should be awarded a doctorate in law for publishing contracts . . . sniff! You couldn't get one up on her! Ah! But she was great for the laughs! And if we can laugh we are living mighty well!

Douglas Nicoll in accounts! Old-school accountant, time for a chat and make sure every penny due came to you.

Amanda Fisher, production assistant, full of youth and bloom – she is like a breath of fresh air! Reminds me every time I speak to her of my sunshine days filled with hope and full of expectation.

Then there is Francesca Dymond, the beautiful actress, been on many a TV soap! The gorgeous voice at the other end of the Mainstream Publishing phone. Wonderful tonic just to listen to her cheerful wit, her kind willingness to help – do anything to oblige, our Francesca.

Ah, finally, Neil, the ghost of Mainstream. He hides himself away from us authors, buried deep in the bowels of production. No, I never spoke to him. My loss.

So, to all of you! May you prosper and go from strength to strength. I wish you good health and happiness, and thank you all for your kindness to me. You all kept me going in your own unique and, yes, Mainstream publishing way. I will miss you all sorely.

Adieu!

AUTHOR'S NOTE

A word to the reader: this is the last book ending the 'Ma' series. This journey may be the end for you, but for me it was only the prelude to the beginning. It marked the first step I would take in beginning a long journey that started with *Ma, He Sold Me for a Few Cigarettes*. This final book, *Ma, Jackser's Dyin Alone*, is the first time I would dare to go back and glimpse behind hidden doors where my childhood lay in darkness waiting for my return.

So, this may be old news to you – you have met little Martha and know her well. But I am only meeting her for the first time in decades. The wheel has turned full circle. Jackser is dying and fate has thrown us together again. The buried child in me is stirring and she will not be quiet. She senses our time has come. Jackser and I must take our final journey together. It is a time to die and a time to be born.

I

I crawled in behind a huge juggernaut delivery truck with more cars and trucks steaming up behind me. Oh, bloody hell! What have I done? Me eyeballs flew around like heat-seeking missiles looking for a parking spot. Suddenly I jammed on the brakes and swivelled my neck with all systems on alert, then leapt into action as a taxi pulled out. I reversed in a puff of smoke, bombing into the parking spot just as a black BMW readied itself to leap in. Then I dived out and tore around to open the boot of the car, leaving it wide open as an ear-piercing roar came from behind me.

'Eh, you! That's my parking spot! I was waiting to get in there!'

My head shot to the BMW, seeing a white-faced fella with steam coming out of his ears glaring at me. I grinned, lifting me thumb and winked at him. 'Better luck next time, matey! Get yourself a faster car like mine!' I said, stroking big Bertha, giving her a loving rub.

'Jesus! I'll be done for you!' he snarled, swinging the head around, getting ready to jump out.

Suddenly there was a blast of horns, with agitated screams coming from the pile-up he was causing.

'See ya!' I waved happily, as he moved off with the mouth flapping up and down, cursing me to hell.

Right, any sign of Hitler? No, no sign of the pint-sized midget with the beady little eyes, I thought, flying me head around looking for sight of the shite-looking brown uniform with the matching hat. Last time, the little runt nearly had me arrested. Lying sod said I assaulted him when I only belted him on the hat with the rolled-up parking ticket.

Suddenly a gust of wind whipped the back of me legs as a roar went through me head. I moved so fast I nearly ended up in the boot of me car.

'You bloody bastard!' I screamed with the fright as a truck inched past with the driver hammering hell out of his horn. He was making for the unloading bay, but an aul one in a battered old two-seater silver Mercedes sports car beat him to it.

I watched as the truck kept going, looking now to mow down the biddy in her sports job. Then he heaved to a stop with the air brakes moaning and keening, blocking her in solid, leaving her trapped.

She erupted. 'You stupid brute of a man! You have blocked me in! How dare you?! Move that monstrosity out of my way at once!' she screeched, hanging her head out the window, chomping on her gums with the rage on her.

Oh, this is good, I grinned, seeing him tear open the truck door then leap down, steaming over to do battle. She grabbed hold of her squashed felt hat. It had fruit dangling on top and now the lot collapsed, blinding her right eye. She watched him coming through the left eye and flew her head back in, locking the window. Madness! Pity I have to miss it, I grinned, making for the shopping centre.

I whipped into the supermarket, making straight for the reception desk then around the counter, seeing my trolley still sitting stuffed with the week's shopping. Good, no one robbed it, seeing as it's bought and paid for!

I grabbed it, saying, 'I'm back, Bernie! Thanks for minding the shopping. I'm off!' I puffed in me hurry, gasping to the blonde with her head buried under the counter. She lifted it, giving me a big grin with the baby-blue eyes dancing in her head.

'Uh-oh! Looks like you're just in time,' Bernie muttered, as her eyes landed on something. 'Don't look now, but guess who's coming?'

Me head swivelled just in time to see 'Hitler' making his way for the exit. Then I spotted a very angry-looking aul fella with a roaring-red face and a flat nose waving a parking ticket. We watched as he leapt out in front of Hitler, shouting, 'Here, you! What the fuck's all this about? You can wipe your arse with that!' he screamed, slamming the ticket against Hitler's chest, creasing his lovely brown uniform.

Hitler stopped dead, making his six chins wobble. 'Get yer hands offa me! Or I'll have you done for assault!' screamed Hitler.

I shook my head slowly. 'That little aul fella is very vicious. He loves his job too much. Only last week he gave me two tickets in one go!' I said, feeling the heart still hammer with the rage. 'This place won't last if they don't get rid of him. You'll be back, Bernie, looking for your old job in the other centre,' I said, thinking, this place is a nightmare.

She grinned, saying, 'Well, let's hope he's picked the wrong one this time. Looks like there's going to be murder!' She whispered, letting the excitement dance in her head. Then she peeled her eyes off him to me, saying, 'One of these days someone is going to kill that little aul fella. Everybody around here knows where he lives.'

'Well, if someone wants to put out a contract on him, I'll take it!' I grinned, getting the lovely picture of setting fire to Hitler's arse. He must have been in having his tea break. That's how I managed to get myself parked right smack outside the entrance.

'Right! I'm off, Bernie! Might see you next week,' I croaked, spinning the trolley in the direction of the exit, then taking in a sharp breath, trying to get my wind back.

'Mind yourself!' she shouted after me, seeing me take off, aiming the trolley straight for Hitler's arse. Nope, not yet, Martha. On the way back with the empty trolley, then you can make a fast escape.

I took off flying back in with the empty trolley, rushing to get me money back. I zigzagged around a crowd jamming Hitler up against the wall.

'I knew ye when ye drank in me local pub after collecting yer dole money! Now look at ye! Actin the big man!' an aul one screamed, trying to hit him with her handbag.

I was still flying, grinning and looking back, when I went smack bang into a 'New-Age husband' manly strutting his stuff as he steamed through the crowd, making a path for his full shopping trolley. My trolley kept going, straight into a stack of special-offer baby nappies, sending the lot crashing down, smothering the head of a poor aul unfortunate pensioner. I keeled over, getting wrapped around something warm and furry. Where am I?

When I untangled meself, I was looking into the face of a big, black, hairy Newfoundland dog. It was waiting very patiently, sitting next to its owner while she rattled a box under the noses of shoppers, hoping to make a few bob for the animal shelter. The dog stared back mournfully, looking at me with big, sad, chocolate-brown eyes, wondering where I just landed from.

'You dozy cow!' roared the eegit after sending me flying. I looked up to see the long string of misery brushing back his thin, wispy hair floating around his baldy head, with the long, skinny legs hanging under a huge pair of curtains – he probably called them Bermudas.

'You blind, four-eyed, baldy gobshite! Look what you just done!' I screamed, still sitting on the dog.

'Help! I'm suffocating!' shouted the old woman, buried under the boxes.

'Get up offa me dog!' screamed the woman behind me, giving me a dig.

'You call yourself a man?' I shouted, leppin to me feet, flying to face the fucker. 'Get home to your kitchen! The wife will be in from work looking for her dinner, you bleedin Nancy boy!' I shouted, losing the rag and sending the trolley flying, slapping him right smack in the belly.

'Get the police! Send for the police! I've just been assaulted!' he shouted, looking around at the crowd for help.

'What's happening?' Bernie puffed, appearing out of nowhere and grabbing me by the arm.

'He nearly killed me!' I screamed, going on the attack as the best method of defence.

'I did no such thing!' he shouted, moving over to snort in me face.

'The police are coming!' someone roared, as we looked to the exit, seeing a police car draw up and three big bull-neck culchie coppers heave, trying to scrape themself out, they were that heavy. They made straight for the row going on with Hitler. The crowd around him was growing and the shouting was hitting the ceiling.

'Quick! Come on,' Bernie said. 'Get out before the lot of youse get arrested!' she hissed, dragging me away as your man snarled, 'You bleedin bitch! What you need is a good ****!' he growled, coming up close beside me and spitting into me face.

I missed the last bit but guessed it anyway. I erupted. 'IS THAT RIGHT NOW?! DO YOU MEAN LIKE YOUR WIFE? SHE GOT SO FED UP WATCHING YOU SEARCHING FOR YOUR LITTLE WORM SHE GRABBED THE NEAREST MAN HANDY!' I screamed, getting pulled away by Bernie.

'Who caused all this?' shouted a fella in a pinstripe suit wearing a badge, as he dug out the old woman from under the boxes.

'He did!' said Bernie, pointing her finger at Four-eyes.

'No! She did!' said the animal woman, waving at me.

'Do you need an ambulance?' said the pinstripe suit, dragging the old woman to her feet.

'No! I just want to get outa here!' she roared, fixing her hat and straightening her coat as he steadied her on her feet.

I looked over, seeing her legs still shaky, and a rage nearly choked me. 'You bloody mutant! Never mind me! Look what you did to that poor old pensioner!' I screamed, picking up a frozen chicken from his trolley and sending it flying at his head.

'Call the police! There's murder being committed!' shouted the animal woman.

'THAT'S IT! I'M HAVING YOU DONE FOR ASSAULT AND BATTERY!' screamed Four-eyes.

'Fuck this, Bernie!' I said, making for the exit. 'I only came in for me shopping, I'm never coming back here again! Where's that manager?' I snorted, looking around me as I flew past the coppers.

'There he is! Over sorting out the riot Hitler caused,' she said as we both looked over, seeing the three coppers trying to break up the crowd and sort out that fight.

'Jesus! I was only going for my tea break when I heard you before I saw you!' she said. 'What happened there?' she puffed.

But I was gone! Heading for my car and bulleting it away, burning the rubber tyres.

Never again! I breathed, snorting out me rage. Brand-new shopping centre my arse. There's nothing to look at! Jaysus! The way that crowd erupted with their tearing and stampeding over each other, you would think the shops were paying everyone to take the stuff away free. Bleedin lunatics! Especially them house husbands! Fuckin wearing aprons and joining the mothers' union. I heard one of them used the Hoover to clean out the hot ashes from the fireplace, then took off to join the mothers for their coffee morning, leaving the smouldering Hoover in the cubbyhole under the stairs. When he got back, the house was burnt to the ground. The insurance wouldn't pay up. They didn't believe anyone could be that stupid!

* * *

Made it! Home sweet home, the shopping done, no parking ticket, flat tyre or a dose of road rage. You get that from the men. They're raging! 'The Missus' or, worse, 'the little woman', has won the revolution for freedom in the battle of the sexes. Now 'She who must be obeyed' has grabbed the car and gone out to work, leaving 'the little man', the husband, to bond with the house, home, hearth and kids. Then she swapped his banger for a new, bigger, faster model. Now the few men still left driving are trying to run us off the road. The only downside is the insurance has gone up because more of us are now getting ourselves killed in these faster models. Pity I wasn't cut out to be a wife, but I'm far too bolshy when a man starts to flex his manly muscles. No, couldn't be doing with that. Sergei and me didn't last five minutes. Russian men are far too raw, macho and militant for me!

'You vill obey!' he told me.

'Yeah,' I said. 'Now, which way would you like to go out the door? On yer feet or head-first through the window?'

But we're still pals . . . well, he's around for the kids. I made sure of that. 'Sergei, to escape me, leave the country; otherwise I will hound you down if you don't come running when them two children shout for their father! Got that?' I growled in me belly.

He laughed and looked down at me, saying, 'The size of you! But I believe, you crazy woman!' he said, straightening himself and pushing out his barrel chest. He's built like a Russian tank!

Grand, so here I am back in one piece. Not just that but I didn't get arrested for causing a riot, and the morning's still early. 'Oh, happy days,' I sang to myself as I switched off the engine, feeling delighted to be home and well out of that.

Gawd, there's nothing like having your own little place to go home to. You can go in and shut the door with no one to bother you or even put you out. Yeah, even after all this time, I still marvel at the wonder of it. No, there's some things you never forget – like hunger or wandering the streets with nowhere to call your own. That sure put a red-hot poker up my arse, the fear of it. I was a driven woman. Yeah, I made up for that with a vengeance, I grinned, leaning over the steering wheel, listening to the quiet. My own bit of paradise carved out of this big wide world, and it's all mine! Me and my own . . .

Well, me and the kids! They were the engine that got me moving. Never would my children ever have a day's want. That's a great encouragement for putting a fire in your belly.

My eyes rested on a corner of the courtyard where there was a statue of a little boy standing pissing down the rocks on a fountain. That's for the kids! Further down the rockery stood a statue of two small children, a boy and a girl. He had his arm protectively around the little girl as she dangled her hand in the running water. The fountain was a blaze of colour, with the flowers fighting to show themselves off. It was one scent getting even better than the next. The sweet pea and William looked like they were winning the battle as they burst down, trying to cover everything in their path. A big old weeping willow stood guard, sheltering it all protectively with its canopy of overhanging leaves. Its companion was a lovely big maple, next to an old cast-iron bench left sitting in the middle. This was for ease and comfort – to let you sit back and enjoy this little bit of heaven.

I opened the car door and walked over to sit down on the bench. Ah, sure, there's no hurry on me. I might as well enjoy myself while I can. 'God, how lucky can you get? What more could I want?' I moaned, closing my eyes and stretching meself for comfort, forgetting all about the shopping baking in the steaming-hot car. I sighed out happily, feeling a lovely sense of peace and contentment wash over me. 'Oh, this is definitely the life,' I snorted, breathing in the heavily scented air as I leant back for comfort. I could hear the rush of the water and feel the heat of the sun with the heavy scents flying up me nostrils. I'll just rest meself here for a minute. Sure, I have all the time in the world. Great idea, Martha! Take it easy.

I woke up feeling me face burning and squinted up to see the sun had moved. Jesus! What time is it? My head flew around trying to make out what happened. The side door was hopping, looking like someone was trying to batter it down. Then I heard the barking.

Ah, holy Jaysus! How could I be so stupid? I leapt up, running for the boot of the car. The meat will be gone off; we'll have no dinner! Oh, curse a Jaysus! Me butter and the ice cream for the kids is well melted by now. They'll probably put that in their news for the teacher tomorrow. Even the milk will be sour! Well now, that's it, Martha. There's no one born yet that can be as stupid as you! You're thick as two short bleedin planks! I snorted, rushing with a mound of plastic bags then trying to lift my hand to open the latch on the side door, leaving a couple of heavy bags clinging to the rest of me shaking fingers.

As the latch went up, the door flew open, letting a hairy ball of wool come flying out. It whizzed between me feet, then leapt back to send me buckling.

'Down, Minnie!' I shouted, giving a roar at the little teddy bear flying past me. Her tiny body wriggled in ecstasy, all delighted to clap eyes on me. 'Ahhh! Did you miss me?' I cooed, feeling my heart melt at the sight of her.

She whined and groaned, sang and howled, lifting the head in a tragic aria, then grabbed hold of a bag, trying to nose it along, thinking she was giving me a helping hand.

'Oh! You're such a good girl, Minnie, helping me with the shopping. Now, just wait until we get inside. Mamma has something lovely for you!' I mewled, dropping the bags to grab hold of her ears, giving them a tickle. 'Now, that's your ration of passion for the day. Go on! Out and play,' I said, opening the kitchen doors then throwing them back to let the sun sweep in, giving the place a bit of an airing.

I lifted the last of the shopping out of the boot and hurried to put it away. Minnie stood guarding her giant sausage left over from the children's tea last night.

'Eat it, you eegit,' I warned, seeing the usual game of the two magpies. One tortured her, running along the garden wall. He was the distraction while his mate grabbed the grub. Suddenly the magpie swooped, snatching the sausage.

'Look, Minnie!' I screeched, pointing at the sausage flying through the air.

She looked up then tore after the bird, keeping her head down for speed. Then the eegit took a flying leap and ended flat on her head, plastered on the next level down. She lay still for a few seconds, wondering what happened, then dragged herself up to give me a mournful look.

I stared with me mouth open. 'Yes! Gone again! Every time! Every bleedin time you fall for that, Minnie,' I puffed, not able to get over it. 'You're pure stupid, you gobshite. The bleedin grub is not for guarding, you're supposed to eat it!' I snorted, leaving her whining her loss, with her wanting me to get it back.

'Right, that's the last of the shopping put away,' I muttered, slamming the fridge shut. Minnie nosed her way under the table, still moaning her loss. Her heart broke with the crying when she discovered the children's tasty droppings were long swept up, leaving the kitchen floor squeaky clean.

'That's it!' I said, opening the fridge and giving her the last sausage. 'Now eat it! Don't take it outside,' I said, putting the plate in the sink and watching as she mewled her way contentedly, heading for her bed.

'Oh, Gawd!' I sighed, listening to the sudden peace. That dog is worse than rearing ten kids. But my two little beauties love her. I hand reared her from five weeks old on soya milk, using a baby bottle. Jaysus, the price a the stuff! It cost more to rear her than the two kids put together; they were breastfed. We were supposed to be looking for a toy poodle – something I could put in me pocket and it wouldn't bite me, but we ended up with her. 'Ah! I'll take her,' I said to the aul one who took me forty quid. 'I don't mind having a mongrel. Sure, I'm one meself.'

'Yes, but I will have you know her parents are both show dogs. It was outrageous, shocking!' she sniffed. 'We were abroad, and the kennels . . .'

I listened as she gasped out a sob.

'They were supposed to have the highest reputation!' she screeched, letting her eyeballs land on her cheeks with the horror of it all. 'My poor Mildred is ruined! We had such high hopes for her.'

'What is she, Missus?' I said, looking at the hairy little worm wriggling against her chest.

'Yorkshire terrier!' she snapped. 'The other brute was a Tibetan terrier! Well, this is the result,' she whispered sadly, flinging the little ball with the head too big for its body into the palm of me open hand.

Yeah, she robbed me, but the kids took one look at what was on offer and went mad. I carried her home in a Dunne's Stores plastic bag, with her little head the size of a golf ball sticking out the top. Aul fucker wouldn't even give me a box!

Plus, poor Minnie looked as if she was half-blind – that, or unfortunate in the wits department. She used to follow me everywhere. But when I went left, she turned right. We took her to the vet. 'She's very young!' he gasped. 'Much too young to be separated from her mother! This is sheer neglect. How dare they take this pup away from its mother? She's not weaned! Who sold you this pup?' he demanded, snorting down his glasses at me like it was all my fault.

'Eh! I don't know! I rang the owner from an advert. She met me halfway down the country,' I snorted, thinking I had been well and truly swindled.

Ah, well! I wouldn't part with her now; no, not for love nor money. She's one of the family, I thought, flicking the switch to boil the kettle as I threw the eye at her, seeing her content now, trying to make short work of a sausage that's nearly bigger than herself. But, Jaysus! She's ferocious! She struts out there, guarding all she can survey. Nothing sets foot on her land without her say so. Even the plumber minced past her, hanging on to his 'what-nots'.

'Will she bite me, Missus?' he shivered, as the pair of us looked down at a miniature Paddington Bear swinging out of the tail of his coat with the four legs left dangling in the air. She was trying to evict him from the house.

'No! Only if ye let yer guard down! But you have been warned. The sign on the gate says "Beware of the Dog",' I sniffed, watching her get a better grip as the two little back paws landed on his arse, then the head flew as she tore into the job of trying to shift him. He leapt outa the house, dragging her with him.

'Get tha dog outa here, Missus, or find yerself another fuckin plumber!' he screamed, losing the rag with the fright.

Ah, lovely! The kettle's boiled. Oh, I'm dying for that cup of tea. I grabbed a mug hanging from the old French dresser and landed in a teabag, then poured in the boiling water just as the phone decided to ring. As I moved to pick it up, the clock hanging on the wall caught my eye. My heart leapt. Jesus, it's nearly time to pick up the children from school and I've wasted half the day. I could have done a million things, but, no, I'm a dozy cow! I had to spend it giving meself sunstroke sitting on that bleedin bench. I snorted, picking up the phone, saying peevishly, 'City morgue!'

They hung up. I made a grab for my tea, then slowly counted, waiting. Sure enough, it rang again.

'Hello!' I sighed, listening to the heavy breathing, making sure they had the right number this time.

'Martha?'

'Yes, Alan! How is everything?'

'Listen, Martha! I just got a phone call from Charlie, your brother!'

'Yeah, I know who he is, Alan,' I laughed. 'Where is he? What's he up to? When did he get back?'

'Oh, don't ask, Martha,' he said giving a heavy sigh. 'He got back over two months ago. I let him stay in the house with us. But, well . . . he's gone again! Back on the aul drink, Martha.'

Me heart sank, listening. 'But did he stick it out in that place in the country? Was he off the drink, Alan?'

'Oh, indeed he was. But now he's back to his old haunts. I managed to get him into the Morning Star hostel, but they threw him out. They won't tolerate anyone there with a drink on them.'

'Huh!' I snorted. 'That's the first I ever heard of them being so fussy,' thinking, they must be looking for more upmarket down-and-outs these days.

'So where is he now?'

'Ah,' Alan sighed wearily. 'He turned up here yesterday looking for the price of a bed for the night. I gave him a couple of bob and rang the hostel. They agreed to give him one more chance, providing he comes in sober. Anyway, listen, Martha, I have to go. Charlie asked me to pass on a message. He says "that aul fella" – he wouldn't give a name but he says you will know who he is talking about. Anyway, this "aul fella" has been taken into the city-centre hospital.'

Hospital? I thought. Jesus! He must be really sick. That aul fella has been ailing all his life. He's a bleedin hypochondriac! But he's never shown his nose near a doctor in his life. He's certainly never been in hospital. Ah, who cares, I thought. He's nothing to do with me.

'Hello! Are you there, Martha?'

'Yes, I'm listening, Alan.'

I was about to tell him I'm not interested when it hit me. Jesus! The ma! She will be up there. She's bound to be all on her own. She won't be able to cope. I better go up and see what's happening, just for her sake.

'Listen, Alan! When did he go in?'

'I don't know. I just got the call this morning. I said I would let you know. Other than that, Martha, I didn't ask any questions.'

'OK! Thanks for letting me know, Alan. I'll talk to you soon. Cheers!'

'Bye, Martha. I'll be in touch.'

I put the phone down slowly, taking this in, thinking about him. JACKSER! So! In hospital, eh? Well, well, well. What goes around comes around, Jackser, my boy! My old taskmaster, my nightmare to end all nightmares. My hound of hell who has chased me down all the days of my life and the long dark nights of my silent screams as I fled him, trying to outrun the terror haunting my nightmare dreams. 'Now it is your turn,' I muttered slowly, feeling my time has come. Yes, I have waited a long time to see you on your knees, Jackser, you evil bastard! I want to be there to see the terror in your eyes! To watch as you take your last glimpse of a world you helped to turn into a never-ending nightmare of pure evil. Yes! I want to see the devil on horseback and watch you ride to hell.

I better get moving. I'll get the dinner on now, then go and collect the children from school and give them their dinner, then get them settled down with their homework. But first I better try to contact their father. He can come here and take over after that, then I can high tail it out of the house. I'll go up to the hospital and find out for myself what's happening. OK, that's settled. No, on second thoughts it would be better to organise the children in bed. So, will I leave it until the morning, then? I thought about that. Yeah, that is a better idea. OK, that's finally settled. I will wait until tomorrow morning before I go to the hospital.

2

I parked the car and headed up the steps of the old city-centre hospital. Jesus! Many's the time long ago when I've sneaked in here, looking for a spare bed for the night. Now, here I am again. Only this time I'm now where I always wanted to be, leading my own life with nothing and nobody to tell me what to do. Right, Jackser, it looks like your day of reckoning has come. You are now the one at the mercy of the world and his wife. So there is a God in heaven! Oh, yes, the wheel turns full circle, Jackser, me boyo! You bandy little no-good whoremaster of a black-hearted fucking godforsaken psychopath! This should be nice, I thought, grinning to meself at the idea of Jackser shivering in the bed. Ha! He's going to be afraid of his life. Hospitals scare the shite outa him.

I rushed to the hall entrance, pulling the heavy door open, then stood looking at the porter behind his desk. Ask him what ward Jackser's in? No, forget him. I know this place like the back of me hand, I thought, yanking open the heavy door leading down the corridors to the wards, deciding I would relish this moment by taking it easy. I'll just ramble around the hospital, looking in the men's part, then give myself a lovely surprise when I spot the little weasel. Hopefully he'll be lying all huddled up in his bed of pain. Well, he better have some pain! I'm demanding it! I'll oblige him myself if I don't see enough suffering. Jesus, the mafia are so right: vengeance is a dish best served cold. Gawd, you're a psycho, Martha! Well, I learned from the best. Nobody could outdo Jackser!

I could feel myself humming with pleasure as I wandered down along the old corridors. Bloody hell! The state of this old hospital! They haven't even bothered to throw a can of paint over the place since I was last here. When was that? Must be at least . . . Jesus! Who knows? I'm too old to remember things like that.

I poked me head in doors, seeing poor aul fellas look up hopefully, then let their face drop back in misery after seeing I was nobody they recognised. No, I wasn't coming to them with a few grapes and a bit of gossip. Thinking of grapes! Forget it, Jackser. I wouldn't piss on you if you were on fire, I snorted to meself. Aul fucker, eating all and any grub that ever came into the house, leaving us nothing but our imagination. Yeah! The only thing he left us with was to wonder what it tasted like. Bleedin starved, we were. The stray dogs and cats rummaging in the dustbins got luckier than us. They were faster; they got there first.

I gasped me way up the stone stairs, clinging to the metal handrail. Jaysus! I better stop for a breath, there's no more fun in this! I must have tramped down every corridor, every ward, and still not a sign of the bandy aul bastard.

I dug me hand into my pocket and came up with the roll-up tobacco. I stared at it. Forget that. Wait till me breath comes back. Right! Keep going. I landed on the top floor then staggered along the passage, making for the first ward. No! 'Not a sign,' I moaned, feeling a terrible thought coming into my head. He better not be gone home! The least I can expect now is to be hearing I can dance on his grave. Or better still, hear he's on his last gasp! Oh, yes, that at the very least. My expectations have been raised too high for anything else. I'll up-end the place if they have sent him home. Oh, no, Jackser, nothing less now will do me than to see you planted. God knows I have waited long enough – a whole lifetime nearly.

What age was I when the ma met him? Yeah! Charlie was only a year old. She carried him in her arms. I was six years old, the year I made my first Holy Communion, the last time I ever knew anything remotely normal. Well, nearly normal. If you can call tramping the streets day and night, looking for somewhere to put our heads down for a weary night's rest, normal. Or listening to the ma talking to herself while I tried to figure out the thinking. What were we going to do for a bit of grub and such mundane but very important little things like that ticked away, teasing my brain.

Jesus, the ma was like a breeding machine for that bandy aul bastard, and all with the idea of getting a few extra quid on the Labour. I don't know why they called it that. The only labouring he ever did was count the money I brought back after me day's robbing, the bandy aul toe rag!

I walked on, beginning to lose heart. Only two wards left; he must have been discharged.

Jesus! Talk about losing the run of yourself, Martha. You should have known it was too good to be true. That aul fella is like Rasputin! The mad monk in Russia. They poisoned him, shot him full of bullets, tried to drown him, and they still couldn't kill him! Yeah! We even had a go at that ourselves when we first went to live with Jackser. Me ma tried to put poison in his tea! Well, that's what she said it was. But being thick, the ma dropped the bottle and smashed it before Jackser could even get a sniff of it! I think even Charlie had a go. Yeah, when he was six years old. The time we ran off and left Jackser to fend for himself. But the poor kids got left behind too. Jesus! Charlie told me he sneaked in to Jackser when he was clapped out blind drunk in the bed – plastered with the drink, he was. Charlie came creeping in with the bread knife but then lost his nerve and flew for his life when Jackser farted and turned over in the bed! Yes, Jackser, you were the spawn of the devil – pure evil. Right! Keep going, Martha. You never know your luck.

I turned into the second last ward and came face to face with the devil himself! Well, well! Would you credit that? Here's the bandy little bastard, large as life and ugly as sin. I've found him at last. My heart gave a lurch and me eyes lit up with the sudden delight in me. I stared, seeing him sitting propped up, with about five pillows keeping him straight. His eyes were slowly flickering open and shut, with his face draped sideways on the pillow, and he was moaning something. I listened.

'Oh, holy Jesus, this is terrible. Oh, mother a God, I'm dyin. Oh, sweet divine Jaysus! Someone get me outa here before I'm dead.'

I coughed and his head turned slightly, then his face dropped at the sudden sight of me.

'Who fuckin brought you here? What's yure game? Gerout! Fuck off! Before I lift ye out of it,' he snorted, with the head shaking slowly and the muddy brown eyes boring holes in me.

I winked with a grin on me face, saying, 'How're ye, Jackser? Heard ye were on yer last legs!'

He started breathing heavily, like he was pumping himself up to lift outa the bed and annihilate me. But there's not much wind left in him and he's shrunk now he's just all skin and bone in a wizened old man's body. I just stared at him, keeping the laugh in my eyes. He stared back, curling up his lip, then turned his eyes away, resting his face on the other side of the pillow where he couldn't see me.

'That's a nice welcome,' I said happily, moving over and standing about six feet away, taking him in.

'Who the fuck let you in? If ye've come here te get a rise outa me,' he muttered, 'then YOU can go an fuck off outa tha!' he snarled, raising his voice in a hoarse whisper.

'Ah, now don't be like that, Jackser. Didn't I just come all this way specially to see you?' I said, grinning at him, thinking he knows I'm not here for the good of his health.

'Well! Ye see me now, so ye can fuck off wit yerself!' he gasped, letting out a fit of coughing.

'What's wrong with you anyway, Jackser? How did you end up here?' I said, whipping me head around to take in all the other poor aul unfortunates who were sitting up now, taking everything in. My eyes landed on one little aul fella lying plastered in the bed.

'How are you? Are you getting any better?' I said, leaning over to him.

'Who, me?' he said, pointing a finger at himself, looking shocked at the idea someone had noticed him hidden over in a corner. Suddenly his eyes lit up and he shot up in the bed, giving the pillows a whack with his fist, then he mooched himself and tore down the bedclothes, getting rid of them. I watched as he stretched his bare skinny legs with the pyjamas pulled up.

'Jesus! This heat would kill ye!' he complained, looking around to see how he could better comfort himself. 'I'm tellin ye, Missus! I'm meltin alive in this bed,' he puffed, looking at me and fanning himself with the sides of his pyjama top. 'I'm not at all satisfied wit this bed neither, it's like a block a cement,' he moaned, creasing his face and wriggling his skinny little body, trying to shape himself into the mattress. Then he curled his toes and swung his arms, trying to get a bit of life back into his bony, wasted frame.

I tried not to laugh, seeing him wriggling around the bed like a worm running for its life. 'Are you more comfortable now?' I said, seeing him settled back now against the pillows, with his hands folded across his belly, studying me.

'Listen!' he suddenly said, pointing his finger over at the big window. 'Would you ever run out an ask one a them nurses te come in here quick an open tha winda before we all die here a the suffocation.'

I looked up at the window, seeing it was shut tight. 'Yeah! You're right. You could do with a bit of fresh air in here. The place is steaming,' I said, flapping the hands over me hot dry face. 'Is there a pole somewhere? Maybe I could open it myself,' I said, looking around the ward, seeing nothing.

'No! Do nothing. Tha sister will only ate the head offa ye!'

'Oh, yeah, OK then. I don't want to cause any trouble,' I said, making for the door.

'Oh! Just before ye go, would you ever take this jug wit ye and ask them te give ye a drop fresh water? I'm parched wit the thirst here but I'll be hanged if I'm goin te be caught drinkin this hot water. Here! Take it. It tastes like cat's piss,' he snorted, grabbing up the jug of water and landing it in me hand.

'Yeah! No problem,' I said, making for the door again.

'Oh! One more thing! Would ye ever just stoop down there an get me slippers an dressin gown outa tha aul locker?'

'Sure,' I said, making back for the locker.

'Oh, Jesus help me! Oh, Missus!' a voice croaked at me from the next bed.

I lifted my head outa the locker, looking over at a grey-faced, tiny old man. He was looking up at me with his mouth open and his hand held out. It looked like a skeleton, with a mass of blue veins running through it. He was trying to reach out to me.

'What's wrong? Do you need something? Are you all right?' I said, forgetting about the locker as I leant into the old man lying prostrate in the bed. He looked like he was dying.

'I need the bedpan. Me insides feel like they're coming apart!' he gasped, letting his face twist in an agony of pain. Then there was an unmerciful splutter and suddenly the air turned blue with the smell.

'Ahh, fuck! He's done it again!' roared the aul fella beside me. 'Ahh, holy Jaysus! Tha's cruel, tha is!'

'What! Did his bowels let loose?' I said, looking at him with his head hanging outa the side of the bed and his hand on his belly, with the tongue stretched out. 'Mind you don't fall out,' I said, grabbing hold of him looking like he was going to get sick.

'Let go a me!' he grunted, sticking his head further under the bed, trying to escape the smell. Then another moan came from somewhere else.

'Is tha you, Leila? Come over! Don't be wastin time. Get me the aul glasses. Where are they? I can't see ye right!' groaned an old man from the other corner.

I looked over, seeing him squinting at me, looking very confused. 'What? Are you all right?' I said, making to go over to him now.

'Here! Don't mind him. He's not all there! Would you ever do us a good turn an get tha nurse te come in here pronto and clean up tha dirty aul git's bed,' the little worm demanded, looking at me like I was his paid maid.

'Yeah, OK, I'm on my way. I'll just run and get the nurse,' I said, gritting me teeth and making for the door, thinking it's a pity it's not him lying in that poor man's shit. Jaysus, life can be very cruel when you get old.

'Wha the fuck! Are you still here?' snorted Jackser, coming out of his doze as I shot past him. 'Go on! Fuck off back te where ye came from!' he screamed, lengthening his nose and throwing it towards the door.

'Don't you start!' I muttered, making it out the door without strangling him or the other aul grumpy fucker!

I made my way back down to the ward after having a smoke to calm me nerves. I was just in time to see the nurses making their way out with the wash trolley.

'Can I go back in now, Nurse?'

'Oh, in you go. Joe is squeaky clean again.'

'Ah, the poor man, he looks like he's in terrible pain,' I said, looking at them, then throwing me eye over at the little man. He seemed a bit easier in himself now, resting with his eyes closed. But he was white as a sheet, though.

'Ah, the poor creature has Crohn's disease,' the red-headed nurse said, studying him, then landing her eyes on me. I could see a look of terribly pity on her face for him.

My heart suddenly ached for the poor man. 'Ah, God love him,' I said, thinking old age is bad enough, but then when you have to suffer that with all the other ailments that come with it . . . Jaysus! I wouldn't wish that on me worst enemy, I thought, seeing the other weasel in the bed lying propped up on his pillows, looking the picture of comfort.

'That fella there is a bit of a bully,' I moaned, whispering to the nurse and throwing me eye in his direction.

'Who, Dickie? Ah, don't mind him. His bark's worse than his bite,' they said, looking over at him and giving him a big wave. 'Are you all right now, Dickie?'

'Wha?! Tha's a stupid question, Nurse, te be askin a man in my condition. Sure, if I was all right, wha would I be doin here, may I ask ye?' he barked, snorting and sniffing at them, then looking away and back, waiting to hear what they had to say about that.

'Oh, go on now, Dickie, ye chancer! Sure, with all that fight in you, aren't you healthier than ourselves?' they laughed, then rushed off with the trolley before he started again.

He stared after them leppin out the door while he was getting ready to let rip. By the time he got enough wind up, they were gone. So he turned the eye on me. I gave him a big smile. 'Are you all better now, Dickie?' I made the mistake of saying.

'Wha?!' he barked, letting his eyeballs bulge with the mouth hang open. 'How could I be anythin but not all right?! Are ye stupid or wha? Can ye not see I'm not long for this world?'

A hot rush of rage hit me at the sudden insult. 'Ye bleedin cantankerous aul . . .' Then I stopped. Don't start him off or I'll be kicked out. Right, change the subject fast. 'Well, you're not doing too bad for a man in his eighties,' I said, lifting my face in a smile, hoping to cheer him up.

'Wha?! Who told you tha? You've some bleedin neck, I can tell ye tha! I'm only 73!' he screamed, going red in the face now, really losing the rag altogether.

With that, before the pair of us could get another word out, there was an unmerciful roar from behind.

'Will youse fuckin shut up outa tha! An stop talkin about me!' Jackser suddenly screamed, stretching the veins in his neck, making his face go purple. 'Or I'll erupt outa this bed an I'll bursts ye's! I'll put ye's through tha winda for a shortcut!' he snarled, snorting from me to Dickie, letting steam spray out through the ears and down his nose.

Dickie got the fright of his life and suddenly found the walls very interesting, then he grabbed for the comfort of his blankets and wrapped them up under his neck. 'It's gone very chilly,' he muttered, leaving his nose above the blankets.

I looked over at Jackser and stared at him, keeping my face blank. He stared back with a flicker of the white-hot madness that once possessed him and made him what he was. I caught it as it flared, showing a demonic rage that once shook terror in me. Then it settled into a hard, icy-cold stare that would show you no mercy.

I locked on to that stare, boring deep into him. Yes, I thought, shaking my head slowly, the face of a mad man. I watched it flare up and rage, the volcanic anger burning brightly, hidden behind that steely cold stare as it flashed in the old-man eyes. But then it died out and he let his head drop back wearily, closing his eyes muttering, 'The curse a Jaysus on the lot a ye's, an a curse a Jaysus on this place,' he sighed, sounding like he was losing all hope of ever escaping back out that front door.

I could feel myself breathing fast and a tightness was gripping me belly. Long-forgotten old terrors was rushing at me. I wanted to go over there and match his anger, stand over him and let him feel I had the power of God almighty. Bring him to his knees in terror, make him scream for mercy. He is now ideally placed for that. He is an old, helpless man, just like a small child, not able to protect himself. I just want him to feel a dose of what he gave me and all the other helpless kids. But especially me. I was his for the taking, the favoured one for the unleashing of his passion for evil terror. No! I will bide my time. I have waited too long to make it easy for him. Slowly, slowly will do it – the Chinese torture. One drip at a time to drive him mad.

I took in a deep breath and looked around at Dickie, seeing he was watching very intently.

'I don't think that man likes you,' he said slowly, shaking his head at me and throwing the eye over at Jackser.

'Ah, no, Dickie,' I laughed. 'Sure, he's delighted to see me, aren't you, Jackser?' I shouted over at him, trying to doze in the bed.

His eyes shot open and he snorted then gave a little whimper in frustration, muttering, 'Ye fuckin whore's melt!' then turned his face to the wall.

'Nah, that's just his way, Dickie! Sure, anyone with a heart would have to love me, Dickie! I mean, here I am on a mission of mercy, coming to see poor aul Jackser and talk to you! Who else would do it on a lovely day like today with the sun splitting the rocks? Now I ask ye, would you not agree with me?' I said, rushing over to fix the blankets around his neck. 'Now, anything else I can do for you while I'm here?' I whispered, determined to get a laugh outa him.

'Jaysus, not only do ye love yerself, but ye must think ye're Mother Teresa of Calcutta wit yer carry on!'

'Love meself? Now ye see! I was right! Someone loves me, even if it's only meself!' I said laughing, staring up into his face, seeing him shake his head and snort at me.

'Jaysus, you're a hard case, there's no doubt about tha!' he laughed, swiping out at me with his hand. Then we sat silent for a minute, just looking at each other, feeling companionable.

'Listen,' he suddenly said, looking around to see if anyone was listening then leaning into me. 'See if ye can find where me aul smokes are. I hid them down inside tha locker there, an now I can't get me hands on them. I think tha bloody aul doctor must have told them nurses te whip them. They have the cheek te tell me! At my age!' he said, thumping his chest, not able to get over it. 'I'm te be doin no more smokin! Me lungs are bet, they tell me. Sure! Wha else have I got at my age? I mean, wha's left te enjoy?' he moaned, looking crucified at all his loss.

'Oh, you're right there, Dickie,' I snorted, agreeing with every word. 'Put your foot down! You put your own nails in your coffin! Why should you die for nothing? Sure, you might as well go out with a bang! I'm the same. I'm coughing and puffing, spluttering and gasping me way into an early grave from the aul smokes! But, sure, as you say, what else is there? I'm not interested in man hunting, I don't drink much, I hate shopping, so I'm easy to please. A scrooge would love to get his hands on me. Just think! Low maintenance for something like me. A Rolls-Royce that runs on fresh air! Yeah, definitely, my pleasures are all simple,' I said, diving into his locker and flying all the stuff on his bed, looking for the smokes.

'I'm tellin ye!' he puffed. 'You really fancy yerself, you do! All I can say is ye must a be born wit a silver spoon in yer mouth te get them ideas about yerself,' he said, flying his head up and down at me with a half-disgusted laugh in his tired old eyes.

I looked at him, seeing he was serious, and even a bit in contempt at the idea I was well off while he had to struggle for a life. 'No, Dickie, it's not like you think,' I said quietly. 'Right from the onset you have to put a high price on yourself or the world will sell you short. Why settle for cider when you can have champagne? Life has always been out there for the taking; you just need something to offer and the world will take you as it finds you.

'Here's what you do, Dickie. You look that doctor straight in the eye, and say, "Listen, sonny! I'm an old man. I smoke, I enjoy me smoke, I'm going to keep on smoking, and they can bury a packet with me when they put me into the ground. I'm here now because I'm ailing, and I'm keeping you in a job. So, get on with it!" Then blow smoke in his face, Dickie, if he gets cheeky,' I laughed, looking straight into his eyes, willing him not to be afraid. For all his bluff I could see it was to cover up a very soft heart.

He stared at me, thinking, then roared laughing, saying, 'Jaysus! Ye're right there! Why should I let them push me around? Bejaysus! Hurry up there an find them smokes,' he snorted, whipping his head around at the stuff all piled on his bed.

'Eureka! Here we go, hidden in the wash bag!'

'Ah, yeah, now I remember!' he said, letting his red rheumy eyes light up with the excitement as his wrinkled old face creased into a huge smile, making him look soft and gentle. 'Right! Get me dressin gown an slippers again. I'm off te tha tilet for a long smoke.' Then he was up and gone, flying out the door on his poor aul wobbly, skinny little legs. 'See ye in a few minutes,' he whispered, disappearing outa sight.

I turned me head back to Jackser, then got up and strolled over to stand beside his bed. 'So, how are you sick? What ails ye, Jackser?'

'Yeah! So well ye might ask!' he croaked. 'Was it me ye came te visit, or are ye in the bleedin Legion a Mary now, comin te see any aul fucker?'

'Ah, stop moaning, Jackser, I'm here to see you' – watch you die roarin, I thought, feeling a perverse satisfaction I had rattled his cage. 'Now, go on, tell me, what ails ye? How did you land up here? Did the doctor say anything? Will you fucking talk to me?' I said, seeing the same old Jackser, always trying to stay on top of people, keep them in their place by getting them first.

'I'm not meself,' he groaned, lifting his shitty-brown bloodshot eyes up at me, then letting his face collapse and the mouth droop.

Jesus! I thought, lifting the eyebrows into the air, letting me face stretch. He looks like a sad, miserable aul bloodhound, waiting to be put down. I moved over and pulled back a chair, sitting myself down. He closed his eyes and I puffed me cheeks out, wondering what to do next. I looked around the ward, seeing all the old men had dozed off, looking like they were waiting for the next exit out of here.

Jesus! This place is like a waiting room for death. I could sense it in the sour smell of decay, as even the false teeth melted in the heat. The room was heaped with tired old bodies sending out gases from every pore, and the heavy snoring with the agonised wheezy breathing made it sound like a train heaving off with the whistle blowing.

You could nearly expect any minute to hear a voice suddenly booming out, *'Will all passengers waiting to take their final journey please prepare to depart,'* then a last whistle blasts out and suddenly everything changes. Ghostly figures start wafting out from everywhere, moving closer together, all gathering in a wide-open space. The air is thick, heavy with the terrible silence. It bodes terror; it is just waiting to erupt from the confusion, the fear. It is all coming from the minds of the bewildered souls who suddenly, without warning, found themselves trapped in this no-man's-land of waiting. The screams of terror stay locked down in their chests. They only know one thing: they are waiting for something. Because in this moment they are neither alive nor yet quite dead. The space has neither sky nor land, it has no stars, no anything. It is neither light nor dark. Then they start to move towards something, or someone.

Yeah, death! I wonder what it must be like for Jackser, knowing he is so close to it? Will he be thinking about heaven and hell? I wonder does it really exist, this heaven and hell, and what it would be like. If I close my eyes, I can see the imagined Angel of Death I thought existed when I was a child, but without the horns and hoofs – something more realistic. I can see him now. He is suddenly appearing, looking very ominous. He stands with the book of life in his hands, looking out over the vast distance at the assembled multitude, the never-ending space thick with the millions of newly dead. His eyes, looking like shiny black coals, glimmer out of the hood of his long black habit. Behind him there is a sudden commotion, as in rushes a ghostly white figure, drifting in a halo of bright light.

Suddenly lights blaze on one side of a great room, while the other is illuminated with a muted red glow, making that side look very cosy. 'Terribly sorry to keep you waiting,' says a man wearing a long, gold-silk coat buttoned to the neck, with matching embroidered pointed slippers. He has a thick mane of white-gold hair wafting down in waves, settling on his shoulders.

The room held its breath as everyone watched his move. He rushed up the steps of a white marble podium, then lifted his striking blue eyes to the crowd, looking out over them, then dropped his head to a big gold book, settling it on the book rest.

The other fella stood waiting patiently watching him. Under his black cloak he wore a red-silk tailed coat with embroidered gold buttons, tight black gaiter trousers, shiny black-leather shoes with gold buckles and a long black wavy wig on his head, with a red scarf tied in a bow at his neck. 'Shall we begin?' he asked politely, dropping his book on the rest, sounding fed up at being kept waiting so long.

'Terribly sorry, Nick dear!' Peter said to the fella standing looking at him with the eyebrows raised and the mouth twisted, looking the picture of fed-up patience.

'Oh, no! By all means take your time, I have an eternity to wait!' said Nick, giving his hair a stroke. 'But if I may, it is Nicolai to you! I am just back from Paris!' he said, giving a slight bow of the head, wanting to look the picture of elegance and dignity. 'Yes, wonderful season they're having! French Revolution, you know. I had the most marvellous time with Robespierre. Lots of blood and gore! The man is simply a genius. Heads, heads and more heads rolled and bit the dust! Wonderful! Haven't had such fun since the . . . Oh, my goodness! How the ages fly!'

Then he suddenly stopped waxing lyrical and snapped, 'Well, do get on with it, Pierre! I am anxious to sort this lot out and get back, see what the brutes have been doing in my absence.

Peter stared, taking in a huge, slow, deep breath, listening, then exploded, 'ME? GET ON WITH IT?!'

Nick nodded, the head watching with the eyes opening wide, then wider as he slowly bit his fingers wondering what he did wrong. Then it hit him.

'Oh! Terribly sorry for being so rude, Pierre old chap!' he gasps, then starts nattering again, the very thing he was just giving out about, forgetting it was himself doing all the talking. 'How did yours go? Did you spend your holiday anywhere interesting? Hmm! Still chasing that little golden-haired bit of fluff thingy, built like Dolly Parton? Haw, haw!'

'Please! Do drop the pretentious nonsense! Peter to you!' he sniffed, looking away then turning back and lowering his voice. 'Actually, I was in conference with . . .' he said, pointing the finger up to the heavens. 'Working out the new living quarters. We have to segregate the husbands from the wives. The men are complaining it was only "Death until us do part!" Now they can't enjoy themselves with all the delectable . . . Ahem! They are demanding their right to freedom!' he said quickly, trying to find the right words.

'Oh, indeed, I do get the picture, Pierre old boy,' Nick smiled, letting a slow grin spread across his face.

'Yes, and oh, please! I do not chase little bits of thingy, as you so vulgarly put it. I am all purity! Sacred. I must maintain my position as I am PETER! LORD, KEEPER OF THE KEYS TO HEAVEN AND HIS KINGDOM ON EARTH!' he intoned loudly, eyes piously raised to heaven, then sniffed and dropped them, giving his locks a twirl, looking down to examine his pointy embroidered slippers.

'Oh, how awfully boring. Well, as you know! I do not have to kowtow to anyone. I own the whole kingdom of hell! Voila!' Nick said, twirling his finger to land down below.

'Oh, how the mighty have fallen!' sniffed Peter, now looking bored himself, letting his eyes wander around the walls.

'Well, actually . . .' says Nick, but then gets interrupted by a great booming voice.

'GENTLEMEN! PRAY! PLEASE! DO GET ON WITH THE JOB! Your guests are waiting,' the booming voice now said gently. 'You may continue your bickering repartee during your leisure.'

'Oh, it is "He" who must be obeyed,' whispered Nick, as they both dropped their heads to the books.

'I shall take first roll call,' said Peter, bowing his head politely, smiling to Nick.

'Do! By all means,' bowed Nick, smiling back.

Peter let his eyes run down the book, then lifted his head and coughed, looking over the masses with the sound of quivering skin and rattling bones as they all shivered, waiting to hear their fate.

'MOTHERS! GRANDMOTHERS! Please step forward and join me to my right.' There was a sudden shocked burst of ohhhs! Crying, laughing with tears, sniffing and squeals of delight as people stood with their mouths gaped open, waiting to hear.

'That's us! Hurry, Nelly, we made it!' one granny shrieked, grabbing the arm of another old woman getting herself lost in the stampeding crowd all rushing to stand beside Peter. Then he smiled and bowed to Nick when that lot were settled – they were now sitting along a golden coach with red padded seats and nuns waiting to drive them away.

'MURDERERS! Please join me on my left,' said Nick, smiling at the crowd now suddenly scattering as the place went mad.

'Noooo! FUCK OFF!', 'Get me outa here!', '*Andiamo*! Where fire escape?', 'MAMMY! Save me!'

'Come along now, don't be shy,' said Nick, trying to encourage them to turn in his direction. They were all killing each other to get out of the way as they tried to make it out first, heading for the fire exit. A door blew open when someone grabbed hold of the bars, then a sudden roaring noise hit the room as red-hot flames burst up from down below. It was even more shrieks of panic as they turned tail now, heading back into the room.

Nick smiled down, turning his head from left to right, his smile slowly broadening into a huge grin as he watched them all suffocating. They were mad with the panic as they blindly crashed around the room, now screaming in fear and choking with the sudden burst of smoke.

'Orderly queue, please. We are British here. RULE BRITANNIA!' he suddenly roared, then let it quieten to a hum. 'Britannia rules the waves. All happy, are we?' he said, smiling when they finally settled themselves down and shuffled into a stop, glaring up at him, knowing they were bet!

'Next,' he said, dropping his head looking down the list. 'POLITICIANS! TAX INSPECTORS! BURGLARS! And ... car-park attendants!' he muttered, giving a dirty look to the car-park lot holding up their placard showing who they were. 'Please join me on my left,' he sniffed.

'We were only doin our jobs!' they complained. 'No, we can't a heard right! It can't be us!' they wailed, looking around at each other in confusion, shaking their heads in denial.

'Come along now, gentlemen, we must keep moving. Long list today. Sunday-morning business always brisk after a boozy weekend,' he smirked, looking over at Peter with the head buried; he was busy checking his lists.

'I wish to speak to God! This is insufferable! I did not fiddle my expenses!' shouted a purple-faced, baldy politician.

'ORDER, ORDER!' shouted the Speaker of the House of Commons, then looked to see the effect on Nick, hoping to curry favour.

'You're a shower of shite gombeen eegits!' shouted a culchie politician from the Irish lot. 'Whose feckin idea was it to take us all on dat heap-of-junk government jet? The feckin thing crashed over the Indian ocean, killin the lot of us!' he exploded, carrying his right arm under his left one.

'No, we're not movin outa this; ye can't make us! We demand an appeal te the labour court!' a skinny little runt roared up, lifting the neck and strangling himself because the peanut head was buried in an overcoat two sizes big for him.

'And you would be?' Nick said, leaning his head over to smile down at the little aul fella.

'Midget! Midget Malarkey, representin decent hard-workin burglars from Dublin! Dead Man Square te be exact. Do ye get tha? A no-go area for youse fuckers, or any other fuckers who think they can come in an act the hound wit us!' he said, stretching the neck and slapping the collar down, making himself look bigger. 'Now! An I was sayin . . .'

But before he could get another word in, a voice roared up from the middle. 'I'm the union spokesman for "Murder Incorporated" . . . I mean car parkers! For all a me brother workers here,' said a huge bull-necked fella swaggering closer to the front. 'Tha right? Am I right in sayin tha?' he dared, looking around him at all the hands waving and heads nodding.

'Be Jaysus ye are! You tell him, Bullocks Ham!'

'Yeah, go on, Hammer me aul son! We're right behind ye, boss. Dublin Ghougers, Animal Gang! My stampin ground. Just call if ye need a hand. Mugser Chickmunk's the name!' roared a fat-faced aul fella with a pot belly and a mass of ginger hair standing to attention. Only problem was, the head had to shout from under his arm as he was carrying it!

'Hmm, interesting,' said Nick, looking down at his list. 'Oh, you crafty old devils!' he smiled, letting his face light up in a huge grin. 'Sorry, old boys! All nine hundred and seventy-four of you hiding under the banner of car parking! You lot shift yourselves over to MURDERERS!'

There was sudden silence and all heads turned on Bullocks Ham.

'The dumb bastard just gave the game away, dropped us clean fuckin right in it!' a voice growled, coming from somewhere deep in the thick of the hiding murderers.

'Oh, for hell's bells! Make an orderly queue, or would you all prefer to take the fast exit?' Nick sighed, pointing at the fire exit, losing patience now.

They all turned in silence then shifted, making a mad dash to stand next to him on the left.

'Quite ready?' he asked mildly, seeing them pushing and shoving, shuffling next to and away from him, then finally settling down to wait.

'Next! LAWYERS!' he boomed, looking down his list then smiling in a saintly way up at the crowd of shifty-looking men wearing wigs and gowns. Some were in Savile Row suits, peering up through Gucci spectacles.

'NONSENSE! We demand an immediate appeal to the supreme being! Send for him at once!'

'HEAR, HEAR!' roared the wigs and suits, slapping their papers and stamping their feet.

Nick shifted his head slowly to Peter, raising his eyebrows with the question, a smile playing around his lips.

Peter lifted his eyes from the list to look down shaking his head, then over at Nick, saying, 'The road to hell is paved with lawyers. No appeal, Mi'lord high above has said in a precedent. Let me see now what the details are.'

'Oh, yes! Mr Justice K.M. Stiffneck, plaintiff in the trial versus the defendants Lord of Heaven and Faust, supreme ruler of hell.'

'Indeed,' chuckled Nick, bowing his head at the acknowledgement. 'It was the year of our Lord, seventeen . . . Oh, that will do. Thank you kindly for that, Peter dear! APPEAL DENIED!'

The words were out just as the ceiling lifted with the sudden eruption of roars and shouts, then the stampede of feet and papers thrown into the air now flying everywhere. One floated down, landing smack in front of Nick's face. He whipped it up reading, looking very interested, then clucked to himself as his eyes shot down the page. 'Tut, tut. Lies, lies! All lies! More lies, Mi'lord!' he whispered softly, then lifted his head, throwing the paper over his shoulder, letting a slow smile break out on his face. It turned into a huge grin as he folded his arms, watching the melee. Wigs flew and gowns flapped as they tore into each other, all fighting to get through the same door – the one with the gold plate marked 'Heaven'. They didn't make it! There was no knob to turn. Their banging, hammering, pushing and heaving did no good. It was made a pure steel.

They turned their attention back on Nick; he was waiting with the ready grin.

'NEVER! We do not accept this ruling!' a scream went up.

'No! Impossible – always but always there is a way out! Anyone got a law book? Oh, may the Lord not have mercy on our souls?!' cried a skinny little man, looking around him confused, wondering if he could spot God himself. Then he eased his head up, spotting Nick giving him the eye. Hope! He shuffled over, filling up with it, then stood praying up at him.

'Oh, surely there must be pity for such a wretch as me! I mean, what about justice and mercy? We are both English gentlemen, held in high esteem for our fair play and . . .'

'Indeed? There was not much justice and mercy shown when you were on the bench, old boy. Actually, I think you were one of my favourites! Quite enjoyably entertaining, in fact,' Nick smiled, nodding down at the little man who was shoving the wig into his mouth, the eyes now turning in the back of his head at hearing this. Nick then dropped the smile and lifted himself, raising the head and sniffing the air, taking in a deep breath. 'Lord Cock-Shoot Featherburns, get thee beside me! I am Satan, Lord of Darkness, your new master!'

With that the doors at the back of the place flew open and flames licked in as a roaring hot furnace belched up fumes and smoke, baking the room. Everyone now started to drown in sweat.

'MERCY! I beg of you, Nick, my good man, do show us chaps a little mercy!' grovelled a fat, white-faced man wearing a three-piece suit and dark sunglasses.

'No deals, old sport. No can do! Your fate has already been sealed by the highest court in the land!' said Nick, waving his finger up above. 'It's not personal, old boy!' Then watched intently, looking very interested, with the eyebrow raised, as the man slowly sank down, disappearing under a mass of heaving bodies all wanting to put distance between them and the open doors. The heap suddenly untangled and took off; a huge rumble shook the big room as masses of lawyers all raced for the front, wanting to wait their turn beside Nick. Nick looked down at the now cleared space, seeing the remains of two lawyers lying spreadeagled, flattened out on the floor.

'Nice work,' Nick smiled contentedly, looking from the splattered to the angry-looking lawyers all lined up now beside him.

'NEXT! TERRORISTS!' shouted Nick, looking around the room.

A group shuffled forward, some with their heads and arms missing. Suddenly a high-pitched voice screamed up, 'DIS IS THE IRA! NOW LISTEN CAREFULLY! Dere's two of us here an we're not tryin te get in, we're givin youse all TWO MINUTES TE GET OUT! DERE'S A BOMB PLANTED!'

'Naughty, naughty! We can't have you wet Nellies bringing the roof down over our heads!' said Nick, looking to Peter.

'Oh, no! Quite out of order that,' Peter agreed.

'DISPATCH!' Nick suddenly roared, pointing his finger at the back doors. Instantly the doors flew open again and out rushed ten hefty bald eunuchs! The Irish Republican Army pair screamed and made a run for it, straight for heaven's door. Gates suddenly appeared and slammed shut with a boom, locking them out. Not to be bet, one dived at the bars, squeezing his head in, then immediately lit up with sparks flying as he got himself electrocuted. He didn't have time to react as he was scraped off and hauled away by surrounding eunuchs. They carried the pair out moaning and screaming – they were now heading fast for the back doors – then it was all quiet as the doors slammed and everyone turned now to see next what was happening at the front.

'I think perhaps my lot next. Agreed?' said Peter gently, waving his finger down at his own list.

'Oh, yes, old boy. One does tend to get carried away when having such fun! Terribly polite of you to let me,' Nick smiled. 'But if I may just beg your indulgence one more tick?' he said, waving the finger then dropped his face looking down, hungrily searching his eyes up and down doing a headcount. 'All present and correct,' he smiled happily, rubbing his hands then giving them all a cheery wave.

The damned glared back, some looking baleful. Others cried up at him but definitely nobody was looking happy.

'Heavens, give me patience,' muttered Peter before lifting his voice to shout, 'SAINTS! Please come forward and stand directly behind me,' he said, nodding at all the faces shuffling past him. Some looked crucified, carrying little black wooden crosses grasped to their chests; others carried shopping bags filled with miraculous medals, whips for flagellation and little statues, and one rattled past with heavy chains strapped around his bony chest covered with a hair shirt.

Suddenly a little man shuffled past, looking up very confused at Peter, still shell-shocked.

'Ah, you look like a newly departed just arrived a smidgen too early. You do not know you are dead yet! Please take your place back among these people at the far back. In time I shall call your group. Some have not quite arrived yet,' he said, looking from his papers then lifting his head, holding his hand over his eyes, trying to see into the far distance.

'In that case I shall now take up again,' said Nick, looking down at his book. 'I do think my list is longer,' he smirked. 'Now then, these shall have to be called by name. They need a little encouragement,' grinned Nick, bowing his head to Peter.

'Oh, by all means carry on. My list is short,' sighed Peter, trying to smile back.

'Jackser, your hour is nigh! Come!' Nick boomed, lifting his wigged head from his notes.

Jackser's spirit lifts out of the bed and travels over, still grabbing hold of his ghostly cap. He has that clutched between his hard leathery hands, mashing it to bits with the nerves on him. 'That's me, Sir!' he gasps, bowing his head and making mincemeat out of the cap.

I grinned as I watched, thinking he's as terrified as he always was when faced with trouble.

'Ah, yes, Jackser!' Nick said softly, lowering his head to take in the shivering mass of jelly that's now quivering and shaking, making its way over to him. 'Yes! You are on the J list,' Nick says politely, while Peter is trying to smile down as Jackser floats past, but his nose turns up as if he's getting a very bad smell.

'J, Sir?' Jackser enquires. 'Wha would tha be, Sir? Ye see I'm not a very edumacated man! I'm not very well up wit this kinda thing!' he puffs, hearing it come out in a hoarse gasp. It's the ripple of fear running through him at the thought, Jaysus! He may not be able to get out of this one. Now he's having a terrible thought. Maybe me hour has truly come? Oh, lamb a Jaysus, no! Not tha! He blesses himself quickly, praying for a miracle.

'J list,' Nick explains patiently, 'in fact it is J.T.H.E.M. It is an abbreviation for 'Journey through hell everlasting more'. But we dropped that recently! Oh, about seven, eight hundred years ago. We had too many black-plague souls to get through!'

Jackser listens with the mouth open and the eyes staring out of his skull. It's all going over his head, but the terror is rising in him. He hasn't figured out why, yet. But, holy Jesus! he's thinking. I'm now at the mercy a these people, an tha bleedin Sally one is nowhere te be seen!

'Eh! Excuse me, Sir, for interruptin!' he bows, blinking the eyes and crushing the cap with the terror. 'But, eh, this J.T.H.E.M. thing ye say. Wha would tha be about, Sir? If ye wouldn't mind me te be enquirin.'

'What are you on about, man? Oh, yes!' Nick says, lifting his head then lowering his voice, after forgetting to be businesslike. 'Yes! You are to be dispatched to . . . Let me see your group again.' He peers down, studying his list, looking very serious with a slight lift of his nose. 'Hmm, yes! Over there,' he points, waving the bunch of papers in his hand. 'That is your transport. It will take you to begin your Eternity. A journey through everlasting hell. *Saecula Saeculorum*. Yes! For everlasting more.'

Jackser looks, letting his face collapse into the pains of hell. Then it hits him! Yeah, he's about to get himself well and truly hanged. The badness has caught up with him. I watched as his eyes flew and the brain ticked. He sniffed, taking in breaths of air, wanting to help the brain cells along. Suddenly his face turned to granite and the eyes stared daggers. Nick smiled as he reached into the pocket of his silk coat, taking out a packet of hand-rolled Havana cigars. He got them when an American gangster ordered a big crate from Cuba, but when he opened the wooden box it exploded, blowing his head off. Someone had planted a bomb in it. Nick found this packet in the pocket of the gangster.

He looked at it, seeing the box still saturated with blood, then took one out, sucking the soggy cigar. 'Delicious. Hmm, the added taste of very fine old wine,' he whispered, taking a long drag then blowing into Jackser's face, seeing him vanish in a cloud of smoke.

'I have me rights!' screeched Jackser, coughing and spluttering as he tried to get his breath back. 'I want the missus up here pronto! Shift yerselves and get me Sally up here this minute. I'm goin te instruct her now te contact Bertlamm Savageman, me solicitor. He'll sort this out quick an proper. Youse landed me in the wrong place! I've no business bein here talkin te the likes a youse! Where's the head man? Who's in charge a this kip?' he roared, waving the fists around then taking off when he saw Peter staring over at him, looking a bit interested.

'Oh, time for a break. I shall indulge you!' Nick said, taking long drags, enjoying his smoke. 'Go on! Trot along over. Perhaps Peter might like a few words with you,' he said, waving him off, then taking another deep drag on his Havana with the head thrown back.

'Are you the head fella a this place?' Jackser demanded, stabbing his finger up at Peter, raising the eyebrow and snorting the nose.

'Indeed!' Peter murmured, looking down at him disdainfully. 'Quite the little list you have stored, all pointing against you. Let me see,' he said, looking down at another list that showed all the wrongdoings for not getting into his place. 'A chartered horror of quite grotesquely inhuman suffering left in your wake. Tut, tut. Your mother suffered a slow and tortured life at your hands, until death brought her to us. First night on arrival, when she should have slept in her eternal peace, alas she rolled in her grave with agony. She watched as you sold the key to her house, leaving your brothers and sisters to sleep on the streets. They never forgave you. Then, of course, you honed your evil ways on little ones. The innocent, unprotected children flowered from your seed, two from the seed of others. These two were held by you in an iron grip through a tortured childhood. Tut, tut. Not an impressive account of your life by our standards. All these children given to you as a gift to nurture, you bent, broke and twisted.

'Mad to escape your poison, one took a premature exit. He, now, is here with us. Others must labour on in a twilight world of no-man's-land. They are neither here nor with the living. Yes, that is your legacy, Jackser. Now! Reap what you have sowed. Go!'

Jackser stares with his mouth open and his body frozen in a half-twisted turn. He is staring at a wide-open, inky-blue space with a hole in the middle. It pulsates with a whooshing vacuum of air roaring into a black void. When you listen, you can hear the rain crashing and the wind screaming. It sounds like the Banshee, the screams of the old woman thought long ago to bring a warning of death. More voices are added. It is the howling of wolves coming from a far distant, dark forest. One that is barren of all human life.

'GO!' commands Faust, giving Jackser a push, sending him moving towards the black void. I watch as he gets sucked in with a smacking of air. Then he is floating away, fast getting carried towards a black space of nothingness. Then the screams erupt. 'No! No, stop! The pain! Get away from me, Mother! No! I don't want yer pain, Harry! For fuck's sake, stop! Jesus! The whole lot of youse are after me! Why are ye's givin me all your torments? Oh, Jesus, I can't take it, somebody help me! The pain! The pain! Oh, Jesus, the pain of it. No! Oh, no!

Don't torture me. I'll be good! Give me another chance! I swear te the lovin Jesus I won't harm anyone ever again.'

The screams grew fainter as he went further into the great emptiness. I could barely hear his last cries of terror as he disappeared into the far distant, suffocating blackness. 'I wasn't all bad, please! Just let me rest,' was his exhausted plea as it came faintly whispering back, an echo from the great deep beyond of all eternity.

Amen! I flicked my eyes open, feeling very satisfied with the thought that Jackser may soon meet his maker. Then I hope he suffers the hellish pains of all damnation, something like my imagination just fired up. Yes, that and more. The bastard damned himself to hell!

I sank deeper into the chair, looking around to see everyone had clapped out. I wonder where the ma is? I thought she'd be up here haunting his bedside, on the alert for further orders to do his bidding. But, no, not a sign. She must have slipped her noose and slinked off while Jackser was taking a snooze. Oh, that's very daring, Ma! Just wait until Jackser wakes up and finds you missing! Tut, tut! I wouldn't mind, but she's normally very obedient. Oh, yes, I can still hear her now. '*Jackser! I'm fuckin suffocatin here! When can I take me next breath?*'

'*You'll fuckin breathe when I tell ye te breathe, Missus, an not before! Do ye get tha?*' he snorts, strutting his stuff as he hikes up the trousers that are hanging at half-mast on his bandy legs.

Hmm, happy days. Maybe she's back in the flat doing a tango, flapping with one of Jackser's plastic flowers gripped between her teeth.

No, Martha, miracles do not happen, I thought sadly. The ma is long a beaten woman. Any life left in her by the time she met him was soon ripped out of her.

'Oh, bloody hell,' I sighed, feeling really fed up now. I looked around, seeing not a sign of life. Even Dickie is back in his bed, stone dead to the world, probably dreaming about his next smoke. I snorted out me breath, peeling the eyes on Jackser in frustration, wanting to play a game of cat and mouse.

'Hey, Jackser! Are you awake?'

I waited – nothing.

I gave him a poke. 'Jackser! Wake up! I want to talk to you!'

His eyes flew open, staring in shock. I leant in, studying him, wanting a good look at the face that drew so much terror I thought I would die young – very, very young – because he would kill me.

He stared back hard, letting the eyes narrow and the mouth curl into a snarl, knowing I was coming the hound with him, thinking I could get the better of him. I stared harder, letting a smile into me eyes, seeing his clear and a sudden look of fear creep in. I nodded slowly, letting the smile play on my lips.

'You're an old man now, Jackser; it comes to us all,' I said, shaking my head sadly, looking tragic until a slow grin spread across my face, lighting it up with a malicious gleam.

'This is your first time in hospital, isn't it, Jackser?' I said, waiting to hear his answer.

Not a muscle moved but the eyes changed, glittering into a rage, now looking more treacherous. My heart leapt! I'm getting somewhere; he's forgetting himself again, thinks he's the old Jackser.

'Gawd, you must be really sick! Does that worry you? I mean, you were always afraid of that. Jesus! It could be serious,' I said, shaking my head at him, looking very worried.

'Fuck off,' he growled, letting it come up from his belly. Then he turned his head away, breathing more heavily now, wanting and wishing he could tear me limb from limb.

I grinned, giving a big sigh of satisfaction. 'That's right, you get some sleep, Jackser, and don't worry yourself. I'll just sit here and pray you wake up again,' I said softly, tapping his big leathery hand.

He shovelled air up through his nostrils, growling, 'Whore's melt, I'm warnin ye . . .' Then he let go and sighed into the pillow, giving a little keen, wanting to cry.

I stayed quiet, just watching him, then a thought hit me. 'The ma's not here, Jackser! Do you think she could have left you? Maybe cleared off and gone to England? I mean, it's very odd. There's not one soul next or near to see whether you're dead or alive. I'm the only one here bothered to come in and look after you. Jesus! You could be dying,' I breathed. 'You look like that to me. But do they care? This is bleedin shocking!' I sniffed, leaning over him to get the message across. 'What a pack of ungrateful swine that lot are!'

I waited, hearing his brain ticking, then he let out a big gasp, 'Ye're right! I'm bad . . .'

'Oh, indeed you are!' I interrupted. 'You are looking very, very bad,' I said slowly. 'You may never get outa here, Jackser!' I warned, lowering my voice to a whisper, putting the fear of God into him.

'The curse a Jaysus on the lot a them,' he moaned, lifting the head to look at me, with the mother of all sorrows crying in the voice.

'Tsk, unbelievable. Not one of them here now to help you in your hour of need,' I snorted, creasing me face nearly crying at the heartbreak of it all. 'Jaysus, Jackser, you're cursed! It looks like you may die alone,' I said quietly, letting it sound final.

'Oh, sweet Jesus, help me,' he prayed, dropping his head on the pillow and closing his eyes.

'Yeah, your worst nightmare come true,' I muttered, gritting through me teeth in satisfaction.

Jackser dozed off and I pulled the chair in closer to the bed. I gave a big stretch, trying to get the tiredness out of my bones. Jaysus, I'm banjacksed. This heat is sapping all the strength outa me. I'm ageing by the minute, I thought, looking around at my future. No, I won't be like these unfortunates; I've looked ahead and planned for all that. Two things is all you need to beat old age. One is health. I might give that a miss but I can get meself one of them fancy souped-up wheelchair jobs – have wheels will fly. The other is money – just enough for independence so I don't get bunged into a home. Too much and the kids might poison me to get at it. No, I intend to get away with murder when I hit old age, because the very old and the very young are not expected to have sense. No way will they get me to make up the numbers in a geriatric ward; they'll be bleedin paying me to leave.

Shagging hell, I'm feeling knackered. This room would kill you. It's like a hothouse. I leaned up, dragging the chair closer and dropped me elbows on the bed, resting my face in me hands. I closed my eyes then stopped breathing. What's that smell?

I opened me eyes, landing them on Jackser's thick woolly socks with the feet sticking out the side of the bed. Bleedin hell, that smell is inhuman! Then I thought of something. Never in all my born days since I knew him did he ever have a bath. No! It would be a shave, wash the neck and ears, then he was done. Washed for another week. That happened on dole day, when he went to collect his money for not working. I wonder did the ma ever do that? No, she very seldom went out. I was the gofer: go for this! Go for that!

Take a bath? Never! That was kamikaze! 'You could get yer death a cold from sittin in one a them!' he would say, shaking his head, not able to get over it.

The ma fed his madness. 'Oh! Tha's very true,' she would agree, sounding haunted and hunted. Then she would repeat her story. 'Sure, I knew a woman ye know, God rest her, she went te an early grave after bein put inta one a them aul baths,' me ma would whisper, blessing herself.

'There's nothin more dangerous, heed my words, mark them well,' Jackser would warn, speaking in a low, deadly quiet voice.

Then I blinked, resting me eyes on the feet, seeing the steam rising from the socks, with me getting the full whack of the poison pouring outa Jackser. I blew out me cheeks, thinking, the world is full of madness; now, here I am, back in the thick of it.

I sat dozing, not stirring meself, then suddenly erupted. Bleedin hell! It's billowing right up me nostrils and I'm letting it. Do something, ye gobshite! At least move, I thought, feeling a helpless sense of having staggered back into an old, dark, familiar world; one I had long ago forgotten but which was now dragging me down, sapping all my strength.

I moved my chair back, folding my arms, wondering if a body could get gassed from these fumes. Jesus, that smell! It's like rotten fat getting boiled.

I turned my eyes on Jackser, seeing he was clapped out with the jaw hanging open, wheezing away in a fitful sleep. I felt for the tobacco in my pocket. Right! Time for a smoke.

I stood up and wandered over to look out the big old window, seeing nothing but the roofs of the old Victorian houses. I could hear the traffic in the distance with the horns blaring and, for sure, tempers flaring. The heat in the city brings the worst out in people, I thought. It's especially hard on a mother trying to do a bit of shopping. Jaysus, you get worn out dragging tired little kids through the crowded shops. Then you have to stagger back out into the baking hot streets, trying to make it through choking, black, smelly fumes belching out from all the traffic. But by the time you reach that far the little ones are caked in sweets, covered in snots, exhausted from all your threats and worn out with all the crying. I bet that's when the murder rate goes up! That and Christmas.

Hmm, grand! Lovely thoughts to drive you mad, Martha. So what's really going on? What has you in this mood? Yeah! The real question. What the hell are you still hanging around here for? Jackser doesn't look like he's in any hurry to die, not at the minute, anyway! I knew it was too good to be true.

I looked over at him with the chin hanging down to his chest. His breathing sounds a bit laboured. But it's strong nonetheless. I lifted myself, taking in a big breath, listening to it slowly snort down through me nose. Jaysus, I'm bored outa me skull. This was a complete waste of good time, and having to look at Jackser's ugly mug lying slumped in that bed is putting years on me. Anyway, him and this place is giving me the creeps. Fuck! I'm getting meself outa here.

'Right, get moving. Home sweet home and don't spare the horses,' I muttered, feeling my heart surge with the relief. I went to move, I could even see myself doing it, but nothing happened. Suddenly I'm paralysed, with my feet cemented to the floor. It feels as if some powerful force is wanting to hold me back, keep me from leaving. I hesitated, staring down at Jackser, sensing it's coming from him.

Ever since I came through that door and clapped eyes on him I had started to feel meself sink. I have been slowly but surely getting sucked back into his world without even knowing it. It was as if the badness that made Jackser who he is had been weaving itself into a net. Now it was wrapping itself around me, drawing me all the way back with him, trapping me. No wonder I had been sitting here acting so viciously, tormenting him even if he deserved it. Badness begets badness. Yet it is not all down to his way; there is something in me wanting to stay close to Jackser. It's like a sixth sense telling me this is no accident, something must happen between Jackser and me, because it was always intended. Or I could still let the fear and the heavy weight of him get the better of me; just get up and run, block it all out. Him and his world of black despair, his dragging me back to the feelings of a child who is forever running in terror. But I have learned to listen to my instincts; they are what helped me to survive. So what are they telling me?

'What's going on with me?' I muttered, trying to work it out. Then something slowly began to hit me. I could feel it coming from a sense that had been laid hidden, buried deep down in my guts until now. I stayed still, easing my breath, and let it come. Then it hit me! I was never going to outrun Jackser because every step I will take since I fled all those years ago will now lead back to him anyway. In plain simple truth, I never escaped him. The terrible effect he had on me was so powerful it half crippled me.

I stared into the distance, thinking, God knows what being here might draw out in me. I could even end up being done for murder. So fucking be it! Jackser and me have some business to settle, and for that he is going to get all my attention. So here I stay, or here I'm stuck. I sighed, wanting to curse the fate that ever made him and the ma cross paths.

3

I closed my eyes, deciding to make a mental list of all the things I should be doing.

'How're ye, Martha?'

I lifted my head, hearing the quiet whisper of my name. Charlie stood looking down at me with a tired look on his prematurely old face.

'Charlie! Where did you come out of?' I stood up and rushed around, grabbing him. 'Give us a hug! What's happening? Jesus! I'm delighted to see you!'

He flapped his arms around my waist, then let them fall back against his sides.

'Ahh! Will you ever give us a proper hug?' I said, grabbing him to me.

He let me hug him – never one for showing his feelings. Hugs were alien to him; they were only for other people who grew up with them.

'When did you get here?' he whispered, rubbing his face, ashamed to let me see him looking so rough, so down and out.

My heart bled as I took in his thin grey face, with the sky-blue eyes now faded to a watery dull, lifeless-looking colour. I let my breath out in a sigh, feeling tired as my heart sank even lower, seeing Charlie was wasting away.

'Oh, long hours ago,' I muttered, not wanting to make him feel worse by passing remarks on how he looks, or to even bother him with questions. What's the point? He has set his course. I can wade in and rescue him for a bit, but then he just slips away into his nightmare memories that drive him to go looking into the end of a bottle, hoping to ease the pain with a drop of cheap alcohol.

'Here, sit down, get a seat,' I said, looking around while he lifted up a chair, holding it out for permission to a sleeping man. 'Come on. It's OK.

Take it, Charlie,' I said, waving him over beside me as I sat myself down. 'How did you know your man was here?' I said, pointing to Jackser.

'Oh! I met tha aul one a while back; she was coming along the road outside. For once, she stopped te talk te me,' he said, with a sad half-smile.

'Yeah! She's very odd that way,' I said, thinking, she might be all over you one minute, then the next, ignoring you like you had done something terrible to her. 'Do you ever go up to see her, Charlie?'

'No, I don't!' he said, shaking his head with disgust. 'Ah! Ye know wha she's like, Martha. For a start, she wouldn't even answer the door after seeing me through the spyhole, never mind let me in!'

'Yeah, I know, Charlie. She's the same with me. She never did have much time for us,' I sighed, feeling weary with all the memories crowding across my brain. 'You know, Charlie! It's a funny thing,' I said, speaking quietly and slowly, thinking about it. 'But I never could really figure out why not in my heart. I know why in my brain. It was her way of surviving; she had to close down . . .'

'Ah! Will ye stop outa tha, Martha. Ye know only too well why. It's because he never wanted us.'

I followed his finger that was pointing at Jackser, seeing him lying gasping in the bed. 'So! She threw her lot in wit him. Tha's all it is, plain an simple. But you always looked the other way, Martha. I can't understand what ye ever saw in her. She doesn't even like you, Martha, no more than she likes me. It's just the way she is. So, I won't even talk about tha aul one, never mind give her the time a day. I bleedin hate tha aul one, I do. She's as bad, if not worse, than tha aul fella there,' he said, throwing his head to the bed.

'Hmm. Maybe I can't understand the workings of my own ways,' I said. 'All I know is, I was her minder for as long as I can remember. It's in the nature of a child to want the mother to come to no harm. It's instinct – that way you ensure your own survival. It must have been something primitive in me,' I whispered, feeling an emptiness inside me with that thought. 'I still have it, that's the reason I came here today – to make sure she's OK. And the added bonus,' I sniffed, looking at Charlie then throwing me eye to the aul fella. 'To see him lying there helpless,' I laughed.

Charlie grinned, looking at Jackser and then at me, giving a little snort. Then he shook his head in puzzlement, saying, 'Jesus, yeah! Wonder wha's wrong wit him? He must be bad, Martha, te let himself be taken in here. Ye know wha he was always like. Jesus! He was afraid of his life of doctors an hospitals. Must be bad,' he said, raising his eyebrows and sucking in his breath, giving me a very serious look.

I stared at him with that thought hitting me. 'Do you think he might be on his way out, Charlie?'

We turned our heads to stare at Jackser. He was lying flat out on the pillows with his head thrown back. I could see his chest heaving in and out with his breath coming in gasps.

'Yeah,' I murmured, 'he really does look bad.'

'Oh, he's bad all right,' Charlie muttered. 'He was a bad bastard, no doubt about tha,' he whispered, sounding very tired and weary as he stared down at his hands left sitting in his lap. 'The pair of them were, Martha,' he said, slowly lifting his head, shaking it, then resting his eyes on mine, letting all the years and the weariness of pain show through now in his dull, but still lovely, pale blue eyes.

The life is really gone out of him, I thought, feeling my heart sink at the idea he is losing the will to live. I know that look only too well. I saw it often enough in my own eyes a long time before I decided to top myself. Thank God for miracles, because I'm still here.

'Charlie,' I said quietly, hearing it come out in a croak. 'Have you eaten anything? Come on! Let's go and get something to eat. Do you want a few cigarettes?'

'No, I'm OK, Martha. Thanks anyway, but I'm not hungry.'

'Ah, come on! You have to eat. There must be a canteen here, or we can go across to the fish and chip shop.'

I stood up. 'Ah, come on! Let's go,' I said, taking his elbow.

He gave me a weak smile, saying, 'No! I think I better be movin. Wha time is it, Martha?'

'Ah, no! Jesus, Charlie! You just got here. Stay another little while. Sure, when will I ever see you again? Listen! Do you want to come back home with me? We can have something to eat there! Huh? What do you think? Wouldn't that be a good idea, Charlie?' I stared at him, seeing him looking into the distance. He wasn't interested.

He puffed out his breath and just shook his head, 'No, Martha, I'm tellin ye I'm OK!'

'Right! Then let's just go for a smoke, Charlie,' I said, getting desperate to hold onto him. I stood up, making for the door. 'Where will we go?' I said, looking up and down the passage.

'There's a waitin room down here. Let's go there,' Charlie said, making for the end of the passage.

'Right! You go on in; I'll be back in a minute. What cigarettes do you want?'

'Major!' he said, letting his eyes light up.

'OK, I won't be long. Now don't move! I'll be back in a flash.'

'Ye're all right! I'm not goin anywhere,' he grinned.

I pushed back in through the entrance door, making straight for the lift. Right! Top floor. This beats walking, I thought, as the doors whooshed open. I belted out, looking which way to go. This end. I turned right, hurrying along the passage, seeing the tea trolleys making their rounds. Jesus! What time is it? I wonder how the children are? Ah, no worries, they'll be well minded. Their father is staying with them; he can manage no problem. He'll expect me when he sees me. Yeah, I told him that. So I can be at me ease.

I turned into the waiting room, letting my eyes fly around. Me heart gave a little lurch, Jesus, Charlie! Don't be gone. Then I spied him sitting in the corner, sucking on a roll-up cigarette, watching the television. I grinned, thinking, he hates smoking them things; he must be desperate.

'I'm back!' I puffed, rushing down and flopping in the chair beside him. 'Here we are,' I sighed, whipping from under the arm a big parcel of hot fish and chips, dripping with vinegar. The smell was killing me, making my mouth water. I landed the lot down on the little coffee table, with the plastic carrier bag sitting next to it.

'Wha did ye get?' he said, sniffing the grub.

'Here, that's yours; let's have a party. Fresh cod and chips for the pair of us and a litre of milk each. Go on! Drink that. It's good for you,' I said, seeing him eyeing the milk, not looking too impressed.

I opened my parcel, taking out a long soft chip, soggy with the salt and vinegar, then stuffed it in me mouth with a chunk of lovely crisp fish, taking a mouthful of cold milk. 'Hmm! Delicious,' I mumbled, trying to make short work of the grub.

'Ahh! This is the life,' I sighed, finally stopping halfway through to get in a word.

'Yeah, lovely!' Charlie muttered, giving a quick lift to his head, then landing it back to the business of eating. 'Ohh! Ahhh!' he breathed, shaking his head after lifting it for a break. 'These are lovely. Where did ye get them, Martha?' he said, looking down at his grub in admiration.

'Across the road. One of them old Italian places. They're better than all the rubbish that's opening up now. Those new places get the stuff in ready-made. Or worse, frozen! You can't beat the old Italian places.'

'No! Ye're right there,' he said, leaning down and grabbing another handful.

'Ohh! I'm stuffed,' he puffed, rolling up the paper and leaning back to rub his belly. 'They were lovely. I enjoyed tha,' he said. 'It was a good idea after all,' he laughed. 'I didn't realise I was tha hungry. I'm not usually bothered about eatin, cos I never feel the hunger, Martha.'

'I know,' I muttered, feeling my heart sinking to the bottom of me belly, seeing how thin and worn out he looks. That bleedin drink is killing him! But there's no point in reminding him; he knows that only too well himself. Anyway, it will only get him running out the door.

'Here!' I said, opening the plastic bag. 'It's not over yet; help yourself.' I took out a couple of doughnuts and a packet of chocolate Kimberley biscuits. 'That's for you,' I said, handing him a bar of Cadbury's chocolate and a packet of Fruit Pastilles for meself.

'Yeah! But I'm dyin for an aul smoke. Them aul roll-ups would kill ye! Did ye get me any smokes, Martha?' he whispered, rubbing his hands and grinning, bending into me, then letting his face drop with the sudden worry I might have forgotten.

'No! Here you go – three packets of Major and a packet of roll-ups for the desperate days.'

'Three packets!' he gasped, grabbing them with the eyes lifting out of his head.

'Yeah, if you go easy on them, that sixty will last you.'

'Jesus! Ye're very good, Martha. Thanks! I wasn't expectin tha,' he said, ripping open the packet of cigarettes and happily lighting one up.

'Gawd! This place is grand an handy,' he said, shaking his shoulders then easing himself back in the chair.

'Oh, yeah, there's great comfort here,' I said, looking around seeing the comfortable chairs and tables, with the big colour television sitting in the corner.

'It even has a lovely view, Charlie. Look at the size of that picture window. It's going from wall to wall. I'd say it's lovely at night if you were sitting here looking out at the city all lit up. Yeah! We've all the comforts, Charlie,' I said, enjoying meself no end. 'Here! Eat, have a cake,' I said, picking up a doughnut and taking a big bite with a drop of milk.

'Yeah, this sure was a good idea of yours,' he said, lying back in the chair looking very contented.

'Ah, yeah! This is just like old times, Charlie,' I said, laughing and thinking. 'Do you remember the time you decided to join the army?' I said, looking at him, letting a big laugh outa meself.

'Aw! Don't remind me!' he said, looking away in disgust.

'How long did you last, Charlie?'

'I didn't,' he said.

'No! You bleedin did not. You were in and out so fast I knew nothing about it. Not until one day these two army policemen marched up to my door.'

'Marched?' Charlie laughed.

'Yeah, marched! Stamped in perfect unison wearing big boots and demanded I hand you over! "Are you Martha Long, sister of Charles Henry Long?"

'"Eh, well . . . What's he done?" I said, giving meself time to think while I stared the length of them, trying to figure out what you'd been up to.

'"He's AWOL, ma'am!" they said. I was miffed to be called ma'am! And me only about twenty-one. I stood gaping at them, waiting for more.

'"Is he your brother? Is this his residence? We have orders to march him back to barracks; he is under arrest!" one said, whipping out a sheet of paper and landing it under me nose.

'"Is that right now?" I said, slapping the paper back against his chest. Then I leaned into them, saying quietly, "Yes, he is my brother all right! No, he's not here, nor does he even live here. But wait until

I get me hands on him," I barked. Then I erupted, "Now, as for you lot! How dare you take a child into the army? He's under age, only sixteen years old. He didn't get my permission, so I'm bloody sure it's illegal!" I snorted, staring daggers as I poked one in the chest, giving a thump for every point.

'He didn't blink while I concentrated on boring holes in his ribcage. Oh, no! He's a real man was the message as they just stood straight as an arrow, boring holes back in me. They were staring me right in the eyeballs, trying to work out if I was hiding you, the missing desperado. "Now, you can clear off and don't come back here again or I'll have the law onto you," I said.

"'Ma'am, if you do see him, please inform him he must report back to barracks. This is a serious matter," they roared, raging I wasn't shivering in me skin at how powerful and important they looked. With that, they turned tail and stamped off down the path, marching in step the pair of them, wearing their matching red uniforms with the military police armbands on the sleeve. A big bleedin army truck was landed outside the door, with the heads of a load of shivering young fellas all gaping out. I went out for a look. There was about ten a them sitting along the planks, with a soldier sitting guard and a rifle in his hand. They were all rattling and shivering with the knees knocking, praying for a miracle. Escapee desperados like yourself, Charlie, only now they got themself caught!' I laughed, looking at him. 'Do you remember that time, Charlie?'

'Jesus, yeah,' he laughed. 'Do ye know where I was all that time?'

'No, where were you? You never did tell me!'

'I was hidin out in your coal shed,' he laughed. 'Remember tha time I turned up one day after been missin for a few weeks?'

'Yeah!' I said. 'I remember. You got in with some troublemakers and lost your apprenticeship,' I said sadly, still feeling disappointed at the loss of it.

'Yeah! I started drinkin and didn't turn up fer work or me classes. I loved the carpentry. Jesus! Tha's where everythin started te go wrong,' he said shaking his head, thinking back with a world of regret.

'Oh, well!' I sighed. 'You won't be the first or the last to make mistakes. God knows I made enough mistakes meself. Divorced by twenty,' I laughed. 'Or at least back on my own again.'

'Yeah,' he whispered, staring at the floor, thinking.

'Do you remember the first time when I managed to find you, Charlie?'

'Wha? When ye came down to the homeless boys' hostel?'

'Yeah! You were only fourteen. I was nineteen. I had the baby then and had got meself married. Well, wait until you hear this! Meself and himself were loading up the motorbike with the week's shopping from Moore Street – we were down on Parnell Street. Anyway, suddenly, outa the blue, who comes flying by me but the ma. I watched, seeing her go past, wondering was I dreaming. Then little Dinah shouts, "Ma, ma! Lookit! It's Martha, back there!" she points.

'Fuck! I'm done for. The game's up, I thought, staring in horror. I gaped, watching the ma come to a sudden stop then turn slowly to lock eyes on me. She stared so hard her eyes were crossing trying to take me in. My heart hit the roof of me mouth with the shock. Move! Fast! I thought, whipping me head to him then down at the wheels. But before I could land meself on the bike and take off with a flying leap, she was on me.

'Up she flew, rushing herself in her excitement shouting, "How're ye, Martha? Long time no see!" she screams, making it sound like the banshee screaming back up Moore Street. "Who's this?" she roars, panting beside me, then steams at your man, making him walk backwards. He thinks he's being molested by a madwoman.

'"Eh! That's my husband, Ma. I got married," I said in a flat voice, just before me hanging.

'"Wha, Martha, ye got married?" she breathes, wondering what that word meant. Her face fell and the jaw hung open as she slowly turned to look at me new husband. "Who? Not te him?" she gasps, letting a sudden silence drop as she stood beside me staring yer man up and down, looking like she didn't think much of him. "Jesus! He's not much te look at, is he? Surely ye coulda done better than tha for yerself, Martha?" she croaks, letting it come out on a choke after losing her breath with the shock.

'"What's wrong with him, Ma?" I snorted, getting annoyed she wasn't impressed.

'"Ye married tha thing! An ye ask what's wrong wit him?" she slowly whispers. "Sure, wha's right wit him? Is he even right in the head?"

she demands, beginning to lose the rag at him standing with the mouth open.

"He's shy, Ma," I said, looking up at him standing frozen with the shock, because never in all his born days did he ever come close to the like a my ma, never mind meet her ghost.

"His mammy was lovely. She even wiped his arse for him until I got me hands on him."

"Jesus, Martha, tha was very unfortunate, landin yerself wit tha thing!" she sniffed, shaking her head with the disappointment. "I thought you had more sense! I don't know, I think ye were very foolish altogether, throwin yerself away for tha article," she mutters, turning her face to eye him with the jaw tightening.

"Ma, don't start. You haven't even said hello! Now you're making a bleedin show a me," I said, beginning to lose me own rag.

"Well! Wha are ye expectin me te say? Don't take yer vengeance out on me because ye're stuck wit tha!" she roared. "The damage is done, Martha! Now look at ye! See tha young fella there?" she pointed, throwing her fist at him. "You're nothin but his slave now, when ye coulda been an old man's darlin! One wit money!" she snapped, looking at me then glaring at him. "An another thing . . ." she whipped, letting rip to get dug outa me.

"Excuse me! Would someone mind telling me what's going on? I don't want to be in the middle of a riot," a voice suddenly croaked.

'Me ma blinked, hearing his voice for the first time. She snapped her head, looking up at him, waiting to hear more. He stood with his face turning all colours; now it was going black with the shock. "But . . ." he said, with his mouth opening and closing, trying to say something but nothing was coming out.

'We watched his mouth moving; mine was doing the same, wanting him to get the words out. Then finally he gasps after taking in a deep breath. "Your mother?" he croaks out in a whisper.

"Yeah!" I said half-heartedly, shaking me head miserably at her. She nodded slowly, wondering what was coming, then narrowed her eyes suspiciously, watching him intently.

"But I thought you said she was dead!" he breathed, staring at me then looking at her, trying to take in the cut of her. She was standing in bare hairy legs buried deep inside a huge woman's coat, after getting herself lost inside it. All you could see was a little head, the legs and dirty long toenails sticking out of a pair of sandals that had probably belonged to a monk.

'Then it suddenly hit her! The air exploded as a mighty scream erupted. "Wha did you just say? Who's dead? Who told you I was dead? Do I look fuckin dead te you?" the ma roars, blinking and shaking with the rage, then chewing the cheek off herself as she made to hit him.

'My nerves went. I leapt in to drag her off him before she tore lumps outa him. "Here, Ma! No, stop! Come on, leave him alone! Let's move up a bit. I want to talk to you on me own," I rasped, hearing me voice gone from shock. "For God's sake, Ma, I'm now a holy show!" I moaned, nearly crying with the rage, then thinking your man had heard enough for one day; the rest was me own business. Oh, Jaysus, Charlie, I'll never forget it. I had only seen her the few times since I was sent away to the convent; that was enough for me. Now I had her dead and buried! And along she comes resurrected!' I said, seeing him break his heart with the laughing.

'Anyway, Charlie, that's how I found out where you were staying. The ma told me.'

'Yeah! Tha's the time when I started comin te stay wit you an the husband.'

'Yeah, that's right!' I said. 'You used to come every week and stay the whole weekend. Every week without fail, I thought. Jesus! Will I ever forget about them days. You were living in that house for homeless boys. Gawd, Charlie, that was a lovely set-up. It was run by a men's business club. They were great, weren't they?'

'Oh, yeah! One of them was a big builder. He let me run free on his buildin sites. "Try out everything," he said, "see what you like, then we'll sort you out a trade." Martha, it was great. I worked with the electricians, the plasterers, the bricklayers, everyone! But ye know wha?' he said, pinning his eyes on me with a funny thought hitting him.

'No, what, Charlie? Tell us.'

'Well, when I first started there, I was only fourteen, ye see?'

'Yeah! Go on,' I laughed, waiting to hear.

'Well, I was the messenger boy, an when it came te doin the runnin about, the older fellas – well, the lot a them, really – used te get great enjoyment outa makin the fool a me.'

'Yeah! Like what?' I said, leaning forward with a grin on my face.

'Ah, Jesus, there was one aul codger – he was the brickie, the bricklayer. Anyway, there I would be, runnin up an down gettin him buckets a water te mix the cement. Then one day he's bendin down, workin along this wall he's buildin. Suddenly he stands up an says, takin the Woodbine outa his mouth, "Listen, son, will ye ever go up over there te tha aul foreman an tell him te give ye a bucket a suds an a rubber hammer? Hurry! Run, son! I need it quick for this aul job here!"

'But I didn't shift, didn't get movin. I'm standin there, Martha, hoppin from one foot te the other, starin up at him because I didn't like the idea a botherin the foreman. He was a cantankerous aul beggar, always comin around an findin fault wit people; the men didn't like him. Anyway, he was a bogman, a culchie from Connemara. So I didn't want te make any mistakes an get meself inta trouble wit him or the brickie. So I says, "Is this right, Joe? Ye want me te get you a bucket a suds an a rubber hammer! Is tha it, Joe?"

'"Yeah! Yeah!" he says, watchin me, lookin very intent. "Now hurry! Go on, I'd a made the bleedin thing faster meself than it takes you te shift yerself. Move, if ye don't want me boot up yer arse!"

'I took off like a bullet. I was a bit afraid a gettin on the wrong side a them, Martha. Anyway, I knocked on the door of the cabin. It was Mr O'Grady's office. "Come in. Whacha want?" he roars.

'"Eh! I'm te ask you for a bucket a suds an a rubber hammer, Mr O'Grady!"

'He sat there starin at me then raised his eyes te the ceilin, mutterin, "Oh, holy mother of Jesus, there's one born every minute!" Then he dropped his head, shakin it, an started writin again, sayin in a whisper, "Get out. Get out of me sight. I'm a busy man."

'I stood starin at him, Martha, still waitin, not knowin wha te do. Then he turned on me an roared, "What de ye want? I just told you to get out!"

'"But wha about me bucket a suds?" I moaned. "He's waitin!"

'"Who's waitin?" he shouted, losing the rag.

'"Joe is! Joey Talbot the brickie, Mr O'Grady," I whispered, nearly shittin meself wit the fright.

'"Jesus!" he hissed, bitin his lip and shakin his head. "If I go down to them fellas, I'll knock their block off! You go back and tell that Joey Talbot for me I'll bring the bucket of suds down meself, quick an proper, because he'll sure need it in a hurry when I put a fire under his arse! Now get going! Out!" he roared, pointin me out the door wit his finger.

'I rushes te the door, stops, turns an comes rushin back again. He wouldn't lift his head te look at me, Martha. So I stood shiverin an wringin me hands, not knowin wha te do. Them fellas would really lift ye out of it, Martha, if ye were thought te be anyway dopey; they always wanted everythin in a hurry. So I coughed at yer man an he lifts the head. "What is it now?" he gasps, really fed up wit me.

"'Eh, wha about the rubber hammer, Mr O'Grady?! Will ye be bringin tha, too?" I asked, lookin up at him.

'I couldn't get out quick enough. He threw a book after me as I flew out the door. When I got outside, there they all were, about twenty a them, leanin against the door listenin. Well! The place erupted with the screams a laughin outa them. An all at my expense, Martha!' Charlie says, with the eyebrows raised, still getting the picture as we screamed like a pack of hyenas, the pair of us roaring with the laugh.

'Oh, gawd, Charlie, ye're a scream.'

'Sure, that's nothin, Martha. Wait till ye hear this. I had te make the tea in the mornins for the workmen, an go for the messages. Ye know – go te the shop an buy their cakes, an cigarettes an maybe a bar a chocolate, or whaever they wanted. So, this mornin anyway, I turned up for work an headed straight inta the men's tea hut where they had their dinner breaks an tha. Well! Anyway, this mornin . . . Jesus, Martha! It was really a brutal day. Absolutely bleedin FREEZIN it was.'

I gaped with a laugh on my face, seeing his neck stretch, making the veins stand out with the word 'freezin'; he really dragged it out.

'Anyway! In I went te the hut, an the first thing they wanted was the bit a heat. Now, they had this "Superser" heater, one on wheels, an ye opened the back an jacked on the lead from the heater onta the gas cylinder. Jesus, Martha! It was so cold, the heater wouldn't light. The gas cylinder was frozen solid. I knew they would lift me out of it, start shoutin an callin me all sorts a names, if I didn't get it workin. I didn't want tha,' he said quickly, shaking his head from side to side, rolling his eyes. 'So! I had a great idea. I turned on the gas stove, lightin it for boilin the kettle for the tea. But instead a doin tha – boilin the kettle, ye see?' Charlie said, leaning his head over to me, making sure I understood.

'Yeah! Yeah, go on,' I said, nodding me head, listening to him.

'Well, I lifted the gas cylinder and stood it over the flame, leavin it to thaw out. Then rushed off te get the messages, thinkin te meself I was very smart, really usin me noodle like, as they were always tellin me te do.'

I started getting hysterical, laughing the head off meself.

'Yeah, yeah!' he roared, trying not to laugh. 'No, wait! Wait till ye hear wha happened. When I rushed back wit the messages, I was just about te go up the steps when there was an unmerciful explosion! I was blown back about twenty feet inta kingdom come nearly! The whole place blew up, Martha. The roof went flyin one way and the two sides with the back went another! I ended up sittin in the ditch holdin onta empty brown paper bags all tattered in me two hands. The stuff was gone! They dug me outa the ditch; I was stuck right down the middle. But there wasn't a scratch on me. Except me hair; tha got scorched!'

I erupted with the laugh, watching his face as he looked so serious. 'Gawd, Charlie. If nothing else, we always kept each other going with the laughs.'

'Yeah!' he said, thinking, then saying, 'Tha's when they decided it was much safer te keep me outa the way. I took te the carpentry because I loved workin wit the wood. They set me up with the carpenter, Old Wally Harris. He was a master carpenter. He had been a cabinet-maker until the old firm he worked for shut down. Then they sent me off te the college te learn me trade. Gawd, Martha, lookin back, I really loved them times. I could a had it made. But I threw it all away,' he said, letting his voice drop, sinking his head, looking at the floor.

I stared at him, wanting to say a million things. But every thought was just words. They meant nothing. Nor could I give him back his time, or even make things right for him now. The drink has too much of a hold on him. Anyway, it's only a symptom. It's the dead weight in his heart he's always carried around that's the problem. I knew that of old. I spent my life trying to help him. No amount of encouragement, giving out, picking him up and dusting him down made a blind bit of difference. It all comes to nothing in the end; sooner or later he's back on the drink, then it's all lost.

No, the weight he carries has always been heavier than my own. So I said nothing. Things are what they are, Martha. You are you, and Charlie's Charlie. But we are bound by a fierce protectiveness towards each other, born from a long, dark and lonely childhood – one that was very treacherous and sometimes deadly. We had to travel alone together, always keeping a lookout. We watched for the someone who didn't want us to exist; that someone was Jackser. Now here we are pulled back together. Once again, it's Jackser, Charlie and me waiting for the final showdown. For now, we just sat quiet, lost in our own thoughts, letting time pass, taking comfort from each other's presence. Then I stirred, seeing Charlie sighing and lighting up a cigarette.

'Do ye want one a these, Martha?' he said, holding out the packet to me.

'No, love, I gave them up years ago. I prefer my roll-up tobacco; it's much stronger.'

'Jesus, Martha. You should give them things up. They'll kill ye. Tha stuff has gunpowder in it, te keep them lightin! Did ye know tha?'

'What, real gunpowder, Charlie?'

He nodded, looking at me very worried. 'Yeah, that's why I can't smoke them aul things; they burn the lungs outa me.'

'Fuck! That's all I need. No wonder me lungs feel like they are exploding these days,' I laughed, feeling half-serious.

4

'Listen, Charlie,' I whispered. 'It doesn't look like anyone's coming up. Where are they? Where's the ma? We're here now all day and not a sign of anyone coming up to see him. I thought there's bound to be someone, surely?'

'I don't think there will be anyone, Martha,' he whispered, shaking his head and taking in a deep breath, letting it out slowly. 'Bit surprised, though, she's not here.'

'Who, the ma?'

'Yeah. When I saw her the other day, she was rushin up here.'

'Maybe we missed them, Charlie. They could have come and gone with us sitting here and not knowing.'

'No! Tha aul one would ask if anyone came up. Ye know her! The nurses would tell her. Sure, they keep fallin over us every time they come in lookin for a patient on the mooch. They know they ramble in here te have their smoke.'

'Yeah, I suppose so,' I said, looking around, seeing patients and their visitors draped in corners, talking quietly and smoking contentedly.

'Anyway, come te think about it, sure, who is there te come in except the ma?' Charlie said, looking annoyed.

'Huh! How do you mean, Charlie?'

'I dunno,' he said, shaking his head. 'Sure, who's left? You've been out of it, Martha. You don't really know wha's goin on any more, not since you had the kids. Even you an me lost touch! Everything's changed, Martha!'

'Like how?' I said, wondering what he was talking about, feeling my heart sink.

'Jesus! Sure, Teddy's been missin for years. Right after Harry died. He disappeared soon after the funeral. Sure, ever since Harry died, they all went fuckin mad. Teddy was bad then wit the drink. But he really hit the bottle, then disappeared over te England. He hasn't been seen since. I don't even know if he's dead or alive. No one knows, Martha,' he said, looking at me with a pained look in his eyes. Then he went quiet, getting lost in his thoughts.

I stared at him, thinking. Yeah, he was bad on the drink, right enough. I saw that at Harry's funeral. Fuck! I felt myself sinking. The weight of years of the ma and Jackser, then the kids getting into trouble, was washing itself all over me. It suddenly felt like I had never left.

'What about the rest of them, Charlie?' I said, feeling afraid to ask.

He puffed out his breath slowly, keeping his eyes on the floor. Then shook his head.

'Agnes is the same. Gone, vanished. Oh, the ma really hated her. Couldn't stand the sight of her from the day she was born! When she was little and would try to sit on the ma's lap, tha aul one would push her away. Yeah. "Ger away from me an stop annoyin me!" she would say. Poor kid. Tha aul one couldn't even stand te look at Agnes. She would turn her head away in disgust. Like the kid had some terrible disease. She used te kill tha child. Funny enough, the aul fella used te go for the ma, shoutin at her te leave the child alone. He was the only one took any notice of Agnes.'

'Did he?'

'Yeah!' Charlie smiled, seeing me look shocked at the idea of Jackser showing a bit of heart.

'Jesus! So he minded her?'

'Oh, yeah! He had te protect her from the aul one!'

Hmm, I wonder why, I thought. Maybe poor Agnes was too desperate. Usually the babies learned very fast not to put out their arms for her. She never showed any feeling towards them, so no one looked for it. It sounds like Agnes was having none of it; she was very soft and highly intelligent. She must have been determined to get her ration of some feeling out of the ma, even if that meant getting it dragged screaming out of her! Never mind if it was only a box landed on the ear – that was better than stone indifference, I thought. At least Agnes could be assured then she really did exist.

'Ahh! But little Agnes was gorgeous!' I said, smiling as I got the picture of her. 'She was like a little doll and she talked like a blue-arse fly, and that was all before she could barely walk!' I keened, letting me voice cry and my face ache with the delight and pain of her.

'Yeah, I know,' he smiled. 'She was, wasn't she?! She was really smart, too. Funny enough, she reminded me a lot of you,' he said, pointing his finger at me and lifting himself up to straighten in the chair. 'Yeah! Just like you.'

'Eh! How?'

'Well, there was nothin she wouldn't do te try te please the ma. If tha aul one wanted somethin, she would ask Agnes te get it fer her. So, Agnes would rob the shops blind te make the ma happy. Just like you! She never got caught either! But it was never enough; the ma always wanted more. The poor kid was desperate te get the ma te like her. But ye know wha tha aul one is like. Once she got wha she wanted, she would turn her nose up at it then start complainin it was somethin else she had wanted. It's funny, the pair of you. You were both smart, yet ye fell for the ma's greed; the two of youse always wantin te make her happy. I knew ye fuckin couldn't! She didn't like me, nor ever did. So I couldn't give a fuck. I did nothin for either a the pair of them! I saw how they treated you. Tha was enough for me. I fucked off the first time he threw me outa the house. I was only about nine or ten. Remember? Tha time when you came back lookin for a bed.'

'Did I? When?'

'After ye got outa the convent an lost the job ye had.'

'Oh, yeah!'

But no chance. I know. I was desperate! But someone had . . . driven me there. I'm not saying who or why. I'm not wanting to be dragging up old memories, I thought.

'No!' I said. 'I took one look at the place. Fucking Jesus! It was a hellhole. No, Charlie! I hadn't the slightest idea of staying there. I was really looking for you, I suppose. I just went in to see the ma because I had been dropped outside the bleedin door. Anyway, just as well – I had no hope of getting a bed outa her for the night.

'Gawd, Charlie! That was a century ago! I was what? Sixteen – you were eleven then.'

'Yeah! I had been living rough, mostly sleeping in the fields for a long while by then, Martha. They never fuckin wanted us, you or me anyway, Martha. Lucky for you them courts sent ye away te tha aul convent!'

'Yeah! I suppose so,' I sighed, wondering which was worse – the loneliness of the convent or . . . what?

'So, what happened to Agnes?' I said, seeing him light up another cigarette. 'Think I'll have a smoke meself,' I said, opening my tobacco and rolling a smoke.

'She ran away,' he said, taking the smoke deep into his lungs. I watched as he let it out slowly, saying, 'when she was around twelve.'

'Did she?'

'Yeah,' he grinned. 'She got herself into a homeless hostel for girls. Then, you wouldn't believe it, she got herself adopted!'

'Adopted, Charlie?!' I said, nearly swallowing the cigarette with the astonishment.

'Well, not exactly tha, but near enough. A woman took a likin te her, someone she met. She was a very nice person an she took Agnes te live with her. She had no kids of her own an she was a widow. So Agnes was like a daughter te her. But then she used te go out te see Harry. They were always great pals. She idolised him; he used te look after her when they were young. He would rob sweets for her when she was little. But by the time she went te live wit the woman, he had gotten himself a flat, too – not far from the ma's. I think he was squattin at the time. Then time moved on. Harry got married an settled down. Then Agnes got a job in a kennels mindin dogs. She loved dogs. I think she preferred dogs te people!' he laughed. 'Anyway, she turned up for Harry's funeral. Then tha was the last anyone ever saw of her. Up till then she would be over wit Harry or ye could bump inta her in town. You were always bound te meet her sometime or other; Dublin is a small place. So I don't know – she hasn't been seen since,' he said, looking worried, with his face creasing like he was going to cry. 'Ye don't think she might a done something, do ye, Martha?' he said, staring at me intently, with a terrible thought just occurring to him.

I stared, feeling my heart sinking even lower. 'No!' I said slowly. 'She's a survivor, Charlie. She's not the type!' I said, trying to picture Agnes giving up on life.

'Wha type do ye need te be, Martha?' he whispered, staring hard at me, thinking I was wrong. 'I mean, look at yerself!' he puffed, shaking his head at me and looking away, then looking back and leaning into me. 'I would have said the same about you. But, bleedin hell! Remember tha time I had te visit you in the intensive care in the hospital? You were a goner, Martha. I don't know how they managed te pull ye through! Ye fuckin up an died! Right in front of me own eyes! I was there! Standin right in front a ye when ye had tha cardiac arrest! Fuck! You nearly gave yourself yer marchin orders, Martha, wit tha overdose ye took!'

'Yeah, yeah,' I sighed. 'I remember, Charlie. And not a day goes past when I'm not down on my knees thanking the mercy of God for sparing me,' I whispered, thinking, God had a plan for me. I now have two incredibly lovely children and a whole lot of living to look forward to.

I lifted my head, seeing Charlie staring at me.

'Who knows, Martha, where she is? Or wha happened te her? She was a bit of a loner. She never bothered wit boyfriends, not as long as I knew her. I never saw her wit a fella, Martha. I think tha aul one an Jackser put her off men!'

'Funny, but the ma put me off women!' I said, thinking I went through my whole life believing women were a nonentity. It was not that I even disliked them. No, it was worse – they didn't really exist as far as I was concerned.

I had few girl friends and when I did, they had to be as mad as meself. But that recognition never even dawned on me. I wasn't aware, not until one day I was stuck with a whole load of women. As usual, they were talking about the holidays they went on, clothes and other rubbish I wasn't interested in. I couldn't get near the men. It was a party, but they had managed to group themselves off in another room. I couldn't wander in there without making it look like I was 'man-hunting'. I wasn't wanting to do that, anyway; I didn't really trust them! I was, underneath, terrified of the idea of a man getting close. But I could get around them. They were the ones with the power. The world was ruled by men, and I at the time could wield a bit of power over them! Play them at their own game, then run for me life when they tried to get their hands on my body. No way! That was the very thing to lose the only bit of power we women had! Men wanted a whore in bed and a lady for a wife. It was a very thin line we walked. Anyway, I figured when you got emotionally involved with a man and started sleeping with him, then you were lost. He could play you like a fiddle any way he wanted. So, just play their game but don't fall into their trap.

But this particular time, the women were on to the subject of men. 'I do think, darling, one should have one's own bedroom,' one very grand woman was saying, holding court among the biddies. She was married to a wealthy toff.

'Yes,' another one says. 'When one gets the mating call, or is summoned, wear out the carpet down the corridor, dear! Absolutely agree with you.'

'Haw-haw!' they all squealed, breaking into peals of laughter that sounded like breaking glass, or some, like bleedin horses neighing. They were the horsey brigade – thundering off with their men, hunting and fishing. Jaysus! It was a very grand do! I was moving in high circles then. Anyway, the one wanting separate beds then went on to say, 'You know, I think we girls sticking together, having one's close girl friends, keeps us sane. Goodness! Without them, I would die. Men! They are such clots. One can't talk to a man, share things and have the same empathy one does with a woman. We women understand each other. Don't you agree?' she whispered, peering at them, letting her eyes stare from one to the other.

'Yes,' they all murmured, shaking their head, looking very definite.

My ears had pricked up and I stood listening with my mouth open, then started thinking. Do they? Are they more understanding? What? You can talk to them? Even love them? Come to think about it, Martha, you never give women a second thought! You look at them but you don't see them; you see Sally, the ma. So you turn off when they try to talk to you. Jesus! Wonder why that is? Then it was dawning.

THE MA! The bloody ma. She was such a shadow to Jackser, she never stood up to him. She never batted an eyelid when he tried to murder us. Well, me and Charlie, if he was handy – 'the two bastards'. But he was mostly gunning for me. I was the oldest of the ma's bastards. The gofer. "Go for this! Go for tha! Hurry, ye whore's melt!" Kick, punch! "Wake yerself up, Missus!" Yeah, the mild times. But then there was the nasty stuff! Trying to kill me. Taking me off and stranding me miles in the country when I was little. Sending me off to jolly old England with a one-way ticket. Nasty fucker! I turned straight up again and found me way back home like a stray dog. But it all went over her head, that ma! She didn't even blink. She let the massacres go on. Lived in a fucking twilight zone enclosed in her own little world, her very own private hell.

Hmm, yeah, I was thinking. I fought like a little demon to make her leave him. But I was too young to understand the ways of that woman. In her mind it was . . . I have a man, a roof over me head. The rest of youse can go an fuck yerselves. Childre comin every nine months was just somethin tha happened when ye got yerself a man. Fuck them! They can lie there in their own piss an shit! Let them starve.

I tried to reach her. Get her to mind us, notice we existed. '*Ma! The babbie is eatin his own shit!! MA! Will ye look!!!*'

'*Ahhh! Leave me alone. Fuck ye's! I'm tormented wit the lot a ye's.*' Then the shutters went down and she was locked in her own world, back to her only enjoyment, which was running her fingers through her hair looking for crawling lice. Yeah, she was caged up in a corner of her own mind, lost in a world of lice, just like a bored monkey. Yes, my ma, the woman that sent me a mile, running from the world of women.

Then Jackser! Hammering up and down the little room in his cobnailed boots, clenching and unclenching his fists, throwing his eyes from left to right, watching, fearing, listening, tormented by imaginary happenings. He was tortured by them. Then he would spring, lashing out at the nearest thing – the babby or me, mostly me! I was the biggest standing thing in his way. Babbies could take quick refuge, a fast crawl under the nearest table, chair, cot. Anyway! Being the bastard, another man's leavings, was a definite torment to him. No, he didn't like the two passengers she brought with her.

Still, I did come in handy. He could get a quick and short relief from the inner demons that tortured him by lashing it back at the bastard! The upside for me? Some very handy skills. Mother Nature compensated with instincts so fine-tuned it looked like I was a mind-reader, even psychic. I could smell trouble a mile away and had reflexes so finely honed I made a bullet seem slow! Hmm, very handy, that. I could have joined the SAS. Yes, nature compensates with the natural law of survival.

A smile crosses my lips as a vision appears of a little aul one coming back from a long distant past. She is an old head on a tiny set of shoulders. '*Don't fret yerself, Martha,*' she mutters. '*We have somethin te be gained from everythin! Keep yer head down, keep goin. It's all there ahead a ye! This'll all be over one day; nothin lasts for ever!*'

A sudden jolt of pain hit my chest as I stared back in time, seeing and hearing the inner voice of the ghostly little Martha. She's not at peace, the once little me.

I pulled myself up, sighing and thinking, so that's when it hit me. Yep! Imagine that! I never noticed women before. Half of the world was missing to me, and I never even noticed. From then on, I strained my eyeballs, my ears, taking them in. I talked to them, really listened. Yes, those posh ladies were right. Oh, indeed women can be a pain in the arse – the way they argue about every single detail, have memories like elephants, get hysterical about nothing! But they are caring. They are maternal, so very protective about their little ones, even the big ones. They would throw themselves in front of a bus to protect their child. They would share their last piece of bread with you. They want nothing from you. Just your friendship and loyalty is enough. They will stand by you. They will cry with you when things go badly wrong. They are brilliantly perceptive. They! We! I suddenly began to realise . . . I was a woman too! So what had I been before? Dunno. A nobody! A nonentity!

Yes, we women really do rule the world. We rock them in the cradle. We rule them when they're men. They're too daft to know it, poor lambs.

'Martha! Martha, listen!'

I shook my head, seeing Charlie shaking my arm.

'Oh! Sorry, Charlie. What? Were you saying something? I was miles away,' I laughed, seeing him staring at me.

'Yeah! You looked miles away all right!' he snorted. 'I was left talking te meself,' he laughed, shaking his head then looking away from me like he was embarrassed.

'What? What were you saying?' I said, looking around me, seeing the nurse come in, look at the pair of us, then rush out again. 'We're the only two left here, Charlie,' I whispered. 'It must be getting late.'

'Yeah! I was just sayin tha te you! Do ye think we should get movin, Martha? Wha time is it?' he said, looking around for a clock.

'I don't know. I haven't got the time,' I said. 'I don't wear a watch.'

I looked again, seeing the night lights were on and hearing how quiet it was now. Visiting time must be well over.

'Yeah,' I sighed, looking at him, not knowing if I wanted to move or not. 'I suppose I better find out what's going on,' I said, seeing Charlie pin his eyes on the television. He was watching a man grappling for his life as he hurtled down a mountain, then landed on a branch, hanging on for dear life.

'Stay here, Charlie. I'm just going to check what's happening,' I said, moving for the door.

He nodded, giving me a bit of a smile, looking distracted, then swung back to watch the drama.

5

'Nurse,' I whispered, creeping up to the desk, thinking how late it was. 'How is Jackser? Is he OK?' I said, looking at her as she lifted her head from writing in notes, then fastened her tired grey eyes that sat in a weary-looking pale face, letting them settle on me. But before she could get a word out, her mouth opened in a sudden yawn.

'Sorry,' she laughed then yawned again.

'I think you should find an empty bed and crawl in for an extra bit of sleep,' I said, leaning down to her and laughing quietly.

'Oh, God! Don't tempt me,' she said, shaking her head then giving a quick look down at the notes sitting in front of her. 'Not awake yet,' she grinned, looking up at me. 'I missed out on a few hours' sleep. Tut! I knew it would catch up on me. Are you with Jackser?' she asked, pointing to the room just beside us.

'Yeah. We've been here all day.'

She nodded, saying, 'Yes, the day staff mentioned you.'

'Listen, Nurse,' I whispered. 'Has my mother or anyone else been in this evening since you came on duty?'

She shook her head, saying, 'No, it's just yourselves.'

'How is he?' I said. 'He seems to be sleeping a lot.'

'Yes, that's the medication. But he's comfortable. It's hard to say with old people; their condition can change very rapidly.'

'What's wrong with him, Nurse?' I asked, wanting to know.

She sighed, shaking her head, saying, 'It's better you talk to the doctor tomorrow. He'll fill you in on everything.'

'OK, thanks, Nurse,' I said quietly, making to move away. 'You're very good; take it easy,' I grinned, taking off quietly to creep into the dimly lit ward.

I could instantly feel the warm dry heat and get the sour smell of bodies mixed with a faint scent of disinfectant. It hit me as I made my way through the dimly lit ward with the light coming in from the corridor outside. A light was on over the snow-white sink, throwing a warm glow into that corner. I could see clearly an old man stretched out in the bed with his mouth hanging open. He was snoring heavily; the rest of the patients were all in shadow. I crept in further, stopping when I caught sight of Jackser. He was propped sitting straight up, with his head gently resting on the pillows. His face looked grey, much greyer than it did this morning. It looked even in that short time as if he had aged. His eyes looked fastened closed, like he was in a deep sleep. I could hear his breathing; it sounded much heavier, and every breath seemed to be a gasp. I followed the length of his legs stretched out straight in the bed, with his arms down beside each leg and his hands stretched out. I stared, sensing something – an emptiness around him. Like he was all alone battling something fearful and there was no one to come to him. He didn't seem like the old Jackser. Just an old man who was terribly alone with no one to care! Something stirred in me. A feeling of wanting to take away some of that loneliness, not let him be too afraid.

I moved over and leant down, looking into his face. His skin lay in folds hanging off the cheekbones. His nose was always big; some people said he had a Jewish nose, and he certainly did look it with his brown eyes and tanned skin. His hair used to be dark brown and very silky looking. Well, it would have been if he had not doused it in hair oil.

I felt him stir inside. His breathing didn't change, not even a muscle in his body moved, yet I could sense he had some awareness of a presence beside him. It was as if on some very deep level he could sense me, my thoughts, my intentions. It was just a fleeting sense, but I sensed him feeling my spirit nonetheless.

I pulled out the chair and moved it in as far as I could get, then tentatively moved my hand on his, barely touching it. Then suddenly his strong powerful hand lifted up and grabbed mine, holding on tight. I paused, taking this in. Wondering what I should think about this. Then I relaxed and held his hand tight, letting him know he was not alone.

'I'm here, Jackser,' I breathed, letting him barely hear me. 'I'm not going to leave you alone.'

He squeezed tighter, holding on. Then his breath seemed to slow, and it felt like he was concentrating on getting the next breath, like he needed all his strength for just that. He was determined to take every breath, fighting to stay alive. I could feel another shift in him, like he was sinking deeper, going away. Yet his hand held fast to mine, as if wanting to let me know his terror was facing death. He was leaving this world all on his own with no words of comfort or the warmth of someone to show him his existence mattered, if even just a little.

I lifted my head, stirring, feeling a sharp pain running along my shoulder and back. I looked up, seeing Jackser breathing fast. He still held my hand in an iron grip.

'Are you all right?' the night nurse whispered, looking at me as she lifted her head from peering down at Jackser, checking him. I stretched my arm and wriggled my hand slightly, pulling away from Jackser.

'Yeah! How is he?' I whispered, looking down at Jackser.

'He's holding his own,' she said, shaking her head, not looking too sure. 'Would you like a cup of tea?' she whispered, smiling down at me with her eyebrows raised, ready to rush off and get me one.

'Oh, yeah, please! That would be lovely,' I said, standing myself up and stretching, then making slowly out after her.

'Go on down to the waiting room,' she smiled, making her eyes look brighter now in the early hours of the morning.

She's exhausted, I thought, thinking she has a lovely smile and she's really very pretty.

I wonder what time it is? Ah, it makes no difference; time doesn't matter at this stage. But I better make a quick run home, though, as soon as it gets light. I need to see how the children are. Oh! Another thing! They'll be starting their school summer holidays on Friday. That's handy – it will be easier to organise them. I better let their father know what's happening; he can look after things until further orders. Ah, he won't mind; he's very easy-going that way, especially when it comes to the kids. He takes everything in his stride and lets hassle run off him like water off a duck's back!

I wonder if Charlie is still here? I thought, as I put my nose around the door and looked up and down the room, but I couldn't see him.

A little lamp was throwing light halfway into the room, leaving the rest in darkness.

Oh! There he is! My heart gave a lift seeing him still here. He was clapped out down in the corner, looking the picture of comfort with two armchairs pushed together and himself stretched out fast asleep. He even had a pillow under his head and a blanket wrapped around him. Jaysus! Good man, Charlie, I laughed to meself. You managed to find yourself a bit of comfort. Ah, I won't wake him.

I looked around and decided to sit by the window and look out at the city lights, seeing them spread out in the distance.

'Oh, lovely,' I sighed, stretching out my legs and rolling meself a cigarette. Then I heard the rattle of teacups and looked up.

'Here we are,' the nurse puffed, steaming down the passage, hanging onto the tray.

I leapt up, rushing to grab hold of the tray.

'Where do you want to sit?' she said, looking around seeing I didn't have a little table.

'Hang on,' I whispered, rushing to lift a table and putting it down beside the window next to my chair.

'I made you a couple of slices of hot buttered toast,' she said. 'We're having our own break, so we have the toaster handy,' she laughed.

'Oh, Nurse, you're very good,' I said, seeing the pot of tea she made sitting with a jug of milk and sugar, and even two mugs! That means one for Charlie. Ah! She even thought about him. My heart really gladdened seeing how good she was to us, especially this time of the early morning. Well, it's still only the middle of the night, really, and hard to get anything.

'Nurse, what time is it?' I said.

She looked at her watch pinned on her uniform. 'Only five minutes since I last looked,' she sighed. 'Twenty past two.'

'Gawd! Is that early or very late?' I laughed, asking myself. Now I gave a sigh after thinking about it. 'It's both too late and too early to go home. I don't want to wake everyone. So I better wait until it gets light. I need to get home and sort out my family.'

'Do you live far?' she said.

'No, just along the coast, but far enough in heavy traffic. Yeah, so I better hit the road before it starts. I'll probably go around six.'

'Yes! Good to get a head start,' she said, nodding in agreement with me. 'OK, I will let you get on with your tea. Eat up the toast while it's still hot,' she said, turning to rush off.

I looked down, seeing Charlie with the head lifted off the pillow, staring up at me through red bloodshot eyes, and the hair standing on end. He was confused after waking himself from a deep sleep.

'Charlie! Do you want a lovely hot mug of tea,' I said, 'with a bit of toast?'

He mumbled something.

'Right! I'll bring it down to you.'

I lifted the tray and carried it down, putting it on a table beside him, then poured out two mugs of tea.

'Here! Have that,' I said, handing him the plate of toast.

He sat up slowly, taking the mug and squinting, trying to get his eyes open.

'What time is it, Martha?'

'Half-two!'

His eyeballs widened, then his face stretched in shock.

'We've been here all night?'

'Yeah! Well, what else is there to do, Charlie? Sure, we're not doing anything. Suddenly all the things I have facing me just now don't seem all that important. The kids are OK – that's all that matters. The rest can take care of itself. Sure, you're not rushing off anywhere either. Don't tell me you are!'

'Well, I don't know,' he said, drinking his tea, trying to work out what it is he is about. Then he sighed. 'No! This place is just as good as any for me, probably better than most!' he laughed. 'Especially when ye wake up te this.'

'Yeah! Go on, eat it, Charlie.'

'It's lovely,' he said, shoving half the sliced toast in his mouth. 'You go on, Martha! Have some,' he muttered, throwing his head at the plate while he made short work of nearly a whole slice of toast.

'No, the cigarette will do me! Gawd, this tea is lovely and hot, Charlie, isn't it?' I said, taking a big mouthful. 'Ahhh! That nurse is very good. I must bring her a box of something, maybe a few sweets, just to show my appreciation,' I said, looking at him and enjoying meself.

'Ah! They're very good all right! How's the aul fella? Were ye down wit him all this time?'

'Yeah! I fell asleep on the side of the bed. He's not looking good, Charlie. I don't think he's going to make it. I'm planning on coming back early in the morning. I want to see the ma! Wonder if I will call over early and bring her up?'

'Yeah, save her gettin the bus,' he said. 'But don't think I'll be here, Martha. I'm gettin out too! I'm not hangin around this place.'

My heart dropped, not wanting him to go then vanish again.

'Where are you off to, Charlie?'

'Ah, here an there.'

'Where exactly?'

'Nowhere! Everywhere! I just have te get movin, Martha,' he said, sounding very definite and even a bit annoyed.

'OK!' I mumbled. 'Are you staying at the Morning Star Hostel, Charlie?'

'Yeah. When they let me in an when I have the money.'

I whipped open my purse, taking out two twenty-pound notes and a ten.

'Here, take that. And don't spend it on drink, Charlie! It's for the hostel and a bit of grub.'

'Wha? Ah, ye shouldn't, Martha. I know you have the kids an all tha.'

'Go on! Take it,' I said, shoving it into his hands. 'We won't starve. But you might!' Then my heart dropped seeing the light in his eyes, looking a bit like my old Charlie, but I know it won't last. He will surely blow the lot in the first off-licence he comes to.

'Gawd! You've always been really good te me down the years, Martha. Thanks!' he said, looking embarrassed because he's very shy. He doesn't like showing his emotions.

'Give us a hug!' I said, grabbing him and landing a smacking kiss on his cheek.

'Cut tha out!' he said. 'I'm not a kid,' he laughed, wiping my spit off his face.

'Ah! I know ye're an aul fella, but you'll always be my little brother,' I said, wanting him to know I love him and someone in the world cares about him even though he forgets it. He doesn't even understand it, really. Yet I would say he is far more intelligent than myself. He actually has a very fine mind. He used to read a lot and he could discuss politics, even some of the great philosophers! Yeah, Jaysus! When I think about it, there was nothing he was not interested in. He hides it, though. The weight he carries gets in the way. He never really got a chance to blossom; the drink took him too early. Now he is just wasting away, putting in time waiting for Godot.

'Charlie, what about Dinah? Surely she should have been up? Come with the ma?'

He shook his head. 'Ah, you have no idea, Martha, what's been goin on these years. Sure, Dinah took bad.'

'What?' I shouted, feeling my heart stop. 'How? Where is she?'

'I'm tryin te tell you,' he said, wanting me to shut up. 'After Harry died, she was never the same. She went very inta herself. She started sayin about hearin things in her head. Then she started actin like tha aul fella, thinkin people were talkin about her, everyone was lookin at her. She could get very aggressive, Martha. Then, Jaysus! You wouldn't go near her,' he said, shaking his head, looking sideways at me as if he feared for his life.

I stared, not able to take it in.

'Do you know something, Charlie, that you are after reminding me about? The night Harry died I went over to the flat, and her and Gerry kept saying they could hear Harry calling them. Gerry was tormented. He was holding his fingers to his ears, saying Harry wouldn't stop shouting at him. Then Dinah started. I remember she kept saying, "Yeah! Yeah! Can you hear him? I can hear him too."'

Charlie kept nodding his head, agreeing with me.

'Yeah! Tha's when it must have started. The two a them!' he said, leaning over to me then sitting back. 'Now they are put away probably for life.'

'What?'

'Yes! Dinah is in a mental hospital. She's been there now fer a while. Gerry is in the same place.'

'But he has the mind of a child, Charlie!'

'Well, he now has a very serious mental condition on top of it. But Dinah is really far gone. She acts just like the aul fella. Very strange tha!' he said, shaking his head.

'Jesus! It must be very, very serious whatever's ailing her, or whatever is wrong with her. I just don't know any more. It's bleedin cruel she should be that unfortunate. Maybe that's what was wrong with Jackser!' I said, thinking that would make sense. 'Poor Dinah, maybe she inherited something from him. Could be it was there all the time, the poor thing. But then the shock of Harry committing suicide finished the pair of them off. It sent them over the edge.'

'Yeah, sounds like that,' Charlie whispered, going into himself, getting very down thinking of all the misery.

'I don't know,' I said. 'They all seem wiped out! So who has the ma got now, Charlie?'

'Not young Sally,' he said, shaking his head. 'She can't manage either. She sits up there in her own flat an hardly ever moves outa the place. She lives on her nerves.'

'Yeah, I remember going to see her in hospital when the children were only babies. I used to go up and take her out for the day. Gawd, Charlie, she was very depressed. Her heart was a dead weight inside her. Bloody hell! Now I see what you mean when you said "Who is there left to come up?" Yeah, now I know what you mean,' I muttered, talking to myself, feeling somehow like the ground was going from under me.

'So that means it's just you and me here now, Charlie.' My heart flew at the thought. 'Everyone is just, what? Gone? Disappeared?' I said, looking at Charlie. 'Out of how many?' I asked, knowing the answer but telling myself anyway. 'They had six kids. One is dead, God rest him, Harry. He was only what when he committed suicide? Twenty-eight years old. Two have disappeared. Then two more went completely over the edge and Sally has no life with her depression.

'This is going to drive me mad if I think about it any more,' I said, seeing Charlie was just staring at the floor, lost inside himself.

I took in a deep breath, saying, 'Right! First thing tomorrow I'm calling up to see the ma. Jesus, Charlie, she's left on her own!'

'Well! What does she expect?' he said, looking at me like I should know the answer because it was so obvious.

'I can't take it in,' was all I could say, feeling my stomach churn with a sick fear. The ma is going to be completely lost and all on her own! I wouldn't want her to go through that. Now I'm really beginning to worry about why she hasn't come up.

I stood up, saying, 'Listen, Charlie, I'm going down to check on Jackser. Come on down with me. Do you want to?'

'OK,' he sighed, walking slowly up behind me. 'I might as well, I might as well,' he repeated, sounding as weary as I felt meself.

'Here he is,' I murmured, creeping back into the ward. Everyone was deep in sleep; you could hear the snores were coming from all directions. 'Grab the chair there. I will sit where I was,' I whispered, seeing him sit down looking very intently at Jackser.

'He's lookin a lot worse, Martha,' he whispered. 'Gawd! I don't think he'll last,' he said, looking like it really worried him.

Maybe he does care somehow, I thought, trying to figure out all sorts of odd feelings that were taking me over.

'No! I think you're right!' I said, taking Jackser's hand, feeling him grab hold and hang on tight. 'Shush! He can hear us,' I said softly, pointing with my free hand.

Charlie nodded, then threw his head at me hand, raising his eyebrows and opening his eyes wide.

I nodded, then shrugged much as to say, '*Why not? What harm can it do?*'

Charlie folded his arms across his stomach and stretched out his legs, resting his eyes on Jackser, seeing and hearing him fighting for his breath. I sat across from him holding Jackser's hand, resting myself on the side of the bed. We were both lost in our own thoughts, just sitting quietly and companionably in the near-dark room.

My mind began to wander, taking me all those years, all them so very many years ago, my spirit now wandered back. All the way back to that little room in Rutland Street with the light thrown out from a paraffin lamp sitting on the table. I could smell the paraffin and sense the wonder of being able to rest, just sitting in the room with a red rosy fire throwing out the heat. My ma is lying in the big bed with Charlie snuggled up beside her; they're warm and contented. We're all so happy just to be in, snuggled up and out of the elements. No more tramping through the rain and the cold, the dark and the wind, with everyone turning away from us. Then, in a matter of days, it changes.

Jackser lunges for the bed, draggin me ma out an throwin her on the floor. He punches an kicks her wit his cobnailed boots, an she keeps tryin te get up. The babby wakes up an starts cryin wit the fright. Jackser stops killin me ma an looks up at the babby. I am terribly afraid. Jackser's eyes are bulgin an he's dribblin from the mouth. I am ready te run an grab me babby, an I watch Jackser's eyes when suddenly he plunges the babby from the bed an charges out the door onta the landin. 'I'll fuckin show you, ye whore.'

Me ma jumps up an I race out after him. He holds the babby by one leg over the banisters, threatenin te drop him down inta the hall. Me ma is screamin an I am screamin, an the babby is givin piercin screams. He is frightened outa his life! Me ma is tellin him not te drop the babby, an the people from downstairs come out an look up. Jackser is foamin at the mouth an tellin everyone she is a whore an these are her bastards. She expected him te take another man's leavins. I creep down the stairs hopin te find somethin te catch the babby in an tryin te think of a way te stop Jackser from killin me babby brother, Charlie.

Jackser asked the people tryin te quieten him te tell me ma how lucky she was an not be drivin him te have te chastise her. Me ma puts out her arms fer the babby an says, 'No! I won't be tormentin ye again. Just give me the babby.'

'Here, take it,' he says. 'An count yerself lucky he's not splattered in the hall.'

Jackser's rage was spent. For the minute we are OK – all quiet on the western front. But we won't have long to wait.

'First thing tomorrow, Missus, you get tha young one inta a home,' Jackser says. Then he ran at me an punched me in me head. He kept batterin me wit his fists. Me ears was bleedin, an he picked me up an threw me across the room. I hit me face against the fireplace. Then he came runnin fer me as soon as I hit the ground. I tried te roll meself inta a ball te protect me head. He was kickin me an punchin me. I was screamin all the time, 'Don't hit me, Jackser! I'll be good. I promise I'll never do tha again.'

Jackser doesn't like te hear me screamin when he's killin me. An he's kickin me an tellin me not te cry!

'No, Jackser, I'm not cryin! Ye see, Jackser? I'm not cryin now. Just don't hurt me any more, Jackser.'

He picked me up an threw me again, an then ran te the winda. He whipped open the winda an ran fer me. Me ma screamed, 'Stop! Ye're goin te kill her!' But Jackser hauled me over te the winda an dropped me out, hangin me upside down by me ankles. The terror in me is like nothin on earth. I'm goin te be kilt! I try te grab on te somethin, but there's nothin te grab on to. Everythin is spinnin.

Ah! Ah! I can't breathe, everythin is black. Me eyes are closed. When will it end? I can't shout. Ah, Jesus, don't let me die!

I'm hauled through the air an swung inta the room. Me ma grabs me, an I'm suffocated between the two of them. Jackser won't let me go, an me ma has me by the head.

'Let her go! Harm her an ye won't see me again!' me ma screams.

Jackser drops me, an me ma grabs me. I don't even feel any pain. I can't hear anythin, an everythin seems far away, like I'm lookin at somethin from a distance. Me mouth feels twisted, an me eyes can only see through slits. I can feel the blood tricklin down me throat, then I realise I'm chokin – there's blood everywhere. It doesn't bother me. I'm just takin it all in, tha's all. I'm just glad I'm not still hangin out the winda an Jackser's not killin me any more.

That old house was next door to the little room where Matt Talbot had lived and died. He was known as the 'reformed alcoholic and sinner'. The church is now making him a saint. I could feel myself edging away, being drawn down deeper and deeper into something, somewhere, some time – centuries mean nothing here. It is a place locked in time. I waited sensing a great divide had opened. Something was coming to meet me. Closer and closer I sense its presence. Then I felt it! I wonder did you – your spirit, Matt Talbot – ever meet and comfort the two little ones as their ghostly screams could still be heard on cold, dark winter nights, crying out on the wind. Did you hush them, whispering, 'Take it easy, little childre. Yer nightmare journey wit Jackser, it won't be the death a ye's. Now, come for a wander wit me, an I'll mind youse!'

I lifted my head, resting my eyes on Charlie. Then stared, sensing a change in him. He looked like he was in command of himself. There was a stillness about him, a quiet power as he stared down at Jackser. As if he was watching out for him, sending him his strength. It was almost as if all his years of suffering had meant for something. He had enough reserves of human compassion to show Jackser what it is to be human. To touch with kindness and ease pain.

I followed his gaze, slowly looking down at Jackser. His breathing was getting heavier and the gasps seemed louder. Yet he seemed at peace, like he sensed our presence and the connection drawing the three of us together. We are now looking down on him. A helpless old man struggling towards his end, terrified of dying alone. He needs us. Once, when we were two helpless little ones, a baby and a young girl of six, we were both outcasts in the world. No one wanted us. You took us in, letting us lie under the shelter of your little room. You were strong and young and very powerful. We needed you. You did not care. You used your power to a terrible end. The wheels of life have turned full circle. Now, it is down to us. You need us; we care. It feels like a terrible beauty is growing. We had so much love to give. Yet we had to wait until you are dying a painful death to understand just how much we are worth.

I measured the passing of time with the light creeping in through the window. 'It must be heading towards six o'clock in the morning, Charlie,' I whispered, stirring myself.

He sighed and lifted himself up in the chair. 'Yeah! I have te go an sort a few things out meself, Martha.'

'OK, come on,' I whispered, looking down at Jackser. I could feel the heat rising out of him. I must mention it to the nurse, I thought, thinking, he has a temperature.

'I won't be gone long, Jackser,' I whispered, leaning down close to his face. 'Come on, Charlie, let's go outside.' I made my way down to the sitting room and opened my packet of tobacco, rolling a cigarette.

'So, are you headin off home now, Martha?' he said, lighting up a cigarette.

'Yeah, I have to go and get the children ready for school then sort out a few things with their father. I need to make sure I've left everything in order, Charlie. That way he can take care of the children and run the home until I get back.

'Right! Listen, Charlie! Will you come home with me and we can get something to eat? Then you can have a nice hot shower. It would really do you good,' I said, seeing him put his cigarettes and lighter away, then taking out his money to check it, wanting to make sure he has everything. But I knew he was playing for time, wondering if this was a good idea. I could see his eyes flickering, thinking, then his face dropping. He didn't want to come. He didn't want the pressure of me pushing him, trying to sort him out, making demands on him, with him not being able to fit in to the routine of family life. Not any more, anyway. He preferred to dance to his own tune, go where the wander took him. Drink when he had the money and when he didn't, spend the time looking for it, just to get the next drink. I waited, watching him, seeing how awkward he felt. He didn't want to say no, but he was going to.

'Ahh, Martha! I won't bother. Not this time. Thanks for askin me. Thanks anyway, but I need te keep movin. Listen, sure, I'll see ye again, soon,' he said, running his fingers through his mousey-blond hair, pushing it back off his forehead.

'But just for a run out to the house, Charlie. It will be a bit of a drive for you. An outing! Ah, go on, Charlie! Do it just for the company. We can eat something, then I'm heading straight back into the city. Sure, I need to see the ma anyway, take her up to the hospital. In fact, while I'm getting the kids ready, you can go for a wash. It will make you feel great. You'll be set up for the day,' I said, hearing myself pleading. I didn't want to lose sight of him again. 'Then I can drop you back in town,' I whispered, letting my voice trail away, knowing I was fighting a losing battle.

'Ah, forget it, Martha,' he grinned. 'I can't, I'm tellin ye! I have te get goin,' he whispered, leaning his head to me, wanting me to understand, then making for the door.

'Are you sure?' I said, feeling the heart going out of me.

'Yeah! Honestly, Martha,' he said, shaking his head, looking like he had serious business to get to. He stopped to give me a wave. I stared after him, not wanting to give up.

'Wait! Charlie! Come back here! What's your hurry? At least give us a hug,' I said, rushing over to grab him and giving him a tight squeeze. 'Anyway, I'll walk down with you as soon as I have a quick word with the nurse.'

'No! No, ye're all right. You go on ahead, do tha. But, really, I'm off now. I'll see ye,' he waved, giving me a weak, tired smile. His face looked grey and haggard in the early-morning light. I knew he didn't want a dose of me trying to drag him back to the land of the living.

'OK,' I said quietly, feeling let down. God knows when I would see him again. Now he would go one way and I would go the other. I couldn't share his life any more, not in a normal way. I wanted us just to be able to meet each other and be together, enjoying each other's company like we used to do. We would eat and laugh and talk and be easy together, like we did yesterday. I have a longing for that now with him. We have experienced things together in life, and only he and I can understand what the other feels. A lot is left unspoken, no words are necessary. We can read it in each other's eyes, and we know. It bonds us together. We have a way with each other that I could never have with anyone else.

I watched as he walked off down the passage, putting his hands deep inside the pockets of his rain jacket. Then he turned to stop and wave, giving me a sad-looking smile. He knew I wanted his company. It pained him to see all his loss. Then he was gone.

I watched the empty space, hoping he would reappear. No, he's gone, Martha. Charlie is gone. He couldn't wait to get going fast enough. He must know some place where he can get a drink. They call them sort of places 'the Early House'. They're down along the quays, handy for the sailors coming in off the ships when they dock. Yeah! And even handier for taking the money off the dockers. Very bleedin handy. Take the money off them first thing in the morning before they even have a chance to go home and give it over to the wife and kids.

6

I slammed the front door shut behind me and hurried out to the car. Right, the traffic has eased off this time of the morning, I thought, looking up and down the road, seeing the few cars moving quickly. Great! So I should make good time into town and hopefully across the city.

I climbed into the car, pulling my safety belt across, and snapped it into place. Now, is there anything I have left undone? I thought, slamming the car door and switching on the engine. I got a picture of the kitchen – everything is washed up and put away there. Yeah, now I left out a clean uniform for the kids. That's sitting on their chairs. A clean shirt and socks and underwear. Good! That's them sorted. Then I put a casserole in the oven. That should be tasty – beef and vegetables. It can cook slowly all day. Did I leave a note? Yeah! 'Dinner in the oven.' Jaysus! Men – he can smell it! But you can't leave anything to chance, I laughed. Knowing it was just me being fussy, thinking if I'm not in control the world will collapse around us. Lovely. After that, if necessary, he can look after things himself.

It's just as well I taught him to cook when I first got my hands on him. Jaysus, but the bother! He used every pot, spoon and anything that would need a wash after, not to mention the mess. 'Me lovely kitchen! I'm desecrated!' I used to scream, wanting to crack the pots over his head. It nearly gave me a breakdown. But I learned to let go, with him humming at me, soothing, whispering, 'No problem, I clean everything myself,' while all the time edging me out the door.

It was him that got fucked out eventually when he tried to take over, turning me into an invalid, taking everything over lock, stock and barrel. Fuck that! But now let him content himself for the minute, ruling all he surveys. Jesus, what more could I want? I sighed happily.

Free from doing me 'little Susie Homemaker' bit, while he wears the apron. He might even put manners on that dog!

I hung up the wine-linen jacket on the car hanger, not wanting it to get creased. Right! I'm off. I indicated, putting my hand out, and pulled into the traffic, seeing a man waving me on. I flashed my emergency lights at him, giving him a smile and a wave. I sighed happily as I drove into town, feeling lovely and fresh as I glanced at myself in the mirror. My hair looked silky soft, shining in the early-morning sun. I pinned it up at the back, holding it in place with a big brown hair slide.

Oh! That shower was lovely, I thought. It really put the life back into me. I shivered with the delicious sense of being lovely and soft. I could feel the crisp white shirt and the black linen trousers sitting nice and easy against my fresh clean skin. 'Yeah, I smell lovely,' I sighed, getting the scent of Chanel perfume and soap off meself. I took in a deep breath and sighed happily, fastening my eyes on the road ahead, not wanting to waste any time.

OK, the ma! I wonder how she is. Maybe I should pick up a bit of shopping for her first, bring it with me over to the flat. No, I thought slowly. See what she needs before you do anything. Right! Get going. But suddenly my stomach dropped and me chest tightened at the thought of facing back into the ma and all the problems around her.

Jesus! What are you doing, Martha? You know what the ma's like! She sits in a fog of depression, the air thick with it around her, screaming, '*Everything is hopeless! All is lost!*' Jaysus, there should be a placard up around her neck warning '*Vacuum of Despair. Danger! You will be sucked, smothered and strangled.*'

Fuck! You're very mean, Martha. Well, it feels like that. Anyway, it's not like I can do any good or even get thanks for me trouble. Jaysus, no! One sight of me and the face drops, then the eyes light up and it's blink with a think! She suddenly gets an idea I'm the fairy godmother come to wave me magic wand.

'Eh, Martha! Can ye get me . . .? Will ye give me . . .?'

'Yeah, Ma, here ye go! More, Ma? No problem, here's more.'

'Wha about . . .?'

'No, Ma, I'm all out, no can do!' Then the light goes out and the smile fades. I watch as the eyes turn to stone and the voice snarls in anger and resentment. No, I am now only the stranger I always was. Up goes the sign: '*You don't run with this herd! Ye don't belong here. So fuck off wit yerself!*'

So where do I belong? I asked myself when Sarah was young. All her little pals had a family. There was the daddy, sister and brothers, even a granny and granddad, with a few aunties and uncles thrown in. When I looked at my list, there was nothing. I didn't want her thinking I came from Mars! We had to have someone to visit. Not the ma? No! So it was back to the convent. I waited for wind of a meeting, reunion, gathering – anything the girls were up to I would turn up at.

'Now, Sarah, this is part of all my roots, I used to live here, you know!' I would explain, rushing in the door full of hope and expectation, thinking I would be welcome because I grew up there for a while. Well, a very short while, a few years. So they know me.

Fuck, they knew me all right! They remembered they hated me. 'The street kid! Look at her now! Jaysus, "Lady Muck,"' they sniffed, throwing the evil eye at Sarah. 'Listen to that young one! Isn't she very posh? An goes to a private school, if you wouldn't mind! An look! Yer woman has a car! Jaysus! Who does she think she is?' they snorted, raging because they had to take the bus.

'Nah, Irish begrudgery,' I sniffed. 'Bleedin gaggle a witches. Come along, darling, we're not coming back here!'

No! I didn't run with that herd either, so I didn't belong. Right, I'm a loner. So get on with it.

There you go, Martha, the past is ancient history; it's all dead and buried. You moved on light years ahead into the future. Why go back now? It will only rip you open, remind you of who you were. So why bother? Do you really need to look back?

Yeah, it's the ma, it's the lot of them. It's Jackser! It's him now lying in that hospital bed, an old man all alone.

But Jackser?

Yes, even him. If he was a dog, you wouldn't leave him there to suffer on his own. So why do it even to Jackser? I thought, trying to work out what's going on with me. My feelings are all contradicting each other. I don't know what's happening to me; I only know I have to go back. The problem is that I care. I don't want to bleedin care, but I do! I'm an eegit, but I can't help caring. It can be my downfall, my weak spot, but I can't go against it. It's not in my nature to kick someone when they are down. On the other hand, if I am cornered or someone tries to pull a fast one . . .! They go home in their knickers without even a pocket to rattle two pennies they wish they now still had. Retaliation is swift and very painful. They curse the day they met me! You're ruthless, Martha Long. Yes! Hitler looks like Mother Teresa when I get going. No! They won't be nominating me and my bones with prayers and petitions to become a saint like poor Matt Talbot.

So here we go, I thought, shaking my head, giving a half-laugh. Then I slammed the car down into fifth gear and roared up the new road, heading towards the ma's flat. It's a lovely wide open, long stretch of road. I could see there was no traffic ahead of me for miles. So I shut up the windows, leant down a bit heavier on the juice and let the car rip.

I drove alongside the flats, looking out for the ma. You never know, she could be walking along, heading to take the bus. I shook my head – no sign of her. I parked the car in front of her side of the flats, then got out and locked it. I could see faces looking out through windows, wondering who I was. Hmm! Hope the little young fellas don't touch my car, I thought, seeing a few of them running around with a stick, hitting anything that could move. Right! Don't let them see you or they'll know it's a stranger's car. They won't touch one of their own, I thought, rushing into the hall and hurrying up the pissy stone stairs.

As I stopped on each landing, I could see chutes overflowing with rubbish. The metal lifts looked like they had been hit with sledgehammers. Then I heard a dog barking – it sounded vicious. I stopped dead, feeling me chest jump, missing a heartbeat. Oh, Jaysus! I hope there's no dogs waiting to leap out at me. Mother a God! I'm terrified outa me life of dogs! Well, other people's!

I stepped onto the ma's landing and took my time about showing me nose around the corner. No! No dogs, I saw, then hurried to bang on the ma's door. I waited. Nothing, no sound. Ah! Maybe she won't open the door until she knows who it is. Yeah! That's right. I lifted the letterbox and shouted, 'Ma! Ma! Open the door. It's me, Martha! Are ye in there, Ma? Open the door! Let me in!'

I waited, listening with me ear to the letterbox. No, not a sound – nothing. It felt like the air wasn't moving, just a dead, inert silence. I stood back, biting my lip. I wonder if she's gone already? Maybe she's making her own way over to the hospital. Sure, how was she to know I was coming? Never mind even knowing I would be up at the hospital.

Right, better get moving, I thought, feeling my heart sink with the disappointment. Or she could be over in the shopping centre getting a few messages. OK! Better just to be on the safe side. I will call over and take a run around.

I leapt down the stairs, taking them two at a time, rushing out into the fresh air. It wasn't all that fresh, what with sour and decaying rubbish left lying around. 'Jesus! This place would put years on you,' I sighed, opening the car door, then taking off.

My eyes peeled on the little young fellas making a beeline for me. They stopped to watch me take off, seeing me driving up the road. Their faces dropped as they stood staring after me, looking disappointed. I grinned, giving them a wave. They're probably thinking they missed out on getting a few bob outa me for sweets! Ah, poor kids. They have nowhere to play; they just end up getting filthy dirty messing around in the dog shit and all the rubbish thrown around. Bastards, the corporation are. They get away with fucking murder, treating the poor like they don't exist.

I pulled up outside the shopping centre, then leapt out of the car, heading straight for the supermarket. I rushed around the aisles, then looked along the checkouts. My heart dropped. No, not in here. I'll take a look around the centre; she might be stopped talking to someone. I looked around, going the length and breadth of the place, seeing no sign of her but hoping she might suddenly appear. No! She's definitely not here.

OK, I better head off to the hospital; that's where she must be. Ah, it's a pity I missed her. I could have saved her the journey of trailing all the way over there. 'It's a good aul long walk too,' I sighed, trying to keep away the idea that she may not be all right, especially seeing as she's on her own now. She's not used to that. All her life she has had someone around.

Jaysus! I better get moving. Yeah, she's gone to the hospital. Just don't go worrying, looking for trouble before it happens, Martha. It will find you soon enough, I thought, trying to lift my heart. 'Oh, bloody hell! I have always worried about the ma,' I sighed. It's like worrying about one of my kids. Gawd knows I am very protective of them, even more so now with these last two. I'm like a clucking hen wanting to still wipe their arse. I always thought when I got older I would be more laid back. It's the bleedin opposite. I'm around too long to know all the dangers. The ma, she never grew up, never got happy. She would drive Jesus Christ to come down off the cross and strangle her, just to shut up her moaning.

'Oh! I'm nearly there!' I muttered, seeing the big old hospital rearing up in the distance. I must have been driving on autopilot; my mind wasn't on the driving. I pulled into the car park, seeing the best place to leave the car. Over there, against the wall. I can keep an eye on it from the top windows. Right! Get moving.

The lift opened and I turned right, rushing down the passage. The place was alive with activity. A woman in a white coat was pushing a trolley with blood samples. I could see three nurses looking at charts in the office. I turned, hurrying into the ward, getting the familiar smell. It felt like I had even added a bit of my own, I was so used to the place now.

My eyes lit on Jackser, seeing the empty chair beside his bed. I stopped, walking more slowly now, trying to make this out. Where's the ma? I thought, stopping beside Jackser. I stared down at him. His breathing was still painful, yet he seemed a bit easier in himself, like he was holding his own. I pulled out the chair and moved in, whispering, 'Are you all right, Jackser? I'm back!'

Yeah, he's awake, I thought, watching as he tried to move. He groaned, then shifted his head, opening his eyes to look at me. They seemed to light up for a minute, then he closed them again.

'Has me ma been in?' I whispered, leaning into him, wanting to hear.

'Oh, God!' he sighed, gasping it out on a long breath. He didn't open his eyes, but I could see he wanted to say something. Then he lifted his hand, barely moving it. I looked down, seeing it open. He wanted me to take it. I put my hand in his and he closed it over mine, gripping it.

'Ahh! Me aul topper! I knew you would come,' he gasped, trying to get his breath and open his eyes.

Oh, he must have been waiting for me, or someone, to come.

'Of course,' I said quietly. 'I'm here now, Jackser. I had to go home earlier, but I came back to sit with you. I'm going to stay and keep you company,' I said, gripping his hand, feeling the even tighter iron grip he had on mine.

Then he opened his eyes, looking at me, staring me straight in the face. I stared back, looking at him very intently, seeing terror staring back at me. I took in the lines and wrinkles deeply cut and dug into his face. It was the face of an old man dying, the eyes looking so very full of regret.

I lifted my face to his eyes again, seeing them change. There was a flicker, then I saw a deep sadness. They were no longer the eyes of an old man but the eyes of a young child. I could see the pain in them. He looked so lost. Confused. Lonely. I felt like I knew that little boy, like I had carried him around with me all of the days I lived with Jackser. He was pleading with me now, the child I saw staring through Jackser's eyes. I wasn't seeing the old man any more. I was seeing the child Jackser had once been. I knew about him. Jackser would sometimes say – very rarely but he would say it – 'I'm sorry I hurt you, but I was only tryin te do wha's right for you. Ye see, the Christian Brothers brought me up tha way when I was in Artane. I was there for nine years, from the age of seven. They were very brutal, them Christian Brothers. But they always told us tha was the way te make a man of us. So ye see, I'm only tryin te do what's right fer ye. But I know I went too far.'

I would look up at him from the floor, where the lumps would be standing up on me head after a terrible kicking. I wouldn't be able to straighten meself. Every part of my scrawny, skinny little body would scream in agony. But I would look at him and see the regret. I would see his hands crossed on his chest in fists. He would have a look of terrible sadness. I could see his mind was gone somewhere. He was seeing the picture of himself as a little boy getting beaten to death, nearly. Just like he had done now to me. I would get meself standing and say, 'Yeah! I'm all right, Jackser. I'm not hurt. I know ye didn't mean it.' The words were coming out of me mouth from sheer terror.

I would be trying to hold back my sobs, because he didn't like that – hearing me sob or cry or show pain – but I would feel my heart ease, knowing the terror was over for now.

So this is the little boy I see now in Jackser. He had no mother to protect him, no one to care except his little brother. He was a year younger and only a six year old. I looked at Jackser's face, seeing him pleading with me. He was so full of regret.

I took my hand away, pulling it back gently, then reached over to him and took his head in my arms, saying, 'I understand everything, Jackser. I know you never really intentionally meant me any great harm. It wasn't all your fault; you had a very hard life, too. Don't worry. I'm not holding it against you, Jackser. I'm going to stay here with you for as long as you need me. I promise, Jackser, I won't leave you alone. When I do leave the room, I won't be very far away,' I whispered, letting go of his head resting in my arms, then lifted him gently back on the pillows and sat down, taking his hand in mine.

'Oh, thank God!' he breathed, gripping my hand and closing his eyes, then opening them again to look and get his breath. His eyes stared, looking terrified, like he couldn't catch his breath.

I saw his colour darken, then he tried to lift his head. I stood up, putting my hand on his chest lightly, feeling it, then on his forehead, whispering, 'It's OK, you're all right. Take it easy, Jackser. Your breath will come.' I kept murmuring, trying to soothe him. Then he let out a huge wheeze and dropped his head deeper into the pillow. He was breathing again.

I stroked his forehead, saying, 'Shush, shush, you're all right. It's OK, your breath just got caught there for a minute.' I could feel his forehead was cold and clammy; he was in a cold sweat. I felt his pyjama top; it felt damp to the touch.

I looked up, seeing the nurse come into the ward. She was washing her hands at the sink. 'Nurse,' I whispered, 'can you take a look at Jackser? He's having a hard time trying to breathe.'

She came over, drying her hands, looking from me to him. 'Hang on, I'll take a look at him,' she said, walking back to the sink to dump the paper towel into the pedal bin. Then she came over and looked down at him.

'Do you know, he's in a cold sweat,' I said, watching as she stared down, giving Jackser her professional eye. 'It's a pity I don't have fresh pyjamas for him, Nurse. Would it be possible to give him a sponge down and maybe put fresh pyjamas on him?'

She said nothing as she reached up, taking the thermometer down from where it hung on the wall just above Jackser's bed. Then she put it under his arm and lifted his wrist to take his pulse. I watched as she read the thermometer. 'Yes, he does have a temperature,' she said, looking thoughtful as she felt his forehead. Then she nodded her head after listening and agreeing with me, while she continued to stare at Jackser, pinning her expert eye on him.

'Yes,' she finally said. 'He needs to be changed. We will give him a bed bath, then I will get the doctor to look at him. I'll be back soon,' she said, smiling at me, then she took off, making for the door.

'Oh, Nurse!' I said in a loud whisper, calling after her. 'Was my mother in today? Did she come in earlier maybe?'

She shook her head. 'No. Just yourself. She was in a couple of days ago,' she said, standing half in and half out the door, waiting while I took this in.

I smiled at her, saying, 'OK, thanks, Nurse,' then she was gone.

A couple of days ago! Wonder what she's doing? Maybe she was still asleep this morning when I called. It was early – it must have been about eleven o'clock. Oh, well, one thing at a time, Martha. Do what you're doing now. Stay with Jackser.

I was sitting thinking about nothing when the nurse came hurrying back into the ward. She had another nurse with her. The two of them pushed a steel trolley over to the bed, saying, 'OK! We're ready. We'll give him a bed bath, so you can take a break outside,' she said, pulling the curtains across.

I stood up, seeing the basin of warm water and washing stuff. Oh, great, they have clean sheets and even a fresh pair of pyjamas. He should be more comfortable after that.

'Thanks, Nurse. I'll be down in the sitting room. Will you let me know when you're finished?'

'Sure! No problem. Why don't you pop down to the canteen and get yourself something to eat? They're still serving lunch. It's not over yet,' she said, checking the time on her watch pinned to the side of her chest. 'Oh, maybe it's a bit late,' she said, letting her face crease into a frown. 'Two forty-five! No, you're out of luck, I'm afraid,' she said, shaking her head and clamping her lips together.

'Ah! Never mind. I'm not hungry, thanks, Nurse, anyway,' I said, moving for the door.

'But you can still get yourself a cup of tea,' she said, looking hopeful that might help.

'OK, thanks again, Nurse,' I smiled, heading off down the corridor. I need a smoke. Maybe I will go down to the canteen even just to take a look, see what's it's like. Then again, I could always go down at teatime; they will be starting to serve the grub again. Yeah, that might suit me better!

7

I was sitting down having a smoke when I heard the ma's voice. 'Where is she?'

'Gawd! I would know that voice anywhere,' I laughed, jumping up and rushing to the door, with me heart taking a flying leap at the delight in hearing the ma. 'I'm in here, Ma!' I shouted, before I even saw her.

'Here you are!' she said, hurrying down to me. 'Ahhh, would you look at you!'

'How are you, Ma?' I said, putting my arm around her shoulder, bringing her into the sitting room. God almighty! I thought, looking at her. She's shrunk. She looks ninety, the poor thing. I stared at her, seeing her hair was nearly stone grey, but her face was an even darker grey. Jesus, the eyes are sunk in the back of her head and she's looking really confused and lost. Like she doesn't know where she's going or what she's doing.

'Are you OK? What happened to you? Where were you, Ma? Do you know I was over at the flat this morning looking for you?' I said, letting her hear the worry in my voice. 'I was really worried about you.'

'Ah! Worry! Sure, who worries about me?' she said sourly, turning her head away from me.

'Well, I was, Ma! You should know that by now,' I said, sounding half-annoyed with her. 'So! What happened, Ma? How did Jackser take bad?'

'Ahh! Don't be talkin! I'm still not the better of it,' she said, turning her eye away from me, much as to say her whole world is upside down.

Ah, bloody hell! I had hoped she might have found it a merciful release with Jackser being in hospital; she would be able to breathe again. But it's the opposite! She's lost without him after nearly more than half her life living with him. Jesus, everything is getting turned on its head. Nothing is ever as simple as we think it will be. It is a bit like the old saying: be careful what you wish for! Now it's come and she's in bits.

'They're in there givin him a wash, Martha, them nurses!' she said, making it sound like they were giving him a crucifixion.

'Yeah, Ma, it will do him good. They're going to change the sheets and put fresh, warm pyjamas on him. He needs the good of that, Ma. It will make him feel a lot more comfortable,' I said, trying to get the idea out of her head that they were trying to kill him.

'Oh, I don't know,' she keened, wrapping her hands around each other like she was cold.

'Come on. Sit down here and rest yourself, Ma,' I said moving her over, wanting her to sit down in a comfortable chair beside the window. 'Take it easy, Ma. Tell us what happened. Where were you?'

'Nowhere! Sure, where would I be? I was at home.'

'When?'

'When do ye think? All day!'

'But, Ma, I was banging on the door this morning, Ma. You didn't answer me! Where were you?'

'Wha time was tha, Martha?'

'About eleven o'clock this morning. I just told you. Why didn't you answer the door?'

'No! No one knocked on my door,' she said, looking like she was miles away.

I stared at her. She must have been there all the time. I knew it! She's lost. Oh, Jesus! Someone has to keep an eye on her. But who? Pity Charlie can't. No, wouldn't work – those two hate each other. Sally! Where is she? I wondered.

'Ma, did Sally come up to see you?'

'No! No one. Sure, who's left te come? They've all fucked off an left me te fend fer meself. That's all the thanks I get for rearin them,' she said, sounding very hard done by. I would laugh, except she is serious! Only it feels more like a crying matter.

'Is them nurses ready wit him yet, Martha?' she asked, looking up at me hopefully.

I shook my head and sighed. 'No, Ma, they'll tell us when they are. Listen, Ma, come and let's get you something to eat. What time is it? We can get something in the canteen when it opens,' I said, wondering what time that will be.

'I'm not hungry,' she said, shaking her head in disgust at the idea of eating.

'Well, you have to eat, Ma. Sit there a minute and I'll get you a hot cup of tea. I need one myself; it will keep us going until teatime. Maybe the nurse might give us one if I ask nicely. Huh, Ma? Will I ask?'

'I don't know,' she muttered, staring at the floor, not seeing it.

'She's lost in her own world,' I sighed, feeling very worried about her. 'Wait here, Ma. I'll be back in a minute.'

I hurried off down the corridor, heading for the nurses' station. No, no one here! I'll take a quick look, see what's around, I thought, looking into the rooms on the side, where the nurses go.

I put me head in a door, seeing a big stainless-steel kitchen. I flew in, taking a look around. A big kettle with teapots stood next to an urn, for instantly boiling the water. Me eyes slid down the room, taking in the trolleys all lined up against each other, with trays already prepared for the patients' evening tea. A huge fridge hummed against the wall on the other side of the room. Great! Just what the doctor ordered, I beamed, feeling me eyes light up. Ah! There's the toaster! Lovely, very handy. Right! I'll just have a quick peep in the fridge, I thought, looking around, beginning to get a bit nervous. I'm afraid someone might come in and think I'm up to no good. Hurry!

I whipped open the fridge and me eyes lit up! Yoghurts, butter, milk. Jaysus! There's eatin an livin in this place. I whipped the head around, seeing the crusty-looking fresh pans of bread. They were all stacked on top of each other, waiting in the corner of the worktop. 'What more could a body want?' I puffed, muttering to meself. Will I make the tea myself? Save the nurses the bother? No, definitely not. They could see it as trespassing. I do not, most definitely, want trouble with them! Ah, they've been very good. They're really nice. Right! Now to find a nurse.

I rushed out, spotting a nurse coming out of a ward. 'Nurse! Nurse,' I panted, rushing after her as she made for another room.

'Yes?' she said, stopping with a bedpan covered in a white paper bag.

I stood back a bit, seeing it was used. 'Nurse, would it be possible to get a little pot of tea for my mother? She's a little upset, you know how it is. She's worried about Jackser. He's down in the ward now, getting looked after by the nurses. They're washing him,' I said. 'The poor mother looks like she's nearly off her feet!' I wheezed, hearing meself grovelling while she stood patiently waiting, listening with the piss pot weighing down her arm.

'Ah, no bother,' she said cheerfully, 'just let me get rid of this.'

'Oh, and, eh, would it be possible to rustle up a bit of toast for her? I don't think she's eaten anything today. Just to keep her going,' I said, following her into the sluice room, seeing her land a pile of shit down the plughole in a toilet-looking thing. Me stomach turned and I moved back fast.

'OK! I'll get you that in a minute,' she said. 'Are you down in the waiting room?'

'Yeah! Thanks, Nurse. I really appreciate it. Where would we be without the lot of you?' I said, grinning at her.

'Oh, tell that to the government!' she snorted, throwing in the paper bag then slamming down the lid of the pedal bin.

'Yeah! Overworked and underpaid,' I said, knowing they don't get their worth. 'Right! Better see how the mother is,' I said, taking off back down to the ma.

'The nurse is going to bring you down a cup of tea, Ma, and a bit of toast, I hope!'

'Is she?' the ma mumbled, lifting her head then dropping it again, not taking me in.

I sat down, giving a big sigh, and rolled meself a cigarette. The ma sat staring at the floor, muttering to herself.

'Where is tha nurse? They must be finished wit him now, be all this time! Jaysus, they've been up there long enough wit him! I'm goin up te see,' she said, standing herself up.

'No, Ma! Wait, sit down, rest. They'll tell us when they're ready.'

'Jaysus! I don't know,' she moaned, sounding like she was crying, then whipping her head around the room, looking at nothing.

'Ah, don't be fretting, Ma. It's hard to kill a bad thing,' I laughed, trying to placate her.

'Ah, leave me alone. None of youse want me. Ye's have no time fer me! Don't be talkin te me!' she snorted, waving me away.

'Right,' I muttered, looking down at my fingernails, then hopped up. 'I'll just see how they're getting on,' I said, making for the door and escape just as the nurse came in with a tray.

'Tea's up!' she said happily, landing the tray down on the table beside the ma.

'Oh, lovely!' I could smell the toast and me belly started to rumble. I hadn't realised I was hungry.

'Now, do you need anything else?' she said, looking at the teapot with the steam coming out and the two plates of hot buttered toast.

'No, thanks, you're really very kind, Nurse. We'll manage. This is lovely!' I said, rushing to pour out the tea, then handing a cup to the ma. 'How many sugars will I put in, Ma?'

'I'm not bothered,' she said.

'Ah, come on, drink this. I put in two. Here, eat that toast,' I said, lifting a piece and handing it to her.

She looked at it, wondering if it would poison her, then supped her tea. I watched as she took a nibble of the toast, then a bigger bite.

'Go on! Eat up!' she suddenly said, looking at me and pointing to the bread, with a lump of it hanging out of her mouth.

'No! You have the lot. I had a lovely big dinner,' I said, wanting to see her get something inside her.

'Did ye? Wha did ye get, Martha?'

'Eh, I can't remember,' I said, trying to think.

'Ye didn't get nothin!' she said, laughing at me. 'Go on! Eat some. It's lovely!'

My heart lifted, seeing her come out of herself. 'Yeah! You're right, Ma, I'm starving,' I said, lashing into a piece of toast.

'Where do they make this, Martha? It's lovely bread, very crusty.'

'Down in the kitchen, Ma. They must bring the hot stuff up from the kitchens down below. But they get the tea from the kitchen down along the passage here. Right! What we can do is, Ma, we'll go and see Jackser. Then later we can ramble off for a while and go down to the canteen, where the nurses feed. We'll get something nice to eat. Wouldn't you like that, Ma?' I said, feeling my spirits lift at seeing a bit of life in her.

'Yeah! But we want te go an see him first, Martha. Ye know I'm not here te enjoy meself! He's not well, an you'd do well te remember tha!' she snapped, giving me a dirty look.

'Ah, yeah, Ma, of course! But we have to eat. Sure, I'm staying here keeping an eye on him. So don't be worrying yourself, Ma,' I said slowly, shaking my head and leaning into her.

'Oh, are ye here long, Martha?' she said, softening, letting her eyes blink, then lifting them with interest to hear what I had to say.

'Yeah. I came in yesterday morning. I stayed with him the whole day and night! Come to think about it, I haven't seen my bed since. Then, in the early hours, I had to rush home and sort out the kids.'

'Did ye?' she said, smiling at me, listening. 'How are they?'

'Growing, Ma. Getting very big.'

'Hmm!' she said nodding, but her eyes were flickering. She was gone again.

'Have that last bit of toast, Ma.'

'No!' She shook her head.

'Go on! Here, Ma, eat it,' I said, holding the plate up to her. 'There's still a drop of tea left in the pot. Have that,' I said, pouring it out and putting it in her hand.

She drank and ate without thinking. Her mind was still lost.

'Charlie was here yesterday. He stayed most of the day and all through the night, Ma. We kept Jackser company.'

'Is he off the drink?'

'Oh, yeah! He was stone-cold sober.'

'It won't last,' she sighed, then sniffed, 'I've no time for tha Charlie fella,' she said, lifting her shoulders and straightening herself, then turning away with a sour look on her face.

'Why not, Ma? What's he done to you?' I said, feeling annoyed, knowing full well why she doesn't like him.

'Ah! Leave me alone. He never was good for anythin. He never gave me nothin, anyway! No time for anyone, tha fella, but himself,' she snorted, whipping her head around to look at the wall, then folding her arms, giving me a dirty look. 'No! Let him keep away from me,' she said, shaking her head, throwing away any thoughts of Charlie.

I sighed, letting myself fall back into silence. No point in arguing. You can't change the ma, I thought, feeling myself pull away inside, shutting off a bit of meself from her. Never fucking changes, the ma.

There always has to be someone she hates. She can be all over you one minute. Then, if someone else comes along and they seem a better bet? She'll talk and moan about you to them, then turn against you, like you are the worst in the world. Oh, well! I'm used to her ways. She is what she is – that's the ma for you!

The nurse appeared in the door and leant over to us, saying in a loud whisper, 'He is all done now. You can go in any time you're ready.' She smiled, looking from me to the ma.

'Is he?' the ma said, jumping up landing herself on her feet. 'Come on, Martha. We can go now,' she said, looking at me, happy with that thought.

'OK, Ma. Thanks very much, Nurse. You're very good!'

'Don't mention it!' she smiled, then took off out ahead of us.

The ma was ahead of me, making straight into the ward, saying, before she even hit the place, 'Where is he?'

I came up behind her, seeing Jackser looking washed and polished. He was much cooler. They had him propped up on the pillows in his fresh new pyjamas and the snow-white, crisp sheets. Me ma stared at him as she slowly walked over, taking him in with her eyes and the mouth half-open.

'Here,' I whispered, 'sit down, Ma,' as I pulled out the chair, sitting her in it.

'He's looking a lot worse, Martha,' she breathed, sounding like she had the fear of God in her.

I laid my eyes on him, seeing his face looking a lot greyer than it did earlier.

'Yeah! He's not looking too good, Ma,' I muttered, seeing him begin to really sink. 'What happened to him, Ma?' I said, after a few minutes of the two of us just staring at him.

'I went over te get the few messages across in the shoppin centre. When I got back, I found him lyin on the floor. He couldn't get up! I don't know whether he fell or wha! I don't know wha happened te him,' she said, looking really pained. Her face was creased up in agony.

I stared from her to him, seeing how bad he looked. My head was flying with the idea, wondering why she seems so heartbroken about him. I can't take it in. She spent her life wishing him dead; she hated him. Never once did she ever use his name and call him Jackser. We all hated him, feared him, wished him dead. So I always thought when the time came and he would be gone, the huge weight he bore down on everyone would be lifted. Especially for the ma, she couldn't even leave the house to go for the messages without him losing the head. 'I'm givin ye minutes, Missus, minutes te get back here wit them messages or you'll fuckin pay fer crossin me!' he would threaten, snarling at her with his fists clenching and unclenching.

Jesus, I made the mistake once of taking her out for a drive to the country. She fretted the whole time, crying and moaning. All I could hear the whole day was, 'We have te get back, Martha. He'll be goin mad. I can't take it, Martha. Me nerves are gone wit him. I wish te the Holy Jesus, tha bastard! Tha whore's melt! I only wish an pray he was dead an buried! Then I wouldn't know meself,' she sighed, getting a faraway look of contentment at the picture of herself, free and easy, with nothing and no one to bother her. Oh, but meanwhile, nothing would suit her better but for me to take her home after spending good money, wasted on a lovely dinner in a country hotel it was. She touched nothing, just pushed away the lot, looking around at people, terrified, expecting any minute someone was going to get her arrested because she was a dangerous criminal on the loose!

Fuck! I'll never understand the human race. I suppose she's too far gone, given herself over mind and body to Jackser. He got complete control of her. Now she needs every bit of him and let the badness continue. It's all she's used to! She can't take a step in her own direction; she needs him to tell her when to take the next breath. So, bang goes the rosy picture of the ma laughing and living, taking delight in waking up in the morning. Me and her and the kids all cosy, with me saying, 'Granny is coming to stay. We're going over to take granny out!' My ma even giving me advice on child rearing!

Well, ye're takin that picture a bit too far, Martha. Still, she just needs time. Maybe when she gets used to the idea of doing things for herself . . . Did she ever? No! Not when she had me. But she shifted herself when the kids grew up. She had to, with all her running after Jackser like a rickshaw man in China, pulling the load behind her!

'Do ye hear me? I'm talkin te ye!'

'Oh! What, Ma? Sorry, I was miles away,' I said, shaking me head and blinking to look at her.

'I was just sayin, but I'm bleedin repeatin meself here!' she snorted, flicking her eyeballs at the ceiling. 'He has a cold. Look at him! The state they have him in,' she moaned, leaning in to get a better look at his face.

'Why do you say that, Ma?'

'Because he's sweatin! That's why!' she squealed, taking her vengeance out on me. 'That's them bleedin aul nurses wit their washin him! Wha did they go an do tha for, may I ask ye? An him in very bad condition. Shouldn't they a known tha better? Sure, ye'd a thinked twice about washin yerself when ye're in the full a yer health! Never mind doin tha te him, an he ailin,' she snorted. 'I'm goin te report them!' she said, dragging the coat tight around her, then folding her arms, looking like she meant business.

'Ma, he was like that before he got the bed bath!'

'BED BATH! They stripped him! Mother a divine Jesus! Sure, no wonder they kilt him! He didn't look anythin like this when he set foot inside this hospital, Martha. I'm tellin ye! They've made him a thousand times worse than he already was!'

'No, Ma!'

'Did you put them nurses up te tha?' she said, leaning into me, looking very suspicious, with the eyes narrowing and her nostrils flaring.

'No! Well, for fuck's sake, Ma, he was soaking wet!'

'Right! Tha's it. Where's them bleedin nurses? They shouldn't a been listenin te you! I'm goin te talk te tha doctor!' she said, lifting herself out of the chair, making for the door.

Oh, bloody hell! She's going to start shouting. She'll make a holy show of herself and bleedin me.

'No, no, Ma! Hold on. He asked for a bath!'

'Wha? Ye mean he asked himself fer them te wash him?'

'Eh, yeah, he did, Ma. He said he was too hot!'

She stared at me, blinking like mad, then rushed out her breath, saying, 'But sure! The last time he saw a bath he was only a babby! Why would he start tha now?'

'I don't know, Ma,' I sighed, beginning to lose me patience. 'But if you make a show of yourself now, they'll ban you from the hospital.'

'WHO WILL? I'd like te see them!' she screamed, waving her arms like windmills.

Oh, Jesus! Me nerves. She's going to let fly!

A nurse came out of a ward and stopped, looking down at us with her eyebrows screwed together, looking shocked and worried, wondering what the roaring was about. I could see the ma's face working. It looked like her cheeks were shivering, and her eyes kept blinking. Then she gave a little cough, gasping in a big breath, trying to find her voice.

'EXCUSE ME, PLEASE, NURSE! I WANT A WORD WIT YOU!'

'Ma! Don't! Stop, Ma!' I croaked. 'If you open your mouth,' I hissed, 'that's it, you are on your own. These nurses have been very good to Jackser! Now leave well alone. Here, come on, let's go and get something to eat!' I said, trying to pacify her.

'Eat? Is tha all you can think of?'

'Yeah! After I sort them out,' I snorted, hoping this might work. 'Now! You sit back in there and I'll handle this. I'll demand we see the doctor!'

She hesitated, letting the eyelashes fly, blinking like mad, thinking.

'Yeah,' I said, seeing her let go. 'It's better not to say too much now, otherwise they'll only take it out on Jackser, maybe start ignoring him. Now we don't want that, Ma. We need them!'

She snorted, then lifted her shoulders, dropping them and letting the wind go out of her sails, saying, 'Well, OK, then, but you tell them for me, if I don't get satisfaction outa them – I want him cured, not kilt – or I'll be up te see me solicitor first thing tomorra!' she huffed, letting her head drop then lift as she pinned her eyes on Jackser, sitting herself down in the chair beside him.

I took off out the door, looking for a nurse. Yeah, we need to find out when that doctor is going to take a look at Jackser. I can't bear to see him suffering like that, gasping for every breath! You wouldn't leave an animal in that state. That's what's upsetting the ma, too. It's seeing all the suffering he's going through. Somehow I don't think all of that is necessary.

8

'He's on his way, Ma. The nurse just told me the doctor will be here any minute,' I said, walking back into the ward, seeing her staring into space. 'The doctor is coming, Ma,' I whispered, leaning down with my hand on her shoulder.

'He's bad,' she muttered to herself. 'I don't know wha happened te him at all. I came back an found him on the floor! It happened when I was gone. I wonder how long was he lyin there? Jesus! The shock it gave me! I'm still not the better of it,' she said, stroking her forehead.

'Yeah, I know, Ma,' I said, feeling a heavy weight dragging me down. It was the weight of me heart sitting in my belly, listening and seeing her look so far into herself. 'Oh,' I sighed, feeling exhausted. 'I need a smoke,' then thinking, if there was only some way to lift her, give her a bit of hope. She's now seeing the future on her own and it's killing her.

'Ma, listen, I'm just going down for a quick smoke. Will you come with me? Or do you want to stay here?'

Just then we heard footsteps. I looked up to see the doctor sweeping into the ward then making straight over to us.

'The doctor's here, Ma!' My heart quickened, hoping he could sort something out for Jackser.

'Yeah, about time,' she muttered, standing up and pinning her eyes on him.

'I'm just going to examine him. Would you mind please waiting outside?' he said, waving us away from the bed. 'I will call you when I have finished my examination,' he said, seeing us staring at him. Then he pulled the curtain around, blocking us out.

'OK, thanks, Doctor. Come on, Ma.' I took her arm, feeling relieved the doctor was here. 'Let's go down to the waiting room. I want to have a smoke.'

'We can't go too far, Martha! You heard him, he will be looking for us!' she said, sounding worried.

'No, Ma, don't worry. He knows where to find us,' I said, as we walked down to the waiting room.

'Let's hope he can do something, Martha,' me ma said, voicing my thoughts.

'Yeah, Ma. They can't leave him like that,' I warned, reaching for my tobacco.

'This waitin would kill ye,' the ma sighed, drawing in a deep breath then letting it out, dropping her shoulders again.

'Yeah,' I muttered, going back to stare into space.

'Hospitals would put years on ye,' me ma sighed again, wanting to hear herself.

Yeah, Ma, good idea to make some noise, I thought. Anything was better than the sheer mind-breaking silence around us. I'm just sitting, listening, waiting, with not even a thought going through my skull to occupy me or distract me. I lowered my head, letting the heavy air, thick with the ma's tension, sit on my chest. Then I suddenly exploded air out, puffing. Jesus! This is going to kill me! It will be her! Or else from sitting around this hospital. The place is full of bloody disease, I thought, thinking that is something the ma would say. Then it hit me! Bloody hell, I have picked up every despairing feeling the ma is carrying and now it has a hold on me. It's managed to wrap itself around me; now it's threatening to strangle me. Jaysus, I feel like I'm suffocating, I thought, wanting to get up and run.

I lifted my head a bit, looking over at her. Then I stared, seeing her stooped in the chair. Her eyes were locked on the floor, staring into the distance. I could see her jaw working up and down, chewing the inside of her mouth. She kept blinking and thinking, with her breath ready, always, to take that little cough. She looked so old, yet she was only sixteen years older than meself. With her thin grey hair and the grey old skin, and the tired old eyes looking like she has spent a lifetime in tears, there was so much pain staring out of them eyes.

Suddenly I could feel a dam burst as an ocean of pain and a sea of tears swelled up inside me. I wanted to cry my heart out as I stared over at her. Oh, Mammy, Mammy! My poor little mammy. I wanted to rush over there and wrap her to my chest. She looks so small and frail and thin, all worn out from living.

I could feel a terrible longing coming over my chest. Oh, if only, if only I could turn back the clock. Images – pictures of pain and misery and mayhem – rushed across my mind. The images kept flying, a grey blur, going faster and faster down through the years. So much time. On and on they go, making me grimace as I fall back, flying down the years of my childhood.

An image stops. I get pulled into a room. A little baby sits on dirty black wooden floorboards looking up at me. He's naked, except for a dirty grey vest that only covers his belly button. His tiny body is purple with the cold, and his huge blue eyes look like saucers as they stare out through his tired, pinched little white face. His blond, matted, fluffy baby hair stands up stiff with the dirt.

He sits with his hands on his knees, looking around. He is wondering if there is something to eat, or touch, or taste, or bang, or squeeze – just something he can crawl to. He has a longing to feel, to be felt, touched. But he sees nothing. Only the dirty floorboards and the dirty bare legs and feet moving around him. There's nothing but to keep well away from the big boots that might stand on him; then he will get himself hauled by the neck and sent flying through the air. Mercifully, if he's lucky, he doesn't get smashed against the bars first; he'll end up safely in the cot.

Other shadowy little figures, bigger ones – they can walk – sit and stare around the room. They are waiting. Sitting waiting for the cold to go. For the food that would never come, for the hunger to pass. For the fear to ease, for the dark to come. Then they can hide under the coats and the blankets. It is just the waiting; the room is thick with it. It is heavy with their wants and the despair of knowing nothing is coming. The air is filled with the emptiness of their wants, so they sit and wait and stare. They have trained their senses to be always on the alert; they are looking out for danger. It will come from the big, black, heavy cobnailed boots. They are, right this minute, slowly marching up and down the room in a rhythmic pounding, making the floorboards rattle.

I see a thin little girl. She stands very still on matchstick legs against a bare dirty wall close to the door. She is inert. Her eyes stare into the distance, but they are alive, watchful. She takes a slow blink, keeping watch on the man walking up and down to the window. She sees as he stops, looks out, turns, then walks back, staring at the floor, having a conversation with himself. He looks very agitated as he snorts air in and out quickly, the madness bulging out of his bloodshot eyes as they stare out of his head. He keeps clenching his fists, hissing in his breath, but he has not noticed her yet. His fight is with himself at the minute, and the demons in his head tormenting him. The girl must not let her mind wander or her guard down. She will sense a hair's breadth of change in the air. Her instincts are finely tuned to spring at the slightest movement signalling danger. This speed protects her, allows her to cling fiercely to this world. Any minute, Jackser can suddenly lift his eyes and see her; she is then the demon. He will lunge for her and maybe this time he will go too far. She could lose her life.

Another shadowy figure sits hunched over by an empty fire grate. She keeps her head down, running her fingers through her thin brown hair, looking for lice. She sees nothing and no one. She sighs and prays, talking to herself with her eyes turned inwards. She is not waiting; she gave that up a long time ago when she met a man who would take care of her, mind her and shelter her and her two children. Their fathers had run, leaving her and them to the elements. Now she would be cherished, looked after properly, better than her five-year-old girl could do. But the man was her worse nightmare. She stopped looking, wishing or believing something better could happen. It was him or walking the streets looking to a five year old to make her dreams come true. So she turned to death. It's the only way out. Now she lives in a twilight world, wishing and praying, getting angry and impatient as she hisses, 'Oh! I wish I was dead. I wish it would hurry up an take me.' Then she falls back into stillness, waiting in a black hole of despair for time to pass and death to finally come and claim her.

As I stood watching, taking in the picture, I could feel the thick, suffocating air of stillness, a feeling of everyone waiting for something that will never come. They know that nothing of their wants, needs, will ever happen – no, they will never be met. So they all sit, desolate of any life that will bring hope. They were born to endure; they must exist only to feel a terrible sense of aching emptiness.

Oh, Ma! Mammy! The pain in me, the longing, the ache in me is making me cry inside. I long, Ma, to be able to go back, to be given that power to stand you on your feet and turn you around. I want to force you to open your eyes, then to pump life into you at what you see. I want to shout, 'Ma! Ma, look! You have your health, you are young, look at all else you have, Ma. Look at your lovely children! Look hard at them; they are dying inside. Oh, but they are so beautiful. Look at the little babby sitting in the dirt. He's waiting for you to pick him up. He longs for you to warm him against your body and chase away his fears. He needs you to feed him, clothe him and make him feel safe and snug. He cries for you to bring him into a world with the sound of laughter and to feel the warmth from a ray of golden light. He wants to know and feel the wonder of it all.

Look at the others – the little ones standing up looking at you with the clothes caked to their skin from the dirt. They're in rags, Ma. Their huge haunted eyes are staring out at you, you who brought them into this world. They want you too, Ma. They need you. They look to you to give them mercy. They ask for so very little. Just to be warm and dry and safe, no more than a cub lion gets from its mother in the wilderness. But their pain is getting deeper now because they know, they learnt, the world is a terribly dark place. Oh, they are afraid all the time. Who is causing it all, Ma? You! Him there! That man! That lunatic rattling the floorboards, walking up and down the room talking to himself. The one taking up all the space, making everyone stand out of his way, leaving them all terrorised, hiding themself crouched in corners.

Ma, the world belongs to you, too! These are your children! Use your rage by thinking as a mother. Say, 'No! No more! No more!' Get him locked up in a mental institution. Look at him! He's stone mad. He's not well! That's an easy thing to do, Ma. Anyone can be locked up! You know that. There's a place for everyone, even the children; they lock them up, too. That was your worst fear when you were on the run with me as a small child. They were looking to take me and put you away in a Magdalene laundry. But you kept running. Now it's time to stop running from your mistakes, Ma. Take the house from under Jackser! Get him locked away! Then go out and beg, borrow and steal. What you can't get, Ma, ROB! Do whatever it takes to rear, protect and nourish your children, Ma. Make their world a place of magical wonder for a child. Just be a mother, be a woman.

If only, if only, I thought, shaking my head slowly. So much suffering, so much pain – what a waste. Oh, Ma! You were fucking hopeless! No! I can't go back. I can't ever undo the damage. Jesus, sometimes I hate and love the ma in equal measures. They both end up cancelling each other out. No wonder I forgot she existed and buried her. Now she's back with a vengeance and dragging me down with her. Fuck! I'm cursed because I love her.

'Martha! Martha, for Jaysus sake, will ye wake up outa tha? I'm tryin te talk te you!'

'What! What, Ma?' I looked up, seeing her bending over me, talking into my face. 'Oh, sorry, Ma! I was just resting. The tiredness is catching up on me. I didn't get to my bed last night,' I sighed, giving a yawn.

'Listen te me, Martha. Tha doctor's been in there fer hours now. I'm thinkin he coulda been finished long ago an may be gone off without tellin us! Will we go up an see?' she said, staring at me with a worried look on her face.

'But sure you could have gone yourself, Ma, and checked!' I said, seeing the dirty look she was giving me, as if it was my fault in the first place Jackser was even sick.

She shook her head, looking like the idea horrified her. 'No! No, come on, you go an see.'

I stood up, saying, 'OK, Ma. I'll just see if he's still there.'

The ma doesn't want to face up to the truth that Jackser is bad, I thought. This is going to be real hard for her no matter what anyone else thinks. In her mind, Jackser is the world for her – a world of horror, but it's still her world. The damage is done for her – she's programmed to obey him.

Then it hit me! I am Pavlov's dog – I must obey. He trained his dog to respond to a bell. Every time he rang the bell, the dog would start salivating. He knew he would get grub! Pavlov showed the world. See, we are all like this dog. We can break your mind and condition you into believing what we want you to. And don't I know it! The world is full of bleedin zombies all marching to the same tune, people following each other like sheep. They have been taught to obey the rules. Even when they know something is wrong, nobody will step outside the line. I think it must be primitive instinct. Stay with the herd, follow the leader. The experts have spoken; they must be right. We have to listen to 'our betters'.

That is why I am grateful now I never set foot inside any learning establishment. Schools are wonderful for the rest of the world, especially my children. They train your mind to think; they help you to develop your strengths. Grand! Lovely! But not for me, thanks! Because the downside to this is they condition your mind to think as they want you to think. I have no knowledge of that. So I wander off happily, discovering the wonder of learning in my own sweet way, with no one to tell me how I should think. Therefore, I may learn the hard way, go the long way about things – discovery is a slow business – but I am daft enough to believe I can move mountains, because no one has told me that is not possible. I know nothing about physics, gravity or other such mundane things. But I have discovered you can move mountains.

The great eminent, learned scientists will tell you it is not possible to move a mountain through sheer mind power alone. We will prove it to you. I know nothing about nothing. But I know what I want – I want that mountain to move. Then the fire in my belly rages – I will move that mountain! That is what makes it move. I am deaf to all around me who say that is not possible. They are taught to believe; I am not!

The ma was a broken woman long before she met Jackser. She carried herself to him. He took her and trained her like Pavlov's dog. She is going to need someone to mind her, Martha! Fuck! The curse of love – I can't say no. This love is not something you feel; it is way beyond that. It is paying back to her for the gift of giving me life. But, Jaysus, if God had sense he would have stayed awake when he was dishing out the gift of a child. A mother can wield an unholy power, then the child will curse the heavens as Harry did. A quick and brutal end, when he took that flying death leap, was preferable to a living hell. 'God rest you, Harry, may you now rest in peace,' I sighed. 'OK, enough, Martha, enough!' I whispered, coming out of my doze.

I put me head inside the ward, seeing the curtain drawn around the bed and bodies pressing against it. Oh! They are still with him.

A nurse appeared out, coming arse first, dragging a long pole with a drip.

'Nurse! What's happening? Is everything OK?'

'Yes, the doctors are with him now. We shouldn't be too much longer. Just take a seat in the waiting room. The doctor will come and see you.'

I wandered back to wait, pulling my tobacco out and rolling meself a cigarette.

'Wha's happenin, Martha? Are they ready yet? Jesus Christ! How long does it take them?' she cried, twisting her face, making her keening sound like a Banshee's wail.

'They'll be ready when they're ready, Ma,' I sighed, puffing out me breath, then suffocating in smoke.

'Here he is! Here's the doctor, Martha. Come on! Gerrup!' me ma whispered, hissing at me with her eyes leppin out of her head. Then she stood herself up, blinking and coughing, getting ready to hear the news.

He marched in, jamming a stethoscope into his white coat pocket, then stood, rocking on his feet, looking from me to the ma. I watched as his big mop of curly brown hair bounced around on the top of his head. We waited while he prepared himself to say what he wanted to say. He was thinking of the best way to get it out, I could see by the way he was watching the ma. He knew she wasn't going to take any news he gave her too well at all.

'Ahem! Yes, well,' he paused, looking from me to her, wondering which one of us is best he should make the eyeball contact with. He plumped for the ma – she looked more desperate.

'We have examined your husband.'

Husband? I thought. She never married in her life! But he was married . . . for a few weeks, I think! Yeah, he told me that in one of his more sentimental moods. I was six, yeah! He said the new missus was stone mad; she tried to kill him! Yeah, she's still my hero! You don't mess with a Moore Street dealer. They'd ram their carrots down your neck.

'Your husband has pneumonia.'

'PNEUMONIA!' me ma squawked.

'Yes, double pneumonia,' he said, his face looking very grave as he bounced back on his heels then let his head bow to her.

'But didn't I tell you this would happen? I knew it! I knew! I was right all along,' she puffed, working up the breath, getting ready to explode.

Me heart started to jig!

'That's youse are fault!' she screamed, stabbing him in the chest with her finger.

Oh, fuck! I thought, grabbing her. 'Ma! Ma! Calm down, take it easy. Let the doctor talk.'

'It's them! It's all their fault!' she shouted, looking at me. 'An yours! You're every bit as much te blame. You put them up te it! He's in there now, fightin fer his life. They have kilt him wit their bed baths!'

'That's enough now, Ma. Calm down!' I said, seeing the young doctor walking himself backwards, standing close to the door. He was turning all colours, mostly white to match his coat.

This is not helpful to anyone, I thought, most importantly not to the ma and Jackser. I could see ourselves now becoming outcasts, with everyone giving us a wide berth. We would lose all respect, seeing as we have no respect for them.

'Calm down, Ma! Calm down, please, or the doctor will walk away and so will I,' I said, being brutal to force some sense back into her.

She started to cry.

'Oh, Ma, come on. I'm sorry, Ma,' I whispered, putting my arm around her. 'Come on over here. Sit down there,' I said, quietly and gently, putting her sitting in the seat to rest. 'Let's hear what he has to say, Ma. He knows you are upset.' I looked up at the doctor, seeing he looked shocked, not knowing how to take this.

'Listen, Doctor. What exactly is happening?'

'Well,' he said, 'the news is not good. He has had a stroke.' Then he looked at me, waiting, saying nothing.

'So it's bad, then?'

'Yes.'

'So what can you do for him? He's in terrible distress. It's almost impossible for him to breathe. What can you do? What about physiotherapy?'

He nodded his head, agreeing, then said, 'But I think the immediate problem is to get him comfortable. We are going to give him oxygen and increase his medication. We will keep him under sedation and, meanwhile, get the antibiotics into him. So we are working on that right away,' he said, making to move away from me.

'OK, thank you, Doctor,' I nodded, watching him take off. 'Ma,' I said, seeing her sitting in the chair, wiping her eyes and nose with the sleeve of her cardigan.

'Wha? Wha did he say te ye, Martha?' she whispered, looking up at me, hoping I might have better news.

'Ma, they're going to make him comfortable. He'll be able to breathe easier in himself. They're going to give him oxygen and give him antibiotics.'

'But will he be all right? Will he get better, Martha? Tha's my big worry!'

'I know, Ma,' I said, feeling my heart break at seeing her look so lost and helpless. 'Listen, Ma, he's in great hands,' I said, getting her to her feet. 'The doctors are doing everything in their power to look after him. Look, come on, let's go down and see him. At least now we know he's getting something to help him.'

9

We hurried into the ward, then slowed down when we saw Jackser. He was snow-white, like all the blood had been washed out of him. We stared, letting our eyes take in the sight of him. He had an oxygen mask wrapped around his face, helping him breathe. We listened, hearing it make a hissing sound, then watched it send out a vapour of white, icy-cold air, heading straight for Jackser's lungs. Some of it was managing to escape and waft up around him, then settle itself on his face. But that was grand, because it was cooling the air nicely around him.

He looks very still, I thought, as if he's dead to the world. The only life you can see is coming from his chest. I watched, seeing it slowly lift and heave, sucking in the air, then pause as it pushed out hard, breathing heavily, letting us know he's still very much alive and kicking.

We both stared, saying nothing, then walked over slowly and stood quietly beside him, with the ma on one side and me on the other. We could see him breathing hard, but it was steady and he looked more at peace now.

'He's lookin better, isn't he, Martha?'

'Yeah!' I nodded, seeing him look more at ease. 'Sit down, Ma,' I said, pulling over a chair for her. 'Ah, yeah, he's definitely a lot better now with that oxygen helping him breathe more easily, isn't he, Ma?' I whispered, looking at her.

'Oh, yeah! Indeed he is,' me ma whispered back, looking more content in herself now as she sat quietly, just keeping her eyes on him.

The time ticked away slowly as the hospital seemed to quieten down. There were long periods of silence with nothing happening. Even the nurses seemed to have disappeared off somewhere. All that could be heard was the coughs and groans and snores of the patients, with them all dozing in their beds. At least the heat is going out of the sun. I sighed, seeing it vanish behind the building, now gone from the windows.

I shifted meself, trying to get more comfortable by letting my hands rest on me chin and the elbows dig into the mattress. Then I thought about slinging me legs across and resting the feet on Jackser's bed. Ah, but no! I better not. It wouldn't look right.

Me ma had her eyes closed, resting herself back in the chair. At least she's peaceful. I hate seeing her getting all upset. Jaysus! What wouldn't I give now just to be able to climb into one of these beds. The heat and the stuffiness is really making me eyeballs feel like lead weights.

Suddenly, the hospital fired up again. I could hear the noise of banging dishes and feet rushing, then the voices of people shouting down orders to each other. I lifted meself up, feeling more alert at the sound of the tea trolley. Must be teatime!

I watched as the tea trolley came crashing into the room. The patients woke up, smacking their dry lips and shaking themselves awake, then rubbing their eyes as they lifted their head, then looked around, landing it on the plate coming in their direction.

'Here ye go, love!' a grey-haired woman in a blue smock cheerfully roared as she slammed the plate down on a bedside tray. Then she sent the whole lot flying up to an aul fella, he was sitting ready and waiting, watching as she whipped off the cover.

Me eyes lit on the rashers, sausages and eggs with the steam coming out and the smell wafting over, making me mouth water and the belly rumble.

Me ma stirred herself, opening her eyes. Then straightened herself up to see what's happening.

'It's teatime, Martha! They're givin out the tea,' she said, leaning forward, looking very interested to see what the patients were getting.

'Yeah,' I smiled happily, feeling meself coming wide awake with the life roaring back into me. It was at the sight and the smell from all the grub. 'They're getting a fry, Ma, or lovely-looking salads,' I said, seeing the plates of meat and hard-boiled eggs. 'Jaysus, Ma! I'm starving. Let's go down and get something to eat in the canteen,' I said, standing up and looking at her.

'Do ye think so, Martha? Wha about him?' she said, waving her finger at Jackser. 'Will they be givin him somethin te eat, do ye think?'

I looked at him, seeing him a dead weight in the bed.

'No, Ma. I think he'll be getting what he needs through that drip there.' His arm was attached to a long tube running up to bags hanging off a pole. I could see three bags hanging down. 'He wouldn't be able to eat anything, Ma. He's fast asleep,' I said, thinking, he is out cold, completely unconscious.

'Are ye sure, Martha? Maybe they should wake him up! He needs te eat, Martha! Will I just ask the nurse? It can't do any harm,' she whispered, looking around herself for sight of a nurse.

'No, Ma, leave it. They know what they're doing. He can't manage. He needs his sleep. Rest is the best thing for him now,' I said, not wanting to say he is probably in a coma. 'His nourishment is going in through the tube attached to his hand, Ma. Come on! A bit of grub will give you energy. You need to keep up your strength.'

We walked into the big canteen and stopped to look around us.

'It's crowded wit the people, Martha. We won't get a seat,' she muttered, looking very down in the mouth with her disappointment.

My eyes searched the room, then clapped sight of a couple of empty tables spread out at the far back.

'Listen, Ma, let's go over and see what they have, then you go down and sit at the empty table at the back. I'll bring the grub down.'

'OK,' she said, blinking and chewing, not looking too sure.

'What would you like, Ma?' I said, feasting me eyes on the delicious-looking hot food. I could see it all lined up, sitting behind a well-lit glass in stainless-steel containers. 'You can have a fry, Ma! Look at them lovely rashers and eggs and tomatoes. Now, if you don't want that, you can have fish and chips. It's cod,' I said, looking up at the sign on the wall. 'Or you can have a roast-beef salad. What would you like?'

Me ma searched her eyes up and down, going the length and breadth of what was on offer, not looking too impressed. 'Ah, I don't know, Martha. I'm not really all tha hungry,' she moaned, changing her mind.

'Come on, get something. What will I have? I would love any of them, but I think I will go for the fish and chips,' I said. 'Do you want the roast beef, Ma?'

'No! Yeah! OK. Wait! Are them chips nice, Martha?' she asked, ready to pass remarks before she even tasted them.

'Yeah! They look lovely. Will I get you the same as me?'

'Yeah! OK, go on then. But hurry! I don't want te be left sittin on me own. Where's tha table ye said, Martha? I don't see it,' she said, squinting around the room, letting her face drop in misery. 'Ah, Jaysus! Didn't I tell ye? Didn't I just tell ye it would be taken? Ye see! I was right! Someone's just gone an taken it!' she snorted, waving her arms like all is lost and that's the end of us! Then she stared at me, giving a look of disgust, saying, 'Tha's it now, Martha! Sure, how can we eat here wit no table? Ah! That's a pity!' she kept moaning.

I whipped me head around, seeing there were still a few empty tables down at the far end.

'Ma! Will ye stop panicking! There's a table at the bottom. Come on – let's go down.

'OK, sit here, Ma, and mind the table. I'm going back up to queue.'

'Don't be long, Martha!' she called after me. 'He'll be waitin,' she squealed, letting everyone look around at us with their mouths gaping open.

'Ah, fuck off, Ma! Does she ever give herself a break and just enjoy something,' I muttered, hissing under me breath, feeling my patience go now. Jaysus, I feel like I'm back visiting the loony bin, only it's the ma I've come to see.

'Right! There's yours, and I got us a pot of tea, and bread and butter,' I said, clearing the tray then putting it down beside our table.

I dug into the fish. 'Oh, Ma, this is lovely and fresh,' I said, enjoying the soft, white, juicy fish with the crispy batter, then taking a bit of the fresh white sliced bread and butter.

'Nooo! I don't like them chips,' me ma said, sucking and biting them, then pulling them out of her mouth and slinging them back on the plate.

'MA!' I wailed, looking around me to see if anyone was watching. 'Don't do that! It's disgusting. Stop spitting out the food, for the love of Jaysus! You're making a show of yourself and me!'

'They're too hard!' she moaned, staring down at them, giving them a dirty look.

'Eat the fish, then. It's lovely and soft.'

'Is it?' she said, taking a bite then coughing. 'No! I can't eat tha either, Martha,' she said, grabbing what was in her mouth then flinging and spitting it out, sounding like she was choking to death.

Me eyes travelled from her, seeing her tongue sticking out with bits still clinging, then followed the mashed fish, seeing it flying through the air, then sailing down only to land on the floor.

'What's wrong with you, Ma?' I said, gasping with the shock at how badly she was acting, then seeing her still trying to get rid of what's left in the mouth.

'It's chokin me, Martha!'

'Right! That's it!' I snorted. 'Ma, you need to get yourself false teeth. You only have a few left in your head,' I said, seeing she only had three on the bottom and two at the top. 'Listen, Ma, leave that. I will run up and get you a salad,' I said, wondering if I took off the slops would they do a swap? They can throw it in the bin – sure, she has hardly touched any of it.

'Wha, the roast meat?'

'Yeah! You can leave that too and just eat the rest of it.'

'Wha?! A bit of green stuff, tha lettuce thing, do ye mean?'

'No! There's eggs as well and something else. Fuck, what would you eat, Ma?'

'I don't know. Sure, they haven't anythin here worth eatin!' she keened, turning up her mouth, giving me a sideways look.

'Well, eat the bread anyway and drink the tea. I'll see what they have,' I said, leaving my tea and grabbing her plate.

'Here, Ma, I asked them to leave out the meat and I got them to put fried eggs and beans with a few grilled tomatoes on it. Now eat that.'

She looked at it, giving me a little laugh.

'Go on! Eat it!'

She swung her head around, seeing if there was anyone watching her.

'Eat, Ma. There's no one minding you,' I said, thinking, not half! Only the world and his wife is watching with the carry-on of her. It's like a bleedin madhouse tea party. Jaysus! She's putting me off me grub, and I was enjoying it no end.

'Right! Hurry up and let's get out of here,' I said, attacking my cold fish and chips. Now I'm really getting fed up with this bloody caper.

Ye can't take the ma anywhere.

'Did ye enjoy tha, Martha?'

'Yeah, did you, Ma?'

'Yeah, them tomatoes was lovely. How did they cook them, do ye think?'

'Oh, under the grill, Ma, a big one!'

She shook her head thinking about it, saying, 'Oh! They were really nice. I must get them again. The eggs were lovely an soft too.'

'Yeah, Ma, they looked really tasty,' I said, putting my arm around her. I was feeling happy now she got some grub into her, and, better still, she even got to enjoy it, I thought, leading her out of the canteen.

'Listen, Ma, you really need to get yourself false teeth,' I said, staring at her gummy mouth. 'Or else you're going to starve,' I laughed.

'It's not funny, Martha. I'm afraid a me life I'm goin te choke!' she whispered, staring at me with the eyes out of her head and the face collapsed, getting ready to cry.

'Yeah, I know,' I said, feeling sorry for her. 'But there's no need for that spitting. It turns people off their food!'

'Yeah, but wha can I do, Martha? I'm afraid I'm goin te choke te me death! I'm put in fear fer me life,' she said, not getting the point at all.

I shook my head, sighing at her.

'It's all right fer you,' she sniffed. 'You have all yer fuckin teeth!' she said, pointing the finger at me.

'Oh, well, anyway! We're out of there now,' I said. 'Mind you! I don't think I will be going back in a hurry,' I laughed, feeling down and worried at the thought me ma was getting worse. But I didn't want to show that – she seems a bit better after getting some food into her.

'Well, at least we're fed, Ma. Now we don't have to go wandering around the streets looking for somewhere to eat. I must say I'm feeling much better after that,' I said, smiling at her. 'Did you get enough to eat, Ma?'

'Oh, yeah. I had me fill all right,' she said, sounding very contented and at ease with herself.

'Right! Let's go up and see how he is.'

'Yeah! I don't trust them nurses, they may want te be givin him another one a their bleedin bed baths!' she snorted, puffing up behind me as I rushed to grab the lift.

We sat for hours, with neither of us saying a word. We were just companionably sitting opposite each other, content to rest quietly and watch the visitors coming and going. Our heads turned, watching as someone new came hurrying into the ward. Then we listened as they made a fuss of the patient. Talking and laughing, giving all the news. We looked to see what stuff they were bringing them up.

'Here! Now, Daddy! Here's two lovely new pair a pyjamas for you. I threw out them old ones! Got rid a them te the binmen! They were in rag-bag order. We want you lookin nice, Daddy! Let them see what a handsome man me ma married! Now! Where's yer false teeth, Daddy? Here, put them in. An look! I got the stuff for cleanin them. I'll leave them out on the locker. I must remember te ask the nurse te throw one in the glass a water at night when she takes them out for ye. Now! How're ye feelin in yerself now, Daddy? Ye're lookin a lot better since I saw ye yesterday! I think the rest is doin ye good. Wha did the doctor say? Will they be lettin ye out soon? I must remember te ask the nurse about tha! Now, is there anythin else ye need? How's yer bowels? Did ye do anythin today? Did they shift? I must remember te ask the nurse about tha!

'Oh, yeah! Now, while I remember, I've somethin te tell ye. Me mammy will be up in the mornin te see ye! She's lookin after Shayleigh an Chanel tonight. Jesus! Tha young one's a demon! I wouldn't wish her on me worst enemy! They have her ruined, Daddy! An all them sweets she gets! Tha poor young one hasn't a tooth left in her head! They're all maggoty rotten, Da! Rotten they are! An the child only four a year old!

'Right! So tell us, what's all the news? Did anyone die in this ward? Oh! Talkin a death! Did ye hear poor aul Mister Kelly next door dropped dead yesterday? Yeah! Very sudden it was. Poor Missus Kelly was carted in here wit the shock. Oh! I must remember te pop in an see her. See how's she's gettin on. Gawd love her, she'll have te be out in time for the funeral. That's only two days away. Yeah! Very sad. It's all very sad,' the fat little grey-haired woman sighed, squeezing her handbag as she leant into it, sitting herself comfortably on the bed.

'So! Let me think! Is there any other news I have for ye? Oh, yeah! The new neighbours moved in. Ye know tha house tha was idle for a long time? Well, the corporation gave it to a fambily! She's a young one! A bit full of herself, I thought. Wit the fake-fur jacket – pink it was! But he seems nice enough. He has a good job. He's on the bins. A corporation binman, Daddy. Come te think about it! Tha's probably how he managed te get himself tha house. He's in the know! Knew someone in the corporation!

'Well, Daddy, I better love ye an leave ye. I promised te get back early an iron them clothes for Melinda-Majenta. She wants me te iron tha good skirt an top for her. She's goin out to a dance later on. Anyway, I better hurry. She'll be waitin! Jesus, Daddy, I'm never done runnin after tha lot a mine! I do often say they'll be diggin me up outa me grave wantin te know where I put this or wha did I do wit tha! OK, Daddy, I'm off,' she said, standing up, hanging on to her handbag in one hand and shopping bag in the other.

'Now, will ye be all right, Daddy? I'm goin, I said! Why are ye starin at me? Are ye not talkin? What's wrong wit ye? Jaysus! Something's just hit me! Hang on a minute, Daddy! Did ye put yer hearin aid in? Let me get a look.' She bent down, squinting into his ear. 'No! Sure, ye haven't got yer hearin aid in, Daddy! Where is it? Let me find it! Jaysus! All this time it's in the locker. They didn't put yer hearin aid in, Daddy!' she shouted into his face.

He stared, then nodded.

'Them nurses didn't bother their arses te put yer hearin aid in, Daddy! I must remember te mention tha te the nurse,' she muttered to herself as she hurried off, rushing out the door.

It took our minds off Jackser. He was struggling more and looking more grey as his breathing got louder, and now it sounded even more harsh. Sometimes he gasped as he tried to draw in the next breath. But I was happy to see me ma seemed at ease to just sit and take everything in. I shifted, making the first move for a long while, as we watched the last of the visitors leave the ward.

'Ma,' I said, leaning over to her. She didn't seem in any hurry to leave herself. 'It's getting late. Don't you think it was time for you to get home? You must be exhausted,' I said, seeing how tired and pale she looked.

'Ah! I'm all right for now, there's no hurry on me.'

'But it's getting late. I don't want you going home in the dark. Anyway, this will do you no good. You need to look after yourself.'

'No!' she said, throwing her head at Jackser, then turning away. 'Wha about him?'

'What about him, Ma? Sure, he's OK. I'm going to stay on here to keep an eye on him. He won't be left on his own. Come on! Let's get you home.'

'Ah! Home! Wha home? Sure, there's nothin there fer me,' she said, sounding like she had really given up and there was nothing left for her.

I sighed, feeling miserable at seeing her misery. 'Look, I'll be back in a minute. I have to make a phone call.'

'OK, everything's grand at home,' I said, walking back into the ward. My heart sank seeing she was still sitting in the same position I left her. 'Come on,' I said, taking her arm and trying to haul her to her feet.

'Wait! Hang on. Leave me a minute, I told you!' she snapped at me, pulling her arm away. 'I'll go in me own time, when I'm good an ready!' she snorted, tightening her face and looking at Jackser, then staring out into the night, seeing it beginning to get dark.

'All right. I'm going down for a smoke,' I said. 'I'll be in the waiting room. Do you want a cup of tea? Would you like to go out and get a bit of an airing with me? We can get something to eat.'

'No! I'm fine where I am,' she said, letting her face look like stone and the eyes pierce with a quick look, then she dropped them away to look into the distance.

'OK, I'm going. I won't be long.'

I finished my cigarette and went out, seeing the night nurse.

'Nurse!' I said, stopping her as she headed into a ward. 'Would it be possible to get a cup of tea and maybe a bit of toast for my mother? She won't eat much unless I sit over her.'

'Course you can. Unfortunately, I'm busy right now with bedpans and temperatures. But listen to me,' she said, looking around to see if anyone was coming. 'If you're quick, you can go in yourself and make it. It's quiet now. We're all busy around the wards.'

'Oh, thanks, Nurse,' I said happily, putting my hand on her arm. 'That would be great.'

* * *

I put the tray down, with the big pot of tea and the two slices of hot buttered toast and jam, resting it on the little coffee table, then rushed off to get the ma. I hurried into the ward, then stopped suddenly to stare at the ma. Ah, God help her, I thought, taking her in. She was clapped out fast asleep, exhausted, stretched out in the chair with her head thrown back.

'Ma, Ma!' I shook her gently, not wanting to give her a fright.

She opened her eyes, looking up at me. I could see they were all bloodshot from the exhaustion on her.

'Listen, come on with me,' I said, getting her to her feet.

'What is it, Martha? Where are we goin?'

'I have a lovely pot of hot tea and toast waiting. I made it myself. The nurse let me,' I said happily, smiling at her.

'Did she? Aren't they very good?'

'Yeah! Let's hurry down before the tea gets cold.'

'Now, you sit there and take that,' I said, handing her the tea and plate of toast.

She looked at it, then started to eat. I rushed over and put on the television. There was nothing on, so we sat back watching the end of the news.

'Now, Ma, I'm going to drive you home,' I said, seeing her looking at me like she was going to put up a fight. 'I know you don't want to go home to an empty house. But for the minute I'm staying in here with Jackser. So there's no point in you staying at my house; you would be on your own there, too. The kids are out at school, and, anyway, they don't know you, Ma.'

'Whose fault is tha?' she snorted.

I said nothing, knowing full well she's not interested in them.

'Right, are you finished? Let's go!' I said, standing up.

'No! I'll stay here. I can sit where I am and watch the television.'

'No, you won't, Ma. You need a proper night's sleep in your bed. Now, come on!'

'Ye can't be tellin me wha I can an can't do, Martha!'

'Ah, no, Ma! That's the last thing I want to do. I'm just worried about you, Ma! I want what's best for you. I'm just looking out for you, that's all!' I said, looking into her face, seeing her let go. She was understanding now I meant only to mind her.

'Well, don't bother te drive me, Martha. I'll take the bus,' she said, getting to her feet and standing up, then buttoning her coat and fixing the collar.

'Ah, no! It's too late to be walking this time of the night. You're in no condition for that.'

'No, let me be! I know wha I'm doin,' she said, getting all annoyed again.

'OK! I'm going to call a taxi for you,' I said, heading for the phone box to see if there was a phone book. I wanted to look up a taxi number. Then a thought hit me. 'Oh, wait, the porter should have one. They call taxis all the time,' I said, turning to look at her. 'Come on – let's go down to the ground floor.'

'Here! Where do ye think I would get tha kinda money fer a taxi, may I ask ye?' me ma snorted, looking with her eyebrows raised and her nose narrowed.

'Ah, don't be worrying about that. Here, I had this for you anyway,' I said, taking out a few rolled-up ten- and twenty-pound notes. 'There, Ma, take that. It's my war-chest money. It will keep you going for a bit,' I said, handing her the notes. 'Now, it should be no more than about five pounds for that taxi. So don't let him rob you!'

'How much is in this, Martha?' me ma laughed, opening the money to count it, with her eyes lighting up.

'There's a hundred quid, Ma. Don't lose it. Now, come on! I'll ask that taxi man how much he's going to charge before he takes you there, then I will give him the fare. So you keep that money to yourself. Don't go taking it out to count it when you get into that taxi or he might start wanting more money!'

'Oh, don't you worry!' me ma said, letting her eyes widen and her mouth tighten. 'No fear a me gettin robbed be anyone!'

'Yeah, true!' I said, laughing. 'You're too well used to hiding money from Jackser! Right, let's get moving. We can take the lift down.'

I put me ma into the taxi after it drew up and stopped alongside us.

'Now! Get straight to bed, Ma,' I said to her as she leant out the window, listening to me.

'I will, an you take care a yerself,' she said, waving at me out the window as the taxi took off, driving her off into the night.

I stood watching, seeing her still waving from the back window as the car turned the corner, disappearing out of sight. I could hear the engine rev, picking up speed, then die away as it faded into the distance, hurrying to get my ma home safely, and then she'd take herself into bed, I hoped.

I sighed contentedly, then took in a huge lungful of warm night air. It felt deliciously soft and mellow going up my nostrils, then it settled itself in me chest and cleared my head. Oh, what a lovely night to be alive, I thought, getting a sudden feeling of well-being. Life can be a bowl of cherries, I grinned, lifting my head to look up at the heavens. 'Yes, I'm so lucky to be alive,' I muttered, feeling grateful for the gift of having so much.

A middle-aged couple strolled past, then he nodded and she smiled. 'Lovely night, isn't it?' I smiled, nodding my head back at them. I watched them walk on, arm in arm, keeping step. They looked very contented with each other, and they were all dressed up for the night. I could see they were heading in the direction of town. It looks like they are going out for the night to enjoy themselves.

But my poor ma has nobody! I thought, feeling a sadness hit me chest at her loneliness. If only she had a nice man to take care of her. She could – it's still possible, but she won't take care of herself and won't even go out anywhere. No, that thought would never hit her; it's not the way she thinks. She's like someone held prisoner, except there's no bars – only the ones put up in her mind. Jackser put an invisible iron fence around her. She's programmed only to go to the shops and do what he allowed her to do. She wouldn't know anything else exists beyond that. Jesus, she's very damaged.

I turned my head, lifting it to look up at the big old granite hospital with the wide stone steps. They lead all the way up to the two heavy oak front entrance doors. Jackser's up there now, out of all harm's way. He won't be leaving this place until they take him out in a box. Even then they will take him out the back way. That's where they have the morgue hidden. No! He will never look on these doors again. The march of time slowly edges, marching on. It stops for no one, not even Jackser. Yes, even the bad times come to an end.

I took in a slow deep breath. 'Right, I better get in,' I muttered quietly, as I braced myself to go back up to the hot stuffy ward and sit by Jackser's bed. I am now here to keep the death watch.

IO

I woke up with my head resting in my arms, collapsed on Jackser's bed. Something woke me. My eyes shot to Jackser, seeing him heaving. He was struggling to get a breath that wasn't coming!

I stood up and leant over him. The oxygen mask was not throwing out any air. I rushed to get the nurse.

'He's not breathing properly, Nurse!' I said, as the two of us stared, seeing him turning purple.

She turned after taking one look and flew out the door, then came hurrying back in with another bottle of gas and hooked it up, quickly getting the oxygen back into Jackser. Then we went still and stood looking at him, making sure he was OK.

Finally the nurse shifted beside me and took in a breath, letting it out, saying, 'Yes, I think he's fine now. He should be all right.'

I nodded my head, seeing he was breathing better. He had sunk back now to letting his lungs gasp in the air that was pouring out through the mask.

I felt his forehead.

'He's cold and clammy; the sweat is pouring off him, Nurse. Maybe I should get a cold cloth, with a little dish of cool water, and bathe his forehead? It will help keep him dry and a bit more comfortable.'

'Yes, I'll get that for you,' she said, turning for the door.

'Thanks, Nurse,' I whispered, as she handed me the bowl of water with the cloth. I moved quietly, not wanting to wake the other patients all trying to sleep through the middle of the night. I dipped the cloth in the water and wrung it out, then leant over Jackser, wiping his face and neck. Then I wrung it out again, leaving it stretched across his forehead, wanting to keep him cool. I could feel the heat coming off the cloth straight away. The smell of his skin was coming with it. It smelled rancid. But it doesn't bother me much now; I'm getting used to it.

I sat looking at him, taking in how old he got, picturing him when me ma first met him. He smiled then, letting it show through his big chocolate-brown eyes and the light tan skin. He had lovely sleek brown hair and, once, he wore a snow-white shirt. Gawd, he looked very handsome then. Me ma must have thought she really landed on her feet when he showed his interest straight away.

I remember that shirt. He bought it especially for himself when they went to get their photograph taken by the fella down in Talbot Street. He wanted a photograph of himself and the ma, with his first-born child sitting between them. That photograph sat on the mantlepiece for years, reminding me that the ma had a new family and Charlie and me were not a part of it. It was just the two of them and their little baby boy, Teddy. It used to pain me then, looking at that photograph. No, they did not include us in that picture. We were just there for them to collect the social welfare money. Many is the day I heard them talking about that.

He was all on for getting rid of us. But then it would hit him: they could get more money with us. But he had to find a way around for himself, to get his hands on the money. Me ma was getting paid for us. They wouldn't give it to him, because he was nothing to do with us. But Jackser had his plans straight from the beginning. He wanted to control me ma. So he came up with the plan, after making his enquiries. I heard them talking.

'Listen, Sally. Here's all we need te do. I talked te the fella down in the dispensary. He told me, if we go to a commissioner fer oaths, we can swear out an affidiate sayin I'm the father of dem two. Then we take it te the births registration office. An bob's yer uncle, we're on the pig's back. We'll be elected. I'll then be able te claim in the labour exchange fer the lot of us. We can then ... I can then go an claim everythin tha's goin. Get everythin tha's comin te us. We'll be entitled te everythin. We can even go after the corporation an get them te house us! Especially when we start havin our own family! When they come along, the more kids we have, the more we get. The more we'll bleedin be entitled te.'

Yes! He did do that. And when it was done, the bastard took me off, miles away from Dublin, and stranded me out in the middle of nowhere. Down in the heart of the country, I ended. We set off early one cold, frosty morning. I remember seeing the mist running off the windows of the few cars then parked along the roads. It was just after Halloween – a few weeks after the ma met and moved in with Jackser. He put me up on the crossbar of his bicycle and pedalled away. Out of the city we went, with him pedalling and me sitting up, hanging on to the bar, feeling me hands stiffen with the cold. He was in a black – oh, a very black – mood that morning. He kept muttering, fighting under his breath. 'Wha's tha bastard lookin at? Wha's she talkin about me fer? Wha's he sayin about me?' he kept mumbling, as he swung his head from one side of the road to the other. All this time, convinced people were staring at him, people were talking about him. People were out to get him – they meant him harm. Once we left the city with people, he went deadly quiet.

I passed the time taking in all the sights to be seen with not a word spoken. Jackser stared ahead, pedalling steadily, never losing his pace. On and on we went, while all this time I was lost in my thoughts, even as we passed the airport with nothing to look at. The couple of planes we had then were probably up in the sky somewhere. I was lost in me own world, thinking about the day when I grew up and could escape Jackser, and even the ma by then.

He cycled up and down through narrow country roads, with hedges and trees blocking out the light. Not many people used them roads. They were covered over by grass and had stones underneath. On and on we still went, with the smell of cowshit in me nostrils. I didn't recognise it then. I had never set foot in the country before. I hardly recognised the grass, only I had seen it growing in places – parks and things. Then, finally, he was satisfied. We had reached our destination.

He stopped the bicycle and hauled me off, leaving me standing looking like I was still sitting. Me arse and the rest of me was stiff as a board; the cold didn't help. Then he lifted the bicycle into the air and buried it in the middle of a hedge. I watched, wondering about that. Then he lifted me without a word and put me under his arm while he scaled a dry wall with a thick hedge in front. Over we went with him dropping to the ground, letting me land on me feet. We had one more gate to climb, then we walked. Through long fields with trees and hedges, on and on we went.

Eventually we stopped – we were there. The sun came out. It was a beautiful, cold, crisp November morning, and the sun brightened the icy white fields, making the green all glisten.

He left me standing in the middle of a field, with trees and hedges hiding the land. You could only get on through a narrow gap hidden between two big old trees. Then he told me not to look around. 'Don't move. Stay there!' Then he walked off and left me.

I did as he told me – I stood there all that day. I stood until the watery sun went down and the light was fast disappearing. Then the terror rose in me. I knew then he had dumped me. I was completely alone in the world. No one would ever find me, I thought. I'm lost! I'll never see me mammy again, or me babby brother, Charlie. Yeah! He had strayed me like a dog that wasn't wanted no more.

I was six years old. His intention was probably to let me die of exposure. But I wonder why he came back for me? He probably talked it over with the ma. She would have sat there saying nothing, just blinking and thinking, chewing her lip, wanting me back but afraid he would kill her. Then he managed to work it out. The authorities would track him down, then he would be up the creek without a paddle. Fucked, as he would say himself.

Yes, I thought, letting my eyes focus on Jackser. There's a special reason for us now being here together, Jackser. Your power to chase me down the days and nights of my life, haunting my dreams, bringing me nightmares, is now going to end. I'm not running from you any more. Not from that horror when I would wake in a cold sweat, my heart thumping, still hearing your footsteps thundering up behind me while I ran in terror, trying to keep ahead, all the time feeling your hot breath whispering at my neck, knowing any moment I was just about to lose my life. Then the room would slowly swim into focus. I would wake and I would know, I am safe from you for now. I have managed to outrun you. You happened so very long ago, I had you dead and buried in my mind, if not in my dreams. Because you left me the legacy of a shadowy little girl who haunts the fringes of my mind. It is just before I sleep, while I am falling between two worlds, she will come. Then I hear her whisper, 'He's not gone away, Martha. He will catch ye when you sleep!'

Enough, Jackser, you are part of my history! Somehow, being here with you like this, it feels so bittersweet. It is like you and I have so much unfinished business. So it is important to you and me, Jackser. You need me – we need each other. So I will sit here with you for as long as it takes, and keep the death watch with you.

No, nothing is more important, Jackser. I have all the time in the world. My children are safe and warm and well with their father. So it is just you and me passing the days and nights as you take your last gasps of breath, heading towards the final moments of your time on this earth. We will soon be meeting at a crossroads, Jackser. Your way is pointing into the unknown, and mine is pointing in a new direction. But for now we are travelling together, back along a road I have a sense, a feeling, it is a road I have travelled before. A long, long time ago.

I lifted my head from the side of Jackser's bed, looking around for a minute, seeing the early-morning light beginning to stream in through the windows.

'Good morning. Did you manage to get a bit of sleep?'

I looked up, seeing the night nurse bending over me.

'Oh! What's wrong?' I said.

'It's morning,' she smiled, looking tired but relieved as she said, 'We're going off night duty now, but I wanted to wake you. I have just this minute made you a pot of tea and some hot toast. I left it sitting down for you in the waiting room. I thought you might be more comfortable there. Run down now and have it,' she said, tipping my arm as she buttoned her cardigan around her, getting ready to go off duty.

I came fully to me senses then, realising the night was over. I felt myself lifting at that thought and the idea of having something to eat and drink. I feel tired, weary and hungry – a bit of grub should help to buck me up.

'Oh, thank you, Nurse!' I smiled, standing to me feet and rubbing her shoulder with appreciation. 'Thanks a million. That really is thoughtful of you. It's just what the doctor ordered,' I laughed.

'Oh, don't mention it. It's nothing short of what I might expect myself if the roles were reversed,' she grinned, letting her lovely velvet blue eyes light up in her porcelain, beautifully shaped oval face. It was framed by a head of lovely auburn, silky hair, pinned up under a white-linen cap.

'Your mother should be proud of you, Nurse! You are lovely,' I said, thinking how kind she is.

'Thanks, I will tell her. She will be delighted to hear that,' the nurse shouted, giving a big laugh as she headed out the door.

Oh, I enjoyed that tea and toast, I thought, as I drained the last of it and stubbed out the cigarette in the ashtray. OK, back and hit the ward.

I turned in, seeing the nurses working around Jackser. They were lifting him up, wanting to get him sitting straight. Then they fixed his pillows, making him more comfortable. I watched as they checked his oxygen. Then I moved over as they were taking down the empty saline bags left hanging on the pole.

'Sorry, Nurse, I'll just take my bag and get out of your way,' I said, stooping down to grab my shoulder bag I had sitting under the bed.

'Yes, just give us a minute. We won't be long,' the tall dark-haired nurse whispered, looking at me.

'Oh, don't worry about me. I don't want to get in your way,' I said, heading back towards the door. 'So I'm just going to go into the bathroom and have a quick wash,' I whispered, pointing my hand across the hall.

She nodded, giving a wave of her hand as I took off.

Then I was back before I even left. 'Nurse,' I whispered. 'Would it be all right to borrow one of those towels?' I said, pointing at the trolley with all the clean stuff sitting waiting to be used. 'I just need to dry my face,' I said, holding my hands to my grubby-looking, still half-asleep face.

'Go on! Take what you need,' she said, nodding her head to the trolley.

I grabbed a lovely big white one. 'Smashing,' I laughed happily to meself as I hurried for the bathroom, wanting to get there before the patients beat me to it.

I washed my face, drying it in the towel from the trolley. That's handy. I'll hang on to it while I'm here, I thought. Then I brushed my teeth and combed my hair. I put a bit of face cream on and looked at meself in the mirror. Right, now you look a bit more respectable. That will have to do until I get home. It's just as well I don't make a habit of wearing make-up. I would be looking a holy show by now, with probably two big black eyes from the mascara. Right, I'm ready for the day, I thought, heading back in to Jackser.

The nurses were just finished, and one nurse pulled the curtain halfway around the bed, leaving only a view of the door. 'We'll just pull the curtain around,' she whispered to me. 'It will give him more privacy.'

'Yeah,' I nodded quietly, looking down at Jackser in the bed. His breathing was slowly and steadily getting worse. His chest heaved, struggled, then let go with a terrible, agonised wheeze.

I stared at his face, seeing his colour had changed now to a very dark grey. Beads of cold perspiration stood out on his forehead. I sat down and took his right hand. The other one was limp, lying stretched out on the bed. His hand closed over mine and held it in his iron grip. I was used to it by now. So, obviously the stroke was on his left side, I thought. I gently took my hand away and got up, walking around the bed, and took up his left hand. I gripped it, to see if he would respond. No, no power at all. It's his left side, definitely. But otherwise, the stroke doesn't seem to show. He hasn't lost the power in his face. That doesn't look collapsed to me, I thought, then leant in closer, carefully searching his face for any sign of slack that would show a weakness. No, it seems fine, I thought, walking back around the bed, and sat down, taking his hand in mine again.

The ticking of time slowly edged away the morning. I looked over, seeing the patients sitting up alert now, eating their dinner. Then I let my eyes slowly wander back to Jackser, seeing him lying so still. The only movement was his lungs as they fought hard and noisy, desperately struggling to do the business of getting air into his body. Otherwise, the rest of him was in a coma. Yet he still held that very firm and solid grip on my hand. There must be a part of his mind that is awake, because he's not letting go easily. He's grimly holding on, keeping a tenacious grip on this life. Jaysus! If he could have harnessed that power into doing something good with his life . . . Think of what he could have achieved with that strength of will he possesses.

Right, I better think about moving, otherwise there will be nothing left to eat in the canteen. Only sandwiches! That's what happened to me yesterday when I left it too late to go down. I wonder if the ma will be in today? She didn't make it here yesterday. I wonder what she's doing. I hope it is something that will do her good.

OK, I better get moving, I thought, gently releasing me hand from Jackser's grip, then easing myself up, getting standing on my feet.

The fourth day here, I thought, as I made my way down in the lift, heading meself off to the canteen. The kids will surely be missing me. This is the first time in their life we have ever been separated. I'm sure they don't know what's hitting them. But they sound happy enough when they are giving me all their news. They even seemed to be taking it as an adventure that mamma is not around! They think they can get away with murder with their father. Still, I can hear a little loss in their voices.

'ARE YOU COMING HOME TODAY, MAMMA?'

'Eh, no, darling, not just yet. But I'll be home soon, I promise! Do I ever break a promise to you?'

'No, you don't, Mamma,' they breathe, letting their voices drop with the disappointment. Then they are off again, fighting each other to give me their news.

'Let go of the phone! I was talking to Mamma first!' he squawks.

'No! You let go, you've been on too long,' she squeals. 'Anyway! You're talking nonsense! I have much more special important news to tell her!'

'MAMMA! TELL HER TO STOP!'

'MAMMA! TELL HIM TO GIVE ME THE PHONE!'

'STOP! The pair of you. One of you at a time, please. Now! He was on first. Let him finish his news. Good girl! I am dying to hear your news, too. But first I want to hear the rest of his. Now, go on with your news, son. Come on! Stop that! Stop laughing, you are tormenting her. Now, finish telling Mamma your news.'

Jaysus! I miss them, rows and all! I wonder how little Minnie is, the dog? She'll be missing me too. Staring at the closed kitchen doors, wondering what has happened to her world. If she could only talk I would say she'd put a flea in me ear for leaving her. I can just hear the moans outa her.

DOORS LOCKED! NO MA! No titbits, no tickles! No one to shout at me, 'Gerraway from tha cat, it has the mange! And, Minnie, ye thick plank, you'll end up riddled with fleas!' We all . . . Well, me and the ma hate that cat next door! It creeps into our house and sits on the best furniture, in the best room, the drawing room she calls it.

Now I'm stuck outside, left to run around the garden with no one to talk to me. The only bit of enjoyment I'm getting is chasing tha bleedin cat next door! What's worse, that foreign fella struttin his stuff! The kids call him 'Daddy'. Well, that creep is treating me like I'm a dog. A DOG! ME! Sure, everyone knows I'm one of the kids. Sniff. I don't like men anyway. I never let them in the gate. They get short shrift from me. Oh, yes! A good bite up the arse. Snort. That's my job! I'm in charge of security. Me ma calls me 'the bouncer'. This is a house of women! Well, we have one boy. But I have to put up with him. The ma would kill me if I laid a tooth on him.

II

I came heading back to the ward after having my lunch and a quick stroll in the fresh air. Five minutes is all I took. I just had a quick walk around the block then back here, leaving the world outside managing to get on without me.

'Here we are,' I muttered, turning in and landing meself back in the ward.

'HOLY JESUS!' I breathed, dropping me mouth and coming to a sudden stop.

They were all plastered to the bed with the head thrown back and the mouth gaping up at the ceiling. I listened, hearing the drone as they readied with the breath, then it came. Out roared a bomb, full blast, letting rip around the ward, then landed itself in an almighty snore, giving me shell-shock. Oh, Jesus help me, the noise! It sounds like racing cars caught up in the middle of a chocka-blocked Hong Kong traffic jam. I've walked straight back into the middle of it. I should have known – the afternoon nap! Why didn't I keep walking? What did I come rushing back here for?

Jaysus, you could set your watch by the routine here. Everything and everyone runs like clockwork. *Did yer bowels move today? Nine a.m.? No! Take this, have that!* I thought, sitting meself back down in the chair. There seemed to be no change in Jackser, I saw as I leaned over to check him. He was still sweating, it was pouring down his face. I better get the cloth and fresh cool water, I thought, standing up and walking around to his locker. I lifted the little stainless steel bowl and walked over to the sink, then came back and starting sponging his face.

'There you are now, Jackser,' I whispered, drying him with the towel. 'That should make you a bit more comfortable,' I murmured, leaving the damp cloth sitting on his forehead. Then I sat down, waiting for it to get hot again, and do the same thing all over again. It won't take long; do it as often as you like. But the poor man continues to bake and cook, with his system going full blast, trying to cure his body.

'Ohh! That's it for the minute,' I sighed. 'I'm just going to relax meself for a few minutes,' I breathed, leaning in and pulling the chair up, getting my arms comfortable on Jackser's bed. Then I put me head down and conked out.

Rushing feet and voices sounding like they were in an urgent hurry woke me. I could hear them getting closer to the ward. I stared at the door, waiting. Then suddenly a group of people appeared.

'Here he is! He's in here!' Then they dashed in.

'Da, Da! Wha happened te ye?' a woman moaned, coming over to Jackser.

'It's Dinah!' I whispered to myself, seeing her slowly moving closer to Jackser, never taking her eyes off him. I stared, seeing Gerry coming up behind her. Two nurses, one of them a male, wearing their street coats over white nursing jackets, looked in, checking to see they were all right, then waved, saying, 'We'll wait down the end for you, in the waiting room.'

No one took any notice, so they looked a bit unsure but took off anyway.

'Dinah!' I said, getting my breath back after the shock of seeing the two of them coming out of nowhere.

'Wha's wrong wit ye, Daddy?' Dinah whispered, looking down into Jackser's face, with the shock and disbelief leaving her mouth open and her eyes staring. They were bulging out of her head. Then she looked around, flicking her eyes past me, saying, 'What's wrong wit me da?' She asked the ward, but not seeing anything or anyone. Her eyes looked blank. All the pain in her was looking inward as she asked herself the question, trying to understand.

'Da! Talk te me. Wake up, Daddy! Wake up!' she started to shout, giving Jackser a shake, but he didn't stir.

'Dinah! Take it easy,' I whispered, standing up and rushing around to stand beside her, putting my arm on her shoulder.

'Get away from me! Don't touch me.'

'Sorry, Dinah! Don't upset yourself,' I said, still wanting to calm her down and stop her pulling the guts outa Jackser.

'HE'S MY DA! Not yours! Fuck off an get away. Who asked you here anyway?' she screamed, letting rip the full force of her anger and rage then pinning it on me, with her eyes staring out of her head.

I moved back, not wanting to get hit. She's bigger and better built than I am. Wherever she got that from? Not from the ma; she's a squirt. No, and not Jackser! He's not a big man, but he has powerful strength. Maybe Dinah inherited that. Jaysus, a box then from her would send me flying straight into next week.

Right, time to make myself scarce. I moved, backing out of the ward into the corridor, keeping me eyes peeled on her, then stayed close by, letting her get her bearings.

Gerry swung his head around, looking out at me. 'Me da is sick, Martha. He's in here! In the hospital,' he said, pointing at Jackser.

I nodded and smiled at him, whispering, 'Yeah, Gerry, he's not well.'

Then Gerry went back to looking down at Jackser and hopping from one foot to the other. Then he flicked his head up at Dinah, seeing her standing over Jackser, crying, telling him to talk to her. I could see Gerry wringing his hands, getting very nervous. He's incredibly gentle and would not even know how to harm a fly. He is the most angelic human I have ever met, other than an innocent little child. All that innocence, that goodness, in the body of a full-grown man, I thought sadly.

But me ma lives for him and Dinah. Dinah is the ma and Jackser's first-born girl. Jackser couldn't get over himself with his delight when she was born. Yeah, it was only a novelty, though; it didn't last long. Then Gerry is the last to be born. Me ma takes in every breath just for him, because he does everything she asks. He follows her around like a little puppy. Oh, gawd, he worships the ground she walks on. The ma likes that! It's what she needs. He gives her pure, unconditional love. It's the kind of love a mother has for her child – give without asking for anything in return. Come what may! Just love them as they are. The ma gets that from Gerry. So the pair of them live for each other. Gawd, why was I not born to see the world so plainly? I question fuckin everything. No wonder I never ended up with a man!

'Come on, Da! Get up. WHAT'S THE MATTER WIT YE?!'

Dinah suddenly roared, letting a blast out that could be heard in the morgue.

Fuck! My body went forward, leaning in, wanting to run to her, but me head said no! She'll attack you. Stay where you are. Well, she might not! I hesitated, afraid, not knowing what to do. With the state she's in, it could make things worse.

At that moment, the male nurse leant himself around the corner, looking up the corridor. He was balanced on one leg. I saw his head whip around, saying something to the other nurse. Then he started to hurry up, then trot, and when he heard the roars from Dinah, he broke into a run with the coat flapping out behind him.

I could see the grim determination on their face. Something told me they were going to cause more trouble than good. I felt meself tense, getting ready for trouble.

Gerry started crying, saying, 'Dinah! Is me da goin te die just like Harry did? Is he, Dinah?'

'No, Gerry! Shrrup, you! HE'S NOT GOIN TE FUCKIN DIE!' she screamed, making me heart barrel inta me mouth as my body leapt inta action, pressing me back against the wall, getting ready for the legs to work up speed. Yep! It's looking like she really is going out of control, I thought, feeling me heart rise with fear for myself and sink with the pain for her. She's my little sister. I wanted to protect her.

I watched, seeing her eyes spin in the back of her head, looking around the ward then back to Jackser. She was wanting to do something, tear at something. I could see her chest heaving with the breath coming very fast as her eyes now stretched, bulging out of her head, coming further and further, trying to pop out of their sockets. Jesus, such rage, and the fear and confusion. It was all written over her red face, with the purple veins standing rigid in the side of her neck bulging. They looked like they were threatening to burst. Fuck! What a mess. Do something, Martha! Calm her down.

I was braced for action, my body tensed, but my mind hadn't yet come up with a solution, because moving wasn't one of them.

Just then, Dinah's nurses flew past, whipping me outa the way. They rushed themself into the ward and took just three seconds to sum up the situation, then grabbed Dinah by the arm.

All hell broke loose. She sent one of them flying, and the other one moved in, making a grab for her arms, saying, 'Calm down, Dinah. Calm down. We are going to take you back now. Just take it easy!'

The other fella was now back on his feet and rushing to take Dinah's other arm. She sent the two of them flying, pushing out her arms and lashing out, managing to get past them and out the door. Gerry was rushing up and down, holding his fingers in his ears, chanting a mantra to himself.

I saw it all happen in slow motion. 'No! Please,' Dinah was moaning as I rushed meself into action, flying out the door after them and straight into the ward nurses coming to see what the fuss was, sending the whole pile of us landing in a heap.

'Sorry,' I said, dazed, staggering to me feet, trying to see around me.

'What happened?' moaned a curly-haired nurse, sitting with her legs spread and the cap dangling on the back of her neck.

'Good God! My heavens,' whispered the other one, scraping herself off the floor. We turned our heads to the melee going on behind us.

'Don't take me back. I didn't mean te hurt anyone! I just want te see me da!' Dinah cried, backing herself down the corridor.

Her nurses kept walking slowly towards her, all the time making soothing noises as they pinned their eyes on her. They were getting ready to grab and bundle her out of the hospital, screaming and shouting. It made me sick to see her being caged in like this. This is my little sister! My heart nosedived with the pain of seeing her so at the mercy of the world and his wife.

I rushed down past the nurses and planted myself standing in front of Dinah. 'Don't worry, darling. I will take care of this,' I said, putting me hand near her shoulder, wanting to touch her.

She looked at me with the fear of God in her eyes, then blinked, letting her anger with me go, and slowly turned to watch the nurses.

I took in a deep breath and put out my arms, saying, 'Wait. Leave her be, let her stay. She's OK. All she wants is to spend time with her father.'

They kept walking towards us, shaking their heads, looking like their minds were made up and they were not interested in hearing anything else. They pushed past me, making a grab for Dinah standing behind me.

'Martha! Save me! Don't let them take me back, Martha. I don't want te go back. Please make them let me stay.'

I felt my heart slicing wide open with the pitiful pleas coming out of her, as I listened to her crying behind me.

'Come on, Dinah, you have had your visit,' the nurse said. 'It's better you don't make a fuss. Now be a good girl. Come on!' He made to put his hand on her shoulder and she erupted.

'Fuck off, ye bastards! I'll kill the lot of youse!'

'THAT'S ENOUGH!' I shouted, pushing her out of his grasp and standing in front of him.

He blinked, then let a little sneer cross his face as if to say, do you really think I'm going to do what you tell me? He didn't think so. The arrogant bastard, I thought. They're drunk with their power. They are so used to control over this family they think we are nothing. Right! Time to show them the other side.

'You will take your hands off my sister, please. She will calm down if you back off and leave her space.'

He hesitated, then shook his head, leaning forward to make another move at her. The other one tried to push me aside.

'I SAID take your hands off me and my sister. Or I will make a scene by calling the police. You may be charged with assault. How dare either of you lay a hand on me or my sister?'

'She's very upset,' yer man said, turning a bit off colour.

'Yes! That is understandable. Now, please, let's all calm down. Look, leave her to me. We are very close. I am the eldest. I will take full responsibility for her.'

'OK,' he said quietly, looking at his watch. 'We will give her another ten minutes, then we have to leave.'

'I'm sorry, I am not sure if I read you correctly. But my sister and brother have barely had time to spend with their father, and you are dictating they should leave when you decide?' I shook my head slowly but firmly. 'No! What time do you finish your shift?'

'What has that got to do with you?' he said, sounding outraged at being questioned on something he felt was a personal matter. 'That is nothing to do with you,' he snorted, looking at me with a face turned to stone.

'Well, she stays here until I say she is ready to go. That will be when she decides she is good and ready! Now I want, and quite reasonably, for her and my brother to spend time with their father. That is clearly what they want. Who are you or anybody else to tell them what they can and can't do in this private family situation?

'He is not going to last much longer,' I muttered under my breath, making sure Dinah, standing behind me, couldn't hear. 'Look, leave them be. I will look after them. I can take full responsibility,' I said quietly, nodding and staring at them, looking around to show everyone had settled down now; we were just waiting to be left alone.

'In fact, it would be good for them to have the day out, sit here with me, and maybe later you could call back and collect them? Would that be OK?' I grovelled, dropping the Missus Bouquet act. 'Ah, go on! It will do them all the good in the world,' I smiled, turning it into a big grin.

'OK, we will see you at seven,' he snapped, suddenly making his decision.

'Cheers!' I said, waving my fingers. Dismissing them, letting them have a bit more now of me cocky self. Hate fuckin dictators!

'OK, Dinah love,' I said, turning to put my arm around her. She looked so young and vulnerable now with the steam gone outa her. All that was left to be seen was the red bloodshot eyes and the nose running while she waited to hear what people would decide for her. That's what drove me mad – seeing her treated like an object, a mental case to be controlled. No, my sister is a human being first, foremost and last. Her illness happens to be a condition, a curse that destroys her day-to-day chance of happiness. But it is a condition that is just part of her. She is not the fucking condition.

But the world does not see it like that. They see only a disturbed woman, someone to be feared and shunned, not someone like them. They don't see the lovely woman behind a mind tormented by a hellish pain, caused by a condition that drives her to be constantly at war, fighting a lonely battle to chase away an inner terror. Because of that, she is further cursed. The world can take everything from you, strip you bare of your dignity. Her life has been incredibly hard enough without now being locked up then treated like a social outcast. Jesus, some people's lives can be more frightening than even the fear of dying. How terrible it must be to have to live like that. 'Yeah, life can be very cruel,' I whispered sadly.

12

'Come on, Dinah, let's go in and sit down with your da,' I said, putting my arm around her, heading us into the ward. 'Where's Gerry?' Then I spotted him. He was rushing up and down with the hands wrapped in fists, trailing the head along the floor, buried in a deep conversation with himself. Then he lifted his head, spotting us. Our eyes latched for a split second, then his slid off and he flicked his head away, not wanting to know us. No, he decided, he's seen enough of us already. So he jammed his fingers into his ears and took off again, getting buried in even deeper conversation with himself. 'Poor Gerry, we frightened the life outa him,' I muttered.

It was then I saw the people with all eyes steeled in our direction. Patients, nurses, cleaners and everyone who was anyone all had their heads swinging out of doors, taking it all in. They leant out with the eyeballs sitting like cauliflowers on the cheekbones and their mouths gaping down to the belly button, enjoying the shock of it all. Nobody was expecting this bit of diversion, and it was great! 'Tut, tut, terrible,' they muttered, waiting to see was there more. Then they saw us coming, me giving the evil eye and landing eyeball contact. That was enough. Mouths clamped, eyeballs flew sinking back in sockets as they turned tail, making for the safety of their own wards. They moved fast, slamming doors so hard the draught blew the hair on me head, taking my hearing with it. I went stone deaf, rocking on me feet, still hearing booming doors exploding shut as I stared down the passage. I looked hard, expecting to see the dead staggering back from the morgue wondering what woke them. No, there is now just sudden silence, except for the ringing in me ears to remind me what happened.

'Right, OK, it's all quiet now,' I sniffed, feeling a bit naked after getting so much exposure. It's OK, I told myself, never mind. I know this is happening a bit too often, what with the ma getting to throw her wobbly. 'Oh, Jaysus, I'm a holy show. They won't be forgetting us in a hurry,' I muttered, shaking me head, then moved, wanting to hide meself in the ward.

'Come on, Dinah, let's take our ease here. Come around this side and sit down and hold his hand. He likes that,' I whispered, seeing the eyes standing out of her head as she took in the sight of her father.

Jesus, he looks like a corpse with holy water thrown over his face. He's ashen grey, I thought, staring at him. But he is very much alive and fighting for his life. The loud gasps from his lungs will tell you that.

'What's wrong wit him, Martha?' she whispered, sitting herself down in my chair then taking up his hand.

'He's goin te die, Dinah!' Gerry flew at her, as he whipped past with his hands joined, interrupting his conversation to let her know that fact.

Dinah stared, watching him hurry down the room, but before she had a chance to open her mouth he was up and straight back in.

'Yeah! He's goin te die, Dinah!' he said, cocking the eye, giving her the side of his head, leaning into her.

She stared, he nodded, then he said ominously, speaking in a very grave tone, 'He looks just like Harry did, an he was dead! Wasn't he, Martha? Didn't you see him as well? Yeah, we all did,' he said, flying to the door then hurrying back.

'We put him in a hole. We buried him! Do ye remember tha, Dinah? An Martha planted a rosebush over him! Didn't ye, Martha? Didn't you do tha? That's wha she told me ma, Dinah! It looks lovely me ma's . . .'

'Me da's not goin te fuckin die, Gerry! So don't be sayin tha,' she snorted, giving me a dirty look to see if I agreed or not.

Jaysus! This is going to get out of hand in a minute if I don't do something fast.

'Or I'll put you in a fuckin hole an bury ye!' she roared, turning her head to shout after Gerry, with the eyes bulging out of her head as she watched him hurrying himself up and down the room.

I burst out laughing hearing the way she said that, and the look on her face saying it. She was keeping the face very still with only the mouth opening in a big wide O, then moving it to emphasise each word very slowly, while the eyes stared out of her head.

I took in a sharp breath when Dinah stared at me, saying, 'Wha's so funny about tha, may I ask ye?'

'Nothing, Dinah,' I said quietly, trying to think fast. If she thinks I'm laughing at her, she'll erupt the place. Then I said, 'I was just thinking, Jackser's in the bed listening to us. Any minute now, I'm expecting him to sit up and say, "If ye's don't stop tha fuckin shoutin an fightin, I'm goin te get up outa this bed, an I'll personally bury the lot a ye's meself! Then there'll be no more trouble outa any a ye's."'

Dinah shot her head to the bed looking at Jackser, then grinned, saying, 'Yeah! Ye're right! That's exactly wha me da would say, Martha.'

'Gerry, love!' I said, trying to get his attention. He didn't hear me as he rushed up and down with his fingers back in his ears. He can't take all the aggravation.

'Gerry, listen to me!' I said, going after him and stopping in front of him, taking his fingers out of his ears. 'Come down here with me,' I said quietly, taking his hand and walking over to Dinah.

'Dinah! Do you want something over in the shop? I'm going to send Gerry over. What do you want to buy yourself, Gerry? Would you like a bar of chocolate? Ice cream?'

He listened, thinking about it for a split second. 'Cigarettes, Martha! Will ye buy me a packet a cigarettes?'

'Yeah,' Dinah said quietly, really looking and seeing me for the first time since she came in. 'Will ye buy me a few cigarettes too, Martha?'

'Yeah, sure, Dinah. Get whatever the pair of you want. What do you smoke?'

'Dinah smokes Players Blue, Martha. But they're no good te me, Martha. I smoke Major! They're much better, they are! Ye see, ye get a better smoke outa them, Martha!'

'Right! Get twenty each – one for you and one packet for Dinah. Then get me a bar of Caramel, Cadbury's chocolate. Ahh, wait, no! Make it Fruit and Nut! What about you, Dinah?'

'No! Get us a choc ice!'

'OK,' I said, turning to Gerry. 'Now . . .'

But he wasn't finished yet. 'Yeah! Can I get meself a packet a chocolate HobNob biscuits? Me ma buys them for me, Martha. They're lovely! Wait till ye taste them. I'll give ye a taste, they're lovely wit a cup a tea.'

'OK! Look, here's twenty quid. Spend the lot! Now don't lose that money, Gerry.'

'No, no, I won't, Martha. Sure! I always used te go fer the messages fer me ma. An I always came back wit the right change. I know how te count, Martha! Me ma showed me!'

'Right. Go on then. Mind the road. Make sure there's no cars coming before you cross, Gerry!'

'Yeah, I'll make sure te take a good look before I get across. Me ma always tells me tha too, Martha,' he said, giving me a big grin, letting his eyes widen, looking straight at me. 'Ye're just like me ma! Isn't she, Dinah?' he said, looking at me with his eyes lit up in wonder at that idea.

'Yeah, now go on, Gerry. Hurry, but don't rush!' I said, hearing the contradiction.

Dinah laughed, hearing it too. 'I meant, Dinah, don't rush across the road,' I laughed, sitting meself down opposite her on the other side of the bed.

'What's wrong wit him, Martha?' she said slowly, staring at him with a worried, puzzled look on her face. 'Why does he look so bad? An he's not wakin up,' she said shaking her head, not able to figure out what's happening to Jackser.

I looked at him, thinking before I said anything. 'Well, me ma and me talked to the doctor. He told us Jackser has a very bad chest infection. So they put that mask on him. It's oxygen to help him breathe easier. The doctor said as well he was giving him medication to help him sleep. That way he won't feel the pain. The more he sleeps, the easier it is for him to breathe. So, between the drugs and him getting plenty of rest, it's all for the good, Dinah,' I said, looking from him to her.

She nodded slowly, thinking about it, with her eyes looking tired, like she wanted to nod off but couldn't with the worry. She had a pained look on her face as she stared at Jackser. 'He's sweatin like mad, Martha. He must be really hot! It's very hot in this place,' she said, looking around, skimming her eyes over the patients resting in the beds, then looked up at the sun, seeing it scorching in through the windows.

'Oh, yeah, Jaysus, Dinah, this place gets very stuffy. It would suffocate you!' I said, suddenly realising how tired I felt. I lay me head back and took in a slow, quiet breath, stretching my legs out, deciding I could relax. Dinah was sitting looking calm and peaceful, like she had decided to content herself with just sitting with her father.

'The sweat's pourin outa him,' she muttered, staring at the sweat streaming off his forehead and dripping down his face.

'Oh, yeah. We better give him a wipe,' I said, standing meself up to grab the bowl and fill it with lukewarm water from the washbasin just in behind the door. I wrung it out and handed it to Dinah. 'Here, do you want to give him a wipe?' I said, seeing her not moving.

'I can't! He won't let go a me hand,' she laughed, looking down at his hand.

'Oh, yeah! When he gets a grip, he won't let go of you,' I said quietly, grinning at her as I reached over to Jackser, wiping his face dry, then letting the cloth sit on his forehead. 'That's grand now. It will keep him nice and cool,' I said, feeling satisfied as I looked at him then sat back down.

'How long are ye here, Martha? Me ma said ye were up.'

'Oh, did she? When did you see me ma, Dinah?'

'Yesterday, Martha,' she said, letting her eyes light up as she straightened herself. 'She came down in the train te see us, me an Gerry. It was then she told us about me da bein in here. Then she told us, she said you an her had a lovely time. Youse ate down in the canteen!'

'Oh, Jaysus! Don't talk to me about that, Dinah! Wait until I tell you!' I said, looking around me, then flicking me eyes back to Dinah. 'She wouldn't eat a thing, Dinah. She kept spitting the lot out! This was the carry-on. First the ma opens her mouth, then the tongue comes out with the finger going in then back out carrying something, heading straight, smack, landing back on the plate. It got worse when she missed her aim. That kept going, nearly ending up on a doctor's plate. He was sitting on the next table!' I snorted, seeing her throw her head back then roaring, letting out a huge laugh.

'Ah, yeah! Me ma worries somethin terrible wit the idea tha she's somehow goin te choke te death. But, sure, she has no teeth left, Martha, only them aul few ones tha ye see in the front of her mouth.'

'Yeah, I know. I must take her to get false ones.'

'No, me ma wouldn't put anythin like tha in her mouth!' Dinah said, shaking her head like mad. 'Anyway! Sure, they'd only keep fallin outa her mouth,' she said, then got a picture of it and erupted with the laugh screaming out of her.

'Yeah,' I said, laughing at the idea.

Then we sat back, falling quiet again, with me staring at nothing. 'Jaysus! The eyes are dead in me head. I could sleep for a week,' I muttered, letting them close.

'I'm back, Martha!' Gerry puffed, whispering in his singsong voice, letting nearly every second word go up in the air.

We looked, seeing him tearing into the ward as he flew towards the bed. Then he dropped the heavy bag, landing it straight on Jackser's legs, and started whipping the stuff out.

'I did like ye told me te do, Martha. I got the lot and spent the money like ye said I was te,' he said, looking at me like I had ordered him to spend me money. 'Here, this is for you, Dinah! I got you yer choc ice, and one for you too, Martha, an one for meself! Wasn't tha a good idea I had, Martha? Then we don't have te look at Dinah eatin hers all by herself! I like them too! Was tha all right, Martha?' he said, leaning into me, looking very worried.

'Gawd, yeah, Gerry! It was a brilliant idea you had, pity I didn't think of that meself. Go on! Show us, what else have you in the bag? It looks full.'

'Yeah, it is. It was heavy. I got meself me HobNobs, the chocolate ones! They're the best. I don't like them aul plain ones. Me ma says they have no taste. Ye can get nothin outa them, Martha. Oh, yeah! An I got one for you!' He threw it at me, letting it miss me hand and land on the floor. Then in his excitement he ignored me and went back to getting at the bag.

'Curse of Jaysus,' I muttered, rubbing me head after hitting it under the bed, trying to get at me biscuits.

'There's one for you too, Dinah! An two packets a cigarettes for meself, and two for you, Dinah! An two bars a Fruit an Nut for us all. I think it's a bad idea if we don't have the same, Martha. So we all have two a them as well! Is tha all right? Did I do the right thing, Martha? Did ye mind me spendin all yer money?' he said, leaning down and breathing into my face, looking straight into my eyes.

'Ah! Ye're the best, Gerry! Now all we need is a pot of tea and we're away!'

'Yeah! Pity we can't get ourselves a drop a tea, Martha. Me ma loves a sup a tea wit the biscuits,' he said, thinking about the tragedy of missing out on that.

'No problem, Gerry. We'll get one. Wait, I just had an idea! Dinah, would you like a bag of chips? And I can get the nurse to make us all a pot of tea. We can even have toast with it – make a sandwich, put the chips in with melted butter?'

'Oh, yeah, Martha, tha would be lovely!' Dinah whispered, happily putting the cigarettes inside her jacket pockets.

'But wha will we do wit the ice creams, Martha? They'll melt!' Gerry said, looking very mournful.

'Eat them now, Gerry! Right, come on, Gerry, listen,' I said, whipping meself down to open my bag and take out the purse, digging deeper inta me 'war chest'. 'Look, you'll have to go back out again and run across the road to the chip shop. Get me . . .'

They looked at me, keeping themself very still, all interest in what we were going to get next. 'Get us three onion rings! Do you like them?' I said, looking at the pair of them.

'Oh, yeah! They're lovely!' Dinah breathed, with her tired eyes lighting up.

'I love them too, Martha. Me ma sometimes used te get them for us. Didn't she, Dinah?'

'Yeah!' Dinah said, shaking her head and dropping her mouth, like that was a lovely memory but is long gone now.

'Go on! Here, Gerry, take this ten quid and get three bags of chips as well.'

'But, Martha! Wha about me ice cream? Wha will I do? It'll only melt on me!'

'Eat it on the way, Gerry. Hurry. But stop when you get to the road. Wait until all the cars are gone.' He was gone, flying out the door not hearing a word I said.

Dinah roared laughing, saying, 'Did ye see the speed on him? He'll break his neck if he doesn't slow himself down.'

'Yeah! He moves like a bullet,' I said, opening me ice cream, then seeing half of it melted into the paper. 'Oh! This is gorgeous,' I said, licking then taking a big chunk with one bite. I stood back, examining it, getting ready to lick me way around the cream dripping from the bottom when it suddenly disappeared. I looked down at the floor, seeing half of it looking up at me. 'Fuck,' I muttered.

She laughed, slurping away on hers as I streeled over to get paper and clean it up. Then I sat down, nursing it gently, hoping to get at what was left.

'These are lovely,' she said, making a shivery face at the cold softness.

'Yeah,' I mumbled, feeling it slide down me neck as the two of us sat watching each other. 'Jaysus! Delicious!' I slurped, smacking me lips. 'Especially on a day like today with the sun out there splitting the rocks.

'We won't eat anything else,' I said, seeing us finished the ice creams. 'Let's wait until we get the chips. We'll have these for after,' I said, putting all the stuff back into the bag. 'Jaysus! The chocolate is soft already,' I laughed. 'It's bleedin melting in the heat.'

'Put it under the bed, Martha, outa the way a the sun.'

'Good idea!' I said, bending down and banging me head again, trying to slide the bag under the bed. 'Fuck! Me head is broken,' I said, rubbing it to get away the ringing in me ears.

'Mind yerself, Martha,' she moaned, looking at me with a laugh on her face.

'OK, now hang on,' I sighed. 'I'm going to see where the nurse is. We can have the tea ready for when Gerry gets back.'

'Yeah, but listen, Martha. Where can I go for a smoke?' she whispered, standing herself up and taking out her cigarettes and lighter.

'No problem. Hold on. We can go down to the waiting room. I nearly live in there. It even has very comfortable chairs and little tables. We can eat down there as well. Come on – no, wait a minute, Dinah. Let's get the tea first.'

'Right! You go on an ask the nurse, I'll just stay here,' she said, looking nervous at the mention of the word 'nurse', but hopeful everything will keep going all right.

I was out the door and across the hall into the tearoom. Quicker to make it myself, I thought, seeing no sign of a nurse. 'Gawd, ye own the place now, Martha,' I laughed, thinking, God helps those who help themself. No, nobody starves around me.

'Come on, Dinah! Quick!' I said, putting me head in the ward, seeing her jump with the shock at me suddenly appearing. I was carrying a tray stuffed with three teapots, mugs, milk, butter and a mountain of toast. I had the whole lot sitting balanced on top of three big dinner plates. 'Let's go!' I said, rushing off down the corridor.

'But, Martha! Wha about Gerry? He won't be able te find us,' she said, looking worried as she stopped to look back down the corridor, seeing if he might suddenly appear.

'We can sit at the window just inside the door. Look!' I said, throwing me head down. 'You can see everything that's going on from just inside the door.'

She hurried after me, saying, 'Oh, tha's great! We can have our smoke as well.'

'Sure we can! We have all the comforts here, Dinah. It's home from home,' I laughed, landing the tray down on the little table and pulling over another armchair.

'Yeah! It's really cosy in here, and look, Martha, they even have a big television over be tha corner,' she said, then swinging her head back to look out the window, with her eyes taking in the view.

'Come on, sit down. Let's have a drop of tea and a smoke while we watch for Gerry. Oh, Dinah, I forgot! Will you run up and bring the bag down from under the bed?'

'Yeah, I'll get tha, Martha,' she said, taking off out the door.

I watched her hurrying up the corridor with her lovely long blonde hair swinging around her shoulders. Gawd! She really is very good looking, there's no doubt about that, I thought, thinking she would really stand out in a crowd. She has lovely baby-blue eyes that can sparkle like sapphires when they stare back at you from under long thick eyelashes. She's even very tall – well, much taller than me and more well built, because she has a bigger frame. But it's the eyes that is the giveaway. They have a faraway, distant look in them, like she's looking at you but not really seeing you, because she's looking somewhere into the distance. Her mind is not really here, in the present with you. Sometimes she goes so far away it can make her eyes look vacant, like there is no one at home.

But when she comes alive, she can focus on you for a while, then you see the life in her. You see the light in her eyes as they dance with merriment, when her humour comes through and you get a flash of wit, showing her intelligence. You will see that light going on and her face beam into a flashing smile as she talks about something that is close to her. She likes to talk about the ma; she misses her. Them two are thick as thieves; the ma always loved her. It was love at first sight from the moment they first clapped eyes on each other. But then comes the flying mood change – the eyes that flash with a dark anger, like something is possessing her. It happens in one blink. You look into her eyes again and you see she is gone. She is now looking and listening to some inner demon torturing her to the very soul. What is happening to her then is so very real only to her alone. Nobody can see it or hear it, so who will understand? They see only her reaction, the screaming pain as she lashes out. Dear God, this must be terrifying for her, I thought. No wonder it drives some to suicide. Jesus, will they ever find a cure to get rid of it? Poor Dinah, she's just existing in a no-man's-land of living hell.

I opened the tobacco and rolled myself a cigarette, thinking, well, at least for the minute Dinah is a bit more at ease in herself. Jaysus, am I glad them nurses let her be. Come to think about it, they're not in here. I wonder where they are? I thought, looking up the passage. No, no sound or sight of them! Good, they must be gone off somewhere. Well, bully for them. Now we can all enjoy ourselves without being under the beady eye of two half-baked eegits.

I gave a big yawn, feeling the life drain outa me. 'Oh, God, what am I getting myself into?' I sighed, suddenly feeling wiped out. This is all really beginning to drag me down, and there's not much I can do to help any of them. I can't help the ma – she would eat me alive if I let her. No, nothing is ever going to satisfy her.

I yawned again, opening my mouth so wide me jaws locked. Jaysus, I must be even more tired than I realise. A good bath and a sleep in a bed would do me all the good in the world. Oh! I have that to look forward to. You don't miss your comforts until they're gone, I thought, thinking of all the things I'm deprived of. Fresh air and freedom for a start . . .

Then suddenly something hit me. I took in a deep drag of the cigarette and nearly choked with the thought. Dinah! She's gone an awful long time! I wonder what's she's doing? Fuck! I hope she hasn't taken it into her head to walk out the door! No, she wouldn't do that. She might, I thought, feeling an icy-cold fear creep up through my belly. She could come to some harm! I'm supposed to be responsible for her! Fuck, Martha, ye're not wide awake. Move!

I leapt up, tearing out the door, then stopped dead to a skidding halt, letting me heart pump again. 'Here you are!' I gasped, letting my face break out into a big smile seeing her large as life, making her way down to me.

'What's yer hurry?' she said, laughing at me. 'Ye looked like someone just set fire te yer arse, the way you flew outa tha door!'

'That's more than you did!' I puffed, feeling a huge sigh of breath surge up then wait to be released into my chest. 'You were gone so long I thought you were making the bleedin things, Dinah! Our tea is getting cold.'

'No, ye didn't, ye liar! You thought I was leggin it out the door, or, even worse, up there eatin all the stuff!' she laughed, landing the bag down on the floor beside the table.

'Come on! Let's have a cup of tea. I'm gasping with the thirst. Where's bleedin Gerry gone with them chips, Dinah? I'm dying with the hunger.'

'He's probably outside the shop eatin them on us,' she laughed.

'I'll swing for him if he is!' I snorted, letting go of me fright, then poured out the tea. 'Here, have that cup of tea. How many sugars do you want?'

'Put two in, Martha.'

'Listen, Dinah, let's start on the toast,' I said, giving up hope of seeing Gerry any time this week.

I munched on the toast, seeing her looking at it. 'Go on, eat, Dinah. There's plenty more where that came from.'

She picked up a slice of toast, saying, 'You always knew how te get around, Martha. Are you robbin the whole place? Did ye leave them any bread?' she laughed, letting her lovely big blue eyes light up, seeing the devilment coming outa me.

'No, plenty for everyone. They won't starve and neither will we. Now, polish the plate. Leave nothing, Dinah,' I said, seeing she was hungry but holding back because old habits die hard. Food on the table was never for her; it was a bit for everyone, then the lion's share for Jackser.

13

'Martha! Did ye not wait for me?' Gerry roared, coming flying in with the lovely smell of chips making its way up me nose.

'Come on, hurry! About time, Gerry. Where did you get to?'

'I had a wait till the man made them, Martha,' he explained patiently, bending his back and leaning into me face.

'Oh, sit down, sit down, Gerry. You're great. These are lovely and hot. There's yours, Dinah. Grab a plate. Take these, Gerry, and here's your onions. Oh, look, there's three battered onion rings in mine, how many is in yours, Dinah?' I said, leaning across to get a look. 'Oh, they're very good over in that place. They don't skimp, and look at the amount of chips we got! There's nearly as many again in the bag as there is in the three singles! Grab some bread, Gerry. Make a sandwich.'

'Yeah, I know how te do it, Martha. Me ma makes these all the time,' he said, putting the chips on the toast one by one, making it look like a very delicate operation.

I grabbed a handful and slapped the chips on, banging two slices of toast together, making a sandwich, and nearly choked trying to get half of it into me mouth.

Dinah stopped eating halfway and roared laughing, tapping Gerry on the arm, wanting him to get a look.

Gerry leapt up and started dancing himself up and down, banging the back offa me.

'Wait! Stop!' I screamed, with chips and bread flying outa me mouth. I tried to push him away, seeing Dinah bent in half and purple in the face trying to get enough wind to let out a scream. It finally erupted, sounding like a braying mare screaming for its lost foal. I waved me hand at Gerry, gasping, 'Yeah,' cough, 'tha's enough, Gerry! Leb me be!' Gasp. 'Oh, Jesus,' I panted, breathing in and out like a rust-bucket banger car on a cold frosty morning, heaving and gasping, spluttering and wheezing, desperately trying to spark inta life on an ailing engine with a dying battery.

'That went down the wrong way!' I croaked, finally hearing me voice again.

'Yeah! An I saved yer life, Martha! Ye could a choked te yer death only for me,' Gerry said, looking at me with his eyes hanging out of his head.

'Ye did, ye did, Gerry!' I shuddered, feeling me breath come all at once.

Dinah was still laughing. 'Tha was really funny, Martha! Ye should a seen yer face . . .'

'Yeah, Martha. It's all red, an so is yer eyes!' he said, munching on his sandwich, letting his head shake up and down.

'It looked like feedin time at the zoo wit the greedy monkeys,' Dinah roared, still laughing her head off.

'Yeah, it was, wasn't it, Dinah?' Gerry agreed, copying her as they pushed each other for bigger laughs, with the eyes peeled on me.

'Tha just reminds me,' Dinah said, looking at me and Gerry, 'we saw them havin a tea party on the telly one time. It was great gas watchin them holdin the cup wit the knees crossed,' she said, laughing and thinking about it.

'Yeah, but do ye know wha, Dinah?' Gerry said, stopping to think like an idea had just hit him. 'I never knew monkeys drink tea. I must tell me ma tha. She won't a heard a tha, Martha!'

I stopped eating with me mouth open, letting what Gerry just said bounce across the air, still hearing it said in such a serious tone. Then I looked at Dinah, seeing her looking at me. The pair of us let out an almighty roar, laughing our heads off.

'Yeah,' Gerry said, laughing too. 'Monkeys drinkin tea – tha's very funny, isn't it, Martha an Dinah? But then how do they get te hold the cup? They only have their toes.'

'Right! Back to the grub,' I said, taking little nibbles. I didn't want another dose of Gerry's heroics saving me life.

'Oh! I've had enough. That was really good. I enjoyed that,' I said, pushing away my empty plate and rolling meself a cigarette.

'Martha! Can ye watch the television? Will they let ye turn it on?'

'Course you can, Gerry! Go over and switch it on yourself, that's what it's there for.'

He was back, with the television going full blast. 'Turn down that, Gerry!' I whispered.

'Oh, yeah, sorry, Martha,' he said, flying over to switch it down, then he was back in the same breath. 'Where's me stuff, Martha? Is it in tha bag? Can I take me stuff out?'

'Yeah, go on, help yourself!'

'Wha about another hot sup a tea, Martha? For me biscuits! Me ma says ye can't eat them witout the tea!'

'Oh,' I sighed, 'I'll go down and make a fresh pot. I might as well bring the tray back and wash these few things anyway. Then we can take it easy over a mug of tea – just relax and watch the telly. Isn't that a good idea, Dinah, Gerry?'

'Yeah, we'll just take it easy,' Dinah said, giving a big sigh, letting her shoulders drop. Then she turned to look out the window, letting her sad eyes rest on the world going on without her. It was all taking place just down below in the streets around us, with the city centre showing just a short distance away. I watched as she stared into the distance, looking out through haunted eyes. They spoke of yearning, a longing to be free from the chains that locked her mind. To be free from a people that feared and locked her away, to be just free to go out among the crowd and walk as one of them. It's not asking so much. Yet it is asking too much. Her burden is mighty heavy to carry alone. But in a time that fears a lonely figure not marching to the world's tune, people will catch, trap and cage you, control you like animals in a zoo.

We lay sprawled in front of the telly, sitting in companionable silence, just happy being in each other's company.

'It's great meetin ye here like this, Martha. Yeah, me ma did say you were up here, all right. I was delighted te hear it, because we haven't seen ye in a long time, Martha.'

'No, time flies, Dinah,' I said, resting my eyes on her, staring without blinking. The tiredness was making me feel heavy, and I just sat, content to let it wash over me. I was enjoying the feeling of being completely still, just listening to Dinah's voice murmuring, telling me whatever was coming into her head.

'I wish me ma was here,' Dinah sighed, looking straight at me. 'She would enjoy this, just sittin an havin us here. Do ye think she might come up this evenin, Martha?'

'I don't know, Dinah, I didn't see her yesterday, so she might. Did she say anything to you, Dinah, about coming up?

'No, she just said she was goin home. She wanted te get a bit a rest. She complained she was tired. Ye don't think there's anythin the matter wit her, do ye, Martha?' Dinah said, giving me a worried look, creasing her eyebrows.

'No, not at all. She's grand. She's just taking it easy, Dinah. Put that thought out of your head.'

She sighed, turning her head to the window, thinking about it anyway.

'How long are you in the hospital, Dinah?'

'Wha? Oh, gawd, too long, Martha. I've been there a few years now. Me da won't let me come home. They won't take me out, Martha!'

'Why, Dinah? How long do they expect you to stay there?'

'Until I'm cured, me da says.' Then she looked down at the floor, dropping her face, letting a feeling of misery show.

'But, sure, there's no cure. It's only a matter of getting things working right for you with the right medication, Dinah.'

'Yeah, I know tha, Martha,' she whispered.

'So how are you getting on? Are you any better in yourself?'

'Yeah, I am. I'm an awful lot better than I was. Wha they have me on now is workin grand. But I still get the voices in me head sometimes, then me mind is not me own, Martha. They keep crowdin me head. It's terrible!' she said, letting her eyes fill up with pain, looking like she was going to cry.

We sat silent, me staring, her looking into the distance, lost in her own thoughts.

'Ye know wha, Martha?' she said, turning to me with her eyes alive, looking like an idea was coming into her head.

'What, Dinah? Tell us,' I said, seeing her eyes wandering off again.

'Maybe while me da is in here me ma might take me home. She's livin there on her own. We'd be company fer each other. Will ye ask her fer me, Martha? She will listen to you!'

'Oh, the ma never listens to me, Dinah!' I laughed, thinking she never listens to anyone except Jackser.

'But she might, if you tell her I'm OK. Ye can see I would be able te live at home, Martha. Will ye ask her? I'm goin te ask her meself. I did yesterday. But she wouldn't take any notice a me.'

'Jaysus, at that rate of going, Dinah, it's just as well them nurses didn't get their hands on you. If they had managed to drag you back, making a bad report, then those doctors would have had a good excuse to hold you!' I said, looking at her, thinking we had a lucky escape.

'Oh, yeah! Ye're right there, Martha. That's wha I was just thinkin meself. I even knew tha today. That's why I didn't want te go back. They would have knocked me out wit more drugs, given me an injection, then watched me all the time. Tha does ye no good, Martha. Because then they keep ye drugged so bad ye don't know day from night. Weeks can pass, an it takes a long time for them te wear off. I do get very sick, Martha.'

I looked at her, seeing the suffering now really coming through her eyes as she thought about it. It was working itself across her face, making her look old, tired and weary. Yet you could still see behind it the young woman with the light blue eyes and the white youthful skin. She went very still, like she was turned to marble with a crease of sorrow frozen on her face. Her eyes stared into the distance, getting a picture that only she could see.

'Are you thinking, Dinah?' I said quietly, putting my arm around her gently.

She blinked, clamping her eyes shut tight, then opened them wide, staring, with the big blue eyes looking straight at me.

I smiled, saying, 'You were lost! Where did you go to, Dinah?'

She shifted her eyes away from me and let a smile come to her face, saying, 'It's funny you ask tha, Martha. I was just thinkin wouldn't it be lovely te be at home now wit me ma an wake up in me own room. There would be nobody there watchin me. I could get me own breakfast in me own time, then go where I want. There would be no door locked te me,' she said, looking at me like it was an impossible dream.

I stared back, thinking about it, trying to work out how it's possible for someone to want and crave so little. Her world must be such a dark, horrible place.

Then she said, letting the smile stay on her face as her eyes lit up and looked into the distance, thinking what she would like, 'I'd love te have nothin better than the worries about wha I was goin te wear an am I gettin me make-up on right?' she laughed.

'Then what would you do?' I said, really wanting to know, thinking these and more, much much more, I never even think about. They are all there for the taking – the freedom to live life.

'Well, it would be great te take me time an wander around the shops, lookin te see what I'd like te buy if I had the money,' she laughed. 'To do it just for the sake of it, because there's no one te stop me. But wait fer it! No! I know what I would really like te do, I would love te get a job somewhere. There must be somethin I can do,' she laughed. 'I could do a job course! Plenty a them around. The mothers are all doin tha!' she said, looking so pleased, like that was the best idea that ever came into her head. 'I could go out wit friends an enjoy meself, go te the pictures or eat out in a cafe! Ye know wha, Martha? I could save a few bob an take me ma on a holiday! Gawd, me ma would love tha. We could go somewhere far, take the train or even go over on the boat te see England.' Then she went quiet.

I smiled, thinking about it with my heart racing, wanting to give her that. My mind was going like the clappers, flying so fast with a buzz in my chest. It was like I get when I am thinking fast, knowing a solution will come, because it has to. But an answer kept coming and going, with the one fact clear that Dinah needs someone to keep an eye on her. How will that happen? Dinah needs someone who loves her, someone very strong and stable, someone who will take the responsibility for looking after her, and above all someone who will accept her illness as just a part of her. That is Dinah, that is the way she is, now on with the business of helping her through life. Jaysus! I could advertise for a man, a widower, someone incredibly kind and understanding who would be glad of a beautiful wife like Dinah! She's really very soft and kind and even shy. It's all there, hidden behind that illness. Where would I get him? Jaysus! Looking for a needle in a haystack.

'Martha!'

I shook me head coming outa me doze, seeing her looking at me like she was waiting to tell me something.

'What, Dinah?' I said, moving closer to her.

'Martha, I'm afraid all the time. Will ye say a prayer to our Blessed Lord tha some day I will find peace . . . All I want is tha, Martha,' she whispered, suddenly letting go as her face crumbled and a huge sob hit, bursting her into tears.

Oh, Jesus! I cried inside myself, feeling her tears wet my cheeks as I grabbed her to me. She's asking for your help, God. But . . . oh, fucking life. Oh, fuck it anyway! I wanted to laugh and cry with rage, knowing I felt inside like Don Quixote, the mad knight pissing at windmills. We come into this world clutching a hand of cards – too many bleedin dummies and you end up blowing like a leaf in the wind. That's your challenge in return for existence. On with it! Go now and play out the game of life! shouts Fate. Yeah, and there isn't even a fuckin complaints department!

'What's wrong?' Gerry whipped, with his eyes flashing on Dinah, then rushing up to put his hands in his ears and take off, hurrying around the room. I let him be, just sat still with Dinah, rocking her as she cried quietly, letting the tears roll as she stared into an emptiness. How does she keep going? I thought, feeling my heart break at how much suffering she has to endure. Imagine, she can't even get up and go home, live with her mother! That's something most people of her age wouldn't dream of doing, not willingly. They want their own families. So must she, but she is content to settle for the basic right just to live as a normal person. Oh, my heart is breaking. Life won't even give her that. For fuck sake, all she wants is to be at ease from one minute to the next, to know she can enjoy herself, laugh with friends and fall in love. All the things we all want and take for granted. No, these things are denied to Dinah.

I stayed very still for a long time, not moving, just feeling my heart sitting in my belly. It was aching for the emptiness that sits hollow in her heart. I never knew these things had all happened just after the death of Harry. How can I ever again say I'm lonely when the night falls and I'm all alone because the children are sleeping in their beds? How can I say the sun won't shine for me when I get a sudden crushing pain of loneliness – it will be on the sight of seeing a couple walk hand in hand while they cradle the little ones safely in their arms? No, I can't ever again, because all I have to do is think about Dinah.

'Right,' I said, thinking about it. 'I will talk to the ma and get her to come with me. Dinah, I am going to have to talk to your psychiatrist, see what he has to say. I don't think you should be stuck in that hospital indefinitely. It depends on whether they have you stable on your medication. Also, the family, the ma – she is going to have to know what to do, make sure you take your medication properly. I think she would be able to handle that – particularly if you are living together, she will want that. Do you know something, Dinah? The ma is not as foolish as she just lets on. She has a very sharp mind when she wants. I'll tell you how I know that. She has a bleedin photographic memory that actually makes her a fucking genius!' I laughed, throwing my head back, really laughing at the idea.

'No! She knows full well what she is about when it suits her,' I said, thinking, it's not the brains the ma lacks; it's her mind, her damaged emotions. The way she sees herself and life. But with Dinah to take care of – well, it might just be the making of her. I think it would be a good idea she take Gerry for the occasional weekend as well. She dotes on him, I thought, looking over, seeing him calmed down now, resting his chin in his hands, glued to the television. He wouldn't be a problem with the support of the hospital. They could help the ma with looking after his medication too, especially if she gets used to it with Dinah. I think it would be the answer to all their problems – just her, Dinah and Gerry now that Jackser is not there driving them all into despair with his madness. Well, the ma is still standing. OK, she may be down, but she's not out! Especially after having survived so long in the boxing ring with him. So she should be able to manage Dinah, especially now she has all the back-up from the hospital and the doctors. Yeah, why not?

'Yes, don't worry about it, Dinah,' I said, reaching over and putting my arms around her. 'Something will be sorted. Just take it easy, be patient. I have a feeling, Dinah, one door is going to close for the lot of you, but another door is going to open.'

'What do ye mean, Martha?' she said, letting her eyes light up with a look of new hope.

'I don't know what I'm thinking, but I just have a feeling, Dinah, things might happen to get better for you,' I said.

'Oh, Martha! It would be just great. I would be over the moon wit the happiness, if me ma took me home.'

'Yeah, I think it would be great too, Dinah. You and the ma are very close.'

'But so are you and her, Martha! Sure, me ma never stops talkin about you! She's always tellin me the things ye used te get up to. She thinks the world a you, Martha,' Dinah whispered, looking into my face, letting her eyes soften.

I was now getting a glimpse of the little Dinah that used to break my heart with her innocence and longing. I remembered the pitifully trusting big blue eyes that believed one day the world would be kind to her. We were very close then. She knew I loved her and I would give her the world if it was mine for the taking. I always felt like that about all my brothers and sisters, and especially the ma.

'Come on! Let's make another pot of tea and have a cigarette. Where's them biscuits? Jaysus! Is the chocolate melted?'

'Are ye eatin yer chocolate, Martha? My two are there as well!' Gerry warned me, keeping his eyes peeled on me emptying the bag onto the table.

'Yeah, we know, Gerry!' Dinah laughed, looking at me and nodding her head over at him.

'Are we havin more tea, Martha? Then we can eat our biscuits!' he said, rushing over with what was left of his biscuits. 'Here! Let me carry the cups for ye, Martha. I'm a man, I'm supposed te do them things.'

'Who told you that, Gerry?' I laughed, seeing him trying to grab the tray offa me.

'Me ma told me, Martha. She said I shouldn't let her be liftin heavy things, Martha. That's wha she has me for! So I do, well, I will, when I'm . . .'

'When you're what, Gerry?'

'I don't remember wha I wanted te say, Martha. Tha happens te me sometimes; it won't come outa me mouth.'

'Right, well, you are a man, so here, carry that tray and let's go. Won't be a minute, Dinah. Just making the tea. Do you want toast?'

'NO! I'll burst. Anyway, I've only got room for me biscuits.'

'Don't touch mine, Dinah!' Gerry said, whipping around with the tray.

'Mind where you're going, Gerry! You nearly landed that teapot down the front of me clothes. Go on, move! Don't be worrying, she won't bleedin touch your biscuits! We all have our own, remember?'

'Dinah, did you ever have a boyfriend, a fella of your own?'

She nodded, munching on a biscuit, saying, 'Yeah, I did, Martha. We were goin out for ages. But he broke it off.'

'Oh, what happened, Dinah? What was he like?'

She stopped chewing and held the biscuit in front of her, thinking, then she said, 'He was very quiet, Martha, very easy-goin, ye know? He wouldn't fight wit ye or anythin like tha; he was real respectable. His family had their own house, ye know. It was a purchase house! They bought it themself.'

'What did he do for a living, Dinah?'

'Oh, he had a very good job. He was a qualified electrician wit the board of works. It meant when he retired they gave him a pension. We were goin te get married, Martha!'

'Really? It was serious, Dinah?' I said, feeling very impressed for her.

'Yeah, he was saving fer us te buy our own place. I wanted fer nothin wit him, Martha,' she said, starting to cry.

'Ah, don't, no, don't cry, Dinah.' I rushed over, grabbing her and rocking her against me, feeling the tears pouring down her face and onto my neck.

'I still miss him, Martha,' she said.

'Shush, take it easy, Dinah. I know it hurts. It's horrible,' I said, feeling her sobbing, making her chest jerk.

'He used te come inta the hospital te see me, then he told me he couldn't come any more. Tha was the last I ever saw of him. Then, last Christmas gone, he sent me a card wishin me a happy Christmas. He wished me all the best fer the future. Then he said he was married an he just had a new baby boy. He just wanted te let me know, just so I would not be thinkin about him. That's wha it said, Martha. I kept the card. It's back at the hospital. I keep it buried at the back of me locker. It's hidden so no one will take it.

'But, Martha,' she said, letting go and standing back to look at me.

'What, Dinah?' I said, looking at her, seeing her trying to say what she wanted to say.

She shook her head, like she was trying to understand. 'I can't stop thinkin about him. He's in my mind day an night. He was me only boyfriend. I never went out wit another fella, Martha. I'll never be able te get married now he's gone! I don't want anyone else.'

'What happened, Dinah? Did it just get too much for him? How long were you going out?'

'We were goin together, Martha, for three years an five weeks! I met him outside the Savoy picture house standin next te us on the queue – me an Sally were goin. It was just after the Christmas. He was wit another fella an they chatted us up. Then I went wit him, an Sally went wit his friend, Paul. But he had a girlfriend. She was away at the time. My fella, Sonny! Everyone calls him tha because he's always laughing, but his real name is Martin O'Shea. So tha was it – we met nearly every day after tha.

'He took me everywhere, Martha. We used te go a lot te his house. In the beginnin his ma didn't like me. I knew she didn't – she wasn't very nice te me. Every time we would turn up she'd walk outa the room, barely lookin at me. I used te say it te Sonny, but he said not te take any notice, she would come around. He used te laugh an say no girl is good enough fer her sons. An she'd want them sleepin at the end of her bed if she could get away wit it,' Dinah smiled, letting the picture sit in her head. 'But he was right! She did get te like me, an we used to sit an watch the telly together when Sonny was playin his football. I hated tha, I did. I had no time for watchin him chasin around a ball. He played fer a team they had at work; it was a club they were all in.

'But me an his ma would sit watchin *Coronation Street* an spend the night waitin fer him te get in. We got along great in the end. But after a while, things started te go wrong. I was hearin them voices. I had been bad before tha, but not tha bad. I used te just get me moods. Anyway, he came one day, not too long after the first Christmas when I went inta the hospital. It was in the beginnin a January, tha's when he told me he wasn't comin te see me any more. He just stood there, Martha, tellin me he still loved me but he couldn't take any more. It was destroyin his health. He was losin weight, an the best thing was te let me go, tha he just had te walk away from me. So there ye are, Martha, he broke it all off. He's gone for good.

'I wouldn't believe it for a long time. I kept tellin meself he would come back. Tha he would miss me like I was missin him. I kept watchin the door, expectin him te suddenly walk through it. But the waitin never came te anythin. He never came back, then I got the card from him. So he really is gone, Martha. I've nothin left. Only me ma!' she said quietly, dropping her voice to a whisper, looking down at the floor. Then she lifted her eyes to me, saying in a dead voice. 'But she doesn't want me.'

We went very quiet, letting the pain of that happening sit between us. Then Dinah sighed, saying, 'Wha will I do, Martha? Can you make her listen? If I don't get outa tha hospital, I'm goin te do somethin!'

'Like what, Dinah? Do what? Harm yourself?' I said, seeing her staring out the window with a terrible look of loss and grief and pain. It was all showing itself in the weary look in her face, making her eyes look so dead, so old, like she had reached the end of the road.

'I'm goin te do away wit meself, Martha,' she said quietly, giving her head a slow shake, then looking away again.

I stared at her, seeing a cold look appear in her eyes, and listened, hearing her say it in such a matter-of-fact way I knew she would. Yes, I thought, no doubt about it. I could feel a terrible fear gripping my chest. I took in a sharp breath, saying quietly, 'Have a smoke, Dinah. I want to tell you something,' I said, rolling myself a cigarette. 'I know what you are saying. Dying is easy; it is the living that is hard. In fact, it can be so hard I have felt the pain of it. Believe me, Dinah, I know something about pain. The kind of pain so terrifying it trapped me, leaving me no escape. I have screamed for mercy to be released from it, but no mercy came. I have lifted my face to the heavens and howled in terror, hoping to be heard. But all I could hear was my own tortured cries echoing back at me. I have looked around and seen no way out. I was locked inside a dark, cold dungeon of despairing hell. Then I lifted my face again and cursed God from the bottom of my soul for ever letting me be born.

'It was after that I was pushed all the way to the edge. I stood looking down, staring into the abyss – a cold, black pit that went all the way to the bowels of hell. It shook me to the core and I screamed in terror. Now I was afraid of dying. Then I turned around, looking back, and screamed even more, because I was too afraid to go on living. I had nothing to do but wait – just wait, buried in a living hell.

Then it came. I rushed to the edge and jumped, not like Harry, but I took that plunge to my death nonetheless. Yes, I know what it feels like, Dinah,' I said, staring into her eyes, seeing hers locked on mine as I spoke quietly. 'But I was lucky. I believe it was the hand of God. It was him that whipped me back from the jaws of death. Clearly he had other plans for me. There was only one place for me to go now and that was up. So up I went, climbing all the way, realising my dreams one by one. Now, Dinah, I have a life that gives me pride. I have everything except a man,' I laughed, thinking if only . . . I wonder where Ralph is! Will I ever see him again? My heart leapt, feeling a longing wanting to come to life.

'No, God only knows,' I sighed, shaking my head, blocking it out.

'Yeah, Charlie told me, Martha, youse didn't work out. He said the fella was really lovely. He was mad about you, but tha he was a bit bossy, an tha didn't go down too well wit you!' she laughed, looking at me.

'No, as much as we wanted to make it work, it couldn't, Dinah. We were both too powerfully passionate and fiercely independent,' I said, getting the memory of that other loss. 'He wouldn't follow and I wouldn't follow. It was against his Russian male dignity,' I laughed. 'We kept locking horns. The screams could be heard in Russia. No, we were impossible together. We just had to cut our losses quickly. So it got a surgical cut before we even knew the second baby was on the way. I . . . I didn't love him, Dinah. We went our separate ways, but he is still the children's father. Other than that, we are strangers. I do not depend on him for anything. No, I paddle my own canoe, Dinah. But you never know what's around the next bend, so get paddling!

'Now, you forget about thinking like that, Dinah. Anyway, you would only be taking the ma and Gerry with you. They wouldn't be able to take it. No, you will have plenty to live for. Just you wait and see, Dinah! It's coming. The ma is on her own now. She's going to need you, so think about that! OK, come on, give me a hug,' I said, wrapping my arms around her.

I could feel her stiffen, holding herself rigid with the tension. 'Take it easy,' I murmured, stroking her back. 'You have to believe me, Dinah. Your time is definitely coming. I promise you, nothing stays dark for ever. Now, just bide your time for a little while longer,' I said, pulling her closer to me.

She took in a big sigh, listening but saying nothing. Then I felt her easing and letting go, falling into me. She trusts me, I thought happily. She still has hope.

We stayed very quiet, letting the sense of peace between us soak into her. I wanted to give her strength, let her know she is loved because she is Dinah. I want her to know she has me behind her, looking out, just like I did when she was a little child. I only pray this will keep her safe and give her courage.

'I love you, Dinah. Don't forget that. You know I would never let you down. Are you listening to me?' I whispered, looking into her face.

'Yeah! I know, Martha. Me ma knows tha too.'

I nodded slowly, seeing a bit more life creep back into her eyes. 'So I'm never very far away, just at the end of a phone call.'

The words I had just said came hurtling back to haunt me. I remember saying those very same words before. It was to Harry! He had said the very same thing to me then that Dinah just said to me now. '*I'm goin te do away wit meself, Martha.*' That day was the last time I ever saw him. The next time I saw him I was looking down at him in the hospital morgue as he lay dead on a cold stone slab. I couldn't bear it to happen again.

'Listen, Dinah, sit down for a minute,' I said, taking her arm and sitting her in the chair. 'I want you to listen to me, Dinah! No matter how bad things get, how black they seem, even when everything has failed, when no one wants to know you, when we're down and out we've hit rock bottom – well, Dinah, we still have one thing left to us, we still have our life. That's the greatest gift we have, Dinah. We have our life. That's why I love the ma. She gave me that gift. It was her that brought me into this world. Nothing else matters, Dinah. Life is everything – hang on to it! You never know what's just around the next corner.

'One more thing – there is plenty of room in the world for everyone. The mad, the bad, the good, the woeful and indifferent! All colours, creed and race – we all have our place; we make up the world. Now, there is somewhere out there specially waiting for you. It is a place in the world where you will be happy. Look for it, Dinah. Look hard and you will find it. You are a very beautiful woman, a man would give his eye teeth for you, but he has to be special. Someone who will see and bring the best out in you. I found him, but . . .' I took in a deep breath, shaking my head, feeling a determination to send flying any thoughts of ever again entertaining that bleedin madness.

Her eyes widened and her mouth dropped open. 'Who, Martha? Who is it? Wha happened?' she said, knowing I have always been alone, never even showed an interest in a man until Sergei.

I shook my head and smiled. 'Forget I said it, Dinah. It is something that is now in the far distant past. I know where I'm heading now and so will you.'

'Do ye really think so, Martha? Do ye really think I could ever meet someone again?' she said, looking at me, not really believing it but wanting to.

'Of course you will! Think about it, Dinah. Some people go through partners like a dose of salts before they meet the right one. Ask any woman how many times she has been in love. Oh, Jesus! Nearly every fella I went out with, they will tell you. Now you only lost one! Mind you, he sounded like a real good one. But, Jesus Christ, you were only getting started. What the hell! That fella wasn't meant for you. He was only a taste of what's to come. The world is full of good fellas, Dinah. Honestly, with your looks and your health getting better all the time – well, your fella is out there still waiting for you. Just believe that, Dinah, then it will happen. Now, keep smiling, darling. The world loves a smiler! OK, pet?'

'Yeah, thanks, Martha. It's great havin ye around,' she smiled, letting the life come into her eyes.

I stared at her for a minute, seeing her face relax, and her eyes looked at me like she was thinking maybe there is something after all, out there for her. I winked, looking at her, saying, 'It's all ahead of you, kid! Just take it nice and easy.

'Right! I think we should go down and see how Jackser is. What do you think, Dinah? Look, the visitors are starting to come in,' I said, seeing a man coming down the corridor. He was carrying a big bag in one hand and gripping a bundle under the free arm, with the hand trying to hold onto a bunch of flowers. 'Let's go down now. We can leave Gerry with his television. Gerry! We're just going down to the ward to see Jackser. You can stay there and watch the television. Will you be all right?'

'Yeah, yeah, Martha,' he said, giving me a quick look with a nod, then the head was whipped back to the goggle box, looking worried he might miss something.

Just as we were walking down to see Jackser the two nurses arrived. 'Ready?' they said, looking at Dinah.

'Yeah, I'm just goin in te say goodbye te me da.'

'Give her a few minutes,' I smiled. 'Gerry is down in the waiting room watching the television.'

The other nurse took off and your man hesitated, looking at me, wanting to say something. Then he looked at his watch and said, 'OK! We better leave or we'll be shot. It's nearly seven-thirty.'

'Is it? Good God! The day has flown! OK, I'll tell her to get ready,' I said, rushing in the ward after Dinah.

'How is he?' I whispered, looking over to the bed as I moved closer. I stared down at him, seeing he looked a lot greyer now. His breathing was worse and it was coming very fast and loud. He really is struggling, I thought, seeing the sweat rolling off his chin and streaming down his neck. No, it's only a matter of time, I thought. He's not going to last much longer.

'He's after gettin worse, Martha. Look at him,' she gasped, staring at him in shock.

I said nothing, just stood beside her, barely nodding and taking in how bad he looked.

'Come on, lean over and tell him you're going, Dinah. The nurses are on their way back. It's half-seven,' I smiled. 'We got away with murder!'

'Yeah,' she whispered, keeping her eyes fastened on Jackser. 'He's me da,' she said, looking away and letting her eyes rest on me.

'I know, Dinah. You love him as much as I love the ma. So there's a pair of us in it.'

She gave a little laugh, understanding without me saying a word. She knew exactly what I meant. Somebody doesn't have to be loveable to love them; blood is thicker than water.

'Are we ready?' the male nurse said, buttoning up his coat and jerking his shoulders, trying to get the coat to settle more comfortably on him.

'OK, bye, Martha. We had a lovely day, didn't we? I really enjoyed it. It was great tha we met, wasn't it, Martha?' she said, moving towards the nurses.

'Yeah, it was smashing having the day together like that. Bye, Dinah. Give us a hug. Now mind yourself,' I said, letting go of her and making a grab for Gerry. He was holding on to the bag with what was left of the stuff.

'Bye, Martha. Thanks for all the stuff,' he said, waving the bag at me, holding it in the air.

'No, think nothing of it, Gerry! It's thanks to you, too. I really enjoyed meself being with you and Dinah. Go on, you better go. The nurses are going without you!' I said, pointing after them rushing to grab the lift.

'Bye!' Gerry shouted, and Dinah gave a little wave, watching me as I stood watching them standing in the lift between the two nurses. The two of them looked like orphans being taken home by a couple of minders after a day's outing, I didn't see the grown man and woman; I saw only the image of how they were inside. I watched as Gerry gave a nervous look at the two nurses then shuffled closer to Dinah. She looked, seeing the sudden movement, and turned her head suspiciously, taking in the two nurses. They were now looking very authoritative as they straightened themselves, hemming in their charges. She said nothing, just protectively moved Gerry closer, wanting him to know he was OK – she was there. Then I saw it: a lonely brother and sister taking comfort with each other in their abandonment. It happened because they were out of step. They didn't march to the same tune the rest of the world played, so they were kicked to the side and the world moved on. What's to do with them, so? Lock them up, says the world.

I watched as the doors closed, then stood staring at the spot where they had been. Then I turned away, carrying the dead weight in my heart. It was heavy from the terrible feeling of sadness that sat in the pit of my belly. I wearily walked back in to Jackser, wanting to keep watch over him, because deep in my soul there is a pain of emptiness. I have carried it too long. Now the time has come. I need to find the missing bits of myself. So much of me was taken – stolen. So much was never given back. Jackser will hold the answer. I will find it with him. He is the link to my past and the link that joined my brothers and sisters to me. So I knew coming back like this would not be easy. It's not. I am running the gauntlet of all the troubles he caused, the lives he crucified, the wreckage of human debris he now leaves scattered behind in his wake. Yes, but I am compelled to stay. I must keep the death watch with him.

14

I heard the sounds of crashing trolleys, footsteps and toilets flushing, doors banging and all before I even opened my eyes. I lay still, listening with my arms wrapped on the side of Jackser's bed and my head resting over them. I opened one eye first, then the other. It's morning already? But I got no sleep! Oh, well, time waits for no one. The hospital is now on the march.

Jaysus, what a night. I sat up through most of it then into the early hours. I must have collapsed only hours after the first light hit the window and the birds woke up. What time was that? About half-six, I think.

I lifted my head, looking to see how Jackser was. Gawd, we had a bad night. I thought he was a goner. Me eyes lit on him. Ah! He rallied. He's still with us. Good old Jackser – keep them on their toes.

We had to get the doctor. He came rushing in here with the eyes wide, scratching the head, not knowing where he was. Then he stumbled over to you, banging into chairs, not waking himself, but he made enough noise to wake the dead and bring the whole ward to life. Jaysus, they were all up with the lights on and the head looking around, asking, 'Is it time for breakfast?'

It didn't wake the doctor, though. He was on autopilot. He went straight into action with a syringe, but I got very worried when he asked me to roll up my sleeve.

'Not me; him!' I said, pointing at Jackser screaming in the bed for the want of air. Jaysus, that poor doctor was like an aul workhorse. Keep them going till they drop. I must remember to discourage the kids from ever going anywhere near the idea of becoming a doctor. The poor doctors are like indentured slaves. No wonder you need a mortgage just to see them when they make it up the ladder. Only then do they reach the top, finally becoming a consultant!

Gawd, Jackser, I just heard your voice grumbling, '*Never mind, make the fuckers work!*' I could hear it so plainly inside my mind, I wonder, are we wired into the same wavelength? Telepathic? With me picking up your thoughts. How fanciful an idea is that? But as they say: 'There are more things in heaven and earth, Horatio, than are dreamed about in your philosophy.' It's that or I'm now getting delusional from lack of sleep.

I yawned, taking a huge long stretch, trying to straighten out my bent frame. 'Listen, Jackser! There is something I want to say to you,' I whispered, pulling around the curtain then sitting down and leaning close into him. 'You knew as soon as you clapped eyes on me swooping into this room I was here on a victory roll. I had come back to beat the drums and watch you on your knees. Now I would act as judge and jury, then throw you to hell. I would sit here mocking and torturing you, taking vengeance for condemning my childhood and that of the others into a living nightmare of never-ending horror. I dreamed about this day, Jackser. It kept me going when I was small. I prayed for it. I bargained and made deals with God! But, Jaysus, he had other ideas for you. You managed to make it. Keep going right into old age! The ma used to say you will go on for ever, because only the good die young! She got that right, didn't she, Jackser?!

'But you know something? My big moment has come and gone. It's not so easy to take vengeance. Since I have sat here with you through your long torturous days and even longer nights, watching you suffer, something has happened to me. Something has shifted in me. It has come right from the core of me, deep down in my soul. I am a woman sitting here now, and I feel as a woman I am getting close to knowing the man you are. I can sense your soul, see who you really are behind the madness. I sense you through Charlie. What did you give him that brought out the goodness for him to sit through the night calmly watching over you without bitterness? I sense you through your daughter Dinah. You caused her a lot of pain but she now cries for your pain. What did you give her that caused that kind of sorrow at your suffering?

'What did you give that causes something deep in me to reach out and try to ease your passing? I realise now I can't judge you because we do not carry the same demons. I have been blessed with the power to control mine. But you, Jackser, you were given a terrible affliction. It stopped you ever being able to find the path out of a dark and terrible childhood you had to endure. I sense all this in you, Jackser. It is coming to me now as we both travel together through these dark days and nights, with each of us having to face our own demons. But we are not alone. I am with you and I sense you are with me. I am sorry for what you're going through, Jackser. This is life at its most cruel. I wouldn't wish this on the devil himself. But, do you know? I can sense you and me going back down through all the years. I can hear an echo of your voice from long ago, saying, "*I wasn't all bad.*"

'Do you know, a picture came flashing into my head just as I heard those words . . . or sensed them. You did show me mercy, a kindness when I was suffering. So I feel you should know this. No, Jackser, you were not all bad.

'Do you remember that time when you said to the ma, "Missus! Would you ever get up offa yer fuckin arse an take tha young one te the doctor?" Remember that, Jackser? I was whispering, whining to the ma with the pain, wanting her to do something because my head was eaten alive with lice. Buckets of them crawled around in my badly infected head, tearing through the scabs. It was that bad my head was bleeding and oozing with yellow pus. So, between me scratching to get at them and the yellow pus and blood oozing outa them . . . Well, even the lice was complaining. They were nearly looking for wellington boots to keep their feet dry. They were bleedin swimming in the stuff, Jackser. But the ma was ignoring me, so I kept on about it. Then she lost the rag. "Leave me alone or I'll tell him!" she moaned, looking over at you, making sure you heard her!

'Jaysus, Jackser! I started rattling, thinking you were going to annihilate me. But you didn't. No, you stuck up for me, and the ma had to shift herself. "She's your young one! Now get fuckin movin, Missus!" So she ended up having to rattle herself out and take me to the doctor. If I had been left to the ma, she would have left my head to rot.

'So, thanks for that, Jackser! Thanks for the memory. That little kindness has gone a long way. You see, now, it stayed in my memory, Jackser. I never did forget it. So, one good turn deserves another. I am making sure you get the best care they can give you here. This is what?

How long am I here now with you, Jackser? Five days. God, it's been gruelling, so what must it be like for you, having to go through this agony?

'Right,' I sighed, stirring to move myself. 'Listen, Jackser, I better get moving. I need to throw a drop of cold water on my face. Oh, do you know what, Jackser? My eyes are scorched in the back of me head, I wish I could take me eyeballs out and drop them into a cup of stone-cold water just to cool them. It's the tiredness, Jackser. Still, it's nothing compared to what you are going through. I hope you can hear me, Jackser. Because I don't want you to go on suffering. I wish there was a way to bring you a bit more comfort. But all I can do is hold your hand and chat to you in the hope that somewhere inside you, you hear me and know I care. Now, I'm off for a few minutes. Just hang on, Jackser. I'll be back soon.'

I looked in the mirror and gasped. Is that me? No! That's not the picture I carry around in me head of myself. The woman I know has fresh youthful skin, bright eyes, shiny hair and nice white teeth. Then, with a bit of help from the cosmetic counter – sure, I'm any man's fancy. Well, that's my fantasy! But I still get the occasional looks from the odd man. True, maybe they are a bit long in the tooth, but well, who cares? Beggars can't be choosers! But now, this woman looking back at me is . . .?

I leant into the mirror. Go on! Be brave, face these things head on. Oh, Jesus! I look like something out of a Van Gogh painting. The one he did of himself. Horrible it was, with mad staring eyes burning like red-hot coals! Yeah, the poor man was demented with madness. Now, did he have his ear in that one? Before he cut it off, that is? Don't remember. Anyway, this poor unfortunate creature staring back at me in the mirror would pass for his sister.

I let the cold tap run and leant down, catching the water in handfuls, slapping and drenching it onto my face, soaking the front of me shirt. 'Oh, lovely,' I gasped, reaching for the towel with water pouring outa me nostrils and pumping down my neck. 'Oh, yes,' I puffed, 'cold water is the cure for all ills.' Drink it after too much booze and wake feeling grand without the hangover. Yeah, works wonders, but it's just as well that's not my problem. No, I'm very wary of the old drink, me! Jaysus, I've got to be. I think I have a propensity to be an addict. How do I know that? The aul smokes – I eat them! Knowing I might die young, leave the kids orphans and others to enjoy spending the money I intend to make. Even the terrible news I now have holes in my lungs hasn't put a stop to my gallop. No, but me and the doctor thought it most definitely would put me off the smokes. It hasn't! I now smoke more worrying about how long I still have left to live! Jesus, life's a bitch and then you die!

'Right,' I gasped, dropping the towel to see what's looking back at me in the mirror.

I stared, seeing a red face to match the eyes. The eyes widened in tragedy, looking more now like Van Gogh himself. Well, there will be no worry about crowd control wanting a look at that face. No, my days of youth and beauty went finally down the swanny with this latest carry-on. Pity, it would be nice to hear the randy little buggers, the young doctors, leppin at the bit to get at me. No, they won't be wanting to know, '*Who is that dynamite bit of stuff with the big knockers and the legs that go all the way up to her arse! Who is she, man? Who? The one sitting with the old geezer, Jackser? Dunno! But I sure intend to find out. She's one I want notched on my bedpost!*'

In your dreams, Martha darling. In your dreams! Never mind. According to the children I am beautiful looking! They keep telling me that all the time. I believe them – kids never lie. They are so sweet and innocent, they tell it as they see it. Right! Enough messing, brush the teeth and get out of here. You can't leave Jackser on his own for too long. He's sinking fast. Jesus, last night I definitely thought he was gone. But, no, he won't let go. He's still holding a tenacious grip on his life. Right, bit of breakfast, then back to the ward.

I walked back into the ward, flying me eyes straight to Jackser. He's pouring with the sweat. I could see it running down his face and sitting in a pool on his neck. I rushed over, checking him. Jesus, the pyjamas are soaked. He's in an awful state, I thought, seeing him blue in the face. He was gasping to get a breath out of an empty mask. There was no air coming out of it! I looked up, seeing the glucose bag was just about empty too. Right, grab the bowl. I hurried back from the sink and leant over him, wiping and drying his face. Then I felt his pyjamas again. Bloody hell, they're sopping wet! But does he need to be disturbed? Yes! If they are quick, they can change his pyjamas, maybe give him a quick rub-down. Very quick. Then dry him with the towel. He can't be allowed to lie in that wet. OK, ask the nurses about that when they are on their rounds with the linen trolley. Meanwhile get them in here fast with oxygen and more glucose before he suffocates, or dehydrates, or whatever may come first.

I sat down beside him and took his hand, seeing him look more comfortable now. They had given him his wash and he was all set up with his new oxygen and plenty of glucose. 'Oh, you poor thing,' I whispered, staring at him. 'God, how much you are suffering, Jackser? But now that I feel your end is very close . . . I don't know,' I sighed, feeling an awful longing inside me – an ache, like I wanted to cry for so much lost.

'Jackser, I feel so sad for you, for me, for all our loss, I want to chat to you. I want to tell you things, share things with you, things that belong to you and me. Do you know, Jackser?' I whispered, leaning meself closer into the bed, looking into his face. 'We never really talked, you and me. Oh, in the beginning, when me ma first met you, you used to take me everywhere with you. I think you liked that, then. You liked the company. Of course, me ma used to make sure I went with you. "Don't let him outa yer sight. Watch wha he does!" She didn't trust you, Jackser, not to lose me and scarper off up around the corner outa sight. Like you did that first time you took me with you. Remember that? "Keep yer eyes peeled on me bike. Don't take yer eyes offa it!" you said. I did! I stood staring at that bike even when it got dark and freezing. Jackser's word was law! So I couldn't watch for "dyed-haired blondes" getting sniffed by you, with you, Jackser, supposedly prowling around after them. Anyway, you were gone! The ma went mad! You went mad! So after that, Jackser, it was "Make sure he doesn't be lookin at other women! Don't let him leave ye and go off by himself." Then, Jackser, she would pump me for info when we got back. "Who was he lookin at? Was he lookin at any dyed-haired blondes?"

'Gawd! Looking back, Jackser, me ma was her own worst enemy. The poor woman was demented with jealousy. She wouldn't let you out of her sight. Do you know, the pair of you made a bad match. Yeah, Jackser. You did make an effort in the very beginning. Remember the coal round you did for Smelly Murphy? Thank God you decided to give that up. Because, do you know what the ma had planned? I was to go with you the next morning and keep me eye on you. I can still hear it. "Yeah, he won't mind," she told herself, squinting into the distance, thinking about her plan. "Sure, you can help him anyway," she told me.

"'Wha, Ma? Am I goin te be a coalman? Sure, I can only carry a few lumps a coal, Ma! I'm only six!"

"'Shut the fuck up. Ye can keep yer eye on him!" Me ma was delighted. Over the moon she was with her plan and thinking of all the money she'd get. But then you took off in the pitch black of the early winter morning, leaving the room quietly without waking me or disturbing her. So she had to get up early and follow you. She was only satisfied when she saw you with nothing more harmless than a horse. Good! Not a dyed blonde in sight, she thought, as she hid, watching you innocently walk yourself and the nag outa the stables. Getting ready for the day's work ahead, you were. But you gave that up in no time at all. You said, "Draggin them bleedin bags a heavy coal round on me back nearly kilt me, Sally! Me lungs are gone, for Jaysus' sake. No! Fuck tha! I'm jackin it in."

'But then you had another go! Remember, Jackser, when you "borrowed" the money from the very respectable grand man who ran the business down in Sheriff Street? His mother and father had great respect for your mother, you said. So, trading on that, you got the money and bought the "Bony Pony". Poor thing was so skinny, you said. We called her Daisy and you hiked her up to the cart after getting me to go over to O'Connell Street, down the quays and across the bridge from Bachelors Walk, then into the toy factory to get the stuff. A box of balloons, a box of windmills and sticks for the balloons. You had to put them on yourself; sticks are separate. Then you hiked Daisy to the cart and we were away in a hack, with me sitting up on the little seat beside you. We were in the rag 'n' bone trade, just like Steptoe and Son. Except we Irish called it the Rag Man. I even got to wear some of the rags, Jackser. But it didn't last.

'You sold the pony and cart – got five pounds, I remember. The ma sent me down to get you outa the pub. You sat there in the height of comfort with another ghouger. Then you whipped out the money, holding up a big note, saying to your man. "Watch this! This kid is smart! How much money is tha, Martha?"

'I stared at it, seeing the colour, and said, "Five pounds, Jackser!" You shook your head and winked at me, then turned to the ghouger sitting beside you helping to spend the money, saying, "I told ye! Any fuckin flies on tha young one is payin rent!"

'Remember that, Jackser? Then you had another go, deciding we were going into the coal business again, working for yourself with me as the helper. Back to the grand respectable man we went, with you telling him the horse was robbed! "Could ye buy another one, please, sir, te feed me family?" The grand man went purple. You never stopped running till you hit the safety of Sally and the room. Maybe, I think, Jackser, with a little encouragement, the right woman . . . you might have made a go of family life. Plus with help for the aul head . . . Maybe not, Jackser. I don't think they had much then. If you had gone looking for help, they would have locked you up. Then again, they still do. Some things just don't change, Jackser,' I said sadly.

'But, you know, come to think about it, you used to tell me things, filling me in on a few memories that would come to you. I would sit and listen while you got lost, remembering all your mistakes. Yeah, that was right back in the early days when we first moved in with you. Up on the bike you would hump me, then we would pedal from one convent to the next. You knew them all, Jackser. Where to get the grey old stale bread, the best place for a mug of tea. Even better – where we could go and be in time for "a drop a hot soup, wit a bit a bread if ye promised te pray for them". They were your words said to teach me, Jackser. "Listen! An hang onta me every words. I'll learn ye everything there is te know," you used to say.

'But it was grand and handy for you having me along, I was as good as money in the pocket. You would land me off the bike and straighten me out. I was a bit bokety from sitting in the icy cold wind.

'"Now," you would whisper, covering the mouth with the cap whipped off your head. "Wit a bit a luck, we could be just in time for the drop a soup. Wait! Better still," you said, tearing your head back to me after spotting the statue. "Go over there quick! Stand in front a tha statue there . . . No! I've got a better move. Kneel! An let them see ye prayin! Tha'll impress them no end. We'll be sure a gettin somethin good outa them – maybe even a bit a dinner!"

'All was at the ready when they opened the convent door. You would then point the nun at me. "Sister, God bless ye an protect ye! But I'm not askin for meself, ye understand? It's tha poor child over there shiverin wit the cold an prayin for the want of a bit a grub. I'm askin if ye could see yer way te a drop a soup. An if ye had anythin I could take back te the other childre waitin at home, I will get them all te pray for ye, Sister!"

'Yeah, Jackser, many's the time you stood staring up at a statue with me on the stone ground, kneeling beside you. "Join the hands in the air, raise yer eyes te the statue," you would say, letting the whisper outa the corner of your mouth in case the nuns were watching and could lip-read. So, between your bowing and your blessing yourself at them nuns, we were sure to get something. It kept us going in the early days.

'Yeah, Jackser, that's how we survived, remember? It didn't last long, though, just enough time to get me trained in. Well, that didn't take you long, Jackser, then I was on my own.

'So that's what you must have been doing before you met the ma. You had been living in the men's homeless hostel, next door to the one for women and children. I remember the first time me ma met you, you were sitting on the steps of the homeless men's hostel, back visiting your pals. You were up there letting them know you had just managed to get yourself that room in Rutland Street. Then it happened – me ma was chasing me down the hill, trying to hang onta Charlie rattling under her arm. She had an aul one chasing her. The aul one wanted her high heels back – the ones I was flapping along in. They were sixteen sizes too big for me.

'There I was, do you remember, Jackser? Hammering down the hill, sending sparks flying outa the heels. The aul one was screaming, "Gimme back me bleedin shoes! I'm warnin ye, Missus! If your young one destroys them shoes, you'll pay for them wit yer fuckin life!"

'Me ma was demented with the worry on her. She roared after me, "I'm warnin ye, Martha! Tha aul one is goin te kill me! Then I'll fuckin kill you!" She was panting, waving her fist at me. Then they saw the men sitting on the steps, roaring their head with the laugh. The ma and her sudden new best friend . . . well! The pair of them stopped to talk to you men! You were all getting along great until the Legion of Mary who ran the women's hostel came and broke up the disgraceful congregating of their homeless women, mixing with you unholy lot of vagabonds! They wouldn't take excuses. Me ma roared she had to take the babby across to the hospital. We could see the patients waving out at us. No, you didn't get a chance to pair off. The holy Legion women who flew the flag for the Virgin Mary were having none of it. They ran the ma and the aul one back indoors.

'I never noticed you sitting there, Jackser! Or any of the men. I was too busy flying baby Charlie up and down in the go-car I borrowed. Someone left it sitting outside the front door of the women's hostel. Oh, yeah! That's how the Legion women found out about you lot! It was when the mother came out carrying her baby! "WHERE'S ME GO-CAR? JESUS, IT'S MISSIN! I'VE BEEN ROBBED!" The screams could be heard across the River Liffey, right over into the old Liberties! The ma was in trouble again! So, Jackser, the next time you met, that one cold dark winter night as we made our weary way back to the hostel – it was after the usual walking the streets from early morning, sometimes with nothing in our bellies for days, not even a drop of milk for Charlie, our baby – there you were! Coming straight at us pushing the bike, with the lot of us taking the shortcut through the church grounds of Church Street. Yeah, it was then the die was cast. We moved in with you. But, Jackser, as I was saying, you must have been a homeless tramp, walking the streets like us. But you did better, because you were getting fed your grub in all the convents! Also, you now had a roof over your head. So we suited you as much as you suited the ma. What a gift, what a find, Jackser, for the pair of you! A match made in hell, really, though, wasn't it?'

Yes, I thought sadly, shaking my head and closing my eyes, remembering. I could feel and see again those cold, grey, blustery days as we stood outside those big old oak convent doors, with the pebble stones crunching under our feet. We would wait, hoping that a nun would bring us out something to warm our cold bodies and fill our empty bellies. I would stand, listening to the silence surrounding that holy place, that convent. I would hear the wind blowing the leaves as it rushed, whispering through the trees, making a low keening wail, sounding like the haunting of the Banshee's crying. It was so desolate, it was like bringing a warning of death, something I could sense deep within me – it was the coming death of my childhood.

I see you now, you are a strong handsome young man in your thirties, but you carry a heavy load. You are full of regret you made so many mistakes. There is a terrible loneliness and desolate sadness hanging over you. It comes of something you endured from your days long ago when you were torn from your mother and abandoned behind high walls and locked doors. That prison showed you no mercy. You were just a terrified little boy of seven years old. You spent nine long years in that place. I can see myself now as I looked up at you. You looked around getting a chill on hearing that cold lonely sound. You gave a little shiver as your breath caught. It was when taking in this place that time seems to have forgotten as it stands still, cut off from the world and keeping its dark secrets well hidden, buried deep inside these fortress walls.

I could see the sudden fear in your eyes as you dropped your head, getting lost in some dark place that still haunts you. It was then you started to murmur, needing to tell about that little boy. He is no older than the six-year-old me. You stand, nervously wringing your hands, sharing your memories and giving me glimpses of your painful world. It all seeps out now, pouring through a gentle voice and your softening brown eyes as you remember. You talk to me, yet you look inward, back to a world of horror that only you can see. I sense this is the first time you let your childhood get a mention as you wandered your lonely life cut off from human warmth and care. The gods held even worse to come for that little boy, when in time he turned a man. Life was not kind to you, Jackser. It afflicted you with terrible demons that stalked your every footstep. On they came relentless, all the days to your end.

But now you are sharing them with me, and then your eyes light up with hope. You talk about my mother – how you would give anything to make her happy. You want to do your best for me because 'I am a little topper. A great kid, who'll go far.' Things will get better for all of us, you say. Yet I know, as you and I share a pain we are both familiar with – the pain of being an outcast. Even for that short moment, with the peace and inner happiness that wraps itself around me, and the ease we have in each other's company, it gladdens my heart and makes me grateful. I think God is in his heaven and he is looking out for me. For now I could sit and be free to take everything in around me.

I have no worries, the ma and me, and me babby brother, have found a home and someone to look after us. You, Jackser, think we are the ray of sunshine that has just walked into your life. The family you have been waiting for all of your life. Now you are not alone, now you can be happy. I am content but wary. It is like someone must feel when the hangman has just told them, 'Your life has been spared for now.' I am an old six year old. The world has imprinted on me that happiness does not last for ever. Jackser's demons could appear back at any minute, then they will start tormenting him. They will tell him people are laughing at him, following him, whispering behind his back. They are going to harm him. They humiliate him. The ma can't help. She has her own demons. Jackser is trapped by the sorrow of that little boy he has never escaped. Somehow I understand that little boy as if I lived inside him.

'Jackser,' I whispered, speaking very quietly. 'Yet it is those same moments of peace and contentment just being there with you in those very early days that has imprinted itself in my soul. I would listen to the silence that wrapped itself around that convent and its enclosed grounds. It was then I could feel God very close, as you and me sat waiting. I would listen to you talking quietly, remembering down the days of your life. I enjoyed that – having someone who would talk and teach me things. In those moments, it was a long way from wandering the streets and listening to my mother muttering to herself as she carried little baby Charlie in her arms. She never talked to me or ever knew where to go or what she was doing. To me, you seemed to know exactly what we should do, and we had purpose. It gave me hope. I could almost have felt safe and even happy we found you. But they were only moments, Jackser. It came when you had purpose, when your mind was occupied, and for a short little while it gave you ease, for now you had peace from your demons. I feel like crying for your loss of so much, for the loss of the little girl who got only a glimpse of what it must be like to feel safe with someone who could protect her. Even if it was only a very fleeting hope lasting a very few seconds. You gave me something lovely, Jackser, I never got before.

'But you loved the horses, Jackser. There was nothing you didn't know about them. I remember now, Jackser, when we first moved in with you. You used to show us a photograph of you in a circus ring. There you are, Jackser, standing proudly between two great big black stallions gripped in your pair of outstretched fists. Your arms are held high in the air with an iron hold of a grip on the beasts as they prepare to prance out of the ring with one front leg each balanced high off the ground. They had big plumes on their heads. The plumes stood straight up between their ears and they looked magnificent. So did you, Jackser – a handsome man, strong, young and so proud you looked, Jackser. "Oh, yeah," you would say quietly, getting a faraway look in your eyes, remembering back to a happier time. "I worked for Billy Smart. I worked for Chipperfields. I worked for all the circuses. Oh, yeah," you would say, shaking your head sadly, "I worked for them all."

'But you know, Jackser. The ma wouldn't let you work when you tried in those early days. She didn't want you leaving her alone. She wanted you to stay and mind her at home, keep her company. It terrorised her that you might meet another woman. Every man and person she had ever been close to always went away and left her. So she couldn't lose you. I know you desperately needed each other. You were both so dependent – one couldn't turn their back on the other without all hell breaking loose. Neither of you had enough inside you to trust. But you knocked the stuffing outa her when you held her little babby over them banisters, threatening to kill him! Oh! On that awful day, Jackser! But then she knocked the stuffing outa you when you tried to work. So you fed off each other's madness. Sometimes you took fits and had a go at sweeping the floor. 'The dirt a this kip, Missus!' you would snort, sending the brush flying one way, the dirt and shit from the kids doing it on the floor . . . Well, the shit would explode in another direction, and the ma would sit through it all. So any ideas about keeping the room clean? Well, you just gave up on that idea.

'You did have your moments of softness, it came to me once. But first let me say this! You did send me off to school. No . . . I know it didn't last, what . . . how long? A few days in one year, maybe even a couple of weeks in the next few years? But you were the one to send me. Thanks for that, Jackser. You showed me your kindness that day when I came back and you were all gone out. You, the ma, Charlie and your new little babby, Teddy, in his lovely big high pram. You picked that up second-hand. Anyway, I came back from the school, running. Your law was "Run! Don't be there till ye're back." When I ran to the shops for messages, you timed me in your head! We didn't have a clock. But this day, nobody was home. You were all gone out for the day, off to do the rounds of the convents.

'I waited, praying I wouldn't be kilt by you for doing something. What? Who knows? Maybe something I forgot. When you came back, I was expecting to be sent flying through the window for a shortcut. You could never tell with you, Jackser! But, no, not that day. You all had a great day out, landing on your feet with some kind nun feeding you the best grub you ever had for many a long day. She even gave the ma a ten-bob note! You went mad with the delight, buying yourselves a hot apple pie and sitting on a bench to enjoy it. It was then you told me you had said, "Ah, poor Martha is missing this. Pity she's not here." Then you put your hand into your pocket and whipped out a shilling. "Here," you said. "Take this and go down and buy yerself a bag a chips!" Oh, thank you so much for that warm kind memory, Jackser! It was so lovely to see you all happy, me ma at ease, with her eyes alive and a smile on her face. Me little brother Charlie – he was tired but not afraid. Do you remember that, Jackser? I do! Oh, it pains me now this minute to feel the loss of that love. It came and it went so fast. I pined when it went. Oh, for such a long time. It still hurts me now, Jackser. You had that power in you, but I don't think it ever came back.

'Do you remember, Jackser, when you and me, we used to go down to the labour exchange and collect your unemployment money? It was on a Wednesday. Me ma used to send me with you. The idea was, "Don't let him run off an drink tha bleedin labour money! Watch him, Martha! Don't let him outa yer sight! We have no coal te make the tea an no tea te drink, or even milk. Or even bread for the dinner."

'"OK, right, Ma, don't worry yerself! I'll keep me eye well peeled on him!"

'So off we would set. You taking me along for the company, knowing that would keep the ma happy.

'When we got there, I would make to go in through the old brass front swing doors with you, then the big shovel hand would land on me chest, pushing me straight back out the same way I just came in, with you saying, "Ahhh! No! You can stay out there. Wait for me. I won't be long. Ye can't come in here. There's no women an childre allowed!"

'So I would wait and wait, watching the face of every man coming back out through them doors. You never came, Jackser! It left me with the worry of the ma killing me with her keenin Banshee cries because I let you scarper, and the terror of you ending me life because I scarpered. Home I lashed, heading for the ma to tell her the news, but then turned tail, hoppin back on the other foot to go in after you. No women an childre! Will I? Hunger and cold got the better a me. We need the money. Yeah! I went in after you.

No! He's not in here, not a sign; the place is empty. Me head is spinning on me shoulders, trying to work it out. All I could see was just a long line of cages with weary-looking culchies sorting out their papers after the morning rush on the money. I leapt over to the one lone person who seemed to be giving me any notice. "Did ye see a man?" I gasped, still in a state a shock. "Eh, I'm lookin fer Jackser. He's gone! But he came in an he never came back out!" I said, waving me arms at the fat policeman looking down at me. He was there to keep the order. He shook his head, sucked in his fat cheeks, then puffed them out, making his cheeks swell, and studied me. Then he lifted his arm and pointed to the back door. I flew so fast his cheeks wobbled, with the head spinnin after me. I looked up and down the laneway. Ah, Jaysus! Me heart sank. No! No sign of Jackser! He's gone! Vanished, leaving nothing to be seen but a mangey black cat standing on top of the dustbin, trying to get the lid off.

'But then one day we managed to make it outa the labour exchange with the two of us still together. We even had the money. Well, you did, Jackser. Out we came, turning left at the gates, heading up Gardiner Street. We were making straight for the lights to turn right down Talbot Street, then left onto Corporation Street. Into the cage, as it was called, and we were home and dry, safe with the money.

'Well, we were hardly up the road when all hell broke loose. First we heard the screams. Then came the bangs, as a car hesitated, looking like it was stopping straight in the middle of the road between the traffic lights. But then the driver took off, steaming across the road, veering to the right, only stopping when he hit another car coming in the opposite direction. The next car stopped dead, getting itself hit from the car behind. Horns blew, people screamed. A man was lying on the corner of the road on the other side to us. He had been hit by the car that got crashed into. That car had slammed onto the footpath, sending the man flying through the air to land on the side of the road. The cars had all been trying to get out of the path of the runaway horse and cart that was tearing down from Gardiner Street, just ahead of us. We stopped dead, you and me, Jackser. You craned your neck, dropping from one leg to the other, letting your body go from left to right, readying yourself, looking to see what was going on.

'I looked with my eyes rolling from one happening to the next, with me trying to take everything in at once. We saw the horse and cart – it was flying through the traffic lights without a driver. Bags of coal with coal and black dust covered the road behind it. The cart was swinging like mad from side to side, with the horse charging for all it was worth. You took it in, Jackser, all in a flash. We could hear the shouts: "STOP IT! STOP IT! FOR THE LOVE A GAWD, SOMEBODY STOP IT! IT'S KILLIN PEOPLE! STOP THA RUNAWAY HORSE!"

'In the next blink I took, I was trying to clear me eyeballs. My mouth was open and me eyes were hanging out! I heard you mutter under your breath as your mind was snapping into action. "Fuck me!" you said slowly, with your eyes narrowing and your breath coming fast, then your eyes widened. Instantly, you sprang, as I saw you do so often. But now you were gone, faster than I ever knew a body could move.

'Within the blink of an eye, you tore off your coat, sprang for the middle of the road, leapt from left to right, dancing from one leg to the other, watching as the runaway horse came thundering down the middle of the road, heading straight for you. You stood your ground, keeping your arms wide, held high in the air; your coat was swinging out of your right hand. You leapt from left to right, blocking the horse as the two of you made eye contact. The horse was wild with fear. We could see the whites of his eyes as they rolled in his head and the steam pouring out from his flared nostrils. As he got closer, he was now into a full gallop with nothing in his path but you. The cart was swinging from one side of the road to the other, threatening to overturn. I watched in slow motion as the horse turned his head to the left. You leapt left. The horse did not break speed; it turned its head to the right, wanting to get around you but still keeping up its speed. Then it thundered at you because you would not give ground. Then it was on you. You waited. Then, in a split second, when it was just a nose away, you flipped your right hand, grabbing the coat open, and dropped the coat over the head of the horse, blinding it.

'Then you were running alongside it. You grabbed the mane and leapt, flying like a ballerina, hauling yourself through the air to land on the back of the horse. You grabbed the reins, shouting, "Whooa, whoooa! Easy, easy!" digging your heels under its belly and pulling the reins tight, bringing the horse's head up, higher and higher, making the horse skid and the cart topple left then right. Then it was over. The horse stopped dead in the middle of the road. We could hear the snorting and see the steam pouring up from its back. Then you, Jackser, lifted your coat from the horse's head, throwing it behind you into the coal dust, then leapt down, patting the horse, all the time speaking quietly while you looked around, making sure there was no sudden movement or noise to frighten the horse. Then you brought the horse safely to the side of the road.

'I stood rooted; my eyes never blinked. I could hardly get a breath with the wonder of it all. How you had just done all that without one glance back; you were so intent on stopping that horse. People came running from all directions. Some stood and looked at you, then at the horse. Others came and patted the horse, lifting their hands to look and see the amount of sweat. Then they were slapping you, Jackser, on the back. People were taking it in turns to shake your hand. I couldn't take it all in. My head flew down the road, taking in others now flying to help the man who was knocked down. I finally let go of my breath when me face turned red and my chest pumped out like a pair of billows. Then I was off, steaming across the road to push in and stand next to you. I watched as you took your jacket off the cart and shook it, then started banging it, letting the black coal dust fly.

'You looked grim. Your jaws were tightened and your eyes were staring hard, like you were thinking. Then you went to rub your hand along the neck of the horse, lifting its head to examine it, all the time talking quietly to it. "Jaysus! Ye're some man," a fella said, shaking his head, then lighting up a cigarette and handing one to you, Jackser.

'"Oh! Indeed he is, an not many a one like him! How many men could a done tha? Wha he just done now I ask ye? It's the mercy a God he was here at all! He's saved many a person wit wat he just done! Without a shadow of a doubt, there would a been more than one poor unfortunate lying dead be now than just tha poor unlucky man lyin up there on tha road! This man should be given a medal for bravery!" a woman said, pointing her finger at you, Jackser. "That's all I can say!" she said, giving her shoulders a shake. Then she stood back, standing there staring at you, not able to get over the wonder of you, with everyone laughing and agreeing, nodding their heads. Others were shaking their head in astonishment. But the air was filled with relief and shock and excitement, with everyone having something to say and all wanting to tell each other with no one wanting to listen, because they all had their own stories of what they had just seen.

'A little young fella mooched closer to me. "Is tha yer da?" he asked me, looking up at you, Jackser, like you were a film star, then back to me, like I was very lucky to have you.

'"Yeah, he is," I said, wanting to be part of you, not just with you. For in that moment, you were a hero to me. I was so proud of you, Jackser! Do you remember, Jackser, when we got home, I was shouting for the ma before we even got near the door? "Take it fuckin easy," you said. "We don't want the neighbours hearin all our business."

'I looked up at you then. You acted like nothing had happened. Inside my heart was flying. I wanted to tell anyone who would listen what a hero you were.

'But I said nothing, not even when me ma came rushing to the door, whipping it open with the fear of God in her eyes. "Wha? Wha is it? Wha's happened?" she said, throwing her head from you to me. She was snow-white with the knowing I wouldn't shout like that when I was with you, Jackser. I said nothing. I looked up at your face first, wanting to see if it was all right to start talking.

"'Wha is it? For fuck sake, will someone just tell me?" me ma shouted, looking at the two of us again.

"'Ah, it's just the young one goin on about nothin," you said, slamming past me then taking off your coat. "Have ye got the kettle on, Sally?" you said, brushing back your sleek black hair, then standing up to look at yourself in the little mirror over the fireplace. I saw you rubbing a bit of dust off yourself, then you sat down and laughed at me. "Jaysus! The way you're goin on, ye'd think I just climbed te the moon," you said, shaking your head and turning away, looking to see if the kettle was boiled.

'When me ma sat down an we all had a sup of tea, I told her, giving her the picture of exactly what happened. She said nothing, just kept blinking and staring and tut-tutting, shaking her head at the terrible bits about a man getting knocked down. All this time, she never took her eyes off me. Then, when I finished my story about you, Jackser, "Did he?" she roared, turning to you. "Jesus! Was tha not an awful dangerous thing fer you te have been doin?" she whispered, not able to get her breath.

"'Ahhh! Will ye stop!" you said. "The lot a ye's. Tha was nothin but a poor little mare tha somethin, or someone, somehow frightened the life outa the poor devil!" Then you shook your head in annoyance and looked away, saying, "If you have worked wit stallions, like I did in the circus . . . Jaysus! You can have them rearin up at ye! I've been cornered wit them, I've chased them! I've cornered them! Wit them big stallions rearin up at me wantin te escape. I've tamed them! I've trained them! Wha the fuck!" you laughed, turning away, snorting out your disgust, letting it show on your face the idea of what we thought was astonishing. Yes, standing in the middle of the road, facing head on a runaway horse tearing a cart behind it, mad with the fear and threatening all in its path!

'Thank you for that memory, Jackser!' I whispered, stroking his face gently.

15

The dawn chorus of the birds woke me. Fuck them, I have barely closed my eyes. I could feel the air around Jackser was heavy. It's wet and humid. I leant forward and touched his chest. Jaysus! He really feels cold and sweaty. Then I checked his forehead. Yeah, it's stone cold, but the sweat feels greasy and clammy.

I stared down at him, sighing, seeing his colour is worse now – it looks more like putty. Dear God. Oh, Jesus! Dying can be so hard.

The day passed slowly and the minutes turned to hours as the time crept on. I watched as the day gave way to the evening, taking with it the sun and the light. Soon it would bring on the agonising loneliness of the long dark night, then I will be alone with Jackser's suffering and the torment of my own longing. I long to bring him peace and to quieten the child in me, crying for all she has lost. All I can do is to keep this watchful vigil over Jackser. He is the link that binds us all to the past. But it is bad for Jackser; the long lonely night is cruel. His suffering is relentless as he lies dying, struggling through the dead of night, making his way towards a long painful death.

'This is always the worst time for you, Jackser, isn't it?' I said quietly, holding his hand and looking into his face. 'Somehow, around the same time between the hour of three and four a.m., the dead hour, that is when you start coming around, waking up. Then I see the pain and the fear and the fright in your eyes. There is so many things going on for you at that one time, isn't there, Jackser? You get the panic of not being able to breathe. You get the fear of it, the sickness, the horrible discomfort of your night chills that get worse then. You suffer the helpless feeling of being trapped in your tired old body, frustrated and angry because it has let you down.

'I remember, Jackser, that claustrophobic fear you always had of getting sick. You always feared that, Jackser, didn't you? That is why you stayed away from doctors. You were never sick in your life, yet you always feared you were. It worried you. You were a bit of a hypochondriac!

'Many is the day I heard you say, as you worried you might be sick or even going to die, "Wha would tha pain be, Sally?" You would say to me ma as you rubbed your chest with your fist, getting a worried look on your face. Me ma would stare, blinking like mad, looking worried, with her eyebrows knitting and her lip getting chewed up and down. Then she would take a couple of coughs after thinking about it, then snap, "Ahh! Will ye leave me alone for fuck sake! There's nothin wrong the matter wit ye at all! It's all in yer fuckin head!"

'You would raise your eyebrows, keeping them up there, with your mouth dropped, getting yourself ready to tell her, "Don't come the fuckin hound wit me, Missus!" But then the sudden annoyance would all drop away, and your face would settle, letting your eyes look happy as you would say, "Ye think so, Sally? So ye wouldn't think it's anythin serious then?"

'"Not at all! Would ye stop outa tha?" she would laugh, relieved to see you're happy with what she just said – that there's nothing the matter with you! Then there isn't. So she has nothing to worry about either.

'Yeah, Jackser, everything you ever feared has now come to you. Most of all, and I think it's true, your worst fear of all is here now. This is what terrorises you the most. The knowing that death is just around the corner, waiting to take you. That must be horrendous for you; I can't begin to imagine what that must be like. All your fears coming true at once, because they are all happening right inside you, now, this minute!

'But, I am with you, Jackser. I will shadow you in your fears, every step of the way. I feel myself reaching in closer to you. I am getting a deeper sense of who you really are . . . were, Jackser. I'm sitting here now with my remembered days of you – rare them so treasured sunny days of my childhood. They warm me, oh, but they pain me too. I want to cry my heart out for the loss. I want to go back and find the man you were, the one who gave me them very few precious memories. He was there all the time inside you, Jackser! You could be so soft, so aware of the simple things we needed. You would shout at the ma to do something for us. She never cared, she never noticed, she barely existed, Jackser. But you were more alert. It is like I said, you would get us taken to the doctor, get me enrolled in school, even though I hardly set foot in the place. Still, you did do it.

'It could be just a moment in time, a little happening that took place in a few minutes. They are so very, very few, them precious little memories. They come out of so many years that we lived, day by day, under your terror, yet they happened. I have them now. I see the man you could have been. I yearn now for the lost child in me – the one you never gave that love to. I feel that pain and loss. I feel the pain for you, for the terrible loss of the man waiting inside you that you never became. He would have made you happy; he would have given us all love. He would have filled the lot of us up with so many happy memories we would have burst with the love. We would never have had to know what it feels like to live in a cold, dark world where we could do nothing but wait.

'Waiting for either this world to end or something good in this one to bring us out into the sunlight. To look up and see the golden rays of the sun warm us and be given something of the good food we knew existed out there. We saw it in the shops, we saw it in people's shopping bags. We saw people smile, we saw happy, laughing children holding hands with their happy, smiling mothers and fathers. We saw them warm and dry, with good heavy leather shoes on their feet. We knew there was a life out there. But we could do nothing but wait and hope. We were young, oh, so very young, but little children will always have hope. I didn't wait, Jackser, for the world to bring it to me, I kept my hope and went out and got what we needed from the world, Jackser. Yes! You know that. I just went out and took it. Nobody will give it to you. Why should they? It is every person's burden to look after their own first – that is the way of the world. But you and the ma left us to the law of the jungle, Jackser. We had to survive because you were trapped inside yourself.

'You could have been so many things, Jackser. You did have gifts. Oh, but, Jackser, you never made it. You had too many things going against you. You had the demons in your head – the paranoia, the voices probably. They held you in an iron grip. You had the little boy inside you screaming out his terror. You had to relieve the screams of his pain as he was whipped by grown men. It never ended for you, your grotesquely inhuman childhood, even though it was so very many long years ago when they caged you up in that barbaric institution.

'Yes, I know, you told me. It was in the 1920s, Jackser. An awful time for poor children to be in an institution. A world war had just ended; Ireland was now in the middle of a devastating civil war. The British moved out and the Church moved in. They grabbed up everything and everyone, and turned the country into a fortress of institutions. Jesus! It was brutal. It drove you mad!

'Oh, I have seen that little boy in your eyes, Jackser, when you would show him to me after a bad beating you gave me. You would look at me with pain, and say, "I'm sorry I hurt you. But ye see, tha's wha the Brothers did te me! They always said it would make a man of me! I lost me head, Martha. I'm sorry. I only want te do wha's right fer ye! You're a good kid. I'm sorry. I know I go too far, but . . . tha's wha they taught me!" you would say, letting your voice trail off, letting me see the pain of that little boy inside you.

'So, yes, Jackser, I know how he felt. I know his terrors. I know you, Jackser! You had too much to carry inside you. The ma ate you alive, Jackser. She had her demons too. She held you in her iron grip, wanting you to save her. She was a woman drowning, and, as only someone will do when they are drowning, she clawed at you, not letting you loose, bringing you down with her. Because you couldn't save yourself, never mind give her what she needed. So you both fed off each other's madness, with us, the children, needing one or the pair of you to show us a bit of mercy. To show us a bit of human kindness, just to know what it feels to be like other people – the happy people who live in the light. We could only look at them and wonder and wait and hope. But it couldn't ever happen, no. So it never did. Jesus, Jackser! You two were like two shipwrecks drifting together in a vast ocean of the world. Then, as angry waves rose, you slammed against each other, crushing everything caught between you. The damage done, the children never grew up they just got older. They too never made it. They are now drowning in a vast sea of misery. So now, like you and the ma, Jackser, they too are forever lost. Harry, we already know, decided twenty-eight years is long enough. The darkness in his world was just too unbearable. He had spent an eternity waiting, hoping and searching. He never did find a path leading into the golden sunshine that waiting world was ready to offer.

'But nature has her own brutal way of keeping up the survival of our species. We can't all die out. Yes, Jackser, I'm bruised but I'm a lucky one – oh, so very blessed. Someone must have been looking down on me all along the way. I muddle my way through, learning from both your mistakes. It was a hard lesson I learned from you, Jackser. Oh, but I learned so much. I use it to nourish myself; it helps me grow. Oh, I indeed did take in so much. I understand the pain of human suffering. It makes me terribly human, Jackser. It makes me want to reach out and wipe tears. It won't allow me to walk away and not offer to ease another's pain. It teaches me not to expect, but to act. It teaches me not to wait for the world to knock on my door. It won't. It teaches me patience. I spent a long time waiting, Jackser, just to control my own destiny. Life prepared me well.

'I learned the power of controlled fury. I will be relentless, without mercy if someone tries to take or to harm me or what's mine. Yes! I learned some of your brutality, Jackser. When I am faced with that, I will sink lower than them. Brutality does not recognise goodness; nothing and nobody will get the better of me. Nothing and nobody keeps me down, Jackser! Life goes on and I'm going with it. This world belongs to me too. Yes, I cannot but be influenced by your brutality, Jackser. I carry that part of you inside me too. As the Christian Brothers taught you, you taught me. I did not just see you as that little boy when you showed him, Jackser. I also saw the face of the Christian Brothers when you were at your most brutal. They were very inhuman – demonic, I would say they were, Jackser. So I also hold that smouldering fire deep inside me too. It lies dormant, sleeping quietly. I only use it when it needs to come out. It does not control me, Jackser; I control it. I try to develop as much goodness in my life to keep out its darkness. Oh, but the rage is useful. I have climbed mountains with it. It has pushed me to endure and keep going with an icy-cold determination to succeed – that fire raging in my belly, Jackser! It could have been a very useful asset for you too, Jackser, if only you could have harnessed its power and brought it under control. Oh, if only it could have been used wisely. If only . . .'

'Martha!'

Someone was calling me. I opened my eyes slowly, very slowly, feeling a hand on me, knowing someone was gently pressing my arm.

'Are you awake?' I heard the voice speaking, whispering close to my face.

'Ohh!' I moaned, making an effort to lift my head.

'Good morning,' the night nurse Brenda laughed, looking down at me, holding her breath, with a smile on her face, waiting for me to surface.

'Morning, did you say, Brenda? Sure, that's been here since five o'clock this morning,' I grinned, squinting up at her with one eye closed. 'Is it time to be on the move?' I yawned, nearly breaking my jaw, then stood up stretching myself, trying to get rid of the creaks and curls, twisting every muscle in my body.

'How is he?' I muttered, looking down at Jackser.

We both stared, with her saying nothing as we closely watched his terrible gasps, seeing him continue to fight for every breath. She just nodded her head slightly, staring at him, then looked at me, taking my arm and whispering, 'Come on, you need to worry about yourself as well.' Then she inclined her head towards the door, saying, 'Let's go! I have your breakfast waiting.'

I followed her out of the ward, then we stopped as she said, 'I'm off duty. Gawd, what a night! Did you see the cardiac arrest we had two wards down?'

'Yeah, I didn't know what happened, but I heard and saw the flap. Everyone seemed to be on this floor at the same time, including James! Doctor Collins. He came hurrying past the ward . . . Well, more like shuffling. Then in his hurry he dropped his stethoscope. Wait till you hear this, Nurse. He bent down to pick it up, then fell over his flip-flops!' I laughed, then said, 'He's not getting much kip these nights on his graveyard shift, is he? Mind you, it doesn't stop him trying!'

'Don't talk to me about that fella,' she snorted, raising her eyes to the ceiling.

'Yeah, he's very dopey, isn't he?' I said, looking at her. 'I think he broke his stethoscope when he landed on it!' Then we gave a roar, laughing our heads off.

'Good enough for him,' she said. 'If ever a doctor fancied himself, that fella does. What he lacks in brains, he makes up for in ego! He thinks he's a consultant already, the way he marches around here in that pinstripe suit, throwing out the white coat behind him.'

'Yeah, wonder where he got the suit, Brenda? It's a bit short in the legs,' I laughed.

'Oh, from his father. One of his cast-offs,' Brenda snorted. 'The dad is a consultant,' she sniffed, sounding like she hadn't much time for them.

'Yeah, I see them. They flash in and out of the place, then they're gone! Off to see the private patients in their private suite, then it's off for a round of golf!' I said, not thinking too much of them meself. Then we went quiet, with the two of us running out of puff. It was too late, or too early in the morning, for us to be showing such energy.

'Did the patient make it last night, then, Brenda?' I said. 'Who was it? I mean, what bed were they in?'

'It was Ellen, Mrs Casey.'

'What? She's dead?' I said, getting a shock.

She nodded, looking at me.

'But, sure, she wasn't that old. How old was she, Brenda?'

'Sixty-one.'

'What happened to her? The first night she came in here, she was sent up from casualty, wasn't she?'

'Yeah,' Brenda said, taking in a sudden breath that got caught in her throat.

I looked at her, seeing the dark shadows under her lovely blue eyes. She's looking very pale and tired, I thought, staring into her face.

'Tetany!' Brenda said. 'She went into shock. There was nothing we could do. We tried resuscitation, but nothing,' she said, shaking her head and drawing her lips together in a straight line, letting a look of regret come into her eyes.

I said nothing, just thought about Ellen. She was grand when she came in. She was sitting up in the bed laughing. I even made a joke to her as I passed her ward.

'Do you know, Brenda?' I said, thinking about it. 'I only went in and spoke to her about two days ago. She was grand! There she was, sitting up in the bed, laughing and joking away for herself. When I saw her laughing like that, I turned and went into the ward saying, "Huh! There's not too much wrong with you, judging by the looks of you. What are you doing in here?" Then I shook me head at her, laughing and joking, saying, "Jaysus! Some women will do anything to escape housework and cooking. You should be at home cooking your husband's dinner! That poor man is probably out there right now, starving to death, fading away fast for the want of a bit of grub. Are you here for your holidays?" I said, laughing. Then she told me, Brenda. She said, "Yeah! You could be right. I don't know wha I'm doin in this place! It was himself, the husband, tha brought me in here in the first place! I had a septic finger, look. I got it caught on a rusty nail. I was gardening. I thought nothin of it at the time; it didn't even bleed, ye see!" she said, looking up at me, showing me the nasty-looking swelling on her hand. It was bandaged, so I couldn't see much.

"'They sent me up here, straight away from casualty," she said, not able to figure out what all the fuss was about. "Then they sent him home. They said they were keeping me in." Then she shook her head, looking up at the drip she was attached to, with the bags of antibiotics hanging out of it.

"'Maybe I should have come in earlier, got a tetanus injection. But ye see, it didn't bleed. If it had, the poison would have come out. But anyway, I wasn't bothered," she said. "Now look at the trouble I brought on meself, an the weather out there is blazing wit the sun. I could a been out there now, enjoyin me bit a gardenin!" she said.

"'Ah, well,' I said to her. "You're in the right place. They will probably let you home as soon as you're off the antibiotics," I said, moving off and making for the door. I wanted to get back to Jackser. Then I waved at her, Brenda. She gave me a big wave back, smiling. A lovely woman,' I said, still seeing her with the big, bright, happy face and the eyes dancing outa her head, looking like she could get up to plenty a devilment! Always ready for a laugh.

'She left it too late,' Brenda whispered. 'If she had come in when it happened, got herself a tetanus injection, it was such a simple thing. But now,' she said, waving her hands, shaking her head.

I stared, letting the shock and sadness show in my eyes and shaking my head with her, saying, 'She's gone! I did see her husband sitting out there on the bench in the middle of the night,' I said. 'I wasn't thinking. I knew there must be something wrong. He was looking very worried. I stopped and put my arm on his shoulder, whispering, "Are you all right?" But he just nodded up to me. So that, when he didn't say anything, I went on about my business, wanting to just leave him in peace. I was heading off down to the waiting room to grab a quick cigarette, because I couldn't leave Jackser for long. I was anxious to get back. He wasn't good.

'So it was Ellen? That's what all the emergency was about. I could hear the rushing and feet flying up and down, with the carts tearing along the passage. I even heard you all shouting to each other, trying to keep it down to a whisper. I did wonder what was going on. Then I could hear your voices getting louder. You were calling backwards and forwards to each other, right outside the ward. Then the lights went on. But I was in there with Jackser. I had to keep on my feet. Remember, Brenda? You came in just before it happened. We were trying to get him easy. He was in a bad way. Then you went off when he seemed over the worst, and I watched him, keeping him dry. I kept damping his forehead with the cloth,' I said, 'then leaving the wet rag sitting on his forehead. I was so intent on him I blocked out everything around me,' I said, thinking all about that happening in the middle of the night. I could hear meself talking, sounding strained, like somehow I had done something wrong. What the bloody hell is wrong with me? I thought, staring at the floor.

'You are exhausted, Martha. Come on! Go down and have that breakfast. It's probably cold now. Put your feet up for an hour or so. You need it. Or I'll have to be adding you to my list of patients,' she laughed, giving me a dig with her elbow in me arm.

'Yeah, but, sure, like yourself, I'm used to prowling the early hours of the morning, what with one thing or another. If it's not one of the children that's sick and having a bad night . . . Oh, yeah, many is the night I had to run to the hospital with the son in the middle of the night. He had bad croup as a baby. Jesus! He could hardly breathe! That's why I got meself a fast car!' I laughed. 'So I could get him in there! Ah, don't bother your head worrying about me, Brenda. I'm well used to it.'

'OK, let me just get rid of this,' she said, lifting up the teapot and rushing off. 'It won't take me two shakes of a lamb's tail to get you a fresh pot,' she said, looking back at me from the door. Then she was gone.

'Here we are,' she breathed, hurrying back in with another tray, as she fastened her eyes on the table. 'Take that, and some more hot toast! Now sit and eat that straight away,' she said, sitting me down, fussing, with the pair of us laughing. 'Eat!' she ordered, pointing from me to the grub.

'Yeah, yeah!' I said, pouring the tea, then grabbing up a bit of hot toast. 'Where did you get the egg, Brenda?'

She pointed her finger at her nose. No questions asked!

'And a yoghurt! Jaysus, I'm spoilt. That's it! I'm moving in here.'

'Go on, you chancer! I'm off. See ya tonight!' she laughed, taking off in a rustle of stiff white skirt and squeaking black laced-up shoes.

'Thanks a million, Brenda!' I roared after her.

16

I looked down at the breakfast, feeling the exhaustion racing through me. I felt like pulling the two chairs together, like Charlie had done. I wonder how he is? I thought, feeling meself worn out. Come to think about it, I bet this is how he feels when many a night he has nowhere to sleep. Oh, bloody hell!

Right, this is getting you nowhere. OK, eat the breakfast. Take your time, have a break. Then go and pour cold water on yourself and go back in to Jackser. I can't leave him too long. God knows what might be happening to him.

OK, might as well have the television on while I'm enjoying my breakfast. I jumped up, rushing over to switch on the box, seeing the news come on, then sat back down, starting on the grub.

I was just in time to see a newsreader get caught napping. She was primping her hair and examining a spot on her chin through a little compact mirror. Then she slowly turned her head to the camera, with the eyes starting to widen in the head and the face lengthening with the dawning shock. 'YOU'RE ON AIR!' I distinctly heard a man whisper. She shot the mirror under the table, grabbing a bunch of papers, then sat up straight, fixing her face into a stony look. That made it worse!

I roared laughing, because I knew her. I lived in the girls' hostel with her years ago. When? Half a century ago! She was at university; I was doing my secretarial course. Ah, come on now, Molly! You're supposed to be a top professional. Tut, tut! Gawd, do I remember you! The nuns threatened to send the bill to her mother for the make-up she used to leave plastered on their sheets and pillowcases!

The aul kitchen nun, who was in charge of the domestic side of things, came marching into the refectory one evening when we were all having our tea. Straight over she went, banging along in her big cobnailed boots, heading herself straight for Molly Murphy. All the girls sat up, knowing trouble was brewing. We could see the nun had something hidden behind her back. Then she whipped her arm around, sending what was in it flying straight for Molly Murphy. It hit her, blinding and smacking the face off her, landing sheets and pillowcases on top of her head. We all sat stunned, watching Molly sitting like a ghost, or looking like Miss Havisham in Charles Dickens' novel, waiting for the wedding that never happened! We watched as Molly's hands and arms flew inside the sheets, trying to wrestle her way out. When her head finally appeared, the hair was plastered to her face, covering the eyes, and the rest of it was still stuck to the sheets. It was the hair stuff she was using. She spat out bits of hair caught in her mouth, shooting out the tongue, letting it dip in and out with the spits flying.

The mad nun – she was a raving bloody lunatic. Many's the day I had a run-in with her, the dangerous aul cow. The creep tried to poison me! Yeah, that mad aul fucker baked a cake specially for me, she said. I was the only one running with the scutters all night! I sat groaning through the whole night, stuck on the toilet, shitting me brains out. The silly aul cow! It was because we had one too many fights. I drove her mad. I wouldn't stop me capers. Well, when you're sixteen, the world belongs to you.

I smiled, thinking about it, then shook my head, getting back to the picture of Molly. While she sat stunned, still spitting out hair, the kitchen nun erupted.

'How dare yeh, ye dirty filthy creature? Who reared yeh? Was it wit dhe pigs? Look at dhem sheets! Look a dhe state a me pillacases! They're destroyed! Yeh need teh take dhat muck offa yore face when yeh climb into my sheets at night! Don't be handin dhe like a dhem up teh me again for washing. Go out and buy yourself a trowel an take dhat plaster offa yore face!' she screamed, letting the culchie voice go full throttle. Then she turned her big fat carcass and steamed off, smacking her way along in the big black boots, making the floorboards rattle and the dishes hop.

We all stared, our mouths hanging to our belly buttons, watching as she thumped her way back out the door. Jaysus! The place went mad. We laughed for months. Molly never got over it – we wouldn't let her.

'Oh, excruciating! I can still feel your embarrassment, Molly,' I muttered, sitting back with a grin on my face, munching on the toast, getting ready to hear what she was going to tell us.

'The government has announced we will soon be lifting out of the country's economic depression. Jobs will be created, with the hope that an American multinational company will set up here. It would give over one hundred jobs initially. But as negotiations are still in the early stages, it is too soon to say as yet what will happen. However, there is good news. A government spokesman who spoke to our reporter on the ground, Sean-Neen O'Fechel-All, says we should be hopeful! But, as the government say, nothing is settled as of yet.'

'Ah, get stuffed!' I said, whipping meself up to switch it off, then stood, stopping to watch as a plane came up on the screen. The steps up to the huge Learjet was knee-deep in politicians all waving happily with their free hand, while the other one held on to their duty-free bags. I waited to hear what they were up to.

'The government is sending twenty-three government ministers off on a junket. They will have the first stopover in Paris, then on to the Far East for a fact-finding mission. They wish to explore ways to help lift our economy off the ground. When our reporter asked the minister heading up this task, MeHall O'GrovelAll, how much it will cost to keep our private government jet in the air through this month-long fact-finding mission, he simply said, smiling as we waved us away from the aircraft, "It will be money well spent, well spent! Sean-Neen, we intend to give it our all!"

'Now for the winner of the Tidy Towns competition. The local council say it has been marvellous, with so much support coming from the local residents. It has also been a great boon in lifting the depression of unemployed people who were only too delighted to have an interest outside the home.'

'Ah, sure, it gets us out of the house,' a fella of about thirty, looking like he was going on fifty, said, nodding his head, trying to give us all a smile, but it never quite reached his eyes. Then he suddenly bucked up as he lifted his back, straightening himself, then puffed out his chest after getting a bright thought in his head. 'Well,' he said, sounding very definite, snapping his head with a shake. 'It has been marvellous for giving my confidence a boost! You see, I have a law degree . . .'

'Really?' Sean-Neen interrupted, moving his skinny body in closer, holding the microphone to his face, looking like he was kissing it. Then he said, bending in, shoving the microphone into the Law Degree's mouth, letting him too get a kiss of it, 'Tell us more!' He squeaked in his woman's voice, flicking the big goggle eyeglasses up off the end of his nose, then staring happily now he could see your man better.

'Yes, I got my law degree up in Dublin. I attended UCD, oh, seven years ago now. I decided to stay home when most of my friends hit the Big Apple! New York. That was a bad mistake. But now with this, seeing what I can achieve – just the simple things like getting myself up out of the bed in the morning, even washing and having a shave. I didn't see much purpose really before this, not when the months dragged into years. In all that time I have never had one job offer in my profession as a solicitor. Well, it is soul destroying. But now I've decided to get out! I'm going to head for New York. I have lots of contacts there now; most of them are doing very nicely for themselves. So, better late than never,' he said, turning to give a big wave to the camera as he said, 'Nice talking to you, but I better keep moving.'

Then the camera turned back to Molly. 'That is the end of the . . .'

I switched it off, then took in a deep breath, looking out at the beginning of an early-morning sun. I could see it rise, starting to soar high up, raising itself into a deep-blue sky, announcing its arrival and the promise to hail in the beginning of a brand-new, glorious day. Not a cloud in the sky, I mused, moving closer to get a look out the window.

Cars and buses all jostled each other, wanting to get ahead. They were all in a hurry to get going into work. Women walked along looking very jaunty in the sun, wearing nothing but frocks or blouses and skirts, while the men wore shirts and trousers, hanging on to their sandwiches caught under their arms. Everyone was on the move. I could see children making their way slowly to school, pushing and shoving each other, then ducking and diving, going backwards and forwards.

I watched as a pack of young fellas ran with their mouths open, laughing. Then one of them tripped over the footpath, plunging himself flat on his belly. He wasn't laughing any more. A young fella who looked like he was shouting for his schoolbag back raced over and bent down, whipping the bag up off the ground next to where the young fella lay. Then I watched as he lifted his foot, giving your man still plastered to the ground a mighty kick up the arse. With that, he took off running for his life, only stopping when he hit the corner. He looked back with a ready grin on his face, only to see your man now on his feet, making straight for him. The young fella got such a shock his head twirled on his shoulders, not knowing which way to run. Then he gripped his bag under his arm, tearing off into the distance, screaming for his mammy. Uh-oh, that little young fella is in for it! 'Run!' I muttered, seeing the bigger fella reaching out his arm to grab hold, only missing a grip of him.

I smiled, shaking my head, thinking, no wonder kids are always late for school, then end up running at the last minute. You can't trust them to get there on time no matter how early you get them out the door. Still, mine get driven the five minutes it takes to get there. I think they would go into shock if I stopped wiping their arses for them!

Right! I better get moving. I can't leave Jackser for too long on his own. I must be here over half an hour. But I still continued looking out the window, beyond into the distance, thinking it was a pity them fucking eegits blew up Nelson's Pillar! It used to be a lovely landmark in the distance. You could see it for miles then. But it was a throwback to the British rule, they said. We want nothing of them remaining to remind us of their imperial rule! The gobshites! Now look at the city! There's fuck all to see, bleedin cretins! We real Dubliners couldn't give a flying fart about the Empire; we liked our pillar! It fuckin belonged te us! Bet it was the fuckin culchies that did it! They've nothin to look at but bogs.

Oh, thinking of that. Today is the first of July! Yes, the anniversary of the first day of the Battle of the Somme! In 1916 it happened. This is a very sad day for those still alive who remember it, especially the ones who went through it. Yeah! It was a day just like today, in Picardy. Except they had the roaring of the guns lasting seven days and seven nights, tearing and blowing the German lines apart, sending them to kingdom come! Then, they finally grew silent. The early morning sun rose, about to climb high into a glorious blue sky. The birds were singing and the heavy scent of the wild flowers blooming in the lovely green fields wafted over the clean fresh air. It was enough to make you believe it is good to be alive. Down all along the trenches, officers waited. The silence was eerie, ominous. The soldiers, especially our very own Dublin Fusiliers, some as young as sixteen, stood pale and wan, at the ready, with bayonets fixed in both hands and heavy backpacks strapped to their backs. Then all down along the line the call went up. 'Ready!' shouted the officers, as they stared at their watches nestled in the palm of their open hands. They looked frozen in concentration as they watched the seconds tick by. Then, at 7.30 a.m. sharp, the signal was given. A shrill of whistles blew down all along the lines, shattering the deathly silence, as terrified men held their breath. Then the shout went up: 'OVER THE TOP! March! Don't run! Walk! Don't fire! No need to, chaps, we have the Huns well buried. There's nothing left alive over there, not even the rats. We have bombed them all to hell!'

Yes! That's what the generals thought, but the officers knew better. They tried to tell the overfed, underworked, gout-ridden fool generals – that lot were twenty miles behind the firing lines! Not a clue as to what was really happening on the frontlines. Yes! The Germans were buried all right. But not the way the generals thought. They were so well dug in even the rats couldn't find them. They had cemented themselves thirty feet under the ground. The only thing getting buried that day was the sixty thousand men who were left lying, blown to smithereens by shells and cut down by machine-gun fire relentlessly mowing out their guts, sending the bits to land in them now unlovely, once green fields of Flanders. All by the time the sun went down. Not a bird to be heard singing after that – the birds had been silenced. The Germans even blew their trees to kingdom come, along with every man and the earth under him who went over the top that beautiful sunny morning.

For some, it was just minutes after they left their trenches for the last time and walked over to meet their terrible death. For others, it was a long hard dying as they lay crying out in no-man's-land, keening for the mercy of a bullet. Their tortured cries could be heard drifting over from that lonely place by men bruised and shaken but now safely back behind the shelter of a sandbag. Through the long night, they lay listening to the suffering, hearing those awful cries for pity. Some took up the call and, leaving safety, crept into darkness, crawling their way under barbed wire, heading out for no-man's-land. They followed that cry, tracing it to a shell hole. Only then was there silence, as the agonised man went mercifully home to meet his maker. To this day can still be heard, as blood-red poppies blow in the breeze of that once no-man's-land, the ghostly whisper, *'Don't run, march! You will not have to fire a shot! Walk in straight line formation'*, comes that haunting general's command. Oh! They did for a while, and the Germans picked them off like target practice at a shooting gallery. The British generals made it so easy for them. Yeah! What a waste of human life. Such a waste.

England would mourn its loss but not its folly, as her finest cream of British manhood lay shattered in a foreign field, all in less than six hours. They erected a statue to that general! He sits now up on his high horse. 'You Will Come Back To A Land Fit For Heroes' intoned the solemn promise. They came back to a land of beggars. A maimed man stood on a street corner rattling a tin can, hoping to get enough for a bed for the night. 'Copper for an old soldier?' went the whispered plea, as he rested on the stick used to replace the missing limb. Next to him stood the blind, the bothered, the bewildered and shell-shocked, all with the same lonely plea, as the rattle of tin cans could be heard up and down the nation. 'Copper for an old soldier?' Three million a day spent to keep the war going, but ne'er a penny for a broken hero.

I still remember you wandering the Liberty streets of my childhood, the people nodding in pity you were one of our own, but now shell-shock sets you apart. Your ducking and diving, shouting and screaming, 'MASKS ON, MUSTARD GAS! RUN! DUCK RIGHT! SHELL COMING FROM THE LEFT! MACHINE GUN AHEAD! DOWN, TAKE COVER!' sent children screaming for a mammy. The terror in your mad staring eyes frightened. Your missing leg made you an easy target for jeering kids and biting dogs. Nobody understood that glazed stare. They are not with you as you still lie praying, waiting in that shell hole for the bullets, the bombs, the smoke and the deafening roaring noise to clear or God's mercy to put you fast out of your misery. 'Yes,' I whispered. 'You are my hero, old soldier, because you just kept on going.'

* * *

Why am I thinking like this? What has me feeling so melancholic? I suppose it's Jackser. I somehow feel the death of something deep inside me, like this is the end of something for me. Jackser is dying and taking it with him. It feels like death is all round me. People die here. I can feel the pain of blurred images and Jackser is in all of them as my mind flies back down through the ages of time. A little girl – she looks like a waif – is there too. I know who she is and I want to back away from her. I can hear her now and sense her presence, sense her young voice as she pleads with me. She is persuasive, desperate.

I sighed out wearily, feeling myself beginning to get dragged down, pulled into her dark world. I leapt up, not wanting to know. I better move and see how Jackser is. I made for the door but my legs wouldn't move. Something was holding me back. I walked slowly back in and sat down in the chair. 'Oh, what the hell. I'll just have a smoke and sit for another bit,' I muttered, feeling a terrible dead weight hit me.

I sat back, sprawling out my legs, and lit up a smoke, dragging it deep down into my lungs, letting myself go with the exhaustion. Without warning, I felt a panic hitting me as a flood of terrible pain gushed through me, making me feel lost and lonely. I want to open my mouth and scream with the loss – Jackser is dying and I'm lost! 'Oh, Jesus, what's wrong with me? I'm lost all over again! I can't take it,' I groaned, burying my face in my hands as the tears rolled down my cheeks and the sobs poured out my mouth. I closed my eyes, letting it all wash over me. Instantly I was back in time.

I heard the little voice whispering to me. I let her come. '*Martha! Don't be afraid a me. I don't want te hurt ye,*' she whispered, staring at me with the blue eyes looking up at me. They looked so hopeful, yet guarded – ready in case I might lash out.

A lot of pain went into making that look, I thought, staring very intensely at her. She was wary, watching back quietly as I stared, taking in the scruffy little thing standing small and helpless just above the floor. I looked down at her little bare feet, black with the dirt. They were covered in bruises from running on the sharp stones and hard ground. Her little matchstick legs, they were covered in purple zigzag bruises. The buckle of Jackser's leather belt, I thought, getting a remembering flash of that lashing.

'*Can I stay wit ye? Will ye let me stay wit ye fer a bit?*' she whispered in a soft voice, letting it rise and end in a high-pitched squeak. '*Just te keep ye company*,' she coaxed when I didn't answer her. '*I don't want ye te make me all dead inside ye. It's not gettin us nowhere!*' she keened, now starting to complain.

'I'm tired,' I breathed, not able to face up to her.

'*Yeah, I know! It's him, tha Jackser fella! He's always causin trouble,*' she warned, waving her hand down the passage.

I sighed, looking at her, saying nothing.

'*He hurt me somethin terrible, tha bandy aul fella did! Now he's all dyin an nobody's happy!*'

I just stared at her, half trying to think about that, but it was too much effort, so I said nothing.

She sat down beside me on the chair, mooching herself up closer, then rested her chin on her fist, letting it sit on her knee, waving her scruffy little matchstick leg. I looked down at it, letting out a snort, wishing she would stop doing that. She gave a shifty look up with one eye, letting the other take in the swinging, and stopped, then thought about it and started flying the toes, heaving in a huge heavy breath.

'*He's takin an awful long time te die, isn't he, Martha?*' she suddenly erupted on a long squealing moan, shattering the bit of peace trying to creep around. Then she dropped the head sideways, shaking it, letting the mouth tighten, clamping it shut with a snort, then stared at me. '*I dunno!*' she puffed, the lips flapping, the eyes blinking hard, then slowly turned, throwing an evil eye down in Jackser's direction, a look of pure disgust curling up the nose.

I turned my head, sighing at her, then looked down at the floor, staring at nothing. She stared at me, looking me up and down with the brain ticking, then let out a little squeak of annoyance.

'Here we go,' I sighed, lowering the head to rest on my elbow.

'*I don't want te start a row or nothin like tha. But ye took yer time . . . Lookit the size a ye now! Tha's how long I . . . me . . . had te wait meself,*' she snorted, stabbing herself in the chest, wanting to start a row.

I slowly shook my head. 'Don't start, little one. I'm not in the mood,' I said, warning in a deadly quiet voice.

'*No, I'm only lettin ye know! I don't mean te annoy ye!*' she breathed, quick as a flash, leaning in with her little grey-white face, trying to placate me.

'Just sit there, let me be in peace,' I said, snapping at her.

'*Yeah, OK then, we'll just sit an be easy,*' she said, nodding the head, giving me a quick smile, showing a row of little white teeth, then dropped her head, looking at the floor.

The silence hung heavy in the stuffy, overheated room. All I could hear was her heavy breathing, sighs, sniffs and the little brain ticking. Then she started to click the tongue, waving and wagging it. I was just about to turn on her when she landed a little grubby paw on my lap, roaring to distract me.

'*Jaysus, oh ma! This place would put years on ye! Wouldn't it?*' she sighed and sniffed, slowly throwing the head around, sounding like a crabby little aul one fed up with all her living.

I felt a laugh trying to ease into me. 'Jaysus, you're worse than a little aul granny,' I muttered, shaking me head down at her.

'*Well! Me ma was right – only the good die young. The bad's left te torment the rest of us!*' she sniffed, now looking the picture of the ma.

'I'm going to go mad,' I keened, wanting to cry with frustration. 'I'm exhausted. Why can't I go home? I feel rooted and trapped inside this place.'

'*Ah, don't be worryin yerself!*' she panted, getting worried I would bail out. '*Listen te me,*' she whispered, leaning in with the head like an old woman, giving me the eye. '*Won't be long now,*' she tapped, drumming her fingers on my hand, '*till the waitin'll be over!*' she whispered, but it all came out in a high-pitched squeak, then she gave me a quick look before turning away nodding, satisfied with her sound advice.

I gave a little nod, agreeing. That mistake got her going.

'*Then wha will happen te me? Will I be still stuck? Left wanderin them streets wit nowhere te go an nobody te mind me? You don't! Ye left me deaded inside ye – ran off an left me, the cheek a ye!*' she roared, snarling at me, looking like a kitten instead of something fierce, hoping to get the better of me.

'*I got,*' she pointed stabbing herself, '*left behind so you can have yer great life! I only got back now cos ye let me!*' she snorted. '*I'm very annoyed wit you. Ye're always tellin lies about me.*'

'What? How?' I said.

'*Oh, go on, ye're ashamed a me! Ye tell a pack a lies about me. Ye pretend I'm someone very fancy, whoever ye do be talkin about, but it's not me. Oh,*' *yeah, I hear ye!*' she warned, shaking the head, giving me a dirty look.

I stared at her, seeing the scruffy little scrap that you would blow away if a puff of wind hit her. But the eyes sparked like flints and the scrawny body was rigid with fight – it was like she has iron running through her soul. She dropped her shoulders, giving me the eye, getting worried now she might have pushed too far, and took in a breath, letting the hands rest in her lap.

'*I heard ye talkin about me te Jackser! I was listenin,*' she said, nodding her head and drawing her lips in now, looking like she was a gummy old woman. '*But you couldn't see the all a me, only bits! Tha's wha ye wanted. Wha am I goin te do when Jackser dies?*' she suddenly whispered to herself, now staring into the distance with the light fading out of her eyes, then the little face collapsed. '*He's goin te go an you'll bury me wit him, then forget, an I'll be lost, just left te wander always stuck wit Jackser! It will go on till the day you die an only then can I take me ease, cos you can't take the pain a me. But I'm still here an it's painin me terrible. Yeah,*' she said quietly, staring into a black hole. She had nothing behind and could see nothing ahead, not even a glimmer of hope. I was her every chance, but she knows in her heart I was her executioner. I dammed her to hell; she never grew to become a part of me.

I felt the heavy dread of her as I stared listening. It was like I was afraid to die and even more afraid to live. Sweet Jesus! This is what it is to be her.

She gave a little nod, whispering, '*Tha's right, but ye don't remember bein me,*' she said quietly, shaking her head. '*Jackser does be after me night an day. He's always shoutin an killin people . . . me! "Here you! Get movin, get this message an don't be there till ye're back," he roars at me. I do be runnin fer me life down through them dark alleyways wit me heart in me mouth, yeah, cos I'm afraid a me life the bogey man'll catch me! Then I have te watch meself fer the rats. Many's the time I leap outa me skin jumpin te fly over them! Yeah!*' she panted, with the eyes leppin out of her head. '*They do be runnin under yer feet, an mebbe even wantin te bite the face offa me an suck me blood, takin lumps outa me!*' she squealed, then paused to stare at me, making sure I got the picture.

I did! Listening to her, seeing the mouth wide open, stabbing every word, she was tearing it out of herself slowly, one breath at a time, I sat mesmerised. I followed what she was saying with my mouth open, face curling and the eyeballs hanging down, with me nodding the head, getting every picture. 'Go on,' I said, 'tell us!'

'*An tha bogey man! He could jump out at ye when he's hidin himself in the dark corners!*' she warned, looking at me with the eyes on stalks. '*It makes ye do shiver! I don't like tha at all,*' she whispered, shaking the head thinking about it. '*An did ye know wha else?*' she squealed, looking at me with the mouth stuck under the nose, looking disgusted now. '*It does smells somethin terrible shockin!*' she breathed, snapping the head on that word. '*Once I did fly through somethin all squelchy! Then when I stopped te get a look, oh, ma! I discovered someone had just had a good shit! They had done an gone te the tilet, Martha! Righ over the spot I just run! Isn't tha terrible?*'

I nodded, breathing and shutting my mouth with her, getting the smell she was getting now.

'*Yeah, then for more shortcuts I do run over waste ground. But tha can do ye harm! Cos I keep gettin me feet cut on all a the broken glass an bricks tha tumbled down. Tha's from the aul tenements tha had fallen, or someone pulled down. So tha's no good if ye got bare feet, cos ye have te slow down! But then I'm off again, flyin like the wind, runnin on the aul cobblestones, only them's very treacherous too, ye know, Martha!*'

I nodded like mad, listening intently. She nodded, looking very satisfied she had my attention.

'*Oh, yeah. Ye can break yer neck on them when they do be shiny an all wet wit the damp. I don't like tha neither! Cos then once I did fall on the back a me skull! I lay swimming, seein stars, cos I couldn't get up!*'

'Poor you!' I said sadly.

'*Yeah, an ye can hit yer big toe as well! Then I have te limp wit me toe stuck in the air. People does be laughin, but I'm not! I do feel the pain, ye know! Yeah, but I do feel pain somethin worse than tha be times. It can hurt somethin terrible!*' she said quietly, letting her voice drop, going very still as she sat staring into the distance.

I could feel it hitting me too – a picture of Jackser moving in for the kill – it suddenly made me shudder. I wanted to get away from the little one. But I couldn't move. I was frozen solid with the overwhelming pain of her. I just sat staring and listening, letting her take me down, dragging me all the way back, wanting to share her world of hell.

'*But it's worse when I'm not runnin fer messages, cos then I'm stuck in the room listenin te the ma moanin an tha Jackser fella roarin the head offa himself, an mebbe hurt me ma or go fer me. Or then other times I do be roamin the streets lookin fer somethin I lost. I don't know wha I'm lookin for! But I do be tormented searchin. An worse than tha is, nobody can see me! They can't hear me cryin. I do look inta the faces a all the people passin, wantin te see if they know, but they don't, so I have te keep goin. Then I'm lost, cos I can't find me ma no more! The fear erupts in me then an I go faster, runnin like mad, but I'm not gettin back te her! I'm rushin past all the streets, but I'm still not gettin home! Me heart does break, Martha! Cos then I'm out in the dark an cold, wit the wind blowin up me an the Banshee screamin at me from knocked-down buildins, an she's keenin outa the dark hallways wit the doors thrun open a the old tenements. I can hear her cryin! Oh, me heart does be crossways in me, Martha.*

'*Then one time I found me babby brother Charlie! An do ye know wha, Martha?*' she said, leaning into me with the face raging and her mouth dropping, creasing the little eyebrows.

'No, wha? Tell us!' I said, forgetting meself and imitating her.

'*He was all on his own! Yeah,*' she said, nodding her head like mad. '*Sittin in the damp, cold ground, lookin around him he was, an it the middle a the night! Me ma must a left him, an he only a babby! He must a been lookin an waitin for her te come back fer him! Then he started roarin an screamin when he sawed me! He put his arms out for me te pick him up, so I sat down wit him on the cold ground an got him sittin on me lap. Then I heard you – yer voice – in me head. Tha happened the night you an Charlie was sittin wit Jackser! Me an me babby brother was lookin at youse, an the babby was starin up at big Charlie. He was tryin te make out who tha was. His eyes was starin outa his head. But do ye know wha I knew just tha very minute? It was fer you I was lookin all tha time. I knowed tha soon as I seen ye! Yeah, all tha time I was lookin an waitin fer you te come back for me, an I didn't even know tha! No, I just knowed I'm lost an I have te keep lookin, cos ye didn't let me live inside ye!*

'*Am I dead, Martha? Am I a ghost? How come you is all growed up an I'm not, Martha?*' she said, with the eyes staring, the mouth open, and the tongue flying from cheek to cheek, trying to figure it out.

I sighed heavily, not wanting to go into this. Then suddenly I took my annoyance out on her. I wanted to lash back for all her pain, now I was steeped in it too.

'Because you were dead to me,' I said viciously, showing an inhuman streak of cruelty.

'*Oh, yeah. So I must be a ghost*,' she said, dropping the mouth and staring, then nodding the head, deciding that was the answer.

The pain knifed through me, seeing her innocence and complete trust in me. Gobshite Martha, hurt her and you hurt yourself! Was she not hurt enough?

We stared at each other, her letting her breath slow down, taking me in, reading me, searching down through the core of me looking for answers. Suddenly she exploded. '*Here! Sure, you're not much better! You're empty without me, cos we're only two halves! We're separate*,' she snorted, flying back at me with a dig of her own. '*He did tha! Him down there. I can't do nothin, ye're only lettin me in now because yer wantin me back! But the way you're goin we'll be stuck fer ever! I can see it wit me senses – any minute ye might just go, walk away an leave me fer ever. Are ye not listenin te wha's happenin te me an Jackser! Ye have te stay an face us. He's tryin te talk te you through be talkin te me. I can see inside him an hear the tormentin an roarin in his head. It hurts him somethin terrible it does, then tha makes him go ragin! I can see the different ways he has. I sawed him when he was little. They kilt him, they did! He was afraid a his life a them men, so he was, Martha! It was terrible, but then ye see he got te be just like them.*'

'What do you mean, little one? I mean . . . how did you see that? He showed you?'

She stared at me with the eyebrows creasing and the eyes pinned on me, looking like she was wondering how I couldn't know that.

'*It was when you an big Charlie was here. Tha night wit Jackser when youse was sittin at his bed. We was listenin cos youse were lettin us come te ye, but not really! Cos ye didn't let me talk te ye . . . I already told ye this a minute ago*,' she snapped, getting impatient thinking I wasn't listening right.

'*I sawed tha Jackser was old, real old, an I wouldn't a known him only I knew it was him. I kept starin at him an so did Charlie, then he gorra fright an started shoutin cryin, an took off fast, crawlin te make his gerraway! I let him rush off, tearin fer his life te find me ma, an I turned back te*

Jackser. He wanted me wit him so he could talk. Then we were watchin a little young fella like meself, he was standin wit short woolly trousers down past his knees an big black cobnail boots wit socks hangin over them. He was shakin wit fright an lookin up at a man wearin a long habit wit a belt wrapped aroun it an a big leather whip in his hand. Then I sawed the young fella was Jackser! He was goin te get kilt! The priest was tearin him aroun the head an legs an anywhere he could get in wit a lash a the whip. It had loads a little bits a leather on it. Jackser was screamin an tryin his best te gerraway. But the man grabbed him be the neck an hauled him inta the air an shook him!

'I heard old Jackser whisper beside me, "I'm sorry for all the hurt I gave ye's! It was them taught me tha was the right thing te be doin, they told me it was fer me own good. I didn't know any better. I should never a harmed ye!" Then suddenly I could hear roarin an ragin voices comin te do harm! Then it was more an more a them! All shoutin an more voices screamin, then whisperin underneath them big roarin voices. They kept at it, all talkin together an very fast! I started screamin cos I could see in the middle a them Jackser holdin his head. He was tryin te stop them drivin him mad. It was makin him ragin! He was wantin te kill them, lash out an kill someone, just make them stop! But they wouldn't. They kept pointin an laughin, shoutin an tellin him they were goin te get him an he was goin te die. I started te run, wantin te get away fer me life, then I heard Jackser say, "No! No, don't run, let me take ye!" An suddenly it was all quiet. We were gone from it, from the roars an the fright an the child gettin kilt, an the cold an dark hidin all them monsters!

'Now I was runnin through a big field an it was very bright. Jackser was laughin an runnin behind tryin te catch me, an the sun was shinin. I could feel the lovely heat of it on me face an I started laughin too, cos it had chased away the dark an all the bad people, leavin them behind in the other places. "Sit down beside me an make yerself a daisy chain," he said, smilin contentedly, lookin around an pointin at all the little flowers in the grass. "Wha? But I don't know how ye do tha, Jackser!" I said, shakin me head an makin a grab, pickin a big bunch for meself. "Tha should be easy," he said, grabbin hold a my stuff then givin a big snuffle while he sorted them out in lengths, studyin them.

'"This is how it should a been, this picture now! But I never had it in me te make somethin a me life. My dream was a family. I had the idea te

work hard an spread a bit a happiness wit a woman at me side. Oh, yeah, tha more than anythin. But nothin turns out the way ye think," he said, shakin his head, lookin like he lost out somethin terrible. "I never thought I would be such a bad bastard. Oh, may the good Jesus forgive me," he said, closin his eyes like he was goin te cry. "I destroyed meself an everyone aroun me! Tha night I met yer mammy, I shoulda did her a good turn an kept walkin. Youse couldn't a been any worse than the way I left ye's," he said, shakin his head an breathin hard, with his mouth gripped shut.

'I said nothing, just listened. Me heart was breakin. The only thing we had te worry us then was hunger, an where we were goin te sleep tha night. But, yeah, I didn't like te see me mammy always talkin te herself an lookin sick wit all the worry. But it was still OK, we was always the happier fer it when we got somethin te eat or found a place te sleep. Yeah, then me ma would laugh an be happy. Oh, I miss them times.

'"Do ye think, young one, ye might find it in yer heart te not think too bad a me? Could ye forgive me?" he suddenly whispered, rubbin his fist an lookin at me wit a pain in his eyes, just like the one me ma gets when she used te be walkin the streets frettin. I said nothin, just stared at him, not knowin wha te answer. I didn't want te be tellin him a lie.

'He stared at me, waitin, then saw wha I was thinkin and said, "If it's any way consolation to ye, I paid a hard price too fer me bad ways. I only ever wanted the best fer yer mammy an youse, but the fuckin bastards in me head got the better a me. Them an them bastardin Christian Brothers tha brought me up an trained me! They turned me out a walkin fuckin bastard! I hated every minute of me life from the day I was born," he said slowly, grittin his teeth.'

I listened, watching her, not able to start my mind thinking. What? He had taken the child and walked her through the dark hidden caves of his mind, somehow giving her glimpses of his soul, travelling her back down through the days of his life as I sat talking to him. All the time he was with me through the child.

'Yeah! Tha's it,' she said, reading my thoughts. *'He wants ye te understand now, so ye will be happy an he'll be at peace. So do I, Martha. I do be cold an lonely, an I don't like livin in the dark an cryin wit no one te take me. You were me a long time ago. Now I'm just nobody any more. I never got te be happy. I thought when I got big, I'd be you, an I'd be somebody an people would love me, but you never even liked me! You grew up without me, an ye left me behind cos I wasn't lovely! I waited, hopin, but ye never came. Ye didn't want te know me, an I can tell tha cos I'm lookin inside you now,'* she whispered, letting the tears stream down her cheeks.

Suddenly I could feel my heart beginning to break, but I couldn't put my hand out to her. She was right! I couldn't get near enough to love her. She had seen too much suffering. I couldn't bear the pain in her. 'I don't know what to do,' I muttered, seeing the tears crash down her cheeks and flood into her filthy, black, bony little neck. I watched them sitting on her throat then mingle in the dirt, softening from the hot wet tears. They left a pool of dirty water showing a speck of white porcelain skin; it was hidden underneath. My heart broke and my chest suddenly convulsed. Fat drops of tears burst out and streamed down my cheeks, then landed in my throat just as hers did.

She suddenly lifted her head up to me, coming very close. *'Martha! Don't let him go an take me wit him. He doesn't want tha. Ye have te listen, hear wha he's sayin. If ye don't do tha, then you'll never get a day's peace. Somethin will always be missin! He robbed me, an you'll spend the rest a yer days draggin them aul torments wit ye. Yeah, we were your torments, Jackser an me, but we all need te get peace now. If you manage, Martha, te let go a him in yer heart, then it will start te come right, but ye have te do it very soon.'*

I listened to the little voice of truth as it all became suddenly clear, so very clear. Out of the mouths of babes and sucklings! I thought, shaking my head at her in amazement. 'How did you work all that out, little one?' I said, astonished at her insight.

'I can hear it comin from you, but ye're not listenin!' she snapped, beginning to get fed up with my stupidity.

'How old are you, little Martha?' I whispered, suddenly leaning in to make eye contact, wondering at her wisdom, yet understanding nothing of my own mind.

'I'm six! Me ma says I'm six! An I think I know more than you!' she said, looking at me with the eyes spitting fire, raging I couldn't or wouldn't help her. Yet beyond that burning was a terrible sadness. She was such a lonely little girl, so terribly alone and vulnerable. But I turned away from her. I can't carry her pain any more.

'I have to go, little one. I'm tired,' I said, suddenly getting up and walking out. I looked back at the door, seeing her staring after me with the mouth open and the eyes staring in confusion, then she dropped her head to one side, hoping I didn't mean I was really going to leave her. She looked so small and frail and so totally alone. But I couldn't think any more with her. Enough, leave me be. I closed my eyes then slowly let them rest on the armchair again. It was now empty, no little Martha. She was gone to do her haunting, back to the old streets of Dublin where I once roamed.

Just before I turned away I heard a little voice whisper, *'I'll be waitin for ye, Martha. Ye know where te find me. Ye only have te come an search for me along the back streets a Dublin. Tha's where me ghost still wanders.'*

17

I looked over at Jackser, seeing he was sweating again. I stood up and reached for the bowl, testing the water. It's lukewarm. Maybe it might be better if I get fresh cold water. No, I don't want to give him a worse chill.

I looked at his face, seeing how grey he was. Poor Jackser, I hope you don't know how much you are suffering; it is bloody horrendous. I leant over him, listening to the screams of his lungs as they struggled to take in air. My stomach twisted and my face tightened with the tension and pain of seeing him going through this, second by second. Oh, Jesus! I can't bear to see a human being suffer like that. No one should have to go through this. 'Fucking hell!' I muttered, feeling like I was beginning to lose my rag. If he was a dog, they would put him out of his misery straight away! There must be something they can do for him. Where's that nurse? I'm going to get that fucking doctor down here. This is unmerciful!

I whipped back the curtain, feeling a slight drop in the temperature. 'Oh, that's better,' I sighed, pulling it out of the way. An old man sitting in the bed opposite lifted his face to look over. I turned around and pulled the curtain again, leaving Jackser shaded from the blazing sun but now getting the steam from his own body heat.

'It's like a furnace in there,' I said.

'Aye! I'd say it is all right,' he said, nodding his head with the thin bits of grey hair still hanging on.

'It's so hot in here,' I puffed, shaking the week-old shirt stuck to me damp skin. I'm going to need a trowel to scrape the filth off me, I thought, brushing back the hair sticking to my face. Every bit of me burned and ached with tiredness.

'Oh! It's like a Turkish bath in this place,' he said, stretching out his legs, trying to cool them, letting the feet sit on top of the blankets. He had them curled down at the bottom, trying to give himself an airing.

'It's a wonder they don't bring in a cooling fan, one of them things on wheels,' I said, looking at him.

'That'd be an idea,' he said.

'Maybe that's a good idea,' I muttered. 'I'll ask one of the nurses. Jackser could do with it, maybe put it next to him.'

'How is the poor aul unfortunate doin? Ahh! Not good! Not good at all. Jesus! He's suffering something terrible. You wonder how it can go on so long, and he still managing to keep going!' he shook his head, thinking about it, looking pained. 'Oh, it's hard pain coming inta the world, an it can be even harder tryin te get out of it,' he said, shaking his head at me, looking in the direction of Jackser. 'I knew him, ye know!'

'Did you?' I said, feeling me heart quicken. It was like meeting someone from my own past, a connection with my childhood.

'Oh, indeed I did. He used te hang around wit all tha crowd, the ones wit the interest in the horses. They all had somethin te do wit them one way or the other.'

'Really?' I said, wanting to hear about Jackser, getting a picture of when he was young.

'Oh, yeah! Indeed, I knew them all. There used te be him an Smelly Murphy!'

'Why did you call him that?' I said, laughing.

'Ah, who knows? Names stick from when ye're very young. No one ever knows where they came outa. But if I was te guess, I would say he probably farted or did somethin te do wit tha line of it.

'Anyway, there was another fella be the name a Squeaky, an Mac the Knife . . .'

'Why did they call him that?' I said.

'Oh! I remember tha one all right,' he said, raising the eyebrows, letting them land in the air, then turning his head away in disgust. Then he turned back to me, talking. 'He was very handy wit a knife! His father was a butcher. But when he was a Chiseller, ye know, only a lad, his ma got herself an ice-cream stand. She was very handy like tha, ye know. Always on the lookout for makin an extra few bob.

Anyways,' he said, drawing in his breath and sitting himself back for comfort, wanting to tell me the story. 'Now ye see, this ice-cream stand came together wit a bicycle. Ye had te pedal the thing! So nobody better fer the job than the Chiseller! So off he sets, him on the bike, headin straight for the Phoenix Park, where the mammy told him tha's the best place fer him te pick up the crowds. It was durin the holidays – oh, lovely weather like we're gettin at the minute, ye see?' he said, bringing the head over to me, leaning his chin on the hand and pausing his breath, making sure I'm following him.

'Yeah, yeah! Go on!' I said, listening all intent with my eyes feasted on him.

'Well! Tha was grand, an off he set. Now natural like, because of wha was in it, all the ice cream, well, the whole neighbourhood a kids, mostly young fellas, his pals, decided te trek along for the outin an give Chiseller a hand. All was goin grand, the young fella was doin a roarin trade, until, it was yer very man over there! He was only outa Artane, sixteen he was,' the man said, pointing his finger and landing it in the air, keeping it pointed in Jackser's direction.

'What, Jackser! He was there?'

'Oh, yeah! Well, when Chiseller, that's wha he was called, even though be now he was around the sixteen mark, too. No longer a Chiseller! But these things stick, ye know?'

'Oh, yeah, you get a nickname for life when you grow up in a small place,' I said, remembering all that from living in places around the city centre.

'Anyway!' the man continued, getting impatient with me after interrupting. 'Chiseller was after cuttin a shillin wafer. Now tha was a big one. You'd nearly get the whole block a ice cream fer the price a tha! But tha was the charge from Chiseller. "Ye can pay up or fuck up!" Chiseller woulda told ye . . . Excuse me language!' he said. 'But anyway, this big lump of ice cream, stuck between two slices a thin wafer, landed down on the little counter. Well!' The old man paused, slowly taking in a breath. 'If yer man over there didn't up an make a sudden move. Quick as a flash he was, made a grab for the ice cream. Oh, he was quick all right! But be Jaysus! Chiseller was even quicker! Like greased lighting he was wit tha knife. Down he brought the huge butcher's knife, one a his father's, smack on the counter, on top a his fingers over there. Missin him be a hair's breadth! Only because he got the hand back in time, he woulda be known now as "Fingers", cos he wouldn't a had any! Not Snuffler, as we used te call him.'

'Snuffler? Is that what he was called?' I said, with the eyes standing outa me head.

'Oh, yeah!'

'Why did you call him that?'

'Ah, he was always snufflin. It was just an aul habit a his.'

'Yeah, he was,' I said, remembering all his habits. He had the same ones – first the snuffling when you got his interest in something, or he was about to do something. Then came the arm lifting inta the air, then the bending, looking like he was examining the ground. When he was satisfied he was now snuffled enough, the arm got a good shaking, swinging it around, and the back got a bit of exercise all at the same time! Then he was off, down to do the business at hand.

I laughed, remembering back to them times, a feeling of bittersweet memories filling my belly and my chest – loss for the little child I once was. Yet, joy for the hope and the dreams and the times back then of being a child. I let the memory go, taking in a sigh, letting the smile on my face fade away, saying, 'So, what did they call you?'

'Ah, go on! I'm not tellin ye tha!' he said, shaking his head and looking away then back with a half-smile half mixed with a look of disgust on his face.

I waited as he took in a breath, letting it out in a snort. 'Canary!' he said, snorting it out on a breath.

'Canary?' I said. 'Why?'

'Well ye might ask. I had yella hair!'

'Yellow?'

'Yeah! It was a cross between white an red, but neither a them.'

'It was gold!' I said.

'Well, lighter, yella!'

'Gawd! You must have been a brute of a handsome man,' I laughed, looking at the faded sky-blue eyes now a bit bloodshot.

'Yeah! Me mother was from a little village in France. Me father met her during the First World War, when he was fightin there. He stayed wit the family after the war just ended. He was in no hurry te get back here te his poor mother waitin on him. She didn't know whether he was dead or alive. He enlisted when he was only seventeen, without tellin her. Then the deed was done, he arrived home in the uniform, an off he went.

'It was durin the big rush! When Mister what's his name? Me memory is not as good as it was,' he said, twisting his baldy eyebrows, trying to think.

'Lord Kitchener,' I said, guessing that's what he was going to say.

'Yeah! Tha's him, the very man. Anyway! Me father used te tell us stories about how they all rushed down an enlisted, him an the pals. But tha was the last anyone ever seen a them again, so me father used te say, God rest him,' he said sadly, letting his eyes stare as he thought about his long-gone father. 'Anyway, he wasn't satisfied until he got wha he wanted. He brought me mother, God rest her an be good te her, back wit him te Dublin an married her here. They set up home in a little place his mother, me granny, got them. That's how I know Jackser. His family – his mother an mine – were neighbours. We lived next te each other down the lane in Sheriff Street. Everyone knew everyone else. Ye couldn't have a good fart without everyone hearin an gettin te know about it.

'But it was grand in them days. It was easy livin for the childre in the long summer days an nights. Jaysus! We would be out playin on them streets from mornin till dusk! Wit no harm ever comin te us. An harmless fun we got up to! We made our own enjoyment. We were so easily pleased,' he said, looking happy and sad, going back down the memory to the days of his childhood.

I said nothing, just smiled with him, going back with him, getting a sense through him of similar days. Golden, warm and even hot sunny days with gangs of children. Girls, they always played together. They were either chasing each other or swinging outa lamp posts with a rope tied to the top and a noose at the bottom to sit your arse in. Then lash out with the foot at the lamp post and off ye flew, flying in and out, twirling like mad. Seeing how many you could get before you came to a sudden stop when your head smashed into the heavy metal lamp post. Yeah! One too many twirls and you didn't get your foot lashed against the lamp post in time to brake! Jaysus, I can still see the stars, with me head swinging from that! But that was a happy memory before we met Jackser, so I couldn't have been even six years old yet!

'It was lovely talking to you,' I whispered, coming back to me senses and stirring meself. 'I better get moving.'

'Ah, yeah! Nice talkin te you too,' he said, fixing his pyjama legs, then nodding at me.

'I better see if I can get something to cool down Jackser,' I whispered, looking back at him with my body out the door, leaving my head still stuck inside. 'That heat in there is not helping him any,' I muttered, looking pained as I shook me head.

'Yeah! Tha would be a wise move, all right. Go on,' he nodded, 'see if ye can get him something. Jaysus Christ! He must be baked over there behind them aul curtains,' he said, throwing the head at me to get moving.

18

'Now, Jackser, is that better for you?' I muttered to him as I dried his face and neck with the clean towel, then wrung out the cloth. 'We have a bit of comfort,' I said, looking over at the big fan blowing out lovely cool air. It was sitting in the corner, right next to Jackser. I sat down and leant meself into the bed, holding his hand, then rested me head down on my left my arm, laying it flat out on the bed.

'Martha! Martha, are ye asleep?'

I opened my eyes, lifting me head looking straight up into the ma.

'Wha's happenin?' she whispered, looking from me to Jackser.

I looked up at him, seeing him breathing faster. I slowly sat up straight, trying to get me bearings. 'I must have conked out,' I said, feeling me head and eyeballs like someone had stuffed them inside a mangle. My nose and chest felt stuffed and dry. I'm dehydrated, I thought, I better get something to drink. 'Ma, how are you? What time is it?'

'Oh, I couldn't get in any earlier,' she said, sitting herself in the chair and looking from me to Jackser. 'How is he?' she said, letting her face twist with worry and her eyes stare at him, looking like she was going to cry or start shouting.

I said nothing for a minute, knowing she could see it for herself. It's better she reach her own conclusions.

'Is he bad?' she said, looking at me, knowing what she saw.

I took in air slowly through my nose, letting my eyes fix on Jackser. I shook my head. 'He's not good, Ma. He's having an awful hard time of it.'

'Is he?' she said, letting her voice go up in the air like it was news to her.

'Yeah! You can see there for yourself.'

'Yeah,' she said turning her head to the door, then looking back at me. 'Where is she? Why won't she come in?' me ma said, looking back at the door again.

'Who, Ma?'

'Sally! I got her te come in wit me. I had te take a taxi. It's quicker. I was waitin the whole day fer her. I had te wait up te now te get her te come in wit me.'

'What?' I said, seeing her suddenly appear in the door.

'Yeah,' me ma said. 'I didn't want te come in on me own.'

I stared at Sally, seeing the white, worn-out face, the lovely blue eyes that could now be any colour if you didn't know them. They were just staring out of her head with a dead, empty look in them. No, there was nothing to read on her face; it was completely closed down.

'How are you, Sally?' I whispered.

'Yeah, hello,' she said, giving a slight nod of the head, then didn't see me as she forgot my presence. Instead, she flicked her eyes to Jackser, then stood beside the ma, keeping a bit of distance, then back to staring into fresh air, or wherever her mind went it was seeing nothing, because her face was a stone mask of emptiness.

I stared at her for a minute, waiting and wanting to hear something, or for me to say something. But the air stayed pregnant between us, with me waiting, wondering if I should say more, then the moment passed and I gave up. I didn't like the idea of her selfishness. She couldn't put herself out for the ma, never mind bother herself to get in and see her father. Oh, to hell with it. Who knows what's going on in her poor mind? Maybe she's hit rock bottom. No, don't be too quick with the boot, Martha!

I stood up, saying, 'Ma, you sit here. I have to move for a few minutes.'

'Where are ye goin, Martha? Will ye be long?' she said, looking up at me.

'No, Ma, but I need to get meself a cup of tea. I haven't eaten much today, or even had time to wash me face. He's not very well,' I said, pointing my finger at Jackser, suddenly feeling very annoyed. The different emotions flying through me at the same time wouldn't let me work out why I was suddenly feeling my chest flare up with the heat of anger.

'Don't be long, Martha! Sally has te get back,' she said, turning herself around to get a look at me heading out the door.

I suddenly felt a surge of anger and lifted me chest with a breath, letting my eyes land on Sally for a minute. I was about to say something, lash into her. But I held my breath, saying instead, 'Right, Ma, won't be long. Sally can rest herself in my chair. She looks worn out from all her hard work!' Yeah, it was suddenly back to killing Sally time!

'Jaysus!' I muttered, lashing meself inta the kitchen to grab a cup, making myself a drop of tea. Then I shoved two slices of bread in the toaster, getting meself a tray.

'Oh! Are you all right?' a nurse said, coming into the kitchen.

'Don't ask,' I said. 'I will only tell you, then you will regret ever asking,' I snorted, then let my shoulders drop, taking in a sigh.

She grinned and pulled out a little milk jug filled with milk. 'Not surprised, Martha!' she said, shaking her head and helping me get stuff on the tray. 'You have been in there sitting solidly for one week. Seven nights and eight days without any let-up. You have not seen a bed since you set foot into this place. I think you should get someone to relieve you. Ask your family in there or someone to come and give you a break.'

'Yeah, that's an excellent idea, Patricia, but, tempting as it is . . . No! Better not, anything could happen. I want to stay with him.'

'Then you better start looking after yourself,' she said, putting her hand on my back and rubbing it, then moving on to lift the tray. 'Come on, have this. I'll take it down for you, then put your feet up for a few hours. Have a nap in the waiting room. Don't worry, we will let you know if we need you.'

'OK, thanks, Nurse. But my ma is here now and the sister. I better go in and keep them company. I haven't seen the ma for a while.'

'Here we are, sitting room. Right! Sit down there and have that first. Do you want the television switched on?' she said, going over and standing beside it.

'No, I better not, otherwise I will get too comfortable. I really have to get back down to the ma,' I said, pouring the tea and taking a bit of toast.

'OK, see you later,' she said, putting her hand on my shoulder as she swished off, making the starched frock rustle. Then she was out the door and down the passage. I listened to the squeak of her soft black-leather shoes on the shiny tiles. 'Thanks, Patricia!' I roared, just remembering to show my appreciation.

'See you!' she said, waving back at me.

I smoked two cigarettes and drank a second pot of tea before making my move back down to see the ma. She was standing up fixing her coat, buttoning it up. Sally stood waiting, getting ready to make it out the door.

'What's happening, Ma? Where are you going?'

'We have te go, Martha. It's gettin late,' she said, trying to make peace between the demands I looked like making and the quiet but surly Sally and what she wanted.

'Are you leaving already, Ma? Sure, you got here no length of time ago,' I said, looking from one to the other of them. Sally turned away, like this had nothing to do with her, she was only doing the ma a favour. The ma was chewing the inside of her lip, blinking, with her face pushed into a half-smile. She was nervous about upsetting me but more afraid of getting left out in the cold by Sally.

'But, Ma, I need a break! I think one of you should stay the night. He's getting bad, Ma,' I whispered, wanting to get her the picture of Jackser. 'I didn't want to leave him on his own. I will be down in the sitting room, just to get a bit of a break, Ma. We can't leave him on his own!' I said, desperate to get them to stay.

Sally moved off, saying, 'I have te go. Come on, Ma, if ye're comin!'

'We can't stay, Martha. We have te get goin,' me ma whispered, wanting to get herself outa here.

'OK then, but . . .' I wanted to say something sharp! Put a fire under their arses! But what's the point? 'OK, bye, Ma. Bye, Sally. See you! I'm going down for another cigarette,' I said, 'then I'm going to get meself a bit of fresh air.'

'Yeah, goodbye now, Martha,' she whispered, then moved herself back in a few steps to get a look at Jackser, feeling herself getting pulled in different directions. But knowing the one she wanted was out the door with Sally, making sure Sally got her taxi home. Fuck me! The idea of it! Getting the bus home? Never! 'Oh, sweet fuckin Sally, you are a priceless piece of work. No doubt about that!' I snorted to meself, rushing off up the passage, getting speed from the fire rushing around me belly with the annoyance and rage coming over me.

I sat down and lit up the cigarette, thinking it is me overreacting because I'm tired, banjacksed! Anything could set me off. But I will never be able to do this again for Jackser. Somehow he needs someone doing something for him without wanting something back. Maybe it's to do with the way he was robbed of his childhood. Maybe it's because I remember the times when he threw me a bit of kindness. Whatever it is, I don't want him to think he was a complete failure. There he is now, up there dying a thousand deaths and all alone. He has children of his own but there's not one here now as he's coming to his end. It doesn't matter if he brought it on himself or not. What matters is he is alone. He just wasn't lucky enough to have had even one person in his family to say, 'Bye, Da. Ye were a bastard. You were a thunderin bollocks! Ye were some fuckin cowboy! But you were my da, an I still love you! We're goin te miss you, ye aul fucker! Do ye hear tha? But, yeah, when all is said an done, you were still my da. So take it easy when ye get there. Don't be askin God if he's tryin te come the hound wit ye, because he won't take any aul guff outa you!'

I dragged the curtains, pushing them back out of the way, seeing the darkened ward lit up from the light on the corridor and the one burning over the washbasin. Everyone was long sound asleep. The dead quiet all up and down the corridor was suddenly disturbed by a lid getting slammed on something metal, then the sound of gushing water. It's probably one of the night nurses washing a bedpan, I thought, letting the sound distract me. But it couldn't drown out the sound of Jackser ailing. I sat and stood, getting up every few minutes to lean close into him. There was a change coming over him – his breathing was starting to get louder and I could hear a rattle in his chest. I stared at him, seeing his chin lift with nearly every breath that hit him. But it wasn't coming like it should, not like his usual breathing. That was bad, but this was like his lungs is getting tired, getting ready to stop. I looked at his face, seeing him look like he was alert, aware of it. It wouldn't show unless you were really tuned in to how he normally sleeps – dead, out for the count. Now, though, he had a pained look on his face.

'Are ye all right, Jackser?' I said, squeezing his hand.

His arm moved, then he gave a little moan, like a cough.

'Can you hear me, Jackser?' I whispered, standing up and bending down, looking right into his face. His breathing got worse then his face moved. He's coming around.

'You're all right! Take it easy,' I said, loud enough for him to hear it. 'I'm here with you. It's me, Martha. Don't worry, you're all right. I'm right beside you. Here, can you feel my hand holding you?' I said, leaning into him and putting me other hand on his head, looking down into his face.

Then his breathing came in loud gasps and his eyes suddenly opened. I leant my head straight into his face, letting him see me. He didn't seem to be looking at me. His eyes were glazed over, like he was seeing something I couldn't see.

Jesus! Something's happening, I thought, feeling my body spring into alert, with my feet keeping me rooted. My mind flew, thinking a million thoughts.

'Can you hear me, Jackser? Me ma was in and Sally. They were here sitting beside you! Everyone came in, but they're gone home for a while. It's late, but you're all right, I'm not going anywhere. Do you need the nurse?'

Then his eyes shifted, coming alive as the hazy look cleared. He looked at me like he really was seeing me. We stared at each other. I could see the confusion and the shock as he wondered what was happening to him. Then his eyes changed, becoming clearer, more intense as the life soared through him. He was looking at me now like he wanted to tell me something.

'It's OK, Jackser. You have made it all this way,' I said, whispering to him. 'Don't be afraid. Nothing can happen to you. I'm here with you! Just hang on to my hand.'

He gripped it, then his lips moved, letting out a rasped whisper.

'What? Are you trying to say something, Jackser? What did you say?' I said, bending down with my ear close to his lips.

'Than . . . *gasp*!'

I held my breath, desperately trying to hear what he wanted to tell me. 'What, Jackser?' I whispered, seeing my breath go inside his open mouth.

'God bless ye, may he forgive me! I'm . . .' he gasped, but didn't finish.

I lifted my head to look at him, but then he let his eyes close again. He now looked so weary. The effort had dug everything out of him; it had used up that surge of life, sinking him even lower.

I stayed still, holding my breath, afraid to break what was happening with making a sound, letting my breath go, or even stirring myself with making a movement. 'Listen,' I whispered, 'I'm going to go and get the nurse. I have to let go of your hand for a minute. OK, Jackser?' I said softly, letting the question lie for a minute, keeping the stillness as he struggled to get another breath that sounded like it wasn't going to come. The gaps were too long and he held his chest rigid, with everything in him trying to force that air to come.

I let go of his hand and moved fast, making for the passage and down to where I thought I heard a sound coming from, trying to find a nurse. I turned me head in and out of darkened wards – no sign of a nurse. I rushed back, heading towards the top end of the passage.

'Nurse!' I shouted, in a loud whisper, seeing a nurse come out of a ward, shoving something in her pocket. 'Quick! It's Jackser!'

'What? Is there a change? What's happening?'

'Can you come quick?!' I said, seeing her walk towards me with her mind on a pin that got loose, letting her bib fall from her chest. She stuck the pin in and pulled down her apron, then took off into a run behind me. We flew into the ward, seeing Jackser with his chest going rigid, suspended in the air. I could hear the rattles.

'He's bad, Nurse!'

She rushed over and grabbed his wrist, then put her hand on his chest. 'We need to get your mother in here, Martha! She's going to have to be quick!'

'Oh, Jesus! How are we going to do that?' I said, looking at her, then down at Jackser.

'I will phone her!'

'What? How?'

'We have her home phone number,' she said, giving me a look that thought I was odd not knowing that! Then it passed and she shook her head up and down, whispering in a matter-of-fact way, 'Yes, she has a phone.'

'Jesus! Brilliant!' I said, shocked at the idea the ma had a telephone in her home.

She was out the door and heading straight for the nurses' station. I went in and grabbed Jackser's hand, leaning over him. 'Take it easy, Jackser. Me ma is coming. We're all here! You're OK, just take it easy,' I kept murmuring quietly, speaking in a low whisper as I stroked his face, squeezing his hand bending over him. I watched as his eyes opened, staring straight at me. I could hear the death rattles getting worse; they were coming louder.

'Jackser! I want to say this to you. Charlie and me sat up all night with you. Charlie wanted to be with you. He didn't like you being sick and in here on your own. I want to tell you something, Jackser. You were not all bad. You see, you couldn't be, Jackser, or what would I be doing here? You had a kind heart. It came out when your nerves weren't getting the better of you,' I said quietly, staring into his terrified eyes, seeing he was hanging on to me, listening to my every word. He is so alone in his terror, it fills him, makes him desperate for the whispered word of mercy, the gentle touch of comfort. He must dare not be alone – the suffering is too great.

'Jackser,' I whispered, 'I have learned a lot through you. Oh, it has been hell sitting here going back down the days of my life with you, but lately, I don't know, but something strange has been happening between you and me. I sensed it all through these days and nights I have been sitting here talking to you. I knew you were listening to me, but now I suddenly have a sense that it was even more than that. It feels like while I was sitting here talking, that our spirits were actually walking together. You wanted to let me feel what it was to be you, and I had a terrible need to understand why we had so much suffering. I felt the heart in you, I felt your suffering, I felt your pain that you couldn't get life right, it wouldn't work out the way you wanted. The demons tormenting your mind persecuted you. You knew it was all wrong the way you made us suffer, and I felt your sorrow. It feels like our spirits have been communicating so very much, but I am only aware of a bit of it. I think it really came, though, from the young you communicating with the child I once was. But I sense you have taught me a lot, because you care and it was important to you. The spirit of the young child in me needed to know and you wanted her to understand. I feel very peaceful now deep inside myself. That's what you wanted to give me – peace and understanding, because deep inside you was a very kind man. I do forgive you, Jackser. Thank you for giving me that wonderful gift. It will set me free. Now I want to see you go in peace.

'Thank you for all the advice you gave me, Jackser. Thanks for teaching me to read the clock. You taught me to write me own name,' I said, wanting to get everything out now in a hurry. Things were coming to me that I didn't even know I remembered.

'Thanks for teaching me about horses! I even went hacking out on them for a while in the Phoenix Park, until I nearly brained meself. But you taught me a lot. I really enjoyed that. I even made a few bob on the Grand National. I picked out a fifty-to-one. But he had what you would be looking for! The ears pinned up, the skinny legs – he was wide awake, Jackser! I just knew he would be the one,' I said, wanting to see the life dance in his eyes and a smile come to his face as the tears for his great loss poured down my cheeks. He will never smile again, or get a second chance.

'Jackser, I want you to go easy in your mind. I want you to have a bit of peace. Let yourself go, Jackser! Just take your bit of peace. There's people waiting for you. Your mother is waiting. Just let yourself ease away, Jackser. You're going to be all right. Your mother will take care of you. Remember how you used to tell me that she was always worrying about you? Well,' I said, bending down into his face, talking straight into his wide-open, staring eyes, with his chest gasping sounds that came out in quick death rattles. 'You're going home to your mother, Jackser. Take it easy now. Let go,' I whispered softly. 'Don't be afraid.'

Suddenly his eyes widened then slowly closed, while his chest collapsed without taking another breath and I held meself rigid, listening to the sudden silence. I watched as his face changed and seemed to relax, then everything went still. I let my breath go so gently I could hardly feel it. I just stayed staring at him, letting my mind take in he's gone. He's gone – he's dead! Jackser's dead, I repeated in me mind.

I lifted up his hand that rested on his stomach, with my left hand still gripped in his. His hand still feels warm, yet he's gone. I released my hand gently and stood back, staring at him. His face had settled into a more peaceful look.

'Rest in peace, Jackser. Your cross was a heavy one. The Almighty Father was a hard taskmaster when he gave you that to carry; it was too much to bear. We all suffered, but your curse was to struggle harder and longer. May you now find the peace you did not find in this valley of tears that was your life,' I whispered, staring down at him.

The nurse crept in behind me. 'Your mother is on her way,' she whispered, taking in Jackser looking very peaceful as she gently let her hand rest on my shoulder. 'He's at peace now, Martha. He looks very peaceful,' she whispered, as the two of us continued to stare at him. Then she looked at her watch, lifting it up off her chest. 'Ten minutes to four a.m.,' she whispered, staring down at her watch then looking up at me. 'That's the time of his death,' she said, dropping the watch and letting it rest on her chest, then saying to me, 'I'll get you a cup of tea. Do you want to go down to the room and have a cigarette? I will let you know when your mother arrives.'

'Yes, Nurse, thanks ever so much for all your help. You were very good to Jackser, and I can't begin to tell you just how grateful I am for all you've done for me. Gawd! I must owe the hospital a fortune in the amount of stuff I've eaten and drank,' I said, not really able to get out much of a smile. I just felt shell-shocked, tired and exhausted, sad and yet peaceful. There was such a stillness inside me, like I had just come through some terrible storm. It felt like at times I would be lifted up and crashed against ferocious waves in a deadly angry sea. Now, it was just the calm inside me – the quiet of the hospital, the gentle whispers of the night nurse looking at me with kindness and tenderly offering me a cup of tea as I stood, looking down at Jackser. He was lying out in the bed looking more peaceful than I ever saw him in life now he was gone to his eternal rest.

'My God, Jackser! Travelling through our journey of life with you was like travelling through a hurricane,' I whispered, talking to his spirit as it was still warm in his body. I wanted to say a few last things to him just before he took flight and went off in search of something in the great far beyond, from where no one has ever come back.

'Goodbye, Jackser! You will be the only one of two people on this earth who ever had such a power of influence over me. Everything I do is influenced by you, always for the opposite. But nonetheless you were the most powerful person in my life. I was well and truly marked by you. No doubt about that, Jackser,' I whispered, nodding my head.

I was just heading back up the passage, making for the ward, when the ma turned up from the stairs with Sally at her heels.

'What's happened?' she puffed, not thinking to use the lift.

'He's in here, Ma,' I whispered quietly, walking ahead of her into the ward.

She crept in, afraid of what she might see. The first thing that hit her and me was the silence coming from Jackser's bed. 'Ohh!' me ma said, putting her hand to her mouth. 'Is he gone, Martha?'

I nodded, moving over to let in Sally. The three of us just stood staring down at him. I was over by the side where I usually sat, seeing his right hand resting on his stomach, where I had left it. His face had settled into a rigid stillness. You would know there was no life left in him. Any traces that had been left of the suffering he had gone through was now disappeared. He was showing nothing was left of him but his body. Yet I could feel his presence; his spirit was all around this bed. No, he hasn't gone quite yet, I thought, still sensing him very close.

Suddenly we heard footsteps, and a priest came hurrying into the ward.

'I will just give Jackser the Last Rites,' he whispered, putting his hand gently on me ma's shoulder.

'OK, Father,' she said, looking up at him with a fleeting light in her eyes, as if suddenly there was a bit of hope. Maybe he could give some help, do something that would make what's happened go away, make things better. Then it passed. The light went out of her eyes and she moved over to let him in. He pressed his lips to the end of the purple stole hanging around his neck and shoulders, then took out his holy oils, blessing the forehead and lips and hands of Jackser, all the time saying the prayers for the dead. Then he spoke up and we uttered a Hail Mary, repeating after the priest. Then it was over. He turned to all of us, nodding his head, giving the ma his blessing, then left.

Me ma stared down at Jackser lying so very still and silent in the bed, then sighed out a whispered, 'Oh, Jesus!' Then she turned, saying in sorrow, 'We got here too late, Sally!'

She said nothing, just stared at her father like it was one more thing to bear. Just one more heavy yoke among the other heavy weights that she carried on her shoulders. She never spoke a word, it's like she has no further use for words, they mean nothing.

We all started to move away, heading for the door, with no one saying they were going. We seemed to just be of one mind – all walking away slowly, following each other out the door. We walked down the empty, dark, silent corridor, with each of us lost in our own thoughts. I stopped at the lift; me ma was heading for the stairs.

'Are you not taking the lift down, Ma?' I said, seeing her heading down.

'No! I don't trust them things,' she said. 'Are ye coming this way?'

'No, Ma. I'm getting in this. I'm too tired to walk,' I sighed out.

'All right, I'll see ye, then,' she said.

'Yeah, Ma. I'll be over to you tomorrow,' I said wearily. Then the lift opened and I got in, pressing the button for the ground floor, then out through the big heavy front doors I had first walked through a lifetime ago, knowing now I was walking back out for the last time. I will only come back to carry Jackser out in a box, I thought, taking no pleasure in that. Yet only a week ago I thought I would be on top of the world. No, we don't know what we are really like, what we are made of, until we are put to the test, I thought, heading around to the car park.

I sat into the car and rolled meself a cigarette, leaving the door open to let out the smoke. Then took in a deep drag of the cigarette, inhaling it, then blew out the smoke, listening to the silent streets hushed in the dark early hours of a dawn not yet risen. I looked up at the stars, wondering if Jackser would now become one of them. Will he now make his mark up there somewhere? 'You certainly made your mark on me, Jackser,' I whispered.

I switched on the engine, feeling a deep sense of peace. Never have I felt so grateful to be alive. I have a sense of what it would be like to be whole, like I really belonged to myself. I would know who I am now, say I am Martha Long, the bastard, the street kid, a successful woman, because I am at peace. I will have come home to myself. I will have arrived. Love me or hate me, world, you will take me as I am. But now that journey only really begins; I will have a long way to go.

I switched on the engine and drove out of the car park heading for home, my two little beauties and a whole new wide world just beginning to open. For now, I am Martha Long, only a woman of substance to the outside world, a perceived great success. But I hear you, little one. I hear you crying. Be patient. One day I will have to come for you! I will be back, then very slowly I will walk down, back through the days of my life, searching for you. I will leave no back street uncovered. No tenement building where you once roamed, or alleyway where you once ran, or street where you once played will I not search.

Yes, I know I will tremble in fear when I come face to face with all of the ghosts that still haunt me. For now they lie hidden, silently waiting in some dark, buried place. But I will not back down. I will find you and make you mine. But first I need courage – that will come. So this is my promise, little one. Hush! Don't cry. One day soon you will nestle, cradle the heart that is for so long now just an aching emptiness. I will carry you with all the love you and your great courage deserve. I will be so proud of you. I will say softly to you, 'You are the little street kid I once was, the little spitfire who lives inside me now and made me who I am. You are my little Martha! I love you, my sweet little angel. Sleep softly, little one. I will keep you safe.'

19

'Bye, Mamma! I love you very much!' he said.

'Yes, I love you, too!' she screamed, raging he got in first.

'Yes, darlings! I love you too.'

'BUT I LOVE YOU MORE!'

'NO! YOU CAN'T!'

'WE LOVE YOU MORE!'

'OK!' I laughed. 'We all love the same.'

'Mamma, we will tell you all our news tonight when you get home. We will be waiting on you!'

'Oh, yes! I'm dying to hear how you got on. I will be all ears. Now, I will want every detail. It's going to be great, so take it easy, the pair of you. OK, I'm off now, darlings,' I said, starting the engine, getting ready to pull away. Then I leant back out the window. 'Now, remember, what's the first rule?'

I could see the pair of them standing there, the eyes steady for a minute while they worked this out.

Then she was off first, with the pair of them roaring together, 'HAVE FUN, ENJOY OURSELVES! Winning is only second.'

'Right! Now don't forget what we learned – count to three after every full stop, then think of what is happening and act it out. Then you can't go wrong! And if it does, what do you do?' I said, looking at the pair of them, wanting to remind them in case they threw a blue fit if, God forbid, they lost! Jaysus, they'll go mad! There'll be killings!

'Throw your papers into the air, saying, "I won't give up the day job!" Then say, "What's plan B?" Yes?' I said listening, waiting with my mouth open, watching them. 'In other words, get something out of it, get a laugh! Have you got that, beauties?' I said, looking at the pair of them standing with their scripts in their hands. They were getting

ready to take on the world and his wife at the Feis, the national
competition for primary school children. It's for poetry. They have to
recite a poem from memory. They have an excellent chance . . . I hope!
The kids and me chose a difficult one written by Hilaire Belloc.

He makes fun of the old English aristocrats and the upper classes
back in the 1920s. The little man chose 'George'. The grandmamma
bought him an immense balloon for being such a good boy. Yeah, I
thought, thinking that poem is hilarious, though it's supposed to be
sad. Because the bleedin thing was filled with gas, it blew the house
up along with the butler, housemaid, chambermaid, the cook and the
whole bleedin lot a them. But the worst thing was the house happened
to be on SAVILE ROW! For Jaysus' sake, that should never happen.
Oh, very posh! I thought.

She chose another one of Belloc's about a naughty little girl. Ah,
bold lump she was, no balloons for her! Well, she choked herself to
death, chewing on bits of string. So, that's it, Martha. They're off to
do their stuff without you. Pity! I should be there to keep order. Wipe
the snots and mop the tears if something goes wrong. Beat up the
judge if they show favour! Fuck! I'm missing it all.

Yeah, they are brilliant the pair of them. I know they won't settle
for anything less than the gold medal. Jaysus! Me nerves are gone,
thinking of them being there without me. Mind you, Martha, it's
probably better you're not there. Someone told me I was like yer
woman in Maureen Potter's sketch. Yeah, Maureen, the brilliant Irish
stage actress. She does pantomime and a lot of comedy acts. Me
favourite one is her doing a Dublin mother whose young fella, Jimmy,
enters for the Irish Dancing Competition. There he is, her little Jimmy,
up on the stage with the mammy sitting in the front row! *Go on,
Jimmy! Lift them legs! Don't kick the judge! Here! Judge! Stop a minute!
His shoelaces is open. WHA DID YE MEAN, JUDGE, HE'S
DISQUALIFACATED?! Sure, he never got started! Are ye blind? Can
ye not see he has the makins of a national champ ping?! Wha did ye mean?
Yer callin the Po-llease! Sure, whaat did I do? I never laid hand act nor
part on tha judge!! She fell offa the stage herself! Sure, look at her! Tha aul
one is blind as a bat! Looka the size a them goggles she's wearin! Get yer
hands offa me!*

Yeah! That's me. I'm a bleedin nightmare. I'm banned from

everything at their school! But it's still a pity I can't be with them. Ah, but sure they have a whole contingent going along for the outing. Their father is going, and he has his best friend going along to give him a hand. Then the wife decided she's not getting left out, she'll bring a picnic. Russians love their grub. Then there's my old friend – he's a lecturer in the university, very keenly interested in their development, he calls it. Of course his wife is going to hold his hand, stop him getting too excited with the aul blood pressure. Then there's my next-door neighbour. He's retired now, so him and the wife are going, so. All the kids are short of doing is bringing Minnie the dog! They would too, but she won't be allowed into the place. Right! But the ma needs me. There's an awful lot to do, so get going, she will be waiting.

I drove up and parked outside the ma's block, then hopped out, locking the car and gave a look up and down. No! No little moochers ready to throw stones at me car. Good! It's lovely and quiet. They must be all still sleeping, I thought, giving a look in at the clock in the car. Twenty past ten. That's grand time I made this morning. I'm fresh as a daisy, I thought, looking down at myself after using half a bottle of shower gel, plus nearly a bottle of shampoo on the hair. I could smell the Chanel perfume off meself. Nothing like a dab of your best perfume to get the day going. Now all me four cylinders are hammering away at full blast, I thought. Yeah, not bad for three hours' sleep. Ah, sure, I'll sleep long enough when I'm dead and buried! Right! Up now and collect the ma.

I flew in the entrance, rounding onto the stairs, taking them two at a time. 'Here we are,' I puffed, forgetting I'm no longer a spring chicken of twenty. I looked at the door, trying to figure what's the best way to bang. Use the car key or rattle the letterbox? Both!

'Ma!' I shouted, banging and rattling, putting me nose and mouth through the letterbox, then I stood back waiting. Silence! Nothing. I held me breath listening. No, not a sound.

'Ma!' I banged, rattling and shaving the skin off me knuckles. Then I waited, me heart dropping. 'Ma! Open the door! Are you in there, Ma? It's me, Martha!'

I stood back, feeling confused. Where could she be? Last time this happened she said she was in all the time. I gave the door a rhythmic kick with me foot. Not too hard, just enough to get it shaking. I waited, listening. Still nothing.

'Fuck ye, Ma! You knew I would be over. Where are you?' I muttered to meself, feeling like nearly wanting to cry with the rage. I gave up my whole bleedin day for you. Oh, Jaysus, talk about being thick as two short planks! Why did I not think of getting her phone number from the nurse when I had the opportunity? Ah, take it easy, Martha. Sure, there was too much going on.

'Right!' I breathed, taking in a full blast of rotten decay. Jesus, the smell! I blew it out just as fast. OK! Head for the shopping centre. Where else might she be? No, nowhere else around here.

I parked outside the cop shop in the naive belief it would be safe! Gobshite – they use them for target practice. No, this is the last place to be. It might attract the wrong attention, I thought, looking around at all the jalopies with the culchie registration plates. They might think this car is one of the coppers'. I threw meself back into the car, reversing out, only stopping when I nearly hit a battered old Cortina! Easy, Martha, no parking by ear! I thought, shooting the car forward, then around to the back of the shops. I stopped to park with the broken glass and the old bicycles left dangling with their locks attached to poles but the wheels now missing. OK, this will do nicely. Only a lunatic would park here if they're not from around the area. Now, a lunatic wouldn't last long enough with a car like this. So, I must be a local. Jaysus, Martha! That's a heavy burden ye carry with being such a genius, I sniffed, grinning at meself with all my cunning. I better be fuckin right!

I came steaming out of the supermarket feeling a terrible hurry on me. Jesus, the day will be gone. No! Not a sign of her, I thought, heading for the post office. Not here either. Oh, bloody hell! Where else? I thought, flying me eyes up and down, seeing a mother strolling along in her pyjamas and matching pink slippers. Me head did a flip. No! She's not even in a hurry, I thought, staring at the three little kids making their way behind her, all intent on their ice pops the ma just bought them. They were in their lovely little teddy bear PJs as well. Oh! That's handy! In and outa the bed, without all that fussing that gets to go with it.

Right, get moving. This won't find the ma. Where the fuck is she? I thought, standing still with me body bent, ready to go in four directions at the same time. I raced out, rushing around the outside, coming back again to the front entrance. No! She's not here. My heart sank all the way to me belly. I wasn't expecting this. I thought she would know we have to get going and sort out the funeral. There's a million things to do! Oh, fuck, Ma, where did you get to? OK! Go back to the flat – maybe she has turned up there.

Me eyes lit up, seeing the car still sitting with its wheels. 'Thank God for small mercies,' I muttered, jumping in and taking off, flying over the huge bumps, getting airborne then landing with a hiss of air. Great suspension! I thought. You can't beat the aul Swedes! Make great cars, they do. OK, go easy. Next one coming up – no need to over test. The bumps were put up by the Corpo. They had to stop scratching their arses for a bit, just while they got this job done. It's supposed to slow down the kids racing the robbed cars. The idea was the flying squad, the cops in their battered clapped-out Cortinas, or whatever the fuck they beetle around in, well, it's supposed to give them a fairer chance to catch up on the big BMWs the kids have a passion for. I believe the minister is going to get the cops newer, faster cars! He'll probably take the money from the old-age pensioners, telling them it's good for their health. After all, it's them is the ones who keep getting themself knocked down. They're just not fast enough getting across the road.

I drove slowly back, stopping the car to look up and down the road. No! Not a sign of her, and she's definitely not here. The next-door neighbour put his head out, then flew it back in when he saw it was only me, not the cops trying to get in with a battering ram. Where could she be? Think! OK, nothing for it but to go over and wait by the bus stop. Maybe she's gone somewhere, then she will be sure to take the bus back.

I drove over, passing the shopping centre again, then whipped the car back in on an impulse – no harm in trying. Then suddenly me eyes lit on her. I pulled up close and switched off the engine, keeping me eyes on her. My heart took a nosedive as I sat staring, taking her in. Oh, ahh, sweet Jesus! The poor ma. She's standing there with one half of her looking like she was going back in the door, with the other half of her rigid, while her eyes stared into the distance with a puzzled look on her face. She looked like she was lost, not knowing which way to go or what she should do next. She looked so lonely, standing there all alone. I could see she was wearing a pair of black stockings. They hung halfway down her legs, looking like they needed to be pulled up. She had a sheer black nylon scarf sitting on her head and tied under the chin.

Then it hit me. She has nobody; there is nobody left. They've all gone! Where? It just has happened. The why or where does not matter. The thing is now she is all alone. I grabbed the key out of the ignition and shot open the door, banging it shut behind me, and started running, calling her with me heart sinking from the pity of her.

'Ma! Ma, are you all right? I'm here. What happened to you? Where did you go? I was worried about you,' I said gently, talking before I even got next to her.

'Lookit! I had te go an buy a pair a stockings!' she said, holding out the black stockings held between her two hands, with them closed over each other. 'An a scarf,' she said, putting her hand to her head.

'Yeah, Ma,' I said, staring into her as I made to take her arm. 'We have to go and arrange to get Jackser buried.'

'Wha?' she burst out. 'No, no! Go on outa tha. Leave him alone, he's fine! There's nothin wrong wit him, he's in the hospital. No, no! Go on, go about yer business.'

'But, Ma,' I said, getting an awful shock at the state she was in, then seeing her pulling away from me and hurrying off, trying to escape. 'Ma! What do you mean?' I said, rushing to stand in front of her. 'We have to arrange the funeral. Jackser has to be buried.'

'I told ye no! Now leave me alone. Go on! Get away from me.'

I stood staring after her, seeing her making her way left, then turn right, then stop and make up her mind, heading herself off outa the car park. She is probably making her way home. If she gets back there I will never get her out. God knows what may happen to her.

I rushed after her and grabbed her arm, trying to turn her around gently. She flung out her arm, pushing me away.

'I'm after tellin ye! Leave me alone! He's fine. I'll sort it out in me own time. Now, go on, just leave me in peace. Ye're tormentin me.'

I could see she was white as a sheet, totally lost, with the confusion written all over her face and an awful pain showing in her eyes. It was like she was so lost, but thought that if she could think her way through it, she could make things better. Her whole world had collapsed from under her. Jackser was her nightmare, but he was the devil she knew. She had never been on her own before and this was her worst nightmare. But as long as she believes Jackser is still only in the hospital, then all will be like it was before – the familiar world she knew and depended on.

'Ma, please come back to the car,' I said, trying to get her to look at me. But it was like I had done something too horrible for her to face. I disgusted and frightened her. I was there when she saw Jackser dead. If I go away, then Jackser is not dead. The picture will go away with me.

'OK, you are right, Ma, let's forget about burying Jackser. Sure, let's forget about it altogether, but maybe we will just do something. Come on. Get in the car with me, let's go off somewhere,' I said, speaking gently and quietly, then taking her arm when I saw her hesitate. She was letting her eyes show interest, while her mind worked out this new hopeful idea.

'OK, Ma? Let's go,' I said, turning her around and leading her slowly back to the car. She got in and said nothing. I kept quiet.

I drove slowly, trying to think.

'Do you know, Ma, what would you think about the idea of calling in on the local priest? We could talk to him about Jackser.'

'No!' she muttered, shaking her head, just staring into the distance, looking quite definite about that one.

'OK,' I said, wondering where the parish priest's house was. I headed over to the church, seeing that in the distance, then stopped outside the house that looked like where he would live, right next to the church. I switched off the engine, then looked at the ma, saying, 'Sure, what harm can it do? It won't cost us anything to tell him what happened. See what he says, Ma.'

She said nothing, just stared ahead, but at least she didn't say no.

I decided to take it easy. I pulled out my tobacco and rolled up a cigarette. 'Are you hungry, Ma? Will we get something to eat?'

'No!' She shook her head, staring straight in front of her.

'Come on, we'll go into the chapel and say a little prayer for Jackser,

Ma. We can light a candle for him. He would like that. Remember all the little penny candles you used to light around the corner in John's Lane church when I was little? Back in the old Liberties, Ma, where you and me was born and all your family? Remember them days, Ma? It was just you and me, then Charlie. You were very young then, Ma, only a teenager. Now look at all you have managed to come through!'

She sat, barely nodding her head, but then I saw her face change, like she was thinking back, getting a wistful look as if she was feeling again the pain of the loneliness, the lack of money. But yet, all the hope and expectation she had back then. She was young, she had her dreams and life was only starting.

'Come on,' I barely whispered, 'let's light another candle. One from you, and one from me, for Jackser.' I waited, holding my breath.

She moved without saying anything. Then I jumped out and rushed around, opening the heavy car door to let her out.

I put my arm around her as we walked into the dimly lit church. Our eyes blinked, wanting to adjust from the bright sunlight beating down outside. It was lovely and quiet; the statues had little red lamps glowing under each and every one.

'Which saint will we go to, Ma?' I said, stopping to look around, seeing one in nearly every corner and in little alcoves, with polished brass gates into some of them.

'We'll go over to the Blessed Virgin, the mother of God,' she said, after looking around for a few minutes.

I knew she had hardly set foot inside a church since she met Jackser, except when he sent her out on the tear, rushing around the churches, trying to find a priest to give her a few bob – it was mostly to get him his Woodbine cigarettes. Then, after that, would come the milk and then the bread, in that order.

'That was nice, wasn't it, Ma?' I said, blinking as we came outa the church, then looking at me ma, seeing a more content, peaceful look on her face. 'Right! Listen, seeing as we're here, Ma, why don't we go in and see the priest, get him to say a mass for Jackser? Wouldn't that be a great idea?' I said, heading straight in to ring the doorbell seeing as she hadn't objected.

I rang and we waited. Me ma didn't look too sure. Her eyes were getting hard and her mouth was clamping tight. Then the door was whipped open by a pale-faced, thin-looking man with grey hair and glasses. He looked at us. I tried to think. 'Eh! Yes, hello, Father! We have come about the mass,' I said, drawing his eyes to me ma wearing the black scarf, not wanting to mention the word funeral.

His eyes took me in, followed the line of us to the car sitting outside, decided we were lost or we wouldn't be driving from the flats just across the road.

'What parish are you in?' he said quick as a flash, getting ready to tell us we had the wrong parish, wrong priest. Brilliant for him – no having to wear himself out doing a funeral.

'This one!' I said, pointing over to the flats.

'Oh,' he said, looking disappointed. 'You better come in. OK, what is the deceased's name?'

'John Fredrick Harold Manzk.'

'How do you spell that?' he said, looking at his big book with all the masses lined up.

I spelt it for him, then he looked at his book.

'Eleven a.m. Mass on the sixth of July.'

'Oh, good, two days' time,' I said.

'Yes,' the priest nodded, waiting for me to digest this. Then he said, 'Removal for burial immediately after, at twelve noon. Where is the burial?' he said, with the pen at the ready, held in the air.

I thought about this. 'He can be buried with Harry, Ma.'

'Yeah,' she said, suddenly realising that was a good idea. It was dawning on her things were happening, but everything seemed to be all right.

'Glasnevin Cemetery, Father.'

'OK, that is fine. Is it your husband?' he said, looking at the ma.

She hesitated, trying to work this out.

'Yes, her lifelong partner, Father,' I said, wanting to make it easy for her.

'I am sorry for your trouble,' he said, taking her hand and holding it gently.

Me ma blinked, giving a grateful little smile. I made a move, saying, 'Thank you, Father. We will see you then.'

'Yes,' he said, opening the front door and letting us out. Then shutting the door quickly behind us.

We walked slowly to the car, with the sun blinding us. Me ma looked more alive now, it seemed she was heading in the right direction.

'Come on, Ma, let's get in,' I said, whipping out me tobacco, wanting to celebrate in my own quiet way, saying nothing to the ma in case everything would be upended. I didn't want to disturb the quiet bit of peace that was settling into her; it was still very fragile.

'Listen,' I said, starting up the engine, 'let's keep going.'

'Are ye sure, Martha?' she said, getting nervous about what might be happening next, not even sure if she was doing the right thing now.

'Oh, yeah, Ma,' I said. 'Jackser would have you doing this himself if he was here to tell you! Wouldn't he? You know what he was like. If something has to be done, he'd say, "It has te be done! Now get goin an fuckin do it!" Can you not hear him?' I said, looking at her with a ready smile waiting on my face.

'Yeah,' she muttered, looking at me with a little light in her eyes and a half-smile of regret on her face, knowing that is exactly what he would say.

20

I pulled the car up outside an undertaker's, seeing straight away me ma's eyes light on it then look away.

'I'm not goin in there, Martha!' she snapped, looking away with her face going tight.

I stared at her, then looked at the undertaker's. It was shaded in blinds with a very solemn-looking sign outside. It rumbled quietly of tears and misery. Fuck, no way can I get the ma in there! She's terrified of anything to do with death. No wonder her mind has gone wandering now with the shock of losing Jackser to it. Go easy, Martha. Think, but walk carefully.

I sat for a few minutes and rolled up a cigarette. After lighting it, I said, 'Yeah, you're probably right. Why don't we get out and go around the corner? Let's get something to eat. There's a fish and chip shop there. Come on! Let's go. I'm starving, Ma.'

She thought about it for a few minutes, looked up at the sign, then looked back at me suspiciously. I nodded, saying, 'Yeah, let's get something nice to eat, Ma. That's all we need do.'

She took in a big breath, then shifted herself. I rushed around to open the door, getting her out while the going was good.

We looked in the window, examining the menu. 'What do ye fancy, Ma?'

She lifted her mouth, chewing it, shaking her head and muttering, 'I don't care. I'm not very hungry.'

'Let's go in!' I said, grabbing her arm and rushing in the door. We smelled the grub straight away. Oh! I thought. I didn't realise I was hungry.

'What about a nice bit of fish for you, Ma? Or a fried egg? That's soft – and maybe a few baked beans. You can nibble on my chips, because you don't eat them anyway. You suck on them, then spit them out. But only when you've sucked them to death!' I added, wanting to make her laugh. 'Come on, let's sit by the window. We can watch the passing parade!'

'Wha parade are ye talkin about, Martha?'

'The people, Ma. The traffic, the comings and goings, see a bit of the world!'

She snorted at the idea of me rambling, but sat herself down, facing the window out onto the street.

'Anything else, you want, Ma?' I said, looking from her to the Italian young one waiting patiently for us to finish. The ma kept changing her mind.

'Oh, yeah! An will ye give us a pot a tea an a plate a bread an butter, love!' me ma said, sounding like she had to be nice, as if we were under compliment by getting it for nothing.

'OK!' the fat young one said, with the mass of jet-black hair hanging around her shoulders. It was frizzy and stood out in all directions.

'Did ye see tha young one's hair, Martha?' the ma said, looking at me like she was going to be sick, with the mouth open in disgust.

'Yeah, Ma. Nice, isn't it?'

'No! I hope she doesn't get tha fuckin hair in me food!' she said, already making up her mind she couldn't eat it.

'What about a knickerbocker glory, Ma?'

'Wha! Wha's tha, Martha?'

'An ice cream, Ma, with fruit in it,' I said, seeing her looking at me like I had just told her we were off on an expedition to the jungle.

'Is it very foreign, Martha?'

'What do ye mean, Ma?'

'No! I don't like the sound a tha! I like te know wha I'm eatin!' she said, grabbing the coat around her and shifting in the chair.

'Yeah, you're right, Ma. Let's get ourselves a big ice-cream banana boat, with melted chocolate and slices of banana.'

'Banana? Can ye do tha, Martha?' she said, looking at me with the eyebrows raised.

'Yeah, course! And you'll be able to eat it, Ma – the banana's soft, OK?'

'Ah, go on then, but I would prefer a cornet!'

'This is the same thing, Ma, except ye get it in a lovely boat-shaped glass bowl!' I said.

'Oh, do ye? Tha sounds lovely. Yeah, get tha, Martha. Where's tha young one?' she said, whipping herself around.

'Now! Are you happy, Ma? That was really nice that meal was, wasn't it, Ma? Did you enjoy that?'

'Yeah, it was lovely an grand, nice an hot!'

'Right, will we get moving?' I said, going over to pay the bill, then opening the door for me ma, heading us up towards the car.

We passed the undertaker's and I stopped to look in the window. There was nothing to be seen. The place was hidden with white-mesh curtain blinds that blocked everything out. I grabbed her arm gently, heading her in the door, holding me breath.

A man sitting behind a desk was instantly on his feet, coming towards us with a big but sorrowful-looking smile on his handsome-looking face. I smiled; he bent down to the ma, recognising instantly she was the widow with the black headscarf.

'Would you like to come and take the weight off your feet?' he whispered, leading the ma over to a chair sitting in front of his desk like she was the most delicate thing he had ever handled in all his born days. Me ma let herself be led, liking the idea of being minded by a man.

'Now,' he said, after allowing the air to fill with sorrow and loss, then he asked in a very gentle voice how he could help us. They sounded like magic words, as if he could, and now would, lift the yoke of sorrow. I said nothing, being too busy letting meself take in the whole atmosphere he was creating. He leaned his head towards me ma, resting his gorgeous, navy-blue, mother-of-all-sorrows eyes on her. I stared at them, thinking they're lovely but very tragic-looking. It was as if every day had brought him a new crucifixion, as if he had spent his life carrying the cross of so many. Now he was ready and willing to take up another cross – me ma's!

I took to him straight away. The ma, now, was not so sure. She kept looking back around at all the coffins sitting behind us. They were lined up against the wall.

I took in a deep breath, then heard me voice coming out in a squeak;

the nerves were getting to me. I started again and he helped me out.

'Do you wish me to arrange a funeral?' he whispered, leaning over to me, covering me in oozing molasses!

I gave a little shiver. Jaysus! Them eyes. I couldn't stop staring. I would even be willing to climb inta a coffin meself if I could get him in with me, I thought, forgetting the ma for a minute.

'Sorry?' I said, losing the track of where we were.

'Would you like me to take down some details?'

I still stared. The ma gave a cough, shifting in her chair. She wanted to move, get out. That woke me up. I galvanised meself inta action. 'Oh, yes. The deceased's name is . . .' I rushed, hearing meself say deceased! Jaysus, he has me mesmerised. I'm hysterical! It's the relief at getting the ma in here.

'Eh, yes! Right,' I said, trying to think where I was. 'Oh, yes, you want the details,' I said, trying to hold onto me senses. The bloody tiredness is hitting in.

'We have arranged the Mass and removal with the priest.' I gave him all the details, including the ma's address. She stayed quiet, listening, then nodding when I looked at her.

'Yes, good,' he nodded, giving me a flash of them eyes again.

Then I gave the hospital name, saying, 'Yes, he's in the morgue there.'

'OK, I will just give them a ring to confirm they are ready to release the body. It could be the coroner might want to do his work first.'

He came off the phone saying, 'No, all is in order there. They are ready to release the body. Now, would you like to choose?' He stood up, showing us the coffins. 'You have a choice of three.'

I took the ma, getting her standing, and walked her over to the wall. 'These are lovely, Ma. Look at the carvings on them. Gawd! Wouldn't Jackser love that?!' I said, running me hand along the wood. 'Eh, which is the cheapest?' I said, keeping an eye on the money.

'Those ones there – you have a choice of three in each price range. These ones here would be the cheapest,' he said, leading us around the corner to more white-looking coffins, but they didn't look much different. That's if you couldn't tell the difference between solid oak, white deal pine and pitch pine. I could! I like wood, antiques. But I shut me mouth.

'These are lovely,' I said to the ma, seeing the two of us staring at the different designs in the cheapest coffins.

'I like tha one,' me ma said, going for a carving with the head of Christ and the crown of thorns around his bloody and bleeding head.

'Yeah. It's very manly looking,' I said, thinking it would suit Jackser grand. He crucified everyone around him – but then, he was crucified himself. 'So, what do you think, Ma?' I said quietly.

'Yeah, we'll get tha one, Martha,' she said happily, feeling good she was doing something for Jackser. My heart bled for her.

'Yeah, that's the one we'll take,' I said, turning and looking at Blue-eyes. He was waiting discreetly over by his desk; he nodded agreement.

'Yes,' he murmured, 'that is very nice, a good choice,' he said, looking gently at the ma. She smiled happily. 'Now, what about a shroud?' he said. 'We do have a choice. They come in two colours,' he said, making his way calmly over to a row of shiny mahogany drawers and opening one of them.

He gently lifted a white shroud and let it drop, showing a cross on the front. 'Or you can have a choice of blue,' he said, whipping open the next drawer.

We stared at it. 'I like the blue one, Martha,' me ma said, after peeling her eyes from one to the other, then making up her mind.

'Grand! We'll take that, the blue one,' I said, pointing, making sure he knew which one.

'Very well,' he said. 'Now, if we may just come and sit down again.'

We followed and sat, with the ma coming alive now, beginning to look more and more happy. Then somewhere deep inside me a little voice whispered, '*Yeah, we're shoppin te make Jackser lovely before we plant him!*'

'What about the newspapers, the death column? We can have the announcements in all the English and American papers, as well as our own at home. It helps with notifying relatives,' he said, waiting patiently while I took three seconds to make me own mind up on this one.

'No, eh, that won't be necessary,' I said.

'No announcements in the death column,' he mumbled, looking at his list, then he said, not marking that in our sheet but looking up to confirm, 'No?'

'No,' I said, wanting to keep down the cost.

'Now, what about flowers? We have, oh, so many to choo—'

'No! I don't think we need flowers,' I said, looking at the ma, seeing her face dropping at the loss of a big send-off for Jackser. 'The cost, Ma,' I whispered. Then looked up at Blue-eyes, saying, 'Well, maybe one then, saying "DAD". Will that be OK, Ma?' I said, seeing her eyes light up.

'Yeah, yes! That will be lovely,' she said, giving me a smile with her eyes lit up.

'Grand!' I said, giving the big go-ahead with a long bow of me head, making that definite.

'Flowers, "Dad",' he wrote, muttering it to himself as he filled in our sheet that looked like it could grow longer.

'Now, what about memoriam cards?' he said.

'No! We don't need those,' I said, looking out the corner of me eye, seeing the ma shift.

'De ye not think, Martha, it would be lovely te have the memory a him?' she said.

'Oh,' he interrupted, helping out the ma, 'we can add his photograph to the cards,' he said, looking very helpful at the ma.

She nodded, smiled and agreed with him.

Then I thought about this. 'Ma!' I said. 'I'll bring the camera and we can get a photograph of him.' Thinking that would be a good idea, the ma would like that.

'I mean when he was alive!' she shouted, getting very annoyed suddenly.

'But, sure, Ma, what photographs have you got of Jackser?' I said. 'The only one we're going to get now is of him lying in his lovely coffin. It will make a beautiful photograph.'

'Jesus!' the ma said, putting her hand on her chest and looking away, then looking back at me like I had two heads.

'Sorry. I'm sorry, Ma. It's just I know someone who did that,' I explained to the horrified-looking Blue-eyes, staring at me with concern on his face. I could see now that had been incredibly insensitive. 'Yes, a friend of mine, he was Continental,' I said, trying to explain. 'His wife, the mother of his three young children, died. He took photographs of her on her deathbed. It looked quite haunting but very beautiful. The Victorians used to do it. It was quite common,' I said, realising Jackser wasn't young and beautiful! It wouldn't look the same. I was afraid Blue-eyes would think me mad and bad, not to mention the sudden worry of giving the ma nightmares.

He listened, nodding his head, seeing where I was coming from. 'But you're right, Ma. Forget I said that,' I said, wrapping my arm around her. 'No,' I shook me head at him. 'We don't need them, thanks.'

'OK, one final thing – you will have to pay to have the grave reopened,' he said, looking from me to the ma.

'What? But we own that grave. It's a family plot. It takes five family members.'

'Yes, but you still have to pay,' he said. 'It is not cheap. The cost will be several hundred pounds. I can give you the exact price when I have first checked with the cemetery. But I will let you know tomorrow. May I take your phone number?'

'Yes.' I gave him mine, then he took down the ma's phone number.

'Oh, hang on, Ma!' I said, looking at Blue-eyes. 'Will you please give me a note of my mother's phone number? It's a new number,' I said, 'so I don't have it yet.'

He handed it to me and I folded it up, putting it in the pocket of my light beige jacket.

'Now, what about the cars? How many do you intend to cater for?'

'Well,' I said, looking at the ma. 'It's only immediate family. There's yourself and Dinah and Gerry. Oh! We need to go and see them, Ma, let them know!'

'Yes, I wanted te ask ye about tha. We will need te go an see them,' she said, nodding her head, looking very serious.

'Yeah! We'll do that right away,' I said, looking back to him, then at the ma. 'So, how many people altogether, Ma? There's you, those two and Sally, and, oh, Charlie! Did he call up to see you, Ma?'

'No,' she said, shaking her head.

'Right! I'm going to have to track him down. Let's hope he is where I think he might be. I can take him in my car, Ma,' I said. 'So that will be four family members,' I said, seeing him write it on the sheet. 'How many do the cars hold?' I asked.

'Well, we have from three persons to seven.'

'How much is the three-person one?'

'Ninety pounds.'

'That's expensive, Ma. We'll go for the three. I can take Sally in my car.'

'Well, her fella should take her, he has a car,' me ma said.

'Yes, so, it seems we have covered everything,' he said, looking at his list. 'Now, removal from the hospital morgue will be tomorrow at four-thirty, and we will be there some time ahead. That is to prepare your husband. Then when you arrive at, say, two o'clock in the afternoon, he will be laid out, at rest. In order that those wishing to pay their last respects may view him in the open coffin. Then we will proceed to the church, where he will repose overnight. We have the times for the Mass, so that is good. Then immediately following the funeral Mass, we will drive on to the cemetery for the burial. Will that be all OK?' he said, looking from the ma to me.

'Yes, thank you very much, that seems to be everything,' I said, then stopping to think. Is there something I should be asking him? What else do I need to find out from him while I'm still here?

'Oh, yeah! Now, when can you let me know the cost?' I said.

'Yes, I can give you a price this evening. I will phone you later. What would be a good time for you?'

'I don't know,' I said, not wanting to take any chance I might not make it home in time.

'I can phone you tomorrow if you like?' he said, fixing me with his 'Tony Curtis' eyes.

'Look, I will give you a call in the morning,' I said, thinking that was best. 'Or phone you this evening if I get home on time.'

'No problem,' he said, then we got up to leave.

The ma was very happy as he led us to the door, opening it for us. 'Thanks very much,' me ma said.

'Yes, it's a great relief to have that all sorted,' I said, turning to the ma as we made our way to the car. 'Right, Ma. Are you happy with all that?' I said, looking at her, seeing her very contented. Her eyes were thinking as her face smiled.

'Yeah! Tha's grand, isn't it, Martha? Now, wha about Dinah an Gerry? Will we go an see them?'

'Yeah, of course we will. We need to talk to them. Get in, Ma. Let's head off while the traffic is still light,' I said, seeing the time pushing on. 'We don't want to lose the rest of the day sitting in heavy traffic.'

21

'Listen, Ma,' I said, seeing we were heading into the grounds of the old hospital. 'What about the idea of you taking Dinah home to live with you for good? You can even take Gerry home at the weekends.'

'Wha? Do ye think that's a good idea, Martha? She can get very aggravated, ye know! She could go fer me an I'd be afraid a me life!'

'Yeah,' I said, thinking, getting the picture of her in the hospital when she came to see Jackser. But she was terribly upset. It must have come as a shock to her seeing her father sick when nothing like that had ever happened to him before. But once they left her space and didn't make her feel threatened, she was grand!

'Listen, Ma, I was thinking. She has been in this hospital now for a few years. She's on medication. I'm sure now she must be nothing like she was. What would you think? Why don't you talk to her doctor? Tell him you are thinking of taking her home for good. She would be great company for you. It's what she lives for now, Ma,' I said, looking at her as I switched off the engine. 'She told me that, Ma. She's desperate to come home and live with you. I think it would work out. You would have your family around you again, with Dinah living with you all the time then Gerry to look forward to at the weekends. He's no trouble, Ma. The hospital would look after him with his medication. They would even do it for Dinah. You wouldn't be left stranded with her on your own. Why don't you think about it?'

'Yeah, I might just do tha,' me ma said slowly, letting her eyes blink and chewing the inside of her mouth, thinking like mad.

I sat on the side of Dinah's bed, while the ma sat on a chair, with the pair of us watching Dinah, seeing her wiping her red-raw eyes and nose. She was dabbing at her face with a big wad of tissues. She took them from the box the nurses left sitting beside her on the bedside locker. I looked around the ward, seeing about eight beds. They were all empty, so the patients must be up and dressed. But Dinah was obviously on bed rest, seeing the trauma she was going through at the minute.

'Listen, Dinah, I won't be long. I just want to check something,' I said, getting up slowly and heading for the door.

'Where are ye goin, Martha?' me ma called after me.

'I'll be back in a minute, Ma. I won't be long,' I said, heading down for the doctor's office.

I came out of the doctor's office and headed straight into the ward. 'Ma, you're wanted,' I said.

'Who? Who wants me, Martha?' the ma whispered, looking worried and curious as she made to stand up.

'Come on. The doctor wants a word with you,' I said, trying to get her to move while the doctor was still there and waiting. I didn't want to let Dinah get worried or have her asking too many questions that might end in her getting herself upset all over again. She got very upset when me and the ma told her about Jackser. She cried and sobbed her heart out for nearly two hours. You could hear her pitiful wails down around the hospital. But the nurses left her alone. They didn't come rushing in with a doctor in tow to give her pills or injections that would put her out for days.

'Did ye see the doctor, Martha?' Dinah whispered, looking up at me with interest.

'Yeah, I just wanted to find out how you're doing, Dinah, hear what they think, you know. So that you and me and the ma can see how you are, but it's them who make all the decisions.'

'Are ye askin me ma te take me home?' Dinah said, letting her eyes widen and the life come into them, lighting up with sudden hope!

'Ah, Jesus, Dinah! It's too early to go into that yet. We still have to arrange the funeral – I mean, there's the burial and everything. Just take it easy, Dinah. But I did promise you things would change for the better, remember? When you and me talked in the hospital?'

'Yeah,' she said, shaking her head, looking a bit more peaceful at letting the hope rise up in her – the belief of better things to come.

'Where is he? Where's tha doctor, Martha?' the ma said, waiting at the door for me.

'Come on, Ma, listen,' I said, walking down the passage holding her arm. 'I talked to the doctor about Dinah.'

'How she is?' me ma whispered, blinking fast with the interest.

'They said she was generally now stable, but naturally she is upset at the present time with her father having just died. That's what the doctor said, but, Ma, they are considering allowing her to come home in a few weeks. It will be into the care of the local community – that is, if you are willing to take care of her. The doctor said they can organise with her local health doctor to take over her medical care. It will be under the supervision of the psychiatrist here. The psychiatrist from the hospital here will visit the health centre once a week – he's there anyway. Then he said you and Dinah will have the back-up of a social worker. You will have one each, even the local health nurse, everyone, Ma! They will be just five minutes' walk away. So, you go in now and talk to the doctor. He wants to see you on your own. I'm going to ask them to let me take Dinah for a walk out in the fresh air.'

'Wha, but, Martha! I don't know,' me ma said, feeling everything was going too fast for her.

'Ma, you can't live on your own, and Dinah and Gerry can't be left to rot in this place. They belong with you – you're their mother. It makes sense for you all to be together. You will even have Gerry to look forward to at the weekends, Ma. Wouldn't that be great?'

'Yeah,' she whispered, letting the word come out slowly as her eyes lit up on that idea.

'Now go on, go in and talk to the doctor.'

The ma took in a breath, saying nothing as she headed in for the doctor's office. I knocked and heard him say, 'Come in.' I opened the door and put my hand lightly on the ma's back, then waited until she was in, and shut the door quietly after her.

'Come on, Dinah, I think we should start making tracks back in. The ma might be looking for us. She's probably finished talking to the doctor by now,' I said, looking at her stubbing out the cigarette, twisting it into the little border wall behind us. It was covered with roses well kept and pruned, obviously even sprayed with poison, to keep away the bleedin green fly! Mine get eaten alive, I thought, staring at the red roses mixed in with the lovely yellow ones – they looked moist and healthy. The scent wafting around us was wonderful, giving a lovely sense of peace to the big sweeping garden. I would love to take all this home with me and plant it in my own garden! Ah-ah! Keep yer hands te yerself, Martha, I grinned inside meself, knowing them days are long gone. They're now dead and buried behind me. These days I don't just have to survive, I can live a decent life. I have what I need.

'There youse are!' the ma whispered, with her eyes lighting up hurrying towards us, giving herself a little rush. 'OK, Dinah, come on in,' me ma said, turning to make back in the door.

'Are ye goin back inta the ward?' Dinah said, not looking in any hurry to get there.

'Wait till I tell ye,' me ma said, blinking and coughing, thinking and looking excited.

'Wha, Ma? Wha are ye goin te tell me?'

'Wait! Let's get inside first,' me ma said, giving Dinah a push, then laughing.

Dinah hurried herself, rushing for the ward, then sat on the bed, pulling her pyjama-covered legs under her.

'Listen! I talked te tha doctor, an he says ye can come home for good in a few weeks.'

'When, Ma?' Dinah burst out, getting the shock of her life. 'Why can I not come home now?'

'No, Dinah! Things take time. The doctor said one month, but ye can stay at home for the weekend next week. He wants te let ye adjust slowly.'

'Yeah! Tha's grand,' Dinah said slowly, shaking her head, looking really happy as she stared at the ma. Then she looked at me, saying, 'I'm all delighted! I'll be goin home, Martha. Ye were right all along,' she grinned, letting the light of her eyes settle on me. 'Ah, come here an give me a hug. I want te hug you,' she said, dropping on her knees to wrap her arms around me.

I held her tight, thinking, they grow up, but to me she will always be my little sister. They all are. They never grow up in my mind. I suppose, too, it's because I left home at such a young age. So, I don't get pictures of how they are now. When I think of them, I think of us all being children.

'Me da always talked about you, Martha,' Dinah whispered. 'Didn't he, Ma?'

The ma said nothing, just looked grim, with her eyes narrowing as she stared off into the distance. She didn't want to be reminded of Jackser still alive now he's gone.

'Yeah! He always said ye were the best. No one could stand next te ye when it came te doin things, an how ye used te fight an kill the young fellas bigger than yerself! He would always be tellin us stories about you, Martha!' she laughed.

I laughed, thinking, yeah! Young fellas then wouldn't think twice of hitting a young one. They saw their fathers do it to their mothers. So it was normal for them to want to keep a young one down in her place. I used to go after the little creeps with claws drawn and skinny little legs flying. My method was speed! Grab hair, swing around, dance up and down on their belly, then take off with me matchstick legs flying, hammering up and down like a pair of pistons! They would be still scraping themselves off the ground by the time I was home and dry. I roared laughing, getting the picture back then of meself! 'Yeah!' I said, laughing with Dinah.

'Come on, we better move,' me ma said, seeing the nurse walk in the door, heading straight down for Dinah.

'Come for your tea,' the nurse said, bending down to put her arm gently on Dinah's back. 'Did you have a lovely visit?' she said, looking from me and the ma, then back to Dinah still sitting with a big smile on her face.

She looks very happy, I thought, feeling my heart gladden. The ma even looks happy too. Oh, thank God everything seems to be working out for the best, I thought, getting up as the ma made a move.

'We'll see ye at the funeral, Dinah, you an Gerry. Where is he?' me ma said, looking around for him.

'He's gone down to his tea,' the nurse whispered, waiting for Dinah to get to her feet, then we all walked together out the door.

'Is he all right?' me ma said, looking at the nurse.

'Yes, he seems to have taken it well, hasn't he?' the nurse said.

'Yeah,' me ma laughed. 'But I don't think it sunk in! He seemed delighted wit himself tha he was right about wha happened. Ye know! Him goin like tha.'

'Yes, I agree with you,' the nurse said, 'he doesn't fully realise his father has passed away. But, nonetheless, he seems to be coping for now. He has gone down to his tea looking like there is not a bother on him. But we will keep an eye on him, especially with the funeral coming up. So, this is the best we can hope for,' the nurse said, taking Dinah off down the passage while we stood at the entrance door, just on our way out.

'Bye bye now, Dinah! Look after yerself,' me ma waved.

'Happy days, Dinah! See you soon,' I grinned, giving her a wave then following the ma out the door.

'Come on, Ma, we have a long drive back to the city,' I said, dreading meeting the traffic as we pull closer to Dublin. 'Will you be OK? I can give you a lift home or do you want to come home with me for the night?'

'No, no, Martha. I would prefer te be in me own place. There's no point goin wit you. I'm funny like tha. I prefer the comfort of me own few bits an pieces around me.'

'OK, if you're sure,' I said, opening the car door and letting her in. 'OK, I'll drop you home if you're happy with that, then I better get home myself. I haven't seen the kids properly for over a week. They are missing me and I certainly miss them,' I muttered to meself.

Here we go, another day, I thought as I headed over to the Morning Star homeless men's hostel, hoping to catch up with Charlie.

'No, I'm sorry I can't help you. As I said, he turned up here two nights ago with drink on him. He was drunk and he knew our policy – you can't come in here unless you're dry. So he hasn't been seen since.'

I stood on the doorstep looking around me, staring into the distance trying to get a picture of where he might be. I stood thinking, muttering, 'Thanks. It's a pity he's not here. I wonder where he might be?' I said, coming back to me senses, looking up into the face of the supervisor.

He shook his head, blowing out his cheeks, keeping the air in his face before letting it out saying, 'God knows where that could be. Sure, they ramble all over the city! He could be sitting anywhere now – probably met up with a few of his drinking cronies, down-and-outs. Who knows? They go where they can get their hands on a few pennies for a drink. Sorry I can't help you,' he said, making a snap move, ready to shut the door.

'OK,' I sighed, standing meself up straight and drawing a big breath inta me lungs. 'Thanks anyway,' I said, walking off as he shut the door and I made for the car.

Where to now, Martha? My eyes lit on the big old building straight ahead. It was just past the Georgian house for homeless women and children and looked like a barracks. When you went in through the gates, you rounded into the grounds of the old Grangegorman mental hospital. It must have been there for hundreds of years. Every Dubliner who ever had a mad relative ended up in that place, including the ma nearly. I laughed to meself, hearing her again when I was very little. *I'm warnin ye, Martha! If ye don't give up tha whingin an keenin outa ye, I'll be done for ye! They'll fuckin lock me in Grangegorman. I'll end up in the mad house! Me nerves are gone wit havin te listenin to ye!* she'd roar, grinding her teeth and making a run at me.

Oh, I believed her. She seldom got raging with me, so when we had a bed I used to head straight for under it, not taking any chances. But, no, she never laid a finger on me, the ma. Except that one time I can remember, she aimed a knife at me. Bingo! It hit the mark, opening the flesh deep in my elbow. That got me a few stitches and a shilling from the doctor. So me and Charlie got something outa that one! It had been worth our trek up to Temple Street Children's Hospital.

Right! I'll head in there, but I better leave the car where it is. I know the drug addicts and down-and-outs are hanging around there now. Jaysus, them bastards would skin alive their grannies for the next fix or drink. But drunkards are not so desperate; it's the junkies you watch out for. The problem is really getting very serious – even the old people now are getting a dirty syringe held up to their necks. They do it while they rob the poor things of their few ha'pence pension money. They are fucking desperate. It would frighten you to look at them. They look like emaciated, half-dead walking corpses, staggering around with red, bloodshot eyes. What's worse is half of them are still only kids. Jesus help the mothers! I would lose my mind. Few of them are even making it beyond their early twenties, but it's mostly only the city Dubliners. We're the ones being wiped out.

Now if it was the south side, where the judges and doctors live? Oh, no! Wouldn't happen. Their outrage would bring the government down. Their sweet little things will not be subjected to the appalling negligence of this government, no, no, no! 'Little Poppet' will not be allowed to suffer, not simply because they are drug addicts. This is an illness, dear! We demand the best care. We pay our taxes. Oh, no! But it's all right to just let the real Dubliners wipe themselves out! Make more room for the culchies, even if they like to think of themselves as 'sophisticated Dubliners' when they travel home to their roots in the bog. The gobshites! Still, got to be realistic now – addicts are deadly. They are like mindless zombies out of their heads on the bleedin drugs. They would drink your blood if they thought it would give them a high!

Jaysus, Martha, very clever, you have just scared the shite outa yourself! Are you going to go in now after all that? I looked up, feeling meself rattle inside. Go on, get going. Charlie might be mooching around in there.

I walked in through the back gate, except the gates are long since robbed. They're probably sitting up now, gracing the entrance to some new rich culchie's *Dallas*-style mansion, with him showing off to all the relatives and neighbours. They're standing with their sharp intakes of breath, not able to take in the style at all at all of Mickey and his new money. '*Ye won the lotto! Good man yureself! I always knew ye had it in yeh! Now, any chance on yeh lettin me have tha auld combine harvester? Sure, yeh won't be needin dat now yeh gave up the auld farming!*'

Fuck! You're going nuts again, Martha. What's ailing you? I let out me wind and paused, trying to get myself back on an even track. Yeah! I suppose it's the week that's in it. I'm exhausted, I miss the kids and now I can't find Charlie. Right! Shoulders back, deep breath, think what a wonderful day it is. You haven't really got a care in the world. You can take it nice and easy. Just be clinical about this matter; it will all get sorted in the end. Even if it doesn't? Well, it's not the end of the world, you are just tired, woman. Right! That's settled.

I wandered around the huge building, taking in all the broken windows. It's getting derelict very fast, even though they only closed down the place a few months ago. There's so many windows! I thought, looking up. The building is powerfully strong. It's made of solid granite. Nobody could break their way out through them iron bars or doors in a hurry! But then I noticed some of the bars had been jimmied back. Suddenly, without warning, I heard voices behind me. I looked back just in time to see a fella jumping out of the lower bottom window; it was over a five-and-a-half-foot drop.

'Wait, will ye!' a skinny young one of about seventeen roared, turning her bony arse on the windowsill. Then she sat looking down, twisting herself, trying to figure out the best way to jump. 'Will ye fuckin come on outa tha, Josie! Help me, ye fucker,' she screamed.

A disembodied voice complained, 'I'm caught between these bleedin bars, so I am! Hurry, come on, bleedin jump! I'm not stayin all day waitin on the likes a you!' roared the voice as it suddenly appeared outa the mouth of a bony-looking head now popping up behind her at the window. 'Jump! Or I'll give ye a hand! I'll fuckin push ye!' screamed Bony-head.

'BUNNY! GIV'S A BLEEDIN HAND! Mockey is sendin me head-first!' she gasped, looking down trying to see how far he was sending her.

Bunny went tearing over, looking like he was going to drag her down himself. 'Fuckin hell! Ye're a bleedin pain in the arse! Come on!' he said, getting his fist and dragging her by the coat, then putting out his arm, stopping her fall.

Uh-oh! I thought, just what the doctor ordered. A new patient waiting for his emergency help – that's me if I don't make meself scarce. I made to fly around the corner, then I heard a roar.

'EH, MISSUS!'

Too late, I'm spotted. My heart slid down into me belly, making me feel weak. Jesus, the game's up. There's no point in keep going – there's nowhere to go! This building stretches for miles, with not even the sign of a front entrance, I thought, desperately flying me eyes up, down and round, taking in the length and breadth of the place. Oh, bloody hell, the main way out must be way up around the other side. Yeah, that's probably where it is.

I suddenly turned around and faced them.

'Hey, missus! Have ye gor a light? Will ye give us a cigarette? Have ye got any change te spare?' the first fella said, limping with a bit of a run on him as he hurried himself up to me.

I took in a deep breath and changed the expression on my face, making it look annoyed and worried.

'Wha? I was just about te ask youse for one! Have none any a ye's not got air a one on ye? I'm gummin for a bleedin smoke!' I said, staring at them with me mouth wide open, looking from one to the other.

'Wha?' your man said, with the bones sticking out on his cheeks and the eyes dead in his head. But you could see the aggression and nervous energy in the shifting of his body from one side to the other, looking like he was gently hopping his feet. While I talked, I kept me eyes on his hands, seeing they weren't slipping to bring out a syringe, and watched his eyes for a sudden shift, then a rigid look in the body telling me he was ready to spring. I kept meself relaxed, letting him stay close, like he was a much-loved relative and I hadn't a fear in the world.

'Did youse see any utters up there? Any a them drinkin? I'm lookin for someone!'

'Nooo! Can't help ye!' he said, backing away, looking disappointed and puzzled as he stared down at the style of my moccasins, black linen trousers and white Brown Thomas crisp linen shirt. They don't match up with the way I'm talking! Plus the well-fed look of me. Yet, when I open my mouth and you see the look on my face and the knowing look in my eyes, you would know I was common as fuckin muck and I probably robbed the clothes.

'Ahh! Bleedin hell, are youse sure? Did ye's ger a good look aroun tha kip?' I said, pointing me hand up at the building, sounding like I was on something meself.

'Yeah! We jus told ye! We should know cos we're stayin there! There's loads a beds if ye're lookin! Go on in, take a look aroun! There's million a beds left in tha bleedin dump!'

'Nah! Thanks anyway. I better keep on the fuckin mooch. Good luck!' I said, seeing them giving me a wave. I walked off, heading back down the hill – not hurrying but moving anyway. Lucky for me I left my bag under the seat in the car. It would be gone now! They were asking for the light, cigarette, money – oh, yeah! I'm well up to their little game. Take out the money and you're fucked. They take it off you or knife it off – whatever it takes.

I stopped when I reached my car, seeing them pass the women's hostel, heading down the hill like meself. They were hurrying, probably down to the quays to get the methadone, or whatever they get down there. I stopped for a split second, judging the distance. Yeah! No problem. I'll be in and off before they catch up. They're about fifteen steps away at least. I only need four moves to be vanishing with wheels under me. I opened the car, slamming the door shut, then started the engine and shot the car to the left, then reversed, shot forward and was pointing down the road. They were just coming up alongside me, half running with their mouths open, looking over at me in shock. Then I saw the eyes gleam and the chin lift as the mouth clamped with the nose giving a snort.

'Fuckin conned us!' they roared.

I couldn't resist! I pressed the down button for the window and grinned, clamping me left eye shut, keeping it tight, and gave the thumbs up, holding it in the air! 'Beautiful day, eh what, boys and girls? Get plenty of fresh air now! Toodle pip, old socks!' Then I took off like a bullet, giving them a cheery wave.

'FUCKIN WHORE'S MELT!' An unmerciful screech erupted after me, sounding strangled with the rage. I bombed down the hill giving a huge sigh of relief. Thank God I got out of that in one piece! Me heart is still rattling. Jaysus, I can do without that caper. I wouldn't have liked to get caught napping by that shower. Just as well I don't need a brain – that was simply pure instinct. If I had a brain, I wouldn't have gone in there in the first place, seeing as I knew what could happen. Ah, but then you wouldn't be Martha Long the gobshite.

Jaysus! Where are you, Charlie? I thought, reaching the bottom of the hill and wondering which way to turn. What would I do if I was Charlie? Now, if I turn up there, I must have something in my pocket to pay for the night's bed. Where would I head off to when I can't get in? Somewhere close. I'm walking. I would go down the quays

– there's a homeless men's shelter down there. Now, that was two days ago. But with a bit of luck he will have met someone or something that will keep him hanging around the area. Right, head down that direction. But first a little detour. Turn left heading up towards the Broadstone. He might be in the park up there – a lot of down-and-outs go there.

No! And now he's not even in the Phoenix Park, up around the Furry Glen. That's a good place for them to sleep on a lovely night – that's if you don't fall over the bonking couples rolling around desperate for their bit of nookey! They're mostly married men and women, but not to each other! Yeah, it's definitely more comfortable than the car. Now, wouldn't that be something nice to try out? Me an ole Blue-eyes!

Jaysus, Martha, ye're going loopy, nuts! Stop kidding yourself. He would have a better chance of getting a corpse back to life than getting me to let the guard down. Oh, well! It keeps me sane. Ye have te dream.

22

I drove back down O'Connell Street, heading around the side streets. No! Not here, I thought, looking at a few beggars sitting on the steps of the Pro Cathedral church on Marlborough Street. Right, it's now late, very late. I better get on and head straight up to the morgue. The ma will be there waiting. She's left there with Jackser on her own, but if she's lucky Sally will be with her. The removal is at half-four. Fuck, it's twenty past now.

I could feel my heart leap and the face get a sudden burst of blood with the shock leaving me staggered. Right, put the boot down. I looked ahead, judging the traffic. I might make it just in time if these buses and cars don't get in me way.

I ducked and dived in and outa the traffic, not getting the nippy speed. This car is far too heavy for this carry-on. It's meant to bullet across continents on autobahns or autostradas. Them motorways keep going for miles with no stopping – then this car is at its best. But this is definitely not good for the engine – all that stopping and starting it has to do in the city traffic.

I drove up, making it just in time. I could see the funeral car outside the entrance of the morgue. It was a dark, grim-looking building, with the once-yellow bricks now the colour of the inside of a chimney. The two church-looking oak doors stood wide open. I flew into the hall and turned left, heading for where the voices were coming from, then found meself looking at a stone floor with whitewashed stone walls and a cold slab in the middle of the room waiting to meet me. I gave a shiver. Jaysus, the dead house!

'Here she is!' the ma said, looking up as I flew in.

'Ma! I got here. I'm on time!' I panted, feeling relieved I hadn't left her stuck as well.

'Where were you? We were waitin,' the ma moaned, looking very woebegone.

'Yeah, I was out looking for him,' I said, standing staring, looking at Charlie, big bold, large as life and ugly as sin. He gave me a shifty look, looking like he had done something wrong.

'Charlie! Where the hell did you come out of? I have scoured the city from morning till now, looking the length and breadth for you.'

'Ah, yeah, sorry! I wasn't te know tha, Martha. I was here, over there, sitting on the steps waitin for ye's. When I came here first, I called up te the ward at dinnertime an the nurse said he was down here. So I waited for ye's.'

'Oh, right,' was all I could say, then went over to take a look at Jackser lying in his lovely new coffin. They had wrapped him in the white silky frill that lined the coffin. It covered him except for his hands and face.

I stared at him. He looked stiff and very old, not the strong, young Jackser of my childhood days. But it was him all right, no mistaking that.

'Jesus, he got very old, didn't he, Martha?' Charlie whispered, moving over to stand beside me, with the two of us staring into the coffin. 'I hadn't seen him fer years,' Charlie said, staring at Jackser's face.

'No, nor me either, not since the time Harry died.'

'So, tha's it,' Charlie said, shaking his head slowly. 'He's gone!'

'Yeah, maybe me ma might get a bit of peace now, Charlie,' I said, getting hopeful the ma's life would be easier.

'No, go way outa tha, Martha,' he whispered, shaking his head at me, looking disgusted. 'Tha fuckin aul one was every bit as bad as him. In fact, I would say she's worse,' he snorted.

I sighed. 'Yeah! I know you don't like her, Charlie. But she is the ma.'

'Yours maybe, Martha. But not fuckin mine. I'm tellin you! She's hard hearted, she has no heart tha aul one. At least he did be times!' he said, throwing his head at Jackser in the coffin.

'Yeah, still and all, I suppose fellas are different,' I sighed, understanding how Charlie felt. She really hurt him. He never could take it. I think it was one thing Jackser being bad, but he couldn't take his mother never having any time for us.

'Martha!' the ma whispered, hurrying back into the room after talking to one of the undertaker men. 'The man wants you,' she pointed, getting me to look at the man in the black suit and white shirt.

'Is it you your mother is talking about? You have to go over and see the boss.'

'Oh! Why? Is there a problem?' I said, seeing something was definitely up.

'Martha! the ma said. 'He rang me this morning. I was waitin on you, but ye didn't come. He's lookin for the deeds a the grave. I haven't got them. You need te go up quick an get tha sorted out!' she said, bringing her voice up to a high note, making it sound like she was going to start wailing.

'What do you mean, Ma, the deeds are gone? What does that mean? Where are they?'

'I don't know. He was looking for them about two year ago! Someone took them an he thought it was Dinah!'

'Why would she take them?'

'How the hell do I know? I'm only tellin ye wha happened,' she roared, then lowered her voice, seeing I could get annoyed too and that would do no one any good.

'OK, I better take a run up there. You will have to go without me. I better get this sorted out.'

'He won't be buried without them, Martha!' she shouted after me as I whipped meself, rushing for the door. 'Go over te Glasnevin. Get them te sort it out! That's my grave. It belongs te this family!' she started, working herself up to challenge anyone who was going to disagree.

'OK! Don't worry. I'll see you back at the house, Ma. I probably won't make it to the church for the prayers with Jackser,' I said, now flying out the door and down the hill, heading for my car. I dived in switching on the engine. A quarter to five – I hope they don't leave until five-thirty.

I parked the car outside the main gates – they were locked – and ran in through the side gate. I belted to the right, looking for the office. A man with keys in his hand stopped and looked at me. 'The cemetery is closed,' he said, ready to wave me back out the way I came in.

'Listen, we have a burial here in the morning and the deeds are lost. Who can I speak to?'

'Me. Come in,' he said, heading me into his office. 'So, is there no chance of them turning up?' he said, whipping open a book. 'Name, deceased's date of death?'

I rambled off all the details he wanted. 'Right! Without the deeds, nobody has ownership,' he said, making it sound very matter-of-fact.

'Well! Then not just me and the family have a problem, but so do you. Unless you can tell me a way around this in a hurry,' I said, standing up straight and fixing me eyes on him, making eyeball contact with his couldn't-care-less, watery blue-grey eyes. They were programmed only to obey bits of paper and what is written therein.

We stared at each other for a few minutes. I could feel meself turning white with the rage. You could hear me breathing slowly but deeply.

'I paid for this grave. It is a family grave for five family members. Now, there are still four people to go into it,' I said. 'One is on his way here in the morning. The father of the young man aged twenty-eight who is already lying there. Now! He will be buried, lying on top of his son. So what is there to do?' I said, rapping me knuckle in time to that.

'OK, we can allow the burial on one condition. You say you are the one who signed the deeds?'

'Yes!' I said.

'OK, you can write your consent to allow this burial. After that, no more will be buried in that grave until the deeds are found.'

'What about my mother?'

'Yes, she has the automatic right as his wife.'

'Good,' I said, thinking, technically they are not married – not a worry at the minute. 'So, what do I do now?'

'Go over to the undertaker's and sign a form with them. They will hand it in here when they arrive with the deceased. All the paperwork will be handled then.'

'So, sign a form giving my consent?'

'Yes,' he said, nodding at me.

Phew, such relief, I thought. 'Thanks for that, that's very good of you,' I said.

'Don't mention it,' he said. 'All in a day's work.' Then he was busy pulling up the black trousers over the white shirt and fixing the suspenders to keep them up. His big belly was getting in the way, though. It stuck out, threatening to burst the buttons on the shirt. I gave a little wave flying out the door. He gave a little wave back, hurrying out after me, then slowed, stopping to lock up the office.

'Jaysus! I just made that on time,' I said, seeing the traffic now beginning to get chock-a-block as I got to the end of the road, then turned, hitting on to the main road trying to turn left. Then ended, getting meself snarled up with the traffic coming to a dead end. The wise thing to do now would be to stop at the nearest phone box and ring. Ah, never mind, keep going. He's only about ten minutes away on a straight run. But this could take an hour!

I crawled to a stop outside the undertaker's, pulling into the parking spot outside the door. Made it! Blue-eyes looked up as I pushed in the door. I was delighted to clap eyes on him. Thank God he's not closed up! He stood up, giving me a look of concern and a smile at the same time. 'Take a seat,' he said, looking at the red face on me, with the eyes blazing now coming with exhaustion. The few hours' sleep last night has worn off. I'm even more knackered now than I was in the hospital.

'I take it you heard about the problem?'

'Yes. I just spoke to the man in Glasnevin. He told me to come here and sign a consent form.'

He lowered his head, making it look like a bow, and went straight to a filing cabinet, opening a drawer.

'OK, you need to write your letter of consent. Then you can sign the deeds over to your mother.'

'But the deeds are lost, so she says. They can't find them.'

'Yes, but you can write a letter giving your interest as the owner over to them.'

'Do you know, I never intended I should have anything to do with that grave. It belongs to the family.'

'Yes,' he said, 'but you signed the forms at the time.'

'Bloody eegits in that cemetery! They should have told me that. I would then have signed the family names on it!'

'But they would have needed to be present at the time to sign their own name,' he said, still seeing a problem.

'Oh, never mind,' I sighed, letting out a big breath of weariness. 'I'll do all that now.'

'No! The letter signing the grave over to your mother would be best kept by you, but she has to sign it. Then it will be safe,' he said, making it sound eminently sensible to me. 'And just sign there – good. OK,' he said, taking up the papers and leaving them in front of him at his desk. 'That is every thing in order now,' he smiled, letting me suddenly see the sunshine.

Hmm! He really is handsome, I thought, knowing it's nice to look – like seeing delicious cakes in the shop window. But you know you won't be buying one, they're not for you. Far too rich for the digestive system, and maybe not good for you.

'Now, what about the cost?' I said, looking at the figures on the invoice he handed me.

'OK,' he said, getting down to business. 'Your mother is entitled to a death grant – that is [x amount]. Then she will continue to receive the deceased's social welfare payment – that will be for six weeks and that should cover the cost, almost. There is a small outstanding balance.'

I had a look at his figures. 'No problem – I will cover that. I will pay you immediately after the funeral,' I said.

'Perfect,' he said, standing up to shake my hand, then led me to the door with his hand held gently on my back.

'Cheers! Many thanks,' I said, waving happily now that was sorted and getting back into the car, heading over to see the ma. She should be back from the church by now. OK, I better stop and pick up a few things at the supermarket.

I stopped at a little shop, looking in at the big blue duck eggs sitting in the window. Oh! I haven't seen them for years. I wonder would the ma like them? Well, if she doesn't, I'm bringing them home and eating them myself. They're lovely. They taste like meat, with a load of protein, and they have to be fresh, not like the bloody battery hen ones you get now. Right! I'll stop in there on the way back from the supermarket, I thought, as I headed through the shopping centre.

I loaded the stuff onto the belt at the checkout. Then, when the trolley was finally emptied, I rushed through, grabbing a handful of plastic bags she left out and started to pack. Jaysus! I went mad with the shopping, I thought, letting my eyes fly up to the prices turning into nothing but zeros, with higher numbers coming in front. Then me hands flew, packing in the food. A roast chicken, a dozen fresh rolls, two large sliced pans, two packs of butter, tea, sugar, two milk, half a pound of the best fresh ham, tomatoes, biscuits, a nice teatime cake, a dozen eggs – I'll get the duck ones for meself if I have any money left! Rashers, carrots, onions, a packet of mince beef. Jaysus! I had four full plastic bags already, with another what looks like double that again. Ah, well. I don't want the ma to starve. Anyway, she's going to need to feed everyone.

Finally the till came to a silent stop. So did I as I stood with me hand on the overflowing trolley. Then I got the damage, feeling me nerves jerk. I hope I have that much in my purse! I thought.

I handed over the money and got eleven pounds and some change back. I stared at it, taking the long ream of receipt, thinking she must have used nearly the whole roll for that! Oh, well. You can't argue with having plenty of grub in the house. This is the second time today I have done a big shop! I was up early this morning with the kids in tow and we flew around getting the week's shopping. Then I left it to them and their father to unload and cook the dinner while I shot off out about my business.

Right! Here we go. You are on the last lap for today, Martha. After this, there is just the funeral to get through. Then you can get back to normal living – wrestle the kids, dog and house back from their father, and sleep! Oh, lovely blissful sleep and plenty of hot baths. Tea at the ready and no worrying about looking over your shoulder in case you're doing something wrong.

23

I turned into the flats and parked the car, then wearily hauled myself out and walked around, opening the big boot of the car. It's lovely and big – I can get half the house into that! Right, drag up two bags, then see what happens. I hope Charlie hasn't vanished.

I banged on the door and it was whipped open immediately. The ma is crafty. She must have seen me from the kitchen window. I could see her eyes lit up and the smile on her face.

'Where did ye get them, Martha?' she said, moving aside to let me struggle in.

'Shut the door fast, Ma. I think the cops are after me. I just robbed the supermarket!'

'Wha?! Ye didn't, did ye?' she said, looking shocked, then standing still with her heart in her mouth, giving a look to the door.

'Only joking, Ma. Jaysus! You would believe anything.'

'Well! Ye shouldn't be givin me frights like tha, Martha! Ye could easily a given me a heart attack!'

'Ah, Ma, would I do that? Don't be ridiculous!'

'Well! Wha am I supposed te know?' she said, getting all huffy.

'Ah, fuck. Why didn't I keep me bleedin mouth shut?' I muttered, landing the bags on the kitchen table.

'How're ye, Martha? Jaysus! Ye got enough shoppin!'

'No! The rest is down in the car, Charlie. Ma, give us a hand and unpack them. Charlie, you come down with me and we'll unload the rest of the stuff outa the boot.'

'There's more, Martha?

'Yeah, I don't want the ma to starve.'

'No fear a tha,' me ma laughed, happily taking the stuff outa the bag.

Just as we got outside and I was heading for the car with Charlie on me heels, Sally passed us and gave a little nod with a weak smile.

'Hello, Sally! How are you, Sally? You are just in time to give us a hand up with the ma's shopping,' I laughed, opening the boot then looking back, seeing she was gone!

'Fuck! Did ye see that, Charlie? She just blanked me!'

'Wha did ye expect, Martha?' he shrugged. 'They're them; we're us! Come on, let's get it done ourselves,' he said, making a grab for four bags. I grabbed three, deciding I was not too bright, it will take me longer to get up and back. Now, if I had only taken two at a time.

'That's the lot!' I puffed, trailing him up the stairs and into the hall. I could hear whispering, then it stopped when we appeared. Sally was talking to me ma in the sitting room. They gave each other a look, much as to say, 'Don't say any more. They're here now listening.' I felt my heart drop at the thought of not being welcome, then fire up with a feeling of annoyance. Fuck! Charlie is so right.

'Listen, Charlie,' I said, looking at him, seeing the look he gave me, like a sad laugh because he was right, but an even deeper pain showed in his lovely, fading, sky-blue eyes. I stared at him and he held my look, then lifted his mouth and eyebrows, shrugging his shoulders, and put out his arms, giving me the message – We're not wanted? Ah, well! That's the way life goes! Nothing we can do about it. He grinned, shaking his head at me.

'Fuck this, their loss, Charlie!' I muttered under my breath.

He took in a huge sigh, rubbing his hands together, whispering, 'Wha's te eat, Martha? I'm starvin wit the hunger! I could eat a scabby babby!'

'Oh, yeah, I was going to say to you. Listen, Charlie, there's two packets of cigarettes in one of those bags for you. Root around and take them out.'

'They're for me? Oh, thanks, Martha. Jaysus! I was just goin te ask ye fer one a yer roll-ups! I'm gaspin for an aul smoke,' he said, happily sticking his head and hands in the bags, whipping out the stuff.

'Oh!' the ma laughed, not really laughing, but that laugh I can now see is manipulative. She is not laughing with me but wanting to get around me. 'I, eh, Martha, gave them cigarettes te poor Sally!'

'Did you now?' I said, knowing right this minute I could very easily commit murder. 'Listen, Ma, please take yourself right this very minute and get them back from yer poor precious Sally!' I said, nearly gritting me teeth, knowing I sounded exactly like Jackser. Then I cooled down, saying, 'I'm sorry, Ma, but those cigarettes were bought for Charlie, and if he even gives one to Sally I will take the fucking things back and keep them. Let her buy her own.'

'Ah!' she hissed, then went rushing in and arguing in a whisper to Sally. I waited, looking at Charlie. He looked nervous. He didn't expect, nor did I, to end up with me in a rage. I hadn't even realised how angry I was. The ma took it for granted they were for Sally, not letting it enter her head Charlie was here and he smokes too. Surely she knew I had bought them for him. Who else would I be buying them for? Sight nor sound has been seen of Sally! Only me and Charlie had made our presence felt. So, now, I am beginning to see the ma through Charlie's eyes.

'Here!' she said, throwing them on the table at Charlie.

He looked at the ma, seeing her face shaking and her eyes blinking, with the mouth going full throttle, biting the lip off herself. She wanted to say something – tell us to get the fuck out. Charlie went quiet and picked up the cigarettes, saying, 'I think I will head off.'

'Yeah, me too,' I said. Then the two of us went off down the hall, leaving them muttering in angry whispers together, knowing it was probably me and Charlie they were going mad angry about, not just the loss of the smokes! Fuck, she can make a fool outa me, but not the pair of us. Fuck that!

'Come on, Charlie, I'll give you a lift into town.'

'Thanks, Martha. Pity about tha, though. I thought fer a minute there I was goin te lorry inta a great big feed a grub.'

'Listen, for the love a Jaysus! Don't mind me! I was just annoyed with the ma and the Sally one for being so bleedin mean. Why don't you go back up and get yourself something to eat? Sure, you did no harm! It was me that lit into her.'

'Wha? Are you jokin, Martha?' he snorted and shook his head away, leaving one eye behind for a minute, then pulled it away. 'There's no way tha aul one is goin te open the door for me, never mind let me in for a bit te eat.'

'Why not, Charlie? Sure, I bought the food for you, too!'

'Well, she won't see it tha way, Martha.'

'But she was talking to you today. You came back with her, Charlie!'

'Yeah, but tha, Martha, was because she was on her own. Now tha she has Sally there, she doesn't need me, or you. She got wha she wanted. Look, I'm tellin ye, Martha. Ye have te get wide te the ma. You don't know her like I do! Sure, she has time for no one. She only cares about Dinah an Gerry! So forget it. Come on, let's go,' he said, making it sound so final.

I pulled up outside the Morning Star hostel and said, 'Here we are. Your bed inside is waiting for you.'

'I haven't the money, Martha. I don't know why ye're bringin me here.'

'Look,' I said, 'I'll get you a few bob tomorrow. Here's what I've got.' I took out the eleven pounds screwed up inside my purse and handed him the remaining twenty. 'There's thirty-one quid. I'm sure you'll spend it on drink. So, tomorrow I'm going to pay for a month's kip in this place, then you're on your own. Get back down the country and get dried out! Get yourself sorted. It's your life. I tried all my days to help you and so did a lot of other people. You let them down, Charlie. You simply do not care what happens to yourself. What can I do but feel the pain of what you are doing to yourself and worry when I think about you? But decide what kind of a life you want, Charlie. Have you made your mind up to die on the streets? Get a premature death? End up buried in a pauper's grave with no mark, no name, to say you ever existed? Huh, Charlie?'

'Yeah, I've been dry since yesterday,' he said. 'I can do it when I want. But it's when I get back te Dublin, Martha, then I meet the same aul crowd and tha's it, I'm back on the drink. Ye see, Martha, I tried it wit Alan when he helped me out. But after I left them, when I had stayed wit them fer a few months, ye know? Anyway, sure, wha life? Who do I know? Where can I go? The only people I know are all down-an-out alcoholics like meself, Martha. I lost me old life and opportunities years ago, when I was still a lad. It's too late fer me, Martha.'

I lit up a roll-up cigarette and sat smoking while he sat beside me smoking his cigarettes. We just stayed quiet, with the two of us lying back in our seats, sitting companionably but lost in our own thoughts.

'Do you see them steps there, Charlie? What would have been once, I suppose, the back entrance to the women's hostel? It was always blocked up. It even looked like that back then when we were little and me ma stayed here.'

'Yeah. Wha about it, Martha?'

'Well, it was on them very same steps the ma met Jackser. That's where he was sitting. Right on them steps he was, with a load of other ghougers from the men's hostel here.'

'Was it?' he said, sitting up and looking over in surprise, staring at them. 'Yeah,' he said slowly, 'I used te hear him talkin about it right enough. Wha age was I then, Martha?'

I shook my head, lifting me lips together. 'A baby! You were only a baby, Charlie. I doubt you were even a year old. Wait, you must have been – I was six years old.'

'Long time ago, Martha,' he said sadly.

'Yeah, long time ago, Charlie.'

'Now,' he said, 'it's all over fer them two an not before time.'

'Yeah, but it was too late for us, Charlie. Or at least too late for you,' I said.

'Yeah, but you were always different, Martha. I never had your nerve!'

'Yeah,' I said, 'well, I never had your brains. You had a fine mind, Charlie. You were very clever.'

'Maybe I was too clever fer me own good, Martha!' he said, snorting as he sat up straight, getting disgusted with himself.

'You know, there's only two buildings along here,' I said. 'The men's hostel here and, up at the end, the women's. Beyond that is the mad house – or was – Grangegorman. Then to the left is the old Richmond Hospital. But there was no entrance here, only the high wall running down the avenue. This is a lovely little quiet cul de sac. I bet you in the old days that women's hostel was a big old private house for the superintendent of the mad house. The staff from the hospital probably lived in the men's hostel, what do you think?'

'Yeah! Ye could be right,' he said, looking around at all the trees and the greenery in against the old high wall coming up the little hill.

'Do you know, Charlie,' I said slowly, almost whispering, 'I remember me and the ma making our way slowly – oh, so slowly, we were so weary. Up that hill we dragged ourselves, every night, with her carrying you. It was always dark. We couldn't come back until eight o'clock in the evening. Then the doors used to be slammed shut after us at nine o'clock in the morning. We had to be out by then, sharp. The doors would then be locked and wouldn't open until the night. If you were late, you got locked out! Fuck! That was the ma's worst fear. I can still hear her, "Come on, hurry! Ye have te walk! We'll be left sleepin out if ye don't get a move on!"

'So, we used to tramp the streets all day long, waiting to come back here and fall into the little narrow, black-iron single beds. We would be weak with the hunger, Charlie. But the funny thing is you seldom cried. You were used to the hunger by then. So was I. It was just something you knew and accepted – that pain in your belly gnawing away with hunger. That and the walking. You would feel very, very tired, lethargic, but just kept on moving. You had no thoughts and didn't expect anything. Except the one thing you knew – that when the night came, you could walk up that avenue in the dark, with the trees whistling in the wind, making it sound like the Banshee was crying and she was getting ready to jump out at us any minute. I remember I would move in close to the ma, with me hand at the ready, on the alert to grab her coat. I didn't do that – hold onto her – because I knew she had the weight of carrying you. Anyway, I needed me two hands free to carry all our stuff. I hauled that around with my arms stretched pressed to me belly. The ma had it wrapped up in a sheet and tied in a knot.

'Jaysus! They were heavy, Charlie,' I grinned, looking at him. 'But you know the ma. She wouldn't leave anything behind in the hostel because she was afraid of it getting robbed. Then one day we went to the ragman – the aul Jew man down on Henrietta Street. He gave us one shilling and sixpence for them – all the spare clothes we had, mostly your stuff, Charlie. She needed to buy milk for you. So, you see, Charlie, I knew them times. I knew her then. I know what she and me and you went through. I lived them times with her. You never knew any other life than the one we had with Jackser. So, you don't see her like I do,' I said, not looking at him, just staring ahead, staying with that time and seeing us all. 'Me ma struggling, me struggling and you just content to be carried in her arms, not complaining whether you were covered and baked in shit from a rag that sat on you for days at a time. No, nor even the empty hole in your belly for the want of a bit of nourishment.

'No, I don't remember you crying then, except in the earlier times when we had a roof over our heads. Then she used to go off and leave us on our own, with you left sitting in the middle of the one bed we had. You had a little cot over in the corner by the window. But it was for the two of us to keep each other company, I suppose – that's why she left you sitting on the bed. You would cry then because the hunger was on you. It would be from early in the morning until the late in the night she would leave us. We would fall asleep together with my finger stuck in your mouth. It helped to ease the hunger, I discovered, having something to suck, but then you got used to it. Come to think about it, Charlie,' I laughed, getting a thought, 'it's a wonder you weren't poisoned. I'm sure me hands were manky with the dirt!' I said, looking at him with a half-grin on me face. 'Huh! I used to even rummage through the dustbins, hoping I would find a bit of stale bread or something. No such luck, I remember. No, people had very little to put on their tables in that place. They certainly didn't throw it out,' I said, speaking in a quiet monotone with my eyes staring back to that tiny little room. But it was home, I thought.

'I don't know, Charlie. But it was them times we had with the ma and the memories of her never hitting us, just being together. In a way it's just occurring to me. I think she was as much of a child in her own mind as we were! That's why she probably never hit me or showed any real emotion. She was so totally lost inside her own mind. It was almost, now I think about it, like she was a robot. We were as much a part of her as the bundle of clothes I carried around caught between my arms and struggled along with them pressed to me belly. She sold the clothes because we needed the money. So, maybe there is something in what you say, Charlie. She sold us to Jackser. He didn't want us, but he kept us because they could get money by keeping us. So she knew we weren't wanted, but he wanted to hang on to us. So we stayed. He ignored us, treated us badly, and she went back to living in her own world.

'Oh, God Almighty, yes! We were to her like the bundle of clothes

I carried. Something she owned, but they could be got rid of or traded if the price was right. So, maybe you are right! You say she had no heart, she was made of stone. Nothing mattered to her except what she wanted. Even Dinah, she would be company. Gerry is her baby, he will do exactly what she tells him; he has the mind of a baby. But she won't harm them. Dinah is not a child, Gerry has the care of the hospital. You know, Charlie! It wasn't that she didn't want to love us; it was simply that she couldn't. The difference between her and Jackser was he did hate us, he felt passion. She felt nothing; she was just like a robot with a heart made of steel.'

'Now ye're thinkin on the right track, Martha. That's exactly wha I saw, right from the very beginnin. I think up te now, Martha, you weren't prepared te face tha fact. Because as you say, it kept ye goin thinkin the ma was still yer ma. Otherwise ye would have te face the fact she made a fool outa you. Everything ye ever did fer her was all for nothin. You couldn't see tha you had nothin te begin wit, ye needed te believe someone in yer life cared about you. Because in yer own way, Martha, deep down, you're a real softie! But now ye know,' he said, looking very worn out because he had been carrying that belief all his life. The knowledge came too early for him.

I managed to keep going by fooling myself that deep down in her heart she cared, it was just that Jackser had killed her feelings, but she had cared one time, I thought. Now it seems that's not true – there had been nothing there all along. That's why Charlie had not even got started in life – he couldn't take the pain of living with the emptiness, because everyone needs someone to love them, even if it's only for a short while. I thought I had been given that care; he knew he never had. So, that was the difference between us. That is why he fell so soon – he had nothing and nobody that mattered to him.

'You never believed there was something waiting ahead in life for you, did you, Charlie?' I said quietly, looking at him, feeling a terrible sadness for him.

'No, but I was always too cowardly te do somethin about it.'

'Like what, Charlie?'

'Like kill meself as Harry did. So I take the slow way. Anyway, I'll go out happy I hope, tanked up te me eyeballs,' he laughed.

'You listen to me, Charlie. You are here for a reason. As long as you're still alive, there's hope. You never know what's around that next corner. I love you – you've always had me!' I sighed. 'I'm going home, Charlie. Go on, they're all giving you looks, them fellas going in there.'

Charlie turned his head, seeing a crowd of aul fellas laughing at him. Then they gave him a wave with a knowing look, like he had gone and landed himself with a woman, the lucky devil.

'Go on!' I said. 'I'll see you tomorrow.'

'Will you be there, Martha?'

'Yeah,' I said.

'OK,' Charlie said. 'See ye then, good luck!'

'Good luck, Charlie!' I said, watching him wave from the door, looking embarrassed with the heads all peeping around, standing behind his back, laughing, watching and pointing.

Jesus, that would be hell on earth for me – no front door to call your own, no way to tell them to fuck off and shut the door in their faces when all you want is a bit of peace and nobody to push you around. Oh, Charlie. If only . . .

I turned the car around and headed off for home and an early night in bed. Jesus! I am banjacksed. I will be so glad when this is all over, I thought, feeling a little lift hit me as I drove down the hill in my big car where once I struggled up on dark nights in the wind, the rain and the cold, walking with a woman carrying a baby, and she was as cold as the grave and as dead as the buried. Thank God I never realised that until now.

'Oh, I think ye always did, but ye saw only wha ye wanted, because ye knew it was the only way,' murmured a wise little voice who stirred sleepily in my heart.

24

On the last lap now, I turned left heading for home. Ohh! The lovely, sweet, familiar scent of the fresh sea air. God, how lucky can you get? Bloody hell, the fumes from that city centre nearly had me suffocated. Yeah! The aul smoking doesn't help.

'Here we are,' I sighed happily, then looking up, seeing the house in pitch blackness. What! It can't be that late? Oh, I just remembered their father has taken them off. He's visiting friends first, the Russian brigade, then he will drop them down ahead of me and leave them with the Wallaces. Jesus! How could I forget that? You didn't. You just hadn't time to think about anything but what you were doing.

Oh, great. I have that to look forward too – a nice few days down in Wexford in the Wallaces' summer house with their three children. The kids are best friends. They're all around the same age and they go to the same school. So, that's how I got to know the parents. We get along great, but the mother and myself are like chalk and cheese. She's softly spoken, blonde, tall, absolutely gorgeous-looking and very sophisticated. But we get along grand. We laugh at the same things, because we have the same sense of humour. Yeah, it's going to be smashing.

So, tomorrow morning is the funeral. I will fix up all the odds and ends, pay the undertaker what I owe him, then hot foot it over to the hostel. I can even take Charlie back there with me, pay for his bed for the month as I promised, then, first light the next day, hit the road before the early-morning traffic starts to pick up. That way I should arrive just in time for breakfast. Ohh! I can't wait. I will have plenty of time with the children – get to hear all their news and see what they've been up to. Brilliant! I wonder if they have enough clothes? I can ring and find out. Maybe phone them as soon as I get in. What time is it now?

I squinted at the car clock. Quarter to nine! Hmm, maybe the kids could be in bed, with the parents having their feet up. Yeah, I'm sure they will be sitting down to a lazy dinner, supping wine and talking. They might even have invited some friends over for dinner. Yeah, best to be on the safe side. It wouldn't be good to disturb them seeing as we are under compliment being their guests. OK, first thing in the morning, around nine, I can let them know when to expect me. Good, that's that worked out! But the best thing about this is that the children will be having a great time. They won't pause to feel deprived about not having had me around. Poor things, they are very good; there was not one word of complaint out of them. On second thought, maybe the little worms are happy to see the back of me! Good, break for me!

Right, first things first – something to eat, I thought, racing around the side of the house, then pushing in the kitchen door. Oh! They took Minnie! No wonder the house is so quiet. No company, so it's just me and me on me own. I should have known – small and all as she is, you would hear that bark a mile down the road. The kids think she looks and acts like me – noisy and all hair! I switched on the light and two came on. One over the Aga and the other one lighting up the breakfast area. OK! What's there to eat?

Talking about that, it's just hit me! Why the hell did I go beetling off, tearing around the supermarket like a blue-arse fly with the kids racing up behind me doing a weekly shop if we were going away? I was wondering why the kids were so keen to know what we were going to do with all the shopping, especially when they kept saying, 'Mamma, are we bringing this to Wexford?'

'Yes, darling!'

'Are we bringing that to Wexford?'

'Oh, yes! Of course, and that.'

I knew we were going, but I never made the connection between the two. I must have been thinking it was . . . Who the hell cares? I'm a right eegit. I certainly wouldn't be doing my weekly shop to take down to the Wallaces'! They would think I'm odd, turning up with grub. They don't need it. If I had their money, I could burn me own.

Anyway, they eat rubbish, chickens stuffed with blue cheese – it smells like a dirty rag! Reminds me of the pissy smell meself and Charlie used to get off ourselves when we were kids after pissing the bed. No, thanks, I will just have to starve and enjoy the fresh air. So what planet was I on? Never mind, the food won't go off. Lovely, so now I can have me pick – something fast, though. I'm not in the mood to start cooking up a dinner now. Then I will have a quick shower and hop into bed with a good book. What's to read? Something light – a book by Franz Kafka, *The Trial*. Light, me arse. Forget that! He would put years on you. Mind you, I love using that word. 'It is sooo Kafkaesque!' It's handy when you meet some gobshite who thinks they're Einstein, dazzling you with their genius or, worse, the snobs! Out comes me, 'It's soooo Kafkaesque.' That gets the grin wiped off their chops!

I stood up, wondering where all this was coming from. Snobs! What about them? Hmm, I think I'm a bit nervous about hanging around for a few days with the Wallaces. It's not them; it's their bleedin friends. When they start, I'm bound to say something . . . off-putting!

'*Love your dress, dawling!*'

'*Yeah, bought it in Oxfam!*'

'*Owh! How lovely. I must do my little bit too, send them some donation!*'

Then they waft off looking for someone normal. Some brilliant, intelligent, sparkling wit and upper crust like themselves, they think. Jaysus, I never know who I'm going to become around that lot! I could be Missus Bucket . . . '*Bouquet, darling. It is pronounced Bouquet!*' she snorts.

'*You speak so beautifully, Martha! Where did you go to school?*'

'*Eh! The Rutland.*'

Blank look then a huge smile. '*Oh, really! Was that the famous public school?*'

'*Oh, yeah, definitely. It was very public!*' I drone, thinking, so public the ma's and grannies could see us clawing at the windows, banging, hammering and screaming to be let out. They locked the doors to stop us escaping back to Summerhill, Sheriff Street, Sean McDermot Street and all the surrounding boltholes.

'*Oh, was it a classical school?*'

'*Oh, indeed, very classic! In vino veritas,*' I lisp, waving the glass, slurping on the wine.

'*Hmm,*' then they wander off, delighted by the high circles they are now moving in after meeting me. Their aim of the game is to develop a network of powerful, influential friends. Help them get on in business, get their children into the best schools. Keep it in the club, darling! Keep it in the club, old boy, is the motto.

Fuck, I don't really need them. But the kids . . . These are the parents of the children that mine are now growing up with. This is their world. If this is the best it has to offer, so be it. Me? I'm wasted on these people. I should have been an actress. Jaysus, I could be running off with all the Oscars! Still, the Wallaces' crowd are great for a laugh. They're all legal eagles. She's a solicitor and he's a tribunal lawyer. That's the latest jackpot to hit the country for that brigade. He's charming, polite, but has nothing to say unless you're in the business. He and the cronies sit huddled in a corner, plotting their latest wheeze on how to fist a few more millions out of the country. That's each, mind! There must be dozens of them. At the minute he's up in the tribunals court, strutting his stuff as a tribunal barrister. All the bent politicians are getting stretched on the rack.

I turned up one day to watch Harold doing his stuff. Antonia got Harold to squeeze me in. Packed tight I was, sandwiched in among the solicitors and their huge bags. They were the donkeys carrying all the papers for their tribunal barristers. Otherwise I would have had to be there at the crack of dawn to get a seat. The place was jampacked – the world and his wife turned up for the entertainment. I enjoyed meself no end. Everyone had the same idea – we all brought sandwiches and flasks of tea, then sat out on the lawn enjoying it during the lunch interval while the millionaire lawyers went off to the pub for their nosh. We did that as none of us wanted to lose our seats, because as soon as we were all sandwiched back in, the doors were slammed shut and locked. Then they posted a big red-necked copper to stand at the door and keep order. One old man came rushing in from the toilet nearly having a coronary when he saw the doors getting slammed just as he was hobbling to the door. Jaysus, there was ructions! He nearly took the door off its hinges. The copper let him in, asking, 'Is that a gun you have there or are you just happy to see me?'

We all looked down seeing he hadn't zipped up his fly! Oh, the craic was mighty! Then we all went quiet as proceedings began.

'Ah, Minister! Do you recall . . .?' Look down at notes. 'Yes, Mister X – we can't name him for legal reasons, m'lud.' He bows to the judge (he's doing the *Times* crossword puzzle under the bench!). 'As we speak, he is presently attempting to get the high court to stop this tribunal from investigating his part in this affair.'

'OBJECTION, M'LUD! PRESUMPTION OF GUILT BY ASSOCIATION ON THE PART OF MY CLIENT, M'LUD!' screams his pal for the other side, dancing to his feet, slapping out the tails of his black gown.

Silence while the judge wakes up.

'So, I may continue, m'lud?'

'What?! . . . Oh, yes, carry on!'

'Minister, as I was saying, do you recall Mister X handing you a brown-paper bag containing seventy-five thousand pounds in cash, in the car park at the back of Dirty Nelly's pub on Saturday the twenty-fifth of July, nineteen seventy-five?'

'I do not! I never saw dhat fella in me life! Is he a constituent of mine? I do favours for all sorts and class a people! I get paid for it – it's me job! I'm a busy man. I meet oceans of people! I'm a minister, a TD, I'm on the board of rakes a things! The bank board, the golden circle board, building society board – I'm chairman a that! I'm on more boards an collect more money than you've had hot dinners!' he splutters, forgetting this is not free speech. In this place he's not under the protection of the Dail Chamber.

'Yes, I would not doubt that, Minister,' bows the barrister, looking around to the packed gallery for applause.

They're staring with the mouth open, drinking in every word. Then it hits them – they're getting a look-in, so they play it to the hilt. There's cheers, roars and rumbles as the creaking floorboards erupt with the stamping boots. He bows again, after milking them enough, and turns back. He's getting his cheers and claps all right! But who are they clapping for? The lot in the front look like a shower of culchies come up on the bus to support their pal, neighbour and minister all rolled in one. But, no, it's Joe public sitting behind them. They're here with the rotten tomatoes and eggs at the ready, waiting to see will the minister put his foot in his mouth again.

'I collect me pensions, me salaries! As I said, I do a job of work, I get paid for it! Sure, why wouldn't I?' he shouts. 'They give it to me in brown-paper bags, Oxo boxes, plastic carrier bags! I don't care how they pay me so long as I get me money for doing a favour . . . I mean a job of work! I'm entitled!' he shouts, banging his ham fist down on the judge's bench, making him shit himself with the sudden fright. He had just managed to work out a missing word that was killing him for the last hour!

'Minister! Contain yourself, please!' gasps the judge, staring down from under his bushy eyebrows, then dropping his magnifying glass. Where is it? He searches, groping around to dig himself under the bench. He needs that for the *Times* newspaper – very small print. He appears back up with the wig twisted. His clerk gives a point with the little pinky finger and dances the eyebrows up and down, trying to warn him. Then we're all ready and heads spin back to the minister.

'Sorry, your honour! But I'm a man of honour meself, as everyone can testify to that! I never took a bribe in me life,' he cries.

'You tell dhem, Mickey boy,' come the roars screaming from the gallery as the rowdy lot start banging and shouting.

'ORDER!' shouts the judge. 'I will clear the court if there is any more misconduct!' he snorts, glaring down red-faced at the shower of culchie rowdies, all sniffing and shuffling, mumbling about Dublin cowboys.

'Continue, Minister,' he then says quietly, looking at the crying minister wiping his snots in a big red hankie he shakes and flops around the place, then shoves it back in the top pocket of his Armani suit.

'No! I have no recollection of been handed any brown-paper bag,' he sniffs tragically, speaking gravely and quietly. 'I wouldn't even have a mature recollection about it if I was to recollect about it till the cows came home!'

'But, Minister! Did you not just tell this court . . . Please allow . . . if I may beg the court's indulgence,' the tormenting barrister mutters, searching for that bit written down on his notes.

He can't find it! The court goes quiet, leaving room for the coughing, scratching, quick rub at the nose, then we all watch as he turns to his junior barrister, who turns to his assistant, then he turns to a solicitor, who turns to his assistant! A big sigh of relief when they finally find that missing damning bit of admission.

The judge mutters something to his clerk. He nods and stands. 'WE WILL RECESS FOR LUNCH! COURT WILL RESUME AT TWO-THIRTY!'

The judge happily agrees, banging his gavel. He's now fully awake, delighted at the thought of escaping for a long lunch and an even longer cool drink to quench his thirst. He needs that after rooting through all them dusty affidavits! Or he would have been perusing the affidavits if he didn't have to do the *Times* crossword puzzle first!

Right, best foot forward for the kids. Behave yourself when you get there, Martha! Now, get moving. I moved fast for the fridge, opening it and bending down, me eyes scanning up and around. 'Chicken – smashing. That's cooked. They must have had that for their lunch. They even left a bit of breast. What else? Eggs, cheese, ham . . . Yep! Just what the doctor ordered,' I hummed, bending down and grabbing the lot.

OK, it's toast and chicken, with a bit of melted cheese on the toast, even a poached egg, and I know I have some spinach. Don't be ridiculous! It's not eggs benedict you're making. It's . . . I lost track of me first exciting idea. Yeah! Hot chicken sandwich, then a toasted one with melted cheese and a poached egg on top with a bit of mayonnaise for extra flavour. How about a can of Baxter's chicken soup with a little cream . . . no! A lot of cream! Right, get going.

I was just taking the bread out of the toaster when the phone started shrilling, demanding my instant attention. Ahh! For the love a gawd! Is there no peace for the wicked? No! No phone calls tonight. I am going to sit and eat in peace.

I ignored it, letting it ring, and continued eating my grub, feeling it stick in my gut. My stomach was going rigid and I couldn't let go of me breath. It was the listening to it ringing, demanding I answer forthwith, or else you will wonder for the rest of your life . . .

I jumped up, reaching for it just as it stopped ringing. Fuck! Who was that? Now you'll be left wondering, I thought, getting a picture of what I might have missed.

'Hello! Can I speak to Martha Long?'

'Speaking!'

'Are you the daughter of Sally Long?'

'*Who is this?*'

'*I am Joe Soft, of "Soft As Grease Ball", attorney at law here in Dallas, Texas. We are trying to find the heirs to the estate of one Joseph Malcolm Rich Long, late deceased of Dallas, Texas, and Dublin, Ireland. We believe he has two heirs, a mother and daughter.*'

'*Oh!*' I gasp, holding me breath.

'*Are you Martha Long, born yakety-yak in the city of Dublin?*'

'*I am!*' I nod, eyes bulging, ears flapping.

'*Are you the daughter of Sally Long?*'

'*I am,*' gasping to get it out.

'*Well, Martha! You and your mother are the inheritors of a multimillion-dollar estate. Now, according to our records here, he met your sweet dear mother . . . Is she still alive, by the way?*'

'*Yes,*' I croak, giving the ear a quick poke to hear better, then settle meself down for the good news.

'*Well, Martha! It seems the deceased came over here from the old sod, back home. But first I think you want to hear how you both came to be his heirs!*'

'*Well! Not . . .*' is all I could get out before he rushes on.

'*Now I can tell you. Well, he came over here back in nineteen hundred and blot. He went west! Got there before the land rush took off again – in ahead of the posse, you might say he was! Staked his claim, bought a couple of hundred acres of land – turned out to be worth its weight in gold nuggets. Sold out and came on down to Texas. Here he bought shares in oil fields, then made a takeover when shares were dropping – took 'em over he did! Lock, stock and caboodle. Yes, sireee! The rest is history. He made J.D. Rockefeller look like a pauper! Then he disappeared – nobody knew where he'd gone! Just up and vanished, leaving behind a multimillion-dollar industry that carried on without him. It ran like oil-greased wheels, you might say!*

'*Then, some time around the nineteen-fifties mark, he turned up in Dublin and wandered around that city like a lost soul. Then, here it comes! He was no destitute, but he was living like one when he met your mother. I think all the big business lost its draw for him. He just up and quit, deciding money had no further value for him. He couldn't spend it even if he wanted to – there was just too much of it! We have been searching for you, going on . . . ohh, nigh on fifteen years, ever since his death! You and your mother are the sole heirs, Martha, to forty billion, nineteen hundred million, seventeen thousand and fifty-seven dollars and twenty-one cents, give or take a few million. The clock keeps ticking on the interest, Martha! Every day that passes, you are both one hundred thousand dollars richer!'*

Then I ask, *'But who was this man? How did he know me?'*

'Oh, well, Martha, that's an easy question to answer. He was your father! We now have your whole history, I would say. So, we will need you to answer these questions, just to be doubly sure you are the person we are seeking, then with clarification of both your identities we can get the ball rolling.

'Now, so far we have established you have the right name, date and place of birth.'

'Yes,' I nod.

'Now your mother is Sally Long, maiden name Sally Josephine Patricia Harrison, born in the city of Cork in nineteen blot. Married in Cork City, nineteen . . .'

'No, me ma is not married,' I interrupt. *'She's from Dublin and her maiden name is Long,'* I say, with my mind crashing and me heart stopping. *'Hello! Are you there?'* I shout into the silence, hearing a barely audible, *'Oh . . .'*

I listen to the long pause, then croak. *'Does that mean I'm not going to get the money?'* I say, hoping I might be wrong.

'That is correct, ma'am. Afraid the search goes on,' he moans, sounding as disappointed as meself.

'But can we still not get the money if he's a Long? We must be related!' I croak, desperate not to let go. The phone goes dead, leaving only the dialling tone.

I blinked, coming back to me chicken sandwich! I stared at it, suddenly not feeling very hungry. Yeah, very funny, Martha! Where did that come out of? I haven't thought like that since I was a young child. No, not since then have I wondered who my father was. I accepted the ma was never going to tell me. So, suddenly why now? I suppose I'm feeling back in the thick of it. The same old ma, same old problems, then facing into Jackser.

It shook me today, I think, sitting in the car talking to Charlie. I was back at them steps where Jackser first sat and met the ma. I could taste the stale chunk of bread and feel the burning hot tea in the tin mug. I looked up, moaning in a whisper, '*I'm thirsty! I want me own bread an tea, Ma. Where's mine?*'

'*They didn't give anythin fer you,*' she said, looking back at the queue slowly making its way towards the hatch.

'*Here, take the rest a me bread,*' she said, trying to sup on the boiling tea as the shouts went up to get moving out – they are locking the doors.

I was smelling, tasting and breathing in that very same air again. I was one of the desperate homeless drunks with the lost, lonely, hopeless look on their face. I was them, looking out at the respectable woman sitting in her big car, but she was from a world that had passed me by. It was like seeing her through a big thick pane of glass window. I am on the outside, only looking in. I felt empty for Charlie, sitting in the seat beside me. I felt a rage with him. I was frustrated I couldn't get him out and away from that homeless place. No, he got left behind, now he is forever trapped there.

The ma had an opportunity today, but she turned her back on him. There he was, waiting patiently for her and me to turn up and everything seems grand. She lets him come home with her, thinking he was welcome, then treats him like dirt when the other one shows up. I saw the way she gave that devious, malicious look at me and Charlie when they were talking behind our back. It was like she knew she had the power to hurt us and it gave her an evil sense of satisfaction. Yeah! She knew what she was doing all right. But she doesn't connect to us as being feeling human beings. I think the silly bitch blames us for being in her way – we caused all her problems. Even with Jackser – we were his weapon to use against her, the evidence she had been leading the life of a whore in his eyes, and hers. So she blamed us for letting out her secrets.

Right, I'm not letting her upset me. So, she thinks she can control me? We will see. She knows she can't control Charlie – he never let her. He took away her power by seeing her for what she was, then blanking her. No wonder she hates him! She's the kind who uses any tenderness you give her as a weapon to hurt you. Worse, she let him walk out that door on an empty belly after me buying all that fucking food. Jesus, she could have called him back. I know he was hurt, but it was so deep he just fell into apathy. He just shrugged, like he couldn't feel it any more. That was fucking cruel! Normally, I take her behaviour as I find her, but she's overstepped the mark this time. I think she may now have lost an opportunity with me too.

Right, eat up, have a quick shower, then get some sleep. I think that's exactly what I need now – just wash off the dust trying to settle in my head. I've had enough of the ma for one day.

I was just heading up the stairs after tidying the kitchen when the phone rang again. I paused, listening to it, hesitating – no! Get down fast and find out who it is this time. It has to be important – they have rung back.

I tore into the kitchen, grabbing it up before it stopped. 'Hello!' I gasped, hearing a sudden intake of breath, then the voice spoke.

'Hello, this is Hector, the undertaker. Look, I have been trying to contact you. I do apologise for disturbing you this time of night. In fact, I was trying to get you earlier.'

'Oh, yes, I am not too long in, Hector,' I said, wondering what the problem could be.

'Well, early on in the evening I had a phone call from your mother. She asked for more cars. I asked how many people she needed to organise. She wasn't sure, but she insisted on two more cars. I thought it best to put you in the picture, as you are both dealing with the arrangements.'

'Yes! You are right. Thanks for ringing me, Hector. But . . . She did say two more cars?'

'Yes, that is what she asked for.'

'Listen, Hector. I think it best you stick to our original plan – one car for the family is enough. I will discuss this with my mother. But I don't think you need bother yourself further with this. You can take it that nothing has changed.'

'Very good,' he said, sounding polite, but knowing this is par for the course. Family politics! Rows nearly always break out at family events, especially when there is emotion involved. Christmas, weddings, christenings and, of course, the funerals. There's bound to be a bit of bother. So, he is obviously experienced. He knows the ma can't afford it. He wanted to check where the money was coming from.

'OK, I'll wish you goodnight. Sorry again to disturb.'

'Oh, no problem, Hector!' I said, liking the idea of his name rolling off my tongue. 'Thank you again for letting me know.'

'OK, bye bye,' he said.

'Thank you once again. Goodnight!' I said.

I put the phone down, blowing air out through my cheeks. The ma would put years on you. What's she up to now? Three cars – for who? I suppose I better give her a quick ring and sort it out. Otherwise, she could end up getting upset in the morning, then drive herself and everyone around her mad. She gets like that. No matter what I ever gave her in the past as a little kid, she would not be satisfied.

'But ye say they had this! An tha as well! So why did ye not go an get it for me, Martha?' she would wail, sounding and looking like she was going to lose the mind. Then she would keep on and on until something else came along. I recognise it now as sheer greed. But at the bottom of it is really a more serious problem, I thought, thinking about it. She expects someone to fill up the insides of her, where she has nothing but emptiness. It seems the ma is like a bucket with a bleedin hole in it. The more you put in, the faster it runs out and the more miserable she gets! Nobody can fill up that emptiness she carries. It has to come from herself; material things will never do it.

25

Right! Get it over with. I don't want trouble.

I rang the number, hearing it ring for the first time. Jaysus! Imagine the ma having a telephone. Jackser must have got that in. Hmm, he sure was getting himself all sorted. I know one thing, he would never have done to Charlie what me ma did to him tonight. No, he was more fair than that. Incredible! I never saw any of the good things about him before. I was always too busy seeing how incredibly demanding and vicious he was. The positive things he did passed me by. I was too busy thinking of the poor ma. If I turned up at the door, she would never answer. She would always shout through the door, 'Who is it?'

'It's me, Ma, Martha. Will you open the door ma and let me in?'

'Ahh, I'm goin out', or 'Ahh! I'm in me bed. I'm not well. I can't let ye in.'

That would be the end of it. I used to go away thinking it was Jackser – he wouldn't let her open the door. 'No,' Charlie used to say, 'it's the opposite. If he's there an he hears ye knocking, he will shout at the ma te open the door an let you in.'

I took no notice of that. I thought that was just Jackser being in one of his rare good moods. It seems I was wrong – got it all arse ways.

'Hello!' a little voice said, sounding very cautious.

'Ma! It's me.'

'Who's this?'

'It's Martha, Ma!'

'Oh, it's you! Wha do ye want? I'm just goin te me bed. I haven't got time te talk te you.'

'Yeah, OK. I won't keep you. I know it's late. Listen, Ma, the undertaker says you were on looking for another car! Sure, we don't need another car, Ma. One is enough.'

'No! I'm gettin wha I want. It's nothin te do wit you! An ye needn't think ye're comin in tha car, you or any a yours!'

'What do you mean, Ma? Sure, I know that.'

'Tha car is only fer me an my family!'

'I know, Ma. Sure, that's what we agreed. It's only for you and Dinah and Gerry and Sally. Just the immediate family.'

'Well! You're not comin in it! An I don't want them kids a yours comin neither! I have enough wit me own family.'

'What, Ma?! You don't want me to bring the children? Sure! Why would I do that? They don't know you, Ma.'

'Yeah! An tha suits me. Tha's the way I want it te stay!'

'OK! Don't worry yourself, Ma. I won't be bringing them next or near you anyway,' I said, feeling her words cutting right through me.

Even though they had never met her, I still had hopes she would be a part of my life now that Jackser was gone. I thought somehow things would be different. Still, she's just upset.

'Listen, Ma . . .'

'No! You listen te me. You're interferin too much, ye're takin over! Like I said, ye're not comin wit me in tha car. I want only me family in tha car wit me.'

'Yeah, Ma. Will you please listen? I told you – sure, I have my own car and I can take Charlie with me, or if someone else wants a lift I have plenty of room.'

'No! I told ye! I'm sortin things out meself. You shouldn't have been takin over an interferin in the first place! Who put you in charge? Sure, you're not family!'

'What do you mean, Ma?' I said slowly, feeling me heart begin to race.

'You're not one a them! You're not belongin te Jackser. You an tha other fella have nothin te do wit this family.'

I could feel myself going rigid and my whole body tensed as I let what she just said sink in. She sounded so distant, like she was angry with a stranger. There was no feeling there for me. I had nothing to do with her. Suddenly a red-hot fire of rage shot up through me. I exploded.

'So! Who am I? Your bloody social worker? I'm not your social worker, or your mother. I'm your fucking daughter! You're supposed to be my mother.'

'Yeah! So ye say,' she said, sounding very cold.

'So! You're denying even that? Of course you bloody are! It never once in yer bleedin life dawned on you that I was the fucking child. Oh, no! You were too fucking busy getting me to mind you. You were too fucking busy letting yourself and Jackser send me out to rob! Week after week I went, and I brought you home the money and the food and anything else I could get me hands on to feed you fucking two and your poor starved kids.

'You fucking bastard! You no-good bitch! You whore! Do you know what you really are? You are a prostitute! No! Wait a minute – that's too good for the like a you! A prostitute sells it for money! You couldn't even do that much. Oh, no! You have to give it away for nothing. A prostitute? A real mother would have sold herself for money to feed her starving children. You fucking dumped us – on that ship, in that little sitting area, when I was only five years old. You went off and left your little baby and me while you fucked your way across the Irish Sea, earning your passage with the fucking sailors!

'We were left tired, hungry and thirsty, and the baby crying all night with me sitting terrified, holding onta him. People sat and watched us, Ma! But then they just turned away. They thought we weren't worth bothering about. Why? Because they knew! We were nobody's bastards. We were only the scrapings of the mother that came in with the sailor. That was you! You did that! Then fucked off and left us. I watched that door from the minute you walked in and dumped us there, then walked straight back out again with that fucking sailor who told you where to dump us. I didn't even see you the next morning when the ship docked in Liverpool! Everyone had left the ship. They walked off turning their backs on us! We weren't worth even the cost of a few minutes outa someone's time. No! We weren't. We were the only two left, fucking abandoned. It took me to start screaming! Running around that ship hysterical, I was. We had lost the only one in the world we knew. Frightened outa me heart I was, for meself and me little baby brother, before that man sweeping the floor went off to find you! The fucking ship had docked, Ma! The passengers were all gone! Long bloody gone! You were still getting fucking screwed!

'YOU'RE THE WORST WHORE'S MELT THAT EVER WALKED ON GOD'S EARTH!' I screamed, right at the top of my lungs with the rage and the tears and the horrible uselessness of it! The whole God-awful life I had wasted on her! 'Do you know? Harry killed himself to get away from you! Yeah, he damned took himself off up to the highest balcony and threw himself off, killed himself, Ma! Just to escape you, to get away from you. Teddy is missing! He ran and he hasn't been seen since. Just to get away from you. Some of them have driven themselves mad just to get away from you! Charlie is drinking himself to death on the streets because of you! So, you want your family around you at the funeral? So have them, so. What?! Because I am not belonging to Jackser, that means I'm nothing to you? Right! So have your fucking car to yourself. I was only trying to help you. I put myself out for you! I have done it all my life. I got locked up in a convent because of you.

'So now you can get on without me. Call yourself a fucking mother? No, you are right! You are not my mother. You never were my mother. You don't know what the damned meaning of the word is. You think I was born for your convenience? So! Fuck off. This is the last time you will ever hear from me again! As far as I am concerned, you don't exist. Goodbye!'

Then I slammed down the phone, seeing different colour stars with my head spinning and me heart threatening to burst with the rage. I had just gotten a terrible insight into the ma. It was her! Her all along! She had hidden her madness and badness behind Jackser all the time! She had escaped for so long. Never had I directed any blame, any wrong, in her direction.

I got pictures of her come flying at me, seeing her looking at me with her cold marble eyes. Then a picture flashes across my mind. It is me looking at myself. I am standing in front of the fireplace. I must be heading on for ten years old. I am naked except for an old frock covering me. It's lightweight, only a summer frock black with the dirt. But it could be winter because I'm trying to warm meself, standing next to the fire. Jackser is sitting on the chair beside the fire, smoking his Woodbine cigarette butt. Then the ma starts laughing, grabbing at me frock, trying to pull it up. She giggles, with a high-pitched laugh, saying, '*Ooooo! Ha, ha! She's wearin nothin underneath tha aul frock!*'

I grabbed my frock with the sudden shock and fright, saying, '*Ma! Ma, leave me frock alone. Don't be doin tha te me!*'

Then she steps back, looking and pointing at me with her finger, losing her breath in the back of her throat, making her face go red. Then she finds her breath and starts saying, like I am the one doing something wrong, '*Ohhh! She's not wearin any knickers.*' Then she darts in again, grabbing, while I try to hold on to my frock, nearly crying. But before I can escape, I can see Jackser's eyes going red with the lust and he says, '*Go on, Sally. Go on, do it again!*', pointing with his finger towards me frock.

She makes a sudden grab and manages to get my frock up, exposing me completely.

It was after that he had no problem raping me whether she was around or not. Because his rotten secret was now out in the open. She had given him permission to do something he was doing anyway. I sensed now she wanted to make a gift of me to him; she wanted some of that lust it would bring out in him for herself. She needed him to feed her a bit of passion. She wanted to feel like a woman; she wanted him to make her feel she was still alive. For that, I would do the job nicely. Nothing and nobody came in the way of her getting her needs fulfilled. She was the child I minded. He told her what to do. The kids were rearing themselves, or at least I was looking after them. The only reality existed was her own self – everyone around her was just 'things'. Not real. They were there to give comfort, like a kettle will boil water to give you a nice cup of tea. That was us!

I felt then suddenly sucked into their world of madness and private things that belong only to them as men and women. I had most evilly and grotesquely been plucked from being the child I was into their grown-up world. Forced to live with something dark, vile and alien, an unholy world, no place for the shining, innocent beauty of childhood. She took it all away. She had made me become just like her. She was telling me I was no longer a child. I was to stand side by side with her, be the toy in the middle between her and Jackser. She was not going to be my mammy any more. I was now to help her keep Jackser happy with his lust – be his wife, so she can get some of that too. She would do anything to keep Jackser happy. If he is happy, he will make her happy. I didn't understand any of it. I just felt sick. I sensed then what I know now, but I had to blank it out. As soon as the nausea passed, and the terrible pain of knowing me ma doesn't want me – she's thrown me away and turned her back on me – when the fright and fear had slowed down to a terrible empty ache, I forgot it ever happened and carried on loving her like I had always done. I had no one else in the world I could call my own. I needed to believe I belonged to her. She was me mammy. What happened to me is just the way of the world. You live with what you have. There was no other way to cut myself off from believing I was totally alone in the world. That would be more unbearable than what had just happened. I thought like a child – I was a child. Children all have mothers – they have to belong to somebody. I had somebody – I had a ma. I had to believe that.

This had all laid buried until now! Suddenly the floodgates were opening – all my nightmares were tearing out of the darkness and roaring at me!

I made a dive for the stairs but tripped and felt a distant burning pain in my knee. I couldn't get a breath with my mouth wide open. I can't see where I'm going. I gasped for air and hot salty water gushed into my mouth, getting caught in a bubble. It's the blinding tears flooding out of my eyes and down my face. I didn't know I was crying. I wiped my eyes with the arm of me shirt and kept running. I tore up the stairs heading for my bedroom, then staggered into the shower. I need to get clean! I need a drink. I need someone to tell me I am worth loving! I need . . . 'God! Hear my prayer! Give me peace,' I screamed, dropping on my bended knees and screaming up at the heavens.

I came down the stairs wrapped in a warm winter dressing gown, wearing cotton pyjamas and soft slippers on my feet. I felt calmer after having the shower – fresh and clean. But I could feel myself icy cold inside. I need something to heat me up, I thought, heading into the kitchen. My eyes lit on the tin of hot chocolate sitting on the open shelf – that will do. I'll have some of that. Normally I keep this only for the children. I took out a little saucepan and poured in milk, then set it on the cooker to boil. The Aga is kept at a very low heat for the summer, but it gives gallons of hot water. I lifted up the saucepan, seeing the milk froth to the boil, and stirred in the chocolate, pouring it into a mug, then took meself over and sat at the kitchen table. I sipped at the chocolate, letting the sweet hot taste bring a bit of life back into me. I could still feel myself icy cold, even though I stayed for what seemed like hours under the shower. Oh, this is better, I thought, gripping hold of the mug in two hands, then lit up a smoke and stared out into the garden. I stayed that way, hearing my breathing beginning to slow down and feeling my heart ticking away, getting more gentle. I could feel a calm coming over me now as I listened to the sounds of the warm, dark summer night, bringing with it the scent of the lemon trees just outside the open kitchen window.

I knew I was now light years away from them terrible times, but I felt like I had been transported back there again and ended up in the middle of an earthquake. It's only now I've just escaped, because I'm still feeling the ripples of the tremors rumbling all the way down to the core of me. Yes, but I know I'm safe. I am back home now in my warm, clean kitchen, with the yellow glow from an old ship's copper lantern throwing out a gentle golden light. It stands in its own place where it belongs, where it has found a home, sitting on the old pine fiddle-front dresser that has seen more life than I ever lived. I feel comforted by that, surrounded by old things that have survived the ravages of time. I like to rescue them, let them share my space and make a safe haven for me and mine. I need that comfort right now.

I feel myself in shock, confused. What happened? How did I arrive at this, end up turning against the ma? From where and why did that awful memory just arrive like a bolt of lightning? I never saw any of this coming. Then it really hit me! Jesus, you have forgiven Jackser, made your peace with him and yourself, then ironically turned against the ma. I could and can forgive anything – it is better to let go. But first I need to understand what it is, or was, all about. I reached that with Jackser. His intent was never malicious; he acted on emotion – anger mostly, driven by madness.

The ma seemed to channel her anger through hate. It was deliberate, it was calculating. She was not giving way to a surge of emotional anger. No! It is psychotic, insanity, a person who enjoys causing intense suffering to someone they can control. That is the Sally I saw today – watching us with a malevolent glint of power and excitement in those icy-cold blue eyes. No, Jackser did not deliberately set out to cause pain; he just did. It was all through his madness. Besides, he was not my flesh and blood; Sally was. She may be crazy, but she deliberately put us in harm's way, knowing what she was doing. She used us both from birth, Charlie and me. She dragged us with her intentionally. We were money in her pocket and could be used to pave the way for her to get her what she wanted.

I feel nothing after saying all those things to her earlier this night. It will not cost me a thought. I feel no remorse; I feel nothing for her. Yes, the ma is completely disassociated from reality. That is what made her what she was, I think – a stone mother. Charlie and me would have been safer and warmer if we had sat clinging and hugging the statue of a woman. At least it wouldn't have done us any harm. Come to think about it, we never did hug her or cling to her! So the statue was definitely a better bet!

I didn't go to the funeral this morning. It did cross my mind that Jackser was being buried so maybe I should go along and just watch him being lowered into the ground. I could watch from a distance. For one last time I could see him being taken from this world and put into the earth, taking with him all the fears, tears and the terrible pain he had once caused to a little waif. But then I thought, no! I don't feel the need to see him laid into his grave. I had travelled enough miles with him searching to find the answers when I had sat through the last agonised days and nights of his life. I know now and understand where he had been coming from. I had found the answer. No, let it rest now. Enough is enough. One day I will have to face into all of this and then the child in me will burst back into life. Jesus, it will then be an all-out battle cry once she is let loose.

This morning, I listened to a little voice inside my head saying, 'You are kicking her when she is down, when she needs you the most.'

Yes, I am. So be it. I am clearly no loss to her, so what is there to kick? She would take what I have to offer her then have no use for me. As she said, I am not belonging to her. She feels she has nothing to do with me. Amen for that mercy. Anyway, be grateful for an even bigger mercy. Jackser is now gone – the two together were pure evil.

Oh, you were so right all along, Charlie. How very astute you were. You knew I was an eegit, because with me she got away with murder. Bloody hell, there is none so blind, Martha, than you who would not see that Sally was the real bogeyman, she was every child's worst nightmare. A 'She Devil' wrapped in a mother's cloak.

26

I turned the book over, setting it down on the little table beside the couch. Gawd, the house is very quiet. I don't know if that is a good or bad thing. 'Oh, I'm bored,' I sighed, listening to the silence in the empty house. That will teach you, Martha Long! You couldn't wait to get them out the door. I thought it was a bleedin great idea at first, having the kids away for the weekend. Now I'm left with an empty nest. They are gone off camping with the Scouts and Guides. I wonder how they're getting on? Let's hope it doesn't rain! Still, they will be able to spend the night in the youth hostel. Jaysus! The excitement was mighty, and the amount of stuff they took! Bloody hell! I'm sure they didn't need a quarter of it. Still, if it keeps them happy. But I did try putting half of it back. 'No! It's on the list,' the little man kept ordering. 'Please put it back,' he would say, looking up from his list while the sister did the fussing and packing and . . . Oh, gawd! Yeah! Maybe the quiet is better after all.

Right! Where's that list of things need doing? On second thoughts forget the list. Take advantage of the freedom, Martha. Right! Do what? Go where? Ring Vivienne! You owe her a lunch! No! Maybe another time. I'm not in the mood.

I picked up the book again, thinking, I'm sure there's a pile of ironing waiting to be done. Forget it, no chance! I flicked back to my page, reading, then slammed it back on the table. I watched it clatter to the floor then stared down at it. Tut, tut – very bad! I'm usually careful with books if they are well written, but that's a load of rubbish! I used to think that fella could write, but these days . . .

Suddenly the feeling in me belly grew. There was something I really wanted to do, but I wouldn't even let the thought surface. Now it was coming anyway. Ring the ma! See how she is. Go on! Too much time has passed. You had your say. You left her high and dry with the funeral. You let her have the full whack of your wrath, now you know where you stand with each other. Go on! Find out what's she up to. You never know! She might have changed. Maybe she's a bit more human now. You might even be able to have a conversation with her. No! What if she doesn't want to talk to me? Then your illusions will be gone. What illusions? I don't know. Maybe we will, eh? Ah, go on! You know you want to. Give her a ring!

I suddenly stood up and grabbed for the phone. I searched my finger up and down the little phone book, having the book already open at the page. My finger landed on the name and phone number. I stared for a minute, then dialled the number, feeling my heart start to race, while me mind went blank. I listened to it ring out, then a familiar little voice said, 'Hello!'

I said nothing for a minute, holding my breath, listening to that sound, but my voice wouldn't come. Then I croaked, 'Hello!'

Cough. 'Hello!' I tried to say in a firmer, more matter-of-fact voice. It came out in a high-pitched squeak. 'Ma!' Pause. 'It's me!' Pause. 'Martha!' I said, making it sound like a threat coming from a rumble in my belly!

There was an almighty silence on the other end. I could hear the shock of lightning rattling itself right through her, shaking the life force out of her. Now it hung deadly quiet in the silence. It sounded like just before the next roll of roaring thunderclaps. I listened, holding my breath. She's going to hang up. She's not going to speak to me. Too much has happened, too much time has passed – three years is a long time!

'Ma!' I suddenly said quietly but firmly. 'Don't hang up! Please don't hang up, because if you do, I will never ring again. I just want to say something.'

'I'm listenin,' the voice said, speaking quietly and coldly, just as firmly as I had.

'Ma! I think it is time we met up and had a talk. We can do that. It won't cost us anything. You have nothing to lose and neither do I. But I think it is a good idea.'

'When?' she said. 'When are you thinkin? You can come over in a couple of hours, just give me a bit of time.'

'Say . . .' I said, looking through the door into the dining room, seeing the big old clock ticking away on a marble fireplace. 'I'll be over around twelve, will that suit you?'

'Yeah. Goodbye.' Then she hung up.

I held the phone, hearing the dialling tone, then put it slowly down, resting it gently in its cradle. So! I'm going to meet her! I thought about this for a minute, then flew to get meself ready. I hope she doesn't change her mind and not answer the door, or rush off out somewhere seeing as she knows when to expect me. Well, if she does, so let her. As you told her, you have nothing to lose.

I turned the car into the old familiar flats. There was a different air about the place. It looked quieter somehow, and my eyes took in the long line of good cars. I pulled into a parking space where I could see up to the ma's kitchen window, then got out, slamming the door and locking it, letting my eyes scan along the block of flats. Get a load of that! Some of them have plants sitting on their window, if you wouldn't be minding. Oh, happy days! A bit of prosperity has come at long last. Then me eyes peeled up to the ma's. She has a bowl of plastic-looking roses sitting in the window! And new frilly net curtains looking very white. Jesus, Ma, things have changed for the better by the looks of it, I thought, then made for the stairs, holding a box of Dairy Milk chocolates under my arm – they were wrapped in a brown-paper bag.

I hit the ma's landing, seeing her waiting outside, looking over the balcony with the door wide open.

'There ye are! I was watchin out for ye. Ye're here!' she said, giving me a half-smile with her eyes lit up at the sight of me. She was a bit nervous, I could see. So am I! I would prefer this not to go wrong.

'Come on! Come on in,' she said, rushing ahead to hold the door, then shut it behind us. 'Did ye not bring the childre, Martha?' she said, looking disappointed, with her voice sounding the loss.

'No, they're away camping, Ma,' I said, thinking that is the last thing I would do.

'How are they? Gawd, they must be gettin very big be now?'

'Yeah, Ma. They won't let me wipe their snots any more!'

She laughed, saying, 'Come on, come inta the kitchen. Are ye hungry, Martha? I made us a bit a dinner.'

'You did, Ma?' I said, getting more than surprised with the shock! She cooked for me? Offering me something to eat and even waiting with the door open! Gawd, it looks like she is happy to see me.

I cleaned the plate, putting down my knife and fork, then licked my lips, looking at the empty plate. 'Gawd, Ma, that was lovely! Did you cook that yourself?'

'Of course I did!' she laughed, delighted I had enjoyed the fried fish with the mash potatoes and chopped-up raw scallions with a load of butter mashed through it. The carrots were cooked lovely and soft, with a really nice sweet taste to them.

'What did you put over the carrots, Ma?'

'Oh, them!' she said, looking and laughing. 'Orange juice stuff. Me an Dinah has tha. We saw them doin it on the television. Ye know, we do watch them cookin programmes. Dinah likes te try out the easy stuff.'

'Really, Ma? You're experimenting with the cooking, getting it all from the TV?'

'Oh, yeah! There does be lovely stuff they show ye how te cook!' she said, closing her eyes and nodding her head up and down.

I stared at her, seeing the massive difference. 'Gawd, Ma, you look great!' I said. 'You got your hair cut! And even dyed?' I said, looking at the light wispy hair framing her forehead and cut around her face in what looks like a long bob. It really suits her! I stared at the lovely cream blouse she was wearing with the lace collar, then down at the light grey skirt with a grey matching belt. She was even wearing nylons – well, tights, I suppose – and they stayed up on her.

'So, how have ye been, Martha? How are the kids gettin on? Would ye bring them this for me?' she said, getting up suddenly and rushing off down the hall, making for a bedroom. I could hear her grunting, sounding like she was stretching up for something, then the muffled sound of a thud as she jumped down. She must have been standing on a chair, probably getting up to reach inside the top of a wardrobe. Then I heard her coming fast up the hall.

'Here, Martha! Take these fer the kids,' she said, handing me a carrier bag from a big store.

I took the bag off her, looking in at the packages. They were all wrapped in Christmas paper. 'What's this, Ma?' I lifted me head, looking up at her in shock, trying to figure out why she had these for me.

'They're a few presents I bought fer the kids, an there's one in there fer yerself. Tha's the little one,' she said, pointing at the bottom of the bag I was still holding open, with me mouth not able to close. 'Ye can open them if ye want. It's a toy car – is he still playin wit them, Martha? I didn't know wha he would like at the time, but it's a good one. It runs by itself! It has a little box tha ye press. Now, I asked them in the shop at the time. They gave me the batteries an all, so it should be all right. I got the little one a Barbie doll; it's in a box. Now, there's a separate one wit all the stuff tha goes wit the doll. Then she has a white little dolly wardrobe to put the clothes in, Martha. I hope she likes it! Do ye think she will, Martha?' me ma said, creasing her face, staring at me with a worried look on her face.

'Oh, yeah! Oh, yeah, Ma. She loves them. She will go mad for that,' I said, nearly losing my voice. I just couldn't believe she was thinking about them.

'An as I said, there's one fer you. Go on! Here, let me get it fer ye,' she said, making a dive for the bag and shoving her head down.

'There ye are, that's fer you, Martha,' she said, handing me a little package that looked like a tiny box.

I opened it, saying, 'What is it, Ma?'

'Open it, go on! I'm waitin to see if ye like them!' she shouted, laughing at me and pointing at the box.

I opened the box, seeing a pair of pearl earrings. 'Oh, Ma! These are beautiful! Jesus, Ma, they came out of a jeweller's. They must have cost an arm and a leg!'

'Yeah, they were dear all right,' she said, staring at them, looking like she was thinking. 'Go on! Put them in an see wha ye look like.'

I pulled out the gold studs I've had in my ears since I was eighteen – a hundred years ago, I thought – and put in the pearls. They were a very pale pink, with gold backs. I always wanted pearls, but someone said it was bad luck to buy them for yourself. I didn't believe that rubbish and bought meself a pair anyway. Now I have these, they mean more to me. I can give the old ones to my daughter.

'Ohh! They look lovely. Come on down te the bedroom an take a look in the long wardrobe mirror,' she said, going ahead then waiting for me.

'Ma, they're lovely,' I said, seeing the classy look they gave to my face.

'Yeah! They suit you,' me ma said, standing back to examine me, keeping her eyes staring at my face.

'When did you get these Christmas presents, Ma?'

'Oh, they're there a few year now, Martha. I got them about two year ago, then when you never did show up Dinah said to leave them. You may turn up one day. They can sit there an wait for ye,' she said, looking at me with a sadness of great loss in her eyes, letting her voice drop.

I could feel my eyes suddenly burn and me chest swell up, then the tears rolled down me cheeks.

'Wha's wrong wit ye?' she said, seeing me turn my head, trying to wipe away the tears. 'Are ye all right? Wha's wrong wit ye?' she said, coming up behind me and leaning her head over me shoulder.

'I'm sorry, Ma,' I mumbled, trying to look at her. 'I said terrible things to you!' I whispered, suddenly getting the pain of how I must have hurt her.

'Ahh! Forget all about tha. Sure, we all say things. I was wrong meself,' she said. 'I didn't hold tha against you, Martha. You were right,' she whispered. 'You were right all along! I knew tha even at the time. I'm sorry. You were always very good te me. You were the last person I shoulda turned on, but I did,' she said, dropping her head, staring at the carpet.

Then the pair of us went quiet. 'Ma,' I said, looking at her.

'Wha?' she said, looking like she was thinking. Then she spoke quietly, looking at me with a sad, worried and even fearful look in her eyes as she let them stare at me. 'Can we let bygones be bygones?' she whispered, saying it slowly as she stared at me with a pained look in her eyes.

'Yeah,' I whispered, realising I had waited a lifetime for this moment. I had me ma back. 'Oh, Ma!' I said, putting my arms around her neck.

'Blood is thicker than water, Martha, no matter wha anyone says,' she said quietly. 'I lost me way. Me mind was never me own after I had you,' she whispered, lifting her eyes to rest them in the distance.

'Why, Ma?' I said. 'What happened?'

'Come on. Let's go in an get ourselves a cup a tea,' she said.

'Good idea,' I said, following her into the kitchen. I knew she might talk to me now.

'Here! Do ye want a few a them cream crackers?' she said, after pouring out the tea and I was putting sugar in mine. 'Come on, they're lovely, have some. I'll put a bit of butter on them, an ye can even put a lump a hard cheese on top. I like the hard stuff; it has the taste. Tha aul sliced stuff ye get tastes an looks like plastic. I don't like them at all,' she said, grabbing the packet of crackers and tearing the paper down the side to get at them. 'Ye can even have some a them salted ones. Here, taste! They're lovely,' she said, shoving a little yellow biscuit into my mouth.

I laughed, gripping it between my teeth. 'Hmm, yeah! I haven't had these Ritz ones in years, Ma.'

'You go on, have this plate,' she said, handing me a white side plate with four cream crackers and a lump of cheese. 'Here, take the knife an cut the cheese up,' she said, pointing at it.

'Not at all, Ma. I'll just slap it between the crackers,' then lit into it. She was right, the lump stuck up in the middle and I bit into it, opening me mouth wide, trying to get at the two of them stuck together, then started to choke.

'Take it easy!' she said, banging the back off me as crackers flew in all directions.

'Jaysus, Ma, give us a drink,' I croaked, grabbing at her tea. Mine was all gone.

'Are ye all right now?' she said, looking and laughing at me.

'Yeah,' I gasped, 'they were too dry.'

'Come on! Let's take the tea inta the sittin room. We can take our ease in there,' she said, going ahead with me at her heels.

I pulled over the big oak coffee table sitting in the middle of the room, bringing it in closer to the sofa, and rested down the plate.

'These are lovely,' she said, with the two of us looking at each other as we munched our way through the biscuits.

I lit up a smoke and sat back, saying, 'Tell us, Ma, what happened to you when you had me?'

Her face changed, then she dropped her eyes, staring at the rug under the coffee table. 'I better tell you this, Martha. It's been goin around in me head fer most a me life nearly. Wha happened te me came as a terrible shock. I was only fifteen at the time. Me mother an father was dead, an everyone had taken the boat te England. Me an the sister was the only ones left. Then when I was fourteen they came an got me; they brought me over. I was nearly the last a them. Ye see, the way it worked was this, Martha. The first one te get the money an make their way te England got themself a job, a place to stay, then saved wha they could. Then, when they got enough saved fer the ticket, they sent on the money fer the next one te come over. So, be the time they arrived, there was a bed waitin for them an a job to go straight inta. Then it went down the line – the next one savin to bring over the one after them. Till my turn arrived.

'I was livin in digs wit some a them; the others had moved on be this time. Well, a fella, I won't say no more, but I knew him well, only too well, Martha!' she said, looking up at me with a bitter look in her eyes. 'Anyway! He got his hands on me. He was drunk at the time. I was dragged up a laneway an left there. Afterwards, I was found screamin me head off; I went inta terrible shock. But worse was te come! I knew nothin about nothin at the time. None of us young ones did. Ye didn't know anythin till ye got yerself married, then ye found out quick enough. But anyway, just before I was even sixteen at the time, one a them suddenly brought me back here. Back to me home in the Liberties.

'Then one Sunday evenin the pains started. Nobody knew, or if they did they didn't let on te me. I was none the wiser wha was happenin te me. By the next day, you came inta the world an I went inta terrible shock. The place erupted in murder. Me sisters an brothers – they all arrived over on the next boat te find out wha was goin on. I didn't know wha was goin on meself! I just kept lookin at you, seein ye lyin contented in yer box – the one Nelly pulled out from the chest a drawers. You were lyin in tha on the kitchen table; it was pushed in at the end a the big double bed, the one an only bed we had. Me an Nelly used te sleep in tha. Well, anyway, there they all were lookin from me te you, wantin to know how tha happened. I had be now had me suspicions! It was somethin tha fella did te me back all them months ago over in England! I was still not over tha, an now I was left lookin at you.

'After all tha pain, an then you suddenly appearin – I was all in a fog! Me mind just shut down. It wouldn't work, Martha. Here I was, barely just turned sixteen, an everyone is shoutin at me, "Who is the father?" Sure, how would I know? I mean, he bleedin didn't leave me wit his callin card, did he?' she said, leaning towards me with her eyes hanging out, looking very annoyed.

I suddenly let out a burst of laughing, seeing the way she said that. 'But you said you knew him, Ma!'

'Yeah, well, I was still not in me senses. I was still tryin te work you out, an how it mighta happened. I only knew then ye had te be married first before ye got a babby. But here you were!' She snorted, sounding annoyed at her ignorance.

Then she eased in herself, saying with a smile in her eyes, 'Oh, Jesus! There was killins, Martha! Even the parish priest turned up! He wanted te get me put straight away inta a convent! I woulda been locked up in one a them Magdalene laundry places – put away fer life, I woulda been. Then they wanted te take you as well, put ye in a convent as well. They said they could get you adopted! I went mad! Everyone went mad! There was killins!' she said, lowering her head, letting her face crinkle up, and her eyes looked like they had tears ready to burst. Then she lifted her head, saying, 'But then Nelly stepped in. She told them all te go about their business. Tha she would mind us. She was three years older than me – nineteen, she was. But she had a terrible temper on her. Nobody would put themself in fear fer their life by gettin inta a row wit Nelly! So, they were satisfied wit tha. But me auntie was havin none of it. She had a worse temper! Even me father, God rest him, wouldn't cross her be tryin te have a go by givin her his aul guff!

'So the two a them, Nelly an me auntie, had a big run-in about it! Me aunt wanted te get the fella responsible, but I wouldn't open me mouth. I was too ashamed a me life, Martha. I couldn't even bear meself te think about it, never mind open me mouth! So I kept quiet. This is the first time I ever told anyone! So now ye know,' she said, looking up at me, shaking her head, still not able to get over it, as she took in a deep breath and held it, letting her eyes stare, seeing the picture of it all happening again. She was remembering that time with the pain and worry as it all came rushing back at her – I could see it showing in her eyes.

'Oh, them were terrible times, Martha,' she said, shaking her head at me and whispering. 'Everyone thought I had done a shockin thing! I thought tha about meself. It didn't matter tha it wasn't my doin – I was the one it happened to, so I was te blame. They kept tryin te get you offa me. Tha parish priest was a demon. He had the bit between the teeth, an he wasn't prepared te let go so easy!

'But the neighbours! Oh, the old Liberty neighbours were very good to you. They all got together an made a collection. They bought you a lovely big pram wit springs on it. They even got the sunshade te match! Oh, it was lovely. It was cream, I remember, wit a lovely fringe all around the edges. It used te shake when I pushed the pram. Oh, we got great innings outa tha pram, you an me. I used to take you off for the day in it. I walked for miles wit you in tha pram, I did. The people used te stop me every few mile wantin to admire you, an I even made a collection for weeks, I did. People – they would keep stoppin me on the street an put money in the pram. Yeah, they would so they would, for you! Shove it up behind the pilla they did. It's for good luck, ye see! That's wha ye did then, fer a new babby! It was a way te help out the mother a course.

'Oh, you were tiny! Lovely ye were, Martha! I couldn't get over you. Jaysus! There was no stoppin ye, though – small an all as ye were. You were up an outa tha pram be the time ye were nine months old! That's when Nelly managed te get her hands on it. She flew off te the pawn wit it. I was ragin! Tha was the last I ever saw a me lovely pram. She kept tellin me ye didn't need it, tha ye were now on yer feet. "But, sure, wha would ye be needin it for?" she used te say te me. I ask ye? The rows we had! I kept tellin her te stop tryin to make herself the mammy a my babby! She never let go a ye, Martha! Jaysus! The pullin an draggin you got between the pair of us! It's a wonder ye were still in one piece,' she said.

Then she suddenly looked straight at me, leaning towards me, laughing. 'But did ye know, I remember one day she was holdin you. She was kissin an suckin the face offa ye! You stayed quiet, lettin her get away wit tha. But then suddenly you erupted,' me ma laughed, losing her wind before she could get the next word out. 'Ye were only six month old, but, outa the blue, ye suddenly had enough, an up came the hand, givin her a clatter on the face, shoutin, "DOP!"'

'What?! Six months old, Ma?'

'Yeah! That's when ye said yer first word! By the time ye were sixteen month old, ye were goin around singin rebel songs, nearly gettin us all arrested. Ye never shut up from the first in the mornin till I got ye down in the last a the night! Oh, you were very cute! Very cute, everyone used te tell me! I got great enjoyment outa ye – we all did! Nelly idolised you! The kids on the street, the little young ones, they used te come bangin on me door at all hours, they did, wantin te take you out for a walk in yer pram. They were always fightin over who was goin te get te mind you!'

'Gawd, Ma, that sounds like my youngest. She's the very same, and you know it's uncanny but she did the very same thing at six months old too! She clattered an aul one, a very old woman, on the chops, who was sucking the cheeks off her! Not just that, but she was talking by the time she was seventeen months old. Isn't that amazing, Ma? She must take after me,' I said, thinking of the wonder of that.

'Ah, will ye bring them over te see me, Martha?' she said, smiling with a longing on her face.

'Yeah! Course I will, Ma!' I said, really looking forward to that.

'Aah! But I would never let a bad word be said against her, Martha. Against Nelly! She was the best in the world. Jesus! There was nothin she wouldn't do for you or me! Then she had a little babby, just after you! Nine months after, it was. Just after she sold the bleedin pram! I think she was hopin te grab the money for tha, thinkin they might then have te make a collection fer her. Then she'd end up wit herself gettin a new pram for her new babby.'

'Oh, yeah! Barney!' I said. 'He was younger than me. I used to mind him, Ma.'

'Oh, don't talk te me. She had tha poor young fella followin her te the lavatory! She used te be moidered wit him! She couldn't go anywhere without him! Oh, he was very attached to her, Martha,' she said, getting lost in herself. I just sat back listening, not saying a word. I wanted to let her talk in her own time.

'Then ye see, Martha,' she said, lifting her face up but not bringing her eyes with it. She was thinking, letting her eyes stare down at the floor. 'It all went wrong because I picked up wit this fella. He was no good, but I didn't see tha. People kept warnin me. Nelly! She wanted te get her hands on him, but I used to sneak out behind her back, just te avoid the trouble it would cause. The less she knew the better, I thought. By then, ye see, everyone had a fella, or they were married be tha time. I thought I could do the same, but it didn't work out like tha. No fella would take me, wit you! They thought I wasn't decent, not respectable – tha's the way things was back then!

'So this fella, anyway, he hadn't two ha'pence te rub together. But he did take notice a me, an bein as foolish, or maybe just as stupid, as I really was, I believed everythin tha he was tellin me. We would go away an make a fresh start, he said. We could go te England, where he would get work. He was on the bleedin streets, Martha!' she roared, not able to get over her daftness.

I nodded, getting pictures, dark-grey images, remembering every bit of him – even the times she used to take me with her when she was meeting him.

'Anyway, he got me te save me few pennies, then he took off, takin all me savings wit him. Tha was the last I ever saw a him. Then I was left stranded wit another babby on the way.'

'That's when you had Charlie, Ma,' I said, looking at her sadly. I remember every bit of that too, even when she went into labour. I was five, and all I could hear when me and Barney woke up was the moaning and shivering coming from the ma, as the two of us sat up, watching her standing holding onto the side of the bed. Then there was the puddle of blood on the floor. We were out of the room as fast as our little legs could move, with Nelly pushing and shoving us ahead of her, then she was off down the stairs leaving us standing on the landing. Within minutes she had made a collection of aul ones, and there she was, back up the stairs with a procession of aul biddies trailing her. They hurried past us, wearing their black shawls tightly wrapped around themselves, keeping their heads and shoulders warm. We sat on the lobby stairs, watching the excitement, seeing as they flew past, rushing themselves. They were nearly falling over each other and themself in their hurry to get inta the room.

I was given a shopping bag and sent for the messages. 'Here!' an aul one roared at me. 'You go down an get the messages for yer poor mammy.'

I stared. The only messages I got sent for was up to the dairy to buy Nelly one Woodbine cigarette and a match to light it. Even then she stopped sending me. I sucked the thing to death, spitting out what was left, trying to hand her the big gobs of mush with the tobacco clinging to a string of spit.

'Go on!' the aul one roared, shaking the bag at me, then landing it in me hand. 'Get the messages!'

I stopped staring and rushed off to the shops, thinking, I thought ye had te have the money? I handed up the bag, holding me breath, after giving the shopkeeper a list of all the lovely things I wanted. The aul one ate the head offa me in the shop! Telling me I was to go back and tell aul Granny Rafters what she could do – wantin somethin fer nothin! The cheek! An she not standin behind tha counter for the good a her health!

'Well! Ye know wha happened after tha, Martha. Nelly up an left. I was stranded. The house was condemned. Me old family home where we had all been born an reared. I couldn't settle in the new place. Well, ye know the rest! We ended up without a roof over our heads. I went downhill. I lost the only life I had ever known, wit me sister an me neighbours an me friends all around me. Tha was all gone. They boarded up all the windas in the old tenement houses an everyone got shifted, all scattered in different directions. I lost me mind. I lost me way, Martha. Then him! Well, tha finished me. He always made sure te remind me I was only a whore. Tha was an awful thing te call anyone in them days, Martha. So, between the babbies arrivin one after the other, wit no let-up, then his badness an the madness – I stopped carin! But I'm goin to tell you this now, Martha. An you might not believe me, but I'm tellin you anyway! When tha man nearly kilt the pair a youse!' she said, pointing and wagging her finger at me, seeing me not taking my eyes off her. Then she took another breath, getting ready to say what came next. 'It was as soon as we stepped inside his door. Do you remember tha, when he grabbed the babby, Charlie, outa me arms he did, then threatened te kill him by hangin him be the leg over them banisters?! Then he went after you! Nearly sendin you te yer death by hangin ye outa tha winda, swingin ye be yer legs, he was, lookin like any minute he was goin te drop you! Send ye flyin to yer death at any second, then ye woulda landed on them spikes stickin up outa tha railings! They woulda gone clean up through ye! Well, the shock a tha nearly finished me off altogether,' me ma said, leaning over to look at me with the fear of God in her eyes.

I watched, seeing her face had gone white by even just remembering it. Then she stared at me, still leaning towards me, waiting to see if I remembered what she was talking about. I shook me head and lowered it, getting the sense of it coming back even worse. It was seeing the fear now in the ma with that memory.

'Well! Tha put such a fear of God in me, I was terrified outa me mind he would kill youse, an that's wha did it fer me. I never said another word te make him come tha close again. He knew he had me, Martha!' she said, raising her voice with the pain. 'He knew I couldn't go back out on them streets again. Sure, there was the risk anytime tha youse two could be took offa me then be put inta a home. Even meself! I coulda still been locked up then, sent inta one a them convents where they lock ye up! You never see the light a day again, Martha! No! I was in fear a me life a him. I had te watch everythin I said an did.

'I thought the world a youse two! You might not have believed me then, but I did, Martha! It's just he kicked out any life tha I mighta had still left in me when I met him. Sure, at one time or another, he tried to kill all of us. He went after me at one time an kicked the child I was carryin outa me. Then he tried te kill me, be holdin me down an he wit a knife te me throat!'

I stared at her, remembering them times too. My heart was sick with the weight of hearing it all again. But the ma looked worse. I could see her shoulders hunched, sitting on the edge of the couch wringing her hands, then resting them on her lap.

'It was a boy, ye know, Martha,' she said, barely above a whisper as she looked at me.

'What?! The baby you lost, Ma?'

'Yeah! A lovely babby boy, six months growin inside me tha child was.'

Then the tears rolled down. I watched her for a second, seeing her face crumple and the tears stream down her cheeks, making her face go red. Suddenly, she looked so small and fragile.

'Ma, it's all over now. Them times are gone for ever,' I said, moving to wrap my arms around her and rock her back and forth.

'Oh, me poor childre, I know they suffered somethin terrible. But I was like someone left sittin in the middle of a bomb explosion! I was outa me mind. I didn't know who I was or wha was happenin around me, most a the time, I wasn't even aware a meself. It was like days had come an gone by, an I missed them passin. I didn't even know they had come an gone. I had no mind a me own,' she said, shaking her head, wiping her nose with the back of her hand.

'Let me get you something to wipe your face, Ma,' I said, heading for the bathroom.

It smelled lovely, with cleaning stuff beside the toilet and a tumbler holding false teeth. They sat in a cup in a silver holder on the wall, hanging over the wash-hand basin. I could see shampoo and a bottle of herbal bubble bath, even creams for your face. I didn't bother getting nosy and opening the press under the sink or the medicine cabinet on the wall. I grabbed a roll of toilet paper left sitting piled on top of each other behind the toilet. Gawd! The place is lovely, I thought, rushing in seeing the ma lift her head to take the tissue out of my hand. She blew her nose and took another few sheets, and wiped her face, showing it roaring red.

'Will I put the kettle on, Ma?'

'Yeah,' she nodded, still looking very down and out, with her shoulders hunched, looking like she had suddenly gotten terribly small and old.

'Will I make you a sandwich, Ma?' I said, stopping to look back at her as I waited at the door.

She thought about it for a minute, then said, 'Ah, no! Sure, I'll have somethin fer me tea later, but you go on ahead an get yerself one. Here! There's a lovely bit a ham in the . . .'

'No, Ma! Let's wait then. I'm not hungry, not after that lovely big dinner you fed me.'

'Yeah! Tha was a lovely bit a fish. It was, eh, wha do ye call tha soft white fish without the bones, Martha?'

'Yeah, Ma, it was plaice. That's very dear, Ma.'

'Don't remind me! But sure, wha good is the money to ye if ye can't get te enjoy it? There's no pockets in a shroud, Martha! Ye can't take it wit you!' she laughed.

27

'**O**h! Did I tell you, Martha! Me an Dinah are goin away on our holidays in the next two weeks!'

'You are?' I said, hearing her shouting in from the sitting room.

I hurried with the two mugs of tea and rushed in, saying, 'How is Dinah, Ma? What's happening with her?'

'But, sure, she's livin here now wit me fer the last wha . . . three year.'

'Is she, Ma?'

'Yes, indeed she is,' me ma said, dragging her head down with her face, making it definite.

'How is she?'

'Grand! Not a bother on her. She's out now – gone off for the day wit her pal, Joanie. The two a them do go off together, an go here an there! Today they're gone off inta town. Jaysus! I bet you anythin Dinah will walk through tha door wit more stuff tha she's after buyin in them shops. I nearly need another wardrobe just te take the amount a stuff she has!' me ma said, shaking her head, laughing. 'Yeah! They're gone te look aroun the shops, then they said they want te see a film. Afterwards, they usually go fer fish an chips in O'Connell Street. But Dinah likes te bring me back something. Usually a bit a fish from across the road.

'Oh, by the way, Martha. Did ye see me new false teeth they made me get?'

'Oh, yeah. The ones sitting in the bathroom, Ma?'

'Yeah,' she said, 'tha's them! Tha nurse down in tha clinic brought me te the dentist down there. I wouldn't go on me own! Anyway, I only wear them when I'm goin out, otherwise I couldn't be bothered wit them! They fall outa me bleedin mouth, Martha,' she laughed.

'So how is Dinah, Ma? I mean, how is her health?'

'Grand! There's not a bother on her. They have her an Gerry on these new pills. They put the two a them on it when tha drug was just new. They wanted te see if it would work better. Well, they're on it now for goin on nearly two year an they haven't looked back since, Martha! Dinah doesn't be tormented wit the voices so much, an even Gerry is much better. He talks more to ye now, because he's a lot better – the same as Dinah. He's not rushin around so much. He's more easy in himself wit the voices not botherin him so much, ye know?' she said, looking at me, sounding very happy. 'He will even sit now an watch the television wit you. But he prefers te listen to his music. He loves tha aul radio I got him. He knows all the songs. Ye should see him, Martha,' me ma said, getting a convulsion with the laugh. It caught her breath, making the face go red.

'He sits up in the bed, roarin his bleedin head off in the middle of the night, Martha, singing he does be! Listenin to his radio, if ye wouldn't be mindin, but no bother on him at wakin the rest of us up. I ask ye! I do have to let a shout outa me, roarin at him to switch off tha radio an get te sleep! An let the rest of us get a bit a sleep, too.

'Ah, but he's very good, Martha. He's very good-natured. He would do anythin you ask him. He fixes things fer me, ye know! Oh, yeah! If I want him te put up me curtains, he does it no bother once he sees how they should go. Sure, me phone was hangin offa the wall, the socket was loose. I was afraid a me life te go near it. He got the screwdriver an fixed it wit no bother to him. He can even put in a bulb fer me! Oh, yes, he's very handy aroun the house,' me ma said, giving her head a big shake up and down.

'Gawd, Ma, that's great,' I said. 'Ma, have you seen any sight of Charlie? I have come across him only rarely. Do you ever meet him?'

'Wha?! Oh, a course I do! Yeah, he does drop up here the odd time. He even stays fer a while, has a bit of dinner, an might watch the television, then goes off about his business. Sure, he has his own place, ye know! Did you not know tha, Martha?' she said, looking at the shock on me face.

'No!' I said. 'Sure, I haven't seen sight nor sound of him for a long time. Tell us, Ma! When did he get the place? What's it like? Did you go there?'

'No, but he told me it's grand. He has only the one room, but he has everything in it.'

'Is it a bedsit, Ma?'

'Yeah! He even has a television set. But I can tell you, Martha, I told him not te come if he has drink on him. I made tha clear, Martha. I won't open tha door for him, because he can start shouting all over the place. It would only start Dinah gettin very upset. Ye can't do tha. There's no call fer it! But, yeah, he can be grand without it. But then again, he might call up to see ye loads a times on the go. Then ye might not see him fer months on end, wherever he does disappear off to. But one thing ye do know fer sure. Wherever it is, he's off somewhere on tha drink. Tha's the way it takes him, Martha.'

'Oh,' I said, feeling my heart sink with the disappointment. 'I thought for a minute, Ma, you were going to tell me he was off that for good.'

'No, more's the pity,' the ma said, shaking her head.

'Still, at least he has a place of his own,' I said, thinking, Jesus! It's just great he has managed to get himself off the streets. 'Pity he can't give up that drink for good,' I said. 'Imagine! He would be landed, Ma. He would have money in his pocket and he'd be able to sort himself out, start to get a bit of life for himself, maybe even meet a woman.'

'Oh, it's the company he keeps,' me ma said, shaking her head, looking frustrated.

'Did he give you his address, Ma?'

'Yeah. Do ye want me te give it te you?'

'Yeah, Ma, that's the first thing I want to do – go and see him.' Then I said, looking around the room, seeing how lovely it looked, 'Gawd, Ma! You have all the comfort here. You even have a plant,' I said, getting up and going over to the corner, seeing the plant pot standing in a bowl of water.

'Yeah, I have the few here and there, Martha,' me ma said, looking around the room with me, letting her eyes light up. 'Tha one is me spider plant. I like tha one, I do! It's growin nice an big,' she said, going over to finger it and settle it onto two sticks holding it up.

'Gawd, Ma, the place is lovely. Everything is so nice and neat and clean and shining,' I said, taking in the big colour television sitting over in the corner. Above that on the wall was a picture of the pope in a frame, looking down, giving us all his benediction with his hand raised and his fingers pointed in the air.

'Oh, yeah, sure, we're grand, Martha. Dinah an meself do even go off on our holidays, now.'

'What?! Oh, yeah, I forgot. You were telling me that. Holidays, Ma?' I shouted.

'Of course! Why not? Sure, we went to . . . Wha was tha place called? Oh, yeah! Bundoran, it's a seaside place. We went fer a week, me an Dinah did. We go te this club down the road – it's run in the community centre. Jesus! It was lovely, Martha! Gettin te be at the seaside, an walkin on the sand wit the water rushin up at us. But Dinah got herself nearly drowned, so she did!' me ma roared. '"I'm goin for a swim, Ma," she says te me. "Sure you can't swim!" I shouted after her, seein her flyin in the new bathin suit she bought herself. She didn't stay in long, Martha!' me ma roared with the laugh. 'I went rushin after her but I couldn't get in, the bleedin waves were tearin at me. But did tha stop her? She flew in till she disappeared. Me heart was in me mouth, watchin te see would she appear back up again.

'I was just gettin meself ready te start roarin fer help when the next thing she manages te get herself thrown back outa the water. It musta taken her minutes, but it was like hours seein her try te pick herself up an get back out. That was the last a tha, I can tell you!'

'Holidays, Ma? Jaysus! You are having the time of your life,' I said, still not able to take in the complete change in her and everything around her. The lovely home and the bit of style on her – it felt like I was only dreaming.

'Sure, we go down there te tha place, the community centre. They do have all sorts a things goin on. Another time we went for te learn the cookin. Jaysus! At first we nearly burnt the place down. "Here," yer woman, the teacher, said, "the pots an pans should be very hot before ye start te cook anythin." Well, it looked grand an easy when we were doin it there with her. But when we got started at home, I was cookin rashers an sausages at the time. Smokin, yeah, tha's wha she said it should be, smoke should be comin outa the pan. So, we left it te smoke. Till the bleedin thing caught fire, Martha. It was all the drippin I put in it! Dinah went mad! She dragged me out, makin me drop the fryin pan wit the cooker goin up in flames. Then she was on the phone screamin her lungs out, roarin at them te send the fire brigade! So we gave tha up. We just watch it now, on the television.

'Then we took up the knittin class another night. Dinah wanted te knit herself a frock, she said! Oh, holy Jaysus! I couldn't make head nor tail at how te get the armpits for me jumper I was supposed te be knittin. I just kept it goin straight, wit holes from all the dropped stitches I was losin. But yer woman told me I was doin grand. She was right. I made a lovely-lookin warm scarf fer meself, fer the winter!

'Sure, we even have a bit of an aul job now, ye know,' me ma said, digging me with her elbow.

'Go way, Ma! What?! You work?'

'Oh, yes! I used te work in England, ye know! Before you were born. Yeah, indeed I did,' me ma said, shaking her head, remembering that. 'Anyway, we put in two hours down in tha nursin home – it's just two bus stops away, facin out onta the main road. Yeah, we clean up after the patients, the old people – sweep the floors an do a bit a hooverin. Tha kind a thing. It's grand an handy, an the few bob – it's not much, Martha – but it gets us outa the house. Then we save up tha money, put it by fer somethin we need in the house, or go on a holiday wit the money when we get enough of it saved, ye know?' she said, looking at me like she was all excited about doing that.

I kept staring. I couldn't take it in at all. I was getting more and more proud of her.

'Oh, yeah! I'm enjoyin meself no end! Me life is a lot easier, Martha. I can come an go now as I please – get me few messages without havin te look over me shoulder or keep frettin about him waitin an goin mad because I left him on his own.'

I grabbed me ma in a sudden hug.

'Here!' she roared, getting a fright. 'Take it easy, mind me hair.'

I stopped to get a look at it, then brushed it down, seeing it fly into the air. 'It's lovely, Ma, the colour really suits you. It's sandy-looking.'

'Yeah! But I didn't want te end up wit me lookin like a dyed blonde,' me ma said, fixing it up with her two hands, giving it a fluff. 'Do ye like it, Martha?' she said, smiling at me, happy, looking all delighted in herself.

'Ohh! I just can't believe the change over you!' I said, sighing with a deep contentment, thinking she has every comfort now a body could want. God knows it was a long time in coming. It's like I've met a new person, someone who is familiar, yet someone who is so alive. I still can't believe she was lying inside the ma, just waiting to get out.

'Oh, yeah! Did I tell you? The club we're in, it's fer people who are retired, old people. Now some a them are not tha old, Martha. They would be like meself. It's all ages, I suppose. But it's mostly the older ones who turn up more often. Anyway! They are off next week on a big foreign holiday. But we wouldn't go.'

'Where are they going to, Ma?' I said, trying to get the picture of me ma and Dinah heading outa the country. 'But you're not going, Ma? That's a pity. Where are they off to?'

'Eh, let me see. They mentioned the name right enough, but anyways, it doesn't mean much te me. But the place is in Spain.'

'Ah, Ma! You should go, you and Dinah. I can . . .'

'Are ye jokin me, Martha?!' she said slowly, giving me a dirty look. 'Sure, wha would we be doin, goin out foreign, Martha? Sure, I wouldn't know where the hell I am! Never mind eat all tha foreign food – tha would turn me stomach! An anyway, how would we understand wha te ask for? Sure, we don't speak foreign, Martha!'

I shook my head, laughing.

'An another thing! Wouldn't we have te get up in an air a plane! No, thank you! I'll stay where I am, if ye don't mind,' she said, folding her arms, shocked at the idea.

'Oh, but we did go a bit foreign,' she said, seeing me looking at her, waiting to hear. 'Yeah, we went off ourselves after bein at tha seaside place. We went on one a them tours. Oh, it was lovely, Martha. They took us all off on a big luxury bus. Now, not them C.I.E. buses, if ye understand me. A big one, it was. It even had white covers on the back te keep yer head clean. Ye know? Ye would be able to see if anyone had a dirty head, so tha ye wouldn't go catchin anythin! Ye know, Martha! Ye can get diseases these days if ye're not careful! Sure, ye remember tha green disease everyone was talkin about?'

'No, Ma! Green disease! What green disease?' I said, shaking me head, laughing.

'Did you not hear about it, Martha? Well, it was spread by monkeys or something – we were watchin it on the television, meself an Dinah. Jaysus! I was afraid a me life fer months after seein tha. I kept thinkin we were goin te pick it up, Martha!

'Anyway! We went on long journeys on this bus, then when it was time te get off . . . Jesus! I forgot te mention – but if we didn't go an land ourself up wit a load of Americans! Jaysus! Them Yanks – the bus was full a them! The roars outa them, Martha! They shout – they must be all hard a hearin. I was nearly deafened listenin te them. Anyway, me an Dinah walked onta the bus. Now, we wouldn't leave our suitcases in under tha place on the bus. I didn't want all our stuff gettin robbed, Martha! The bus driver said he wasn't movin till we shifted it. We kept sayin, "No, leave it where it is. Go on! Drive the bus." It was grand where it was . . .'

'Where was it, Ma? Was the suitcases big?'

'Oh, indeed they were! I paid big money fer the two a them in Dunnes Stores. They were very modern, Martha, ye know. Good ones, on wheels, wit a big handle te pull it behind you. They were great, Martha. There was no pullin an draggin on them.

'So! I wasn't takin no chances wit them, an all our good stuff inside, gettin whipped!' she said, looking at me as she folded her arms, showing me she meant business and was prepared to fight.

'Did you move them, Ma?'

'Yeah! Them bleedin Americans, mighty mouths, started shoutin an roarin. They didn't want te trip an break their necks. Sure, no one was goin anywhere. But, yeah, I suppose we did make a few stops te go in an get a cup a tea an tha. So the bus driver grabbed them, wit me shoutin he was responsible if them suitcases went missin, tha he better be prepared te pay up! An ye know wha, Martha? He said he would. So, we were appeased. We let him take them. Now! Wha was I goin te tell ye, Martha?' she said, dropping her mouth and narrowing her eyes, staring at the wall trying to remember. 'Oh, yeah! It's come te me! We stayed in this big mansion . . .'

'A what, Ma?' I said, letting me jaw drop.

'Yeah, of course. Sure, why wouldn't we? We spent all the money we saved from the work. It all amounts up, ye know. Anyway, the place was a palace when we got inside. Oh, Jesus, Martha! I never saw the like of it in all me born days! It was like somethin ye'd see on the television! We were swankin wit the style. The bedrooms! We got one big bed, because Dinah an meself sleep in the one bed at home anyway. So here we were, livin in the lap a luxury. We had a lovely big bathroom an our own television, an even a phone at the bed. I kept lookin at it, but we had no one te ring, I couldn't remember any the phone numbers. I was ragin, I was! So we missed out on tha! I coulda rang Gerry, but he was gone too, wit the people he's livin wit in the new house.'

'New house, Ma?'

'Yeah, he's outa the hospital, Martha. Oh! Did I not tell you tha, Martha? Oh, yeah, he's livin in a big house now wit other patients who are left the hospital. They have nurses an all te mind them. Then he sees his doctor once a week when he comes fer their check-up! Oh, yeah, Martha, sure, he now has a job as well! He's workin wit all the others – they roll plastic bags or somethin. But anyway, he gets a few bob fer it. Then he comes home by taxi every Friday. He'll be here tomorra, Martha, if ye have the time an ye want te come over? He stays the weekend an then goes back on a Sunday evenin. I do ring him every night, just te see how he is, so he looks forward te tha. Anyway! He went off on his holidays too; the nurses go wit them.'

'God, that's great, Ma. Everything is going really well. Jesus! This is like a miracle! You're having the time of your life, Ma! I just can't get over you! You're really living now,' I said, laughing with the happiness of it all.

Then an idea hit me. 'Ma! Why don't we all go off somewhere during the summer, say around July? I could bring the children, Ma. Would you like that?' I said, thinking it would be marvellous for them having a granny, my ma.

'Yeah!' she roared, letting her face break into a huge smile. 'Would we do tha, Martha? I'd love tha an so would Dinah. She's goin te be delighted now when she comes in an sees you here. Are ye in a hurry?'

'Not at all, Ma. There's nothing stopping me. I have the time on me hands, as the kids are away camping with the Scouts.'

'Ahhh! They must be really growin! I'd love te see them. When will ye bring them over, Martha?' she said, getting a bit nervous I might still refuse or make some excuse as I didn't really trust her.

'Of course, Ma!' I said, grinning and putting my arms around her.

'Sure, listen! Why don't you and Dinah come over and see me? You could stay the night. I have plenty of room, Ma.'

'Yeah! Tha would be lovely. When were ye thinkin about, Martha? I couldn't come at the weekends because of Gerry. He gets worried. It's best te keep te wha he knows, Martha, he doesn't like ye te change things.'

'No, Ma. Sure, it's the summer holidays. We can do what we like. Oh, Ma, this is great. We'll be able to do lots of things together. The lot of us, as a family, Ma.'

'Yeah! Tha will be lovely,' she said, sighing and sitting back, thinking about it.

28

'Gawd, we're in the height a comfort wit this car, an it's lovely an roomy, Martha,' me ma sighed, shifting herself down into the seats, letting her head rest then turning to look out at the green fields and farmhouses as we flew past, keeping at a nice steady pace.

'Yeah! I still can't believe we're goin away like this,' Dinah whispered, letting her eyes shine as she smiled over at me.

'Great, isn't it?' I muttered, raising my eyes and smiling, agreeing with her. Then I turned me head back to the road, concentrating on keeping up my speed.

Dinah suddenly laid her two hands on my arm, giving them a gentle squeeze, saying, 'I'm so glad, Martha, I have you fer a sister,' she breathed out in an excited laugh.

'Gawd, Dinah! I wouldn't swap you for a Rolo!' I laughed.

'Not even two?' she said.

'No, they would have to go up as far as four packets!' I laughed, getting a little dig in the arm for meself. Then we drove on in silence, with everyone contented, taking it easy looking out the windows.

Suddenly I could hear a muted argument starting up in the back of the car.

'No! We will take turns,' Little Madam said.

'No! I want my map back.' Then there was a squeal.

'Stop! Let go! You're hurting my hand!'

'No! You let go!' he roared, bringing the volume up. 'You have to have the two together!'

'Let's take turns, OK?' she pleaded, trying to bargain.

'No! Hand it back! I don't care! I am the navigator!' he shouted.

'No! You can't find your way without me and my compass!' she screeched.

I listened, watching progress in the rear-view mirror, then I said in a monotone, 'Hand back the map, please!'

They didn't hear me.

'Hand back the map,' I droned.

'Here! Wha's goin on? Stop the fightin, the two a ye's. Whose te blame? Who started it?' me ma said, trying to separate their hands, with them pulling and dragging the map off each other, strangling themselves. It was sitting inside a plastic cover, with a thin rope to carry around on your neck.

'Wait! Stop! I have a few sweets for ye's if ye stop this fightin now!' me ma shouted, getting herself all excited, with her trying to stop the pair of them throttling each other, because the rope was hanging on one neck, then getting yanked off to hang on the other.

'Ahhh! Wait! Hold on!' she suddenly screeched, whipping her head around the car. 'Where's me handbag gone to, Dinah? Wait, Martha!' she said, letting her voice drop to a whispered panic.

'What, Ma? Your handbag?' I said, getting worried. 'Where did you have it last?'

'Back in that Texaco place. When we stopped for tha tea an sandwiches, I bought them a few sweets. Jaysus, Martha! I musta left me handbag wit all me money! An everythin I have in the world is in tha bag!' she cried, turning white.

I quickly looked in the rear-view mirror, getting ready to move into the overtaking lane and find a turn back. 'Ma! We're on the motorway! The next turn-off won't be for about ten miles! But, don't worry . . .'

'Here it is, Sally! Under the clothes on the back window!' Little Madam screamed, standing on the seat, lifting the bag, then handing it triumphantly over to the ma. 'I found it!' she gasped, sounding outa breath, all delighted with herself.

'Ohh! Good girl, darling,' I breathed.

'Oh, ye got it! Oh, ye're the best, a great girl! How did it get there?' me ma said, trying to figure how she managed to let go of it. 'Oh, thanks be te God an his Holy Blessed mother fer tha, Martha!' me ma moaned, putting her hand on her chest, letting go of all her breath.

'Yeah! You can say that again,' I breathed, thinking I am going to end up in threadbare order if there's any more shocks like this.

We drove on in peace and quiet, with everyone biting and chewing on something outa the ma's big handbag, then suddenly there was another moan.

'Dinah! Did we turn off tha cooker? I think I turned it back on just te check it was not workin. Did you pull down tha fuse thing in the electric box te turn off the electricity like I told ye to, Dinah?'

'Yeah, Ma. We turned off everythin a million times!' Dinah grinned, lifting her head to look back at the ma.

'Are ye sure?' the ma muttered, pinning her eyes on Dinah but not seeing her, with the eyes blinking and fluttering, trying to get a picture of her flat, wanting to see what she did, or didn't, turn off.

'Ma,' I sighed, 'everything is off. I should know. I spent two hours there trying to get you out the door.'

'Do ye think so, Martha?' she said, wanting to believe me.

'Yes, Ma. Now sit back and relax. You are just nervous and excited – that's all it is. You don't think like that when you are just heading over to the shops for your few messages. So no more worries. This is a holiday.'

'Yeah, ye're right,' she sighed, letting go and easing her breath out, then feasting her eyes back on the scenery.

A few minutes later I could see her rooting in her bag. 'Did I lock the front door? Where's me keys?'

'There they are, Sally,' the kids said, helping her look in the bag with their eyes locked on the two packets of chocolate eclairs they were hoping to get their hands on. They were still left sitting there in the handbag.

'Wait, Martha! Just stop here for a minute,' me ma said, spotting people coming out of a shop sucking on ice-cream cones as we passed through a little village along the harbour.

'Now! Don't you two drop any of that ice cream on these seats,' I warned, seeing them now sucking happily on a big chocolate flake. It was stuck right down in the middle of the ice cream. 'Ma! You have those children ruined!' I said. 'They normally only get sweets at the weekend with their pocket money. They'll end up with holes in their teeth, and you get diabetes from all that sugar,' I said, feeling myself beginning to fret now, worrying about the kids.

'Ah, a few wormin powders will clear them out. Ye need more than wha they ate te be gettin disease,' the ma grinned, winking at the kids.

I snorted out my annoyance, feeling sick meself from all the rubbish I had just gluttoned down.

'Does that mean we won't be able to eat more sweets?' they whispered, looking worried at the ma.

'Wha?! Course ye will! Ah, go on, childre. Enjoy yerself – if it doesn't kill ye, it'll cure ye!' me ma laughed, looking at them.

Then they all went quiet, watching me to see would there be a row. Oh, she's right. What the hell – we're on holiday, I sighed, thinking they will go high as a kite from all the bleedin sweets the ma picked up.

I wasn't too happy, but she wouldn't let go. 'We'll be a long time dead,' she sniffed, giving me a dirty look, then patted the kids saying, 'Sure! We still have yet them bags a sweets left te get through!'

'Oh, Holy Jesus!' I moaned, then heard Dinah burst out laughing, saying, 'Yeah, Martha, then just wait till they all start gettin sick over the ma, an she wearin her new jacket an skirt! I'm OK – I'm safe in the front!'

'Ah, go on, Dinah! Youse're problem is youse just can't remember wha it was like te be a child! Sure, wha else is there but sweets? Isn't tha wha childre live for?' she snorted.

'Oh, yes, Sally! We're having a great time. This is just like having a party!' the little man slurped, with the young one gasping out her agreement, not getting the ice cream down fast enough.

'You know, Ma, Dinah never spoke a truer word,' I said grimly, speaking quietly as I looked at her in the mirror. 'He can get very, very sick, go down with a roaring temperature and severe vomiting. He has even ended up in hospital and do you know what?'

'Wha?' she said, sounding shocked.

'It has been sometimes after he has eaten too many sweets! I think he must be allergic. It lowers his immune system or something. He has even been tested for diabetes. But thank God he seems to be clear of that, because I'm borderline diabetic, Ma, but I'm grand. I just watch what I eat!'

'Yeah, ye're right. Me sister has tha. It's in the family,' she said, going very quiet, thinking about it.

'Anyway!' I sighed. 'Jaysus, what brought all this on? You would think we were heading to a funeral,' I said giving a big sigh, deciding to wake meself up. 'We're off on holiday. Let's enjoy ourselves!' I shouted, sitting up and pushing the car a bit harder.

'Here we are! We made nice time,' I said, opening the sunroof then pulling into line, getting in behind the last car. Instantly, the kids were out of the seats and pushing the top half of their bodies out through the roof.

'Oh! Tha gives in a lovely bit of air,' me ma said, looking up at the kids hanging out.

'Yeah, it's grand, Ma, if you make sure to close it properly. Otherwise it leaks,' I said, pointing to the water stains showing on the inside, spoiling the look of the lovely cream roof.

'We're movin, Martha! Lookit, the cars are movin!' me ma shouted, getting all excited in case we would be left behind.

'Sit down, children, and put on your safety belts. I don't want to go losing the pair of you out through that sunroof. It can happen very easily,' I said, getting into me mother-clucking, 'Here! Let me wipe your arses clean yer snots' fuss-and-worry mood.

I sat watching as they cleared the car ahead of me, then we got the all-clear. We followed the car just disappeared inside and plunged onto the ramp, then flying up and in, seeing the fella with the ship's logo on his jacket. He waved me in towards the next car up, then came checking to make sure I was close enough. I wasn't, so he waved me on, watching with his palm raised, then slammed it down.

'OK! That's it! Stop!' Then he was off, marching to get the next car directly in line behind me.

'We're on the ship!' the kids roared.

'Yeah! Isn't it lovely?' me ma said, looking around in wonder, hearing the screech of tyres, getting the fumes of cars as they thundered onto the ship. Jesus, the noise was deafening.

I pointed to the door ahead, saying, 'When we arrive, Ma, them doors will open and we will drive through them, then down the ramp.' I paused then gave a big excited shout, saying, 'We will all be in France! Then on our way to Disneyland Paris!' I roared, then laughed, seeing the ma blink and Dinah saying, 'Jesus! We're all goin foreign!'

'Who wants to eat escargot? Because I do!' the little man said.

'Oh, tha sounds lovely. Wha's tha?' said the ma, looking at the kids, thinking it was something sweet.

'Snails! And we can have frogs' legs, Sally. They're very tasty. I love them,' he said with relish, smacking his lips together. 'We can get them here in the dining room.'

'Wha? But ye can't eat the like a them!' she whispered. 'I never heard a the like a tha! Sure, tha would only poison youse,' me ma said, turning green.

'Oh, yes, you can eat them! It's true, Sally,' he said, shaking his head, not taking in that she was going into shock. Then he was off out of the car, trying to drag her with him. 'Come on, Sally, hurry! Get out. We'll show you when we get to the dining room.'

I said nothing, just felt a perverse delight seeing the ma thinking her worst nightmare had just come true! I couldn't help meself – it was so awful for her, yet so great for him. Then the young one says, catching on at seeing the ma turn all colours, 'They might even be hopping around the table; then we'll have to chase our dinner.' She laughed, taking after her father for devilment. She didn't get that from me, I thought, hearing him saying in my head, '*Martha! You must allow the children to run free!*'

'*What?! But they'll be kilt! They're running wild!*'

'*So, they will be killed!*' he says, lifting his jaw, shrugging the shoulders.

Yeah, spoken like a true mad, pragmatic Russian, I think. Pity he is . . . Oh, fuck off, Martha! This is the best time of your life. It has never, but never, been better. Enjoy, woman! Enjoy.

Suddenly me ma erupted, looking at me. 'I knew it! I knew I shouldn't a listened te you an yer foreign holiday! This is all youse a fault if I'm carried back in a box. An you too, Dinah! You put me up te this! I wouldn't a listened, only fer you tellin me it wasn't foreign. It's just like England! ye said. How the hell would you know anyway? You never even got as far as England yerself!' she roared, going red in the face with the fright.

Dinah started screaming laughing, and the ma went mad, shouting, 'Get me offa this ship! Fuck!' Suddenly she dived outa the car and went flying, shouting, 'Mister! Don't let this ship move! I'm gettin off!'

I went tearing after her, shouting back at the others, 'No more! We're frightening the shite outa the ma, Dinah.'

Fuck! This is turning out to be a disaster, I thought, seeing the ma getting herself run down with the cars flying towards her.

'GET BACK!' a man shouted at her, waving and stopping the cars heading onto the ship. I could feel the life leaving my body with the fright. Such a fucking simple thing, but to the ma it can mean hell on earth.

'MA! WAIT!' I screamed, bombing to grab hold and pull her around into my arms. 'No, wait, Ma! Listen to me! The kids were only joking. There's no such thing! I swear, I promise you it is just like England. You can have all the fish and chips you want, just wait and see. Please! I wouldn't tell you a word of a lie,' I said, seeing the lost look of shock in her face. It was the thought of getting stranded in a place without the comforts of her own home, and not having all the familiar things and places around her. She stared up at me, blinking and chewing her gums, trying to read me.

'God, yeah, Ma. France is even better than England. They know how to cook lovely stews and fish and anything you want. Wait until you get to the hotel and see Disneyland. It's a paradise for kids and grown-ups alike,' I said, leading her back to the car.

I could see all the others watching, looking shocked and worried now. Nobody was expecting this. 'OK,' I sighed in a whisper. 'Now you two!' I said, pointing my finger at the two faces staring back, wondering why their world had suddenly and without warning turned upside down!

Me ma got worried seeing the kids go so quiet for a change, knowing they had pushed their luck. 'Ah, no! Leave them be, Martha! Sure, they were only tryin te get me goin! Weren't ye's, childre?' she said, still looking a bit pale from her sudden loss of nerve.

'But it's true, Sally,' they laughed quietly, starting off again.

I couldn't believe it! I opened my mouth but nothing came out!

'Jesus, Martha, them two take after you! Yet, still an all ye're tellin them they're bold? Jesus, you were a demon. You were very wild,' she said, shaking her head laughing.

'Not at all!' I snorted. 'You wouldn't hear a peep outa me!' I said, eyeing the kids, not wanting them to be hearing this stuff.

'Oh, yeah? Not half!' she laughed.

'Tell us, Sally! What did . . .'

'Get going, you two. Come on, everybody, let's start the holiday!' I shouted, making to open the doors. 'Come on, grab your bags, everyone.

Now, only the stuff we need for overnight, remember. We have a big berth; we can sleep our way over! So let's find our family cabin, get settled in and head for the restaurant. You can even take a rest first, Ma. We'll come and get you.'

'No, I'm grand,' me ma said.

'Yeah! I didn't come just te sleep,' Dinah said. 'I want te miss nothin. God knows, Ma, we waited long enough for this day te come,' she said.

'Oh, indeed we have,' the ma said, narrowing her eyes, starting to think about it then getting woken up fast enough.

'Come on, Sally! We want to show you everything! We know this ship; we've been on it before,' the kids roared, getting impatient to be on the move. 'Come on!' they shouted from the entrance, flying their head down the stairs, then looking back up to the ma, seeing her muttering and laughing, trying to hurry herself.

I slammed the car door shut, locking it. Then stared after Dinah, seeing her wobbling on her big high heels trying to tear after the ma, with the ma trying to catch up with the kids. I watched, seeing Dinah's ankle suddenly buckle as the overnight bag waved in her hand threatening to topple her. 'Hey, wait! Don't lose me,' she roared, getting her balance back, then taking off even faster.

I knew it, she won't last long in them high heels, I grinned. Oh, God, I'm so happy! My heart soared with the joy, listening to the life and the laughter coming out of them. Now the ma can feel the wind in her hair and the breeze on her face as she rushes on, trying to catch up with the life she lost down through so many years. The only weight she carries now is the handbag. She has that weighted down with the pension she collects and all the money she saves. Her and Dinah are like two little kids – they are now seeing all the wonders of the world as if they are only looking at it for the first time.

God, Ma, you have finally arrived. Would you ever have thought so long ago when you were down and out, with nothing staring ahead of you but a nightmare journey, always travelling through the darkness of night, with nothing and nobody to protect you and yours but the power of God. Truly, it was him that kept us safe, even though some got lost along the way. But you have safely arrived to find a little haven in the world you can now call home.

Hope now lies with the next generation. They carry a blazing torch of privilege that lights the darkness of poverty. My little ones are not branded social pariahs by its evil mark. Doors will not slam as they are turned away by a frosty world, its inhabitants heaving with a spiritual poverty, one that welcomes only a winner. One day they may grow strong and caring enough to continue on and pass down that burning light. My hope is that the curse of misery and poverty that fell on all of us may then be once and forever broken. That then will be the legacy I leave to all them and theirs that come after me.

Jackser, I will never forget that what you did was evil. But you, Jackser, were not evil. That is what redeems you in my eyes. Poor Jackser. I hope now, wherever you are, you are happy. Some things were never meant to be. You just never found a place where you could be at peace.

Rest in peace now, Jackser. Harry, look after your poor father. He was very unfortunate. Oh, Harry! Wherever you are, my sunshine, I still miss your smile and your bawdy humour. Gawd, you made me laugh. Sleep well, darling little brother.

29

'No! We are . . .'

I let the phone drop into its cradle, still hearing the voice talking, explaining, insensitive, uncaring; worse, completely unaware just how much pain they had caused me. I shook my head, not knowing whether I wanted to cry, commit murder or do both. So, Martha, you think you have lived long enough, seen it all! But no. People's cruelty coming from the most unexpected of places can still knock me for six, amaze and sicken me. 'Put the kettle on,' I muttered to meself, feeling the pain easing into a dull ache.

I sat drinking a cup of tea, dragging on the roll-up cigarette, giving a splutter. Jesus! These things are going to kill me, I thought, staring at the half-smoked cigarette, thinking to jam it in the ashtray. No! I took another suck on it, thinking me nerves are bad at the minute. I need something to keep me going. Then it hit me. Right! Fuck that. I'm going to sit down and write a letter. I am going to say exactly what I think about that bastard. NO! I'm not letting this go. Right, where's my Basildon Bond notepaper and the good Parker pen?

I shot into the study and opened the writing desk. It's only for keeping my papers. I never write letters, never! They can be used against you later down the road. I don't like putting my signature to anything. Jaysus! I'm paranoid about keeping my privacy. It runs too deep in me. It's always better to keep the head down and say nothing to no one. Anyway, I have the knack of talking like a blue-arse fly but really saying nothing!

OK, here goes. Hold back nothing, Martha. Let rip, give the full blast.

'. . . And furthermore!' I droned, feeling myself getting worked up. Then suddenly, a cold hard anger hit me. The enormity of how I was being treated rippled through me like a simmering volcano that was now getting ready to erupt! Fuck this. I screwed the paper up into a ball and fired it at the wastepaper basket, watching it land satisfyingly – smack – inside the bin. Then, like my arse was on fire, I was up and out of the room, tearing up the stairs and into one of the kids' bedrooms. Right! I need a jotter. I picked up a new Tesco A4 notebook, looking at it thinking, yeah, good, this will do. Then I whipped meself around and shot back down the stairs into the study.

Right! Fuck that. I will show them. Think they are too good for me, do they? They just do not know who they are dealing with. Nobody knows me – the real me! I am not what everybody thinks I am, and that includes them. They are fucking not fit to even walk in my shoes. They have had everything handed to them on a plate!

So, I will now reveal the true me. I will hold nothing back. I want a record of who I really am, or was. It's about time I now stopped running. Anyhow, nobody will ever get to see this in my lifetime. No! I will hide it away. Then, by the time they find it, I will be pushing up daisies. I hope they don't throw it out with a load of papers, thinking it is all rubbish when they are clearing out the house. Never mind that. Worry about that later. Just get on with it. I want the kids and their kids to know who they really are, where they came from, warts and all. I don't want them ever looking down on anybody the way that fucker has looked down on me. Yeah, right! So, where will I begin? Where else! Start at the beginning. Oh, wait! Shouldn't I give it a title? I thought, sucking on me biro. The Parker is only to impress; it's too good to waste.

Think! Hmm, I thought, slowly getting the picture of a vague, grim memory!

'Ma, He Sold Me for a Few Cigarettes'.

30

Ilifted my head, rubbing my eyes, sighing and taking in a deep breath. No, that's the end of it. I can't go on any more. This is killing me. For six long months now I have lived that nightmare all over again. God, I never knew any of this really. I had no memory! But the child in me knew it all and she just exploded back into life. It felt like I was not here at all, like I had disappeared. All I do is sit, pick up the pen, then it is her. The pen flies across the paper, letting her come back to life. She is living again. The person I am now does not exist. It is as if she has found a way to use me to live, breathe and talk. My hand is only the instrument. It is her in control, her words, her world, she has broken free! Now I have to live with her sitting in my head. She still wants to go on. She has so much more to say. But I can't take it. I don't know who I am any more. I feel so lost. I am just her again, feeling everything she felt, seeing the world through her eyes. I need to stop – enough is enough.

I closed the last notebook for the last time, then stared at it. Two full thick notebooks, five hundred and sixty-three pages all written by hand. I have never read it back. I have never even crossed out one word. No, not a single one. Everything that child said and lived and breathed I have now recorded. I must have used up a hundred biros. I have cried more tears in the last months than I have cried in many a long year. I need to put her back down inside me. She has so much to say, but I can't listen to any more. No! That's it.

I lifted the books, putting them into a big padded envelope, and carried them up to my bedroom, then I stood up on a chair and hid them at the bottom of a cardboard box pushed down deep, well into the back at the top of my wardrobe. The box is stuffed with old letters and cards, and all sorts of memories. It's been left lying undisturbed, gathering dust for years. I will never throw them out, though, even if it's years since I looked at them. No, because they are a lifetime of memories.

I pulled out a rolled-up coloured print, thinking I would have it framed. Then my eye caught the cardboard box sitting deep into the corner. Oh! I should really take a look in that. I have stuff from the kids when they were small, little notes they sent me and cards for Mother's Day. Jaysus! My whole life is in that box, I thought, as I leaned in to grab hold of it. I humped it down, landing it on the bed, then the big brown package caught my attention. I stared at it for a minute, then pulled it up from the bottom of the box. Hmm! Maybe I will take a look at this, I thought, deciding to put the box back and take a look at the notebooks.

I opened the package sitting at the kitchen table, thinking it might be interesting to read a bit. I couldn't bear to think of it for the last two years. It took me that long to get over it. Just as I was turning over the second page, the phone rang. I jumped up grabbing it.

'Hello!'

'Hi, Martha! What are you up to? I'm just passing your house now. Are you at home, I mean free?'

'Yeah! Come on in, Evelyn. I'm delighted to hear from you.'

'Right, get the kettle on,' she said, letting the line go dead.

'Have you got one of those mobiles, Evelyn?'

'Yeah, on the table there. Take a look,' she said, as I put my attention back to pouring boiling water into the mugs, making her a coffee and a tea for myself.

'Do you want a biscuit?' I said, rooting in the larder then looking down at her, seeing her buried in me notebooks.

'No, Evelyn! Close that book. It's private, my dear!' I said, half-laughing but very serious.

'Ah, go on! It's really interesting,' she said without lifting her head, letting her eyes fly across the pages.

'No!' I said, whipping it from under her nose. 'For my eyes only!' I said, trying to put the notebook back in the envelope.

'Ah, will you stop, Martha! Go on. Just let me take a look. I was enjoying it! What's that about? Did you write that?'

'Yes, I did, Evelyn. OK, I'll tell you what. I'll just read you a bit from it, OK?'

'Yeah, fine,' she said, lighting up a cigarette, supping her coffee and settling herself back in the chair.

I read aloud bits I thought were not too personal, then said, 'OK, that's it, Evelyn.'

'No, no, no! Go on, it's really interesting! I want to hear more!' she said, getting very impatient, waving at me to carry on. 'Listen, start at the beginning, Martha. That's you, isn't it? I even recognise your ma.'

'Oh, God! Don't remind me! Do you remember the time she turned up to the convent on Children's Day?' I moaned, giving her a crucified look.

'Yeah!' she laughed. 'That was a scream. The nuns never got over the shame of it! Do you know, Martha, listening to this reminds me so much of my own mother,' she said. 'They even have the same name. We didn't live too far from the Liberties of Dublin either; we were just across the Liffey. Well, my mother was. I was in the convent.'

'Yeah, but you got a great education out of them nuns, Evelyn. They sent you to a top secondary school. God, you were one of the very few,' I said, looking at her, seeing her nodding at me, with her baby-blue eyes dancing in her head. 'But you were very clever, Evelyn.'

'Yeah, I know,' she laughed, grinning at me with a mouthful of snow-white teeth. 'Well! Go on! Start reading,' she said, lighting up another cigarette. 'Wait, before you begin, let's have another coffee. I'll put the kettle on, so don't start yet,' she laughed, looking at me, then pinning her eyes on the notebook as she filled the kettle.

I finished the last line and closed the book, looking up at her. We both stayed still as she stared back at me, getting lost in her own thoughts.

'That's it!' I muttered. 'The whole story all written down now for posterity. Let the kids do what they like with it. But I am so glad I wrote it, Evelyn. It was worth all the snots and the tears and the heartbreak.'

She kept nodding her head slowly, then she took in a big sigh, shaking her head, saying, 'That has brought back so many memories to me, Martha. Everything became so vivid in my mind. I could see myself as a child, going out with my mother sometimes when she came up to bring me home.'

'Yeah, Evelyn, I know. I've seen more of you now in the last few weeks than I've seen of you when we were in the convent together. I've laughed more too. Some of those stories you told me about your mother, Evelyn, remind me so much of my own ma.'

'Listen, Martha,' she said, lighting up another cigarette. 'Jesus! I'm nearly out of cigarettes,' she said, seeing there was only two left in the box. 'I hope the garage is still open. I better get some. Anyway! You have to listen to me. You really should have that published. I keep telling you, there are people out there who would love to hear about those times again. It will remind them of their own childhood. But you should do it fast, Martha, before they all die off! Frankly, I think it would be a terrible loss to history if you didn't. There are very few records of old Dublin life. Mostly they are written by scholars or people just writing short stories about their memories. But what you have there is unique. Nobody has written a book like that in the dialect of old Dublin-speak. Be glad the nuns didn't educate you,' she laughed. 'It would have spoilt your natural brilliance.'

'Oh, I don't know, Evelyn,' I said, terrified at the idea of letting myself be unmasked. 'I have to think of the children! What would they think, Evelyn? And, Jaysus! I was a street kid! I don't mind that now. I'm secretly proud of myself. But I don't want to broadcast it.'

'Listen, Martha. It's because of that very fact! Because you were a street kid! You had a really tough life. Well, that puts you in the rare position of having the depth inside you to write that stuff! So, take my advice – share it with people. It's their life too! Everyone was poor then, Martha. Jesus! I well remember it,' she said, shaking her head and getting up to make her way towards me. 'Bye, love, thanks for everything. I'll see you soon,' she said, reaching over to grab hold of me in a tight hug. 'I better get home. It's two o'clock in the morning,' she said, looking mournfully down at her gold wristwatch. Then she laughed, saying, 'The only good thing about ending that book was now I can be in bed early and get some sleep.'

'Right! I'll see you out, Evelyn,' I said, watching her climb into her big black BMW. Gawd, Evelyn is a scream, I thought, waving as she drove off roaring out into the night.

Another year had passed when I picked up the notebooks again. I could feel a nervous flutter in the chest as I stared at the thick package envelope. OK, Evelyn was right – this stuff is part of our history; this is how it was. This is the voice from a child long ago, once again come alive to tell her story in her own words. Her voice speaks for the hidden millions. There were many little Marthas out there, some a lot worse off than me. Hunger and disease was rampant in my mother's time, and death was always close. I came barrelling in on the tail of new developments – vaccines about to be discovered – yet not much had changed through them early years. Children were born and died, while the mothers held their breath waiting for the new vaccines to limp in.

Nobody ever saw the silent tears of a mother as she sat cradling her infant child wasting away to death. Slowly it was being clawed from that mother's arms as she watched it perish from hunger and disease. Nobody ever heard the pitiful cries from that tenement house as death came howling back. It rushed in, blowing a cold wind under the door, ready to swoop again. The little ones' tortured screams for another loss – this time their worn-out mother – was just a keening sound being carried on the wind, then it would be heard no more.

So, let this little scrap of a child be the voice for the many generations who never had a voice.

31

I wandered home thinking about that publisher, the one in the UK. Yeah, nobody was bothered until he showed an interest. Weeks, those other publishing houses had it. But as soon as they got wind of the fact someone was interested! Now, suddenly, they are all rushing to make me an offer.

Yeah, well, the question is: do I really want to publish it? The idea sends me into a nightmare. Jesus, I might never be able to hold my head up again. Dublin is only a village. I could see people pointing me out in the street. I could just hear them all.

'Look! There's yer woman!'

'Who would have thought it, Barberalla, dear?'

'And she looks so respectable!'

'Goodness, one never knows who one is fraternising with.'

'I'm off! Quick, she's coming in our direction.'

Oh, fuck! No, I would have to emigrate!

No, think again. You sent this out to the publishers because you had made your mind up; otherwise, you would not be letting it see the light of day. Now you're just getting cold feet. Right, you're going to have to take the risk and run the gauntlet. You may become an outcast again, and everything you've worked for, especially for the kids, will be wiped out. They will suffer. That is the risk. But you would not be where you are today if you had let fear get in your way. Think of it! You have plunged in and taken many a risk, sometimes even sailing close to the wind, with the potential to lose everything. Well, you haven't come a cropper yet, because first you always move slowly, calculate the risk, do the groundwork, then do or be damned. This is a calculated risk and – bloody hell! – the calculation is simple. What have I got to lose? Everything! What have I got to earn? Very little compared to what I have. Jesus! Too much of a risk!

But there is a fire now in my belly. It is something I feel duty-bound to do. I owe it to myself and the people out there who lived through this too. A lot of them are not here any more; they're long gone. So, do it for them, let the little voice of this child speak for them. This is their history too. It should be recorded!

Fuck! You're getting very noble, Martha. Yes! Well, if it is the right thing to do, then do it.

I took in a deep breath, making my mind up. So, let it be published and be damned! Right! That's settled. Now to make the best deal. I'm getting the idea publishers are a hungry lot! Better keep wide awake! Right, I still have a few people to see.

I dived into the back seat then turned, saying, 'Thank you for a lovely evening. I really enjoyed the party.'

'OK, tomorrow morning then. I will phone you around ten-thirty. Have you read the contract yet?' he said, sounding hopeful I might give him an answer now.

'Well, I'm still ploughing through it,' I smiled, not wanting to commit myself.

'OK, we'll talk tomorrow,' he said, smiling and slamming the door shut as the taxi moved off, heading me for home.

I looked around, seeing him head back to the party. He walked with a very erect bearing. Quite the aristocrat, I thought, seeing him hurry, wanting to get in out of the dark night with the rain bucketing down on his big, black, man's umbrella. It even had a gold tip on the handle.

Hmm! He's quite the debonair, I thought – very suave, sophisticated and certainly charming. I have been wined, dined and now met the 'glitter-literati' of Dublin. He was intending to show me there could be weight behind his words of 'You will be famous. You shall be feted! You have done for the twenty-first century what blogs have done for the twentieth century,' he said, with me letting it go in one ear and out the other.

Oh, yeah, very smooth! He's trying to swell my head so big I won't be able to resist parting with me manuscript to him. Anyway! Believing that rubbish would only get me locked up for being delusional! No, second thoughts, maybe there could be something in it. Otherwise, why would he want to publish it? Maybe I do believe he meant what he said. He knows his stuff when it comes to literature. He's not just a publisher but a very erudite and learned man. But still, he may be the only one that sees it like that. Most people are blind – that's why they don't see opportunity under their nose.

He's also made me a handsome offer. It's not really the money but the weight he can put behind the book. He has some very serious contacts. Yet I'm still holding back. So, my antenna is telling me this is not the deal for me.

Others are talking about a huge campaign with an appearance on the 'Late Late' no less! Yeah! I'm sure they could do it. Ireland is an island of nepotism. Scratch my back and I'll scratch yours, dearie!

Yeah, but I'm thinking I might be better with the UK. I met the publisher from Mainstream again yesterday and I have a strong leaning to go with him. He's serious – no smothering you in honeyed words that could be a fly-trap! No, he's a straightforward, hard-headed businessman, with the feet firmly planted on the ground. Plus, he has very strong back-up – he can do what he says. And there's no doubt he's razor-sharp. I see that in the penetrating look he gives you. Like he's not just listening to the words but he's even reading the air around you. That should make it easier for me to do a deal with him. I'm not clever enough to deal with fools – they're much too much hard work. No, this fella is the type that, if he ran a shop, he wouldn't let you out the door without taking something out of your pocket. He's a deal-maker! Good, should be easy. Funnily enough, I even feel I can trust him! Yeah, there's a homeliness about him. You can see the man behind the business front. He has an innate kindness – like he feels what you tell him, like he actually cares. Yeah, I think he's a decent man and would play fair. Right! UK it is, and am I the lucky one? Very lucky, Martha. I sighed contentedly, sitting deeper into the seat for more comfort.

My eyes took in the old Liffey walls, with the river continuing to make its way up along the quays as it headed itself out to sea. It still flows, undisturbed by all the changes that screamed in with the 'Celtic Tiger' now chewing up everything in its path. It's then spitting it out as soulless apartments and giant glass office blocks, with the whole lot held together by giant skeletons of nothing but steel. Pity – the old charm of the Georgian city is nearly being wiped out.

The taxi glided along the dark quays, whirring over the rain-lashed streets with the neon lights flashing ahead in the distance. They winked and dazzled, promising a warm welcome to late-night stragglers desperate to still hang on to the air of gay abandon. I stared out through the rain, seeing the remains of the old Georgian houses tarted up, looking more like painted whores now than the 'grand old dames' they were. That was before the investors got their hands on them. Now they're all show on the outside, but the rot and decay is still eating them away. They sat silent now, looking lonely and empty as business people locked up and went home for the night. At least they're still standing, I thought, getting something for a bit of comfort at seeing me old roots.

Over the other side of the river I stared moodily out at the new apartments. I could see very few of the windows showed a light. I bet they're all in there now sleeping the sleep of the dead, knowing they have to get up in a few hours, then it's back to the salt mines, working all the hours that God sends. And for what? Just so they can pay for them bleedin little dog boxes. Bloody hell, it depresses me. Everything has changed too fast, gone too far. I feel lost now without my old city. I don't recognise the faces on the people, or the places where I lived. I think when this blows over it will leave a lot of devastation in its wake. Oh, yes, there will be hell to pay!

A crowd of people came tumbling out of a nightclub just as the taxi pulled up for the lights on O'Connell Bridge. They made a rush for this taxi then staggered back, seeing it was taken. I watched as they turned, the women falling over each other on high heels trying to make a run for it. They were dashing for the shelter of the awning that hung over the flashing lights of the entrance. I could see now they're already soaked to the skin, with coats thrown over their heads. It happened even before they could make it back to the shelter. Then they started shouting at each other.

'OK, don't forget, next week!' one young one was shouting as she made her way back into the club.

'Happy Christmas!' her friend shouted after her, but it was lost in the wind and the rain as the young one vanished back in, anxious to be in out of this treacherous, dark, wet and stormy night.

The taxi pulled off, heading across the bridge, leaving me looking back at the thinning crowd. They had changed their minds and gone back inside. Christmas week! Gawd, I better get ready, I thought, staring at the flashing lights, seeing them make rainbows of coloured jewels as they sat in fat droplets of rain before pouring down the windowpane.

32

'It was lovely to talk to you, Martha. I am looking forward to working with you on the book.'

'Yes, thank you. I have really enjoyed talking to you, too.'

'Oh! One more thing, Martha. Are you using a pseudonym?'

I listened to that, knowing what it meant. 'Oh, yes! Definitely! Let's see now, what would I like to call myself?' I wondered, thinking about it. 'Something exotic? No, a nice Irish name. Biddy Murphy!' I said, wondering what she might think of that.

Silence.

I waited, but then it went on a long time. 'Hello? Are ye still there?' I whispered into the heavy breathing.

'But, Martha, is it a good idea when you are writing non-fiction? Shouldn't you use your own name?'

'Well, no! Because I don't want anyone to recognise me!' I puffed, knowing that made eminent sense. I just thought of that. It's a brilliant way out. Then it hit me – so, what's the bleedin point in having the book published if you're still going to go on hiding?

'Right!' I said, taking in a sharp breath. 'Leave my own name! You're right – it is my life, so I want my name plastered all over the cover. I might as well, seeing as I've already hanged meself, letting the world and his wife know my business.'

'Fine. I think that just about covers it. OK, I will be in touch soon, when we are ready to start the editing.'

'Lovely, I'm really looking forward to that,' I said, wondering what she was talking about.

'Bye!'

'OK, bye now,' I said, putting down the phone with a smile on my face. Ahh! She really sounds lovely, so nice and gentle. Great! Get started on the work, she said. Well, the sooner the better. I just want to get this over with then vanish back into the woodwork. Jaysus, this idea of having it published has me rattling like a bag of bones. Anyway! How many Martha Longs are there in the country? No, they'll never cop on it's me!

I wandered into Tesco looking for a computer. The publishers said I have to get one for the editing. They said we will be doing it by email, whatever that is.

I stood looking at a big white machine.

'Can I help you?' a young fella said, stopping to look down at me. He was wearing his Tesco jacket with the logo on.

'Oh, yes, please! How much is this computer? Are they dear?'

'Is it a PC you want?' he said, looking at me with a puzzled look on his baby face.

'No, a computer,' I said, wondering if he was deaf.

'Yes, that's what I said – a PC ... personal computer!' he said, looking like he was trying to explain, because I was a bit light in the brain department.

'Oh! Is that what they're called?' I said, letting a smile appear on me face. I nodded happily. 'Yeah! I want to buy a PC. What about this one?' I said, pointing at the white machine with the glass in front.

'No, that's a microwave.'

'Oh! Is it?' I said, whipping me head in to get a better look. 'I don't have one a them, I don't like the sound of them. I heard once on the radio, the waves from that thing can give you cancer! Do you know?' I said, feeling outraged. 'The government is trying to stop us reaching the pension! This must definitely be a conspiracy! Keep the population down – it's exploding too fast! Bet that's the thinking,' I huffed, getting carried away with the annoyance on me. Then I looked around, seeing the young fella had vanished.

I rushed off looking for him, thinking, fuck, stop talking rubbish, Martha! You've been watching too much *Logan's Run*. Then your man flew back around a corner, knocking the wind outa me.

'There you are! I was looking for you,' he said, wanting me to stay with him.

'Oh, grand, here you are. Found you! Where's the computer PCs?'

I said, straining me neck to look up at him. Jesus! The height of him. What do they feed them on?

'OK! Follow me,' he said, flying off, with me having to rush up behind him, six runs for his two strides – running like a coolie, all I needed was the rickshaw.

I struggled out of the shop with a huge box that would barely fit in the trolley. 'Here, young fella, will you give us a hand with this? Help me to get it into the car,' I said.

'Ahh! Grand, thanks. You're very good,' I said, waving as I drove off with me new computer PC. I can't wait to get started!

'Come back! You've only shown me how to turn it on! How the bloody hell do you get to use this thing?' I screamed, seeing the kids break their necks down the stairs, making to get away from me. I sat staring at it, looking at the lovely picture of the green fields and white clouds floating in a blue sky. Yeah, lovely, but how do I get going?

OK, have a go yourself. Press this. Now, what does that mean? Jaysus! Ah, Jaysus! Them kids are not worth feeding. I started moaning and crying, nearly tearing me hair out with the frustration. They do all this in school. How mean can ye get? I'm getting nowhere on me own. Now think. Who do I know with a computer? I can ring them up and they can tell me on the phone.

'OK,' Evelyn said, speaking slowly down the phone line. 'Bring the mouse . . .'

'What mouse?'

'The little gadget at your hand.'

'Oh, yeah! I have that,' I said, getting all excited.

'Now drag it across.'

'How do I do that? Do I lift it?'

Sigh – she's getting impatient – 'Martha, your best bet is to do a course!'

'Ah, forget that, Evelyn. Sure, just tell me what to do! Then I'll be grand. I can work away meself.'

'OK, I'll come over tonight and run you through the basics.'

'HELP! Kids! Come quick! The computer PC is acting peculiar. There's a funny little man down in the corner, grinning and pointing at something. What's that about?'

They sighed, shaking their heads, and turned for the door. 'Mum! We can't keep tearing up and down these stairs, all the way to the top floor. We have our own work to do,' she said. 'Anyway! Why did you not put it down in your study on the ground floor? You are up here in a garret!'

'Yeah,' he said, 'she's starving for her "Art", and starving us as well. Mum! When's dinner?'

'So, are you not going to help me?' I said, staring daggers at the pair of them, only thinking about their bellies! 'This is my work too!' I said. 'Did it never occur to either of you that this is serious work?'

'We know, Mum, but this has to stop. We're not running up and down these stairs again and that's that!'

'Whadeye mean? This is the first time I have asked for your help today! You scatter when you hear me calling. I never realised how mean the pair of you were,' I snorted, going back to me computer.

'That's it, Mum. We're going to have to put ourselves up for adoption if this continues.'

'Why? Because I'm not at your beck and call? If you must know, try burying your nose in the fridge. I've already cooked a casserole! Now it's the weekend, I'm only on this thing for the last four hours. I need to learn to use the bleedin thing for the emalling . . . the editing,' I said.

The kids roared laughing. 'Mum! Emails!'

'Yeah, well, whatever they're called! Now, give me a bit of peace for just a few more minutes, then I'm all yours. Agreed?'

'Agreed!' he said, then nodded at the sister, hiding with the head in the door and the body buried on the landing. She's cute – she knows when to let him do all the talking.

'Bye! See you later,' I shouted to the door as it banged shut behind them, leaving the floorboards rattling under my feet.

Dear Martha, you cannot put a full stop in front of 'And'. It is a conjunction.

Oh! I know what that word means, I thought, I came across it once in the kids' grammar book.

Dear Editor, you can. I have just done that!

Dear Martha, you cannot have all these commas. The sentence is not making sense.

Dear Editor, it makes wonderful sense, try reading it again.

Dear Martha, you really cannot put 'And' with a full stop in the middle of a sentence.

Dear Editor, yes indeed you can, it's the way the language runs.

Dear Martha, what language would that be?

What does she mean? How the fuck do I know?! It's the way I used to speak! Right! I have had enough of this.

Dear Editor, please do not change one word, this is the voice of the child!

Dear Martha, I have spent months on this editing. We are not making progress!

Dear Editor, I have spent bleedin weeks poring over your work, then changing it back to the original. I didn't have one idea, of what this was all about, I just went on following you, answering your questions! Then it dawned on me . . . in fact! May I let you know! I spent weeks putting to rights, the 'Work' you sent me, because I could see me book was getting desecrated! THIS IS NOT THE QUEEN'S BLEEDIN ENGLISH YE KNOW!

Dear Martha, so what is it? Really, I am trying to understand.

She's trying to understand! Think, Martha! How do you explain the old Dublin way of talking? Fuck! I don't really even understand her question! Tell her . . . It is, eh? A mixture . . . Think, Martha – a mixture of what? Oh, I have it.

Dear Editor, this language is not English, in fact, it is not even Irish. It is Dublin-speak! Yes, we Dubliners are unique. Not like the culchies! I do hope now, with this information, it is becoming more clear.

Dear Martha, what is a culchie?

Dear Editor, it is a clodhopper.

Dear Martha, we are not making progress. We must move on.

Dear Editor, where in the name a Jaysus is all me commas, exclamation marks, dots and dashes, GONE TO? You have annihilated them! Please reinstate them, forthwith!

I'm really getting inta this literature business; it's beginning to flow off me tongue, I thought happily. Yeah, I'm definitely a fast learner!

Dear Martha, I am afraid work has come to a standstill. We have not managed to get past the first page after four long months. I therefore think it is best we withdraw from any further attempts. We will now have to wait until the publisher returns from New York. He will have to deal with this. So goodbye for now. Yours, the editor.

Dear Editor, that suits me fine. While you're at it, tell him for me, If one word of that book is changed! He can have his cheque back, then send me back me book. Goodbye for now. Yours, Martha.

I picked up the phone. 'Hello, Martha! This is the publisher! What's going on? What's the problem?'

'Well, that editor of yours is trying to turn my book into the Queen's bleedin English!'

'Martha, that is her job. Let her get on with her work. You have to edit a book, Martha. Be reasonable!'

'No, she can edit somewhere else, no one is changing one word of my book . . .'

'It's not a book! It's a manuscript! It has not been published!' he snapped, really beginning to lose the rag.

'Right!' I steamed, 'so don't bleedin . . .'

'I'll tell you what I will do, Martha!'

I listened, then a smile came on me face.

'OK, grand, I'll let her . . .' Then it hit me. 'No! She cannot change one word, not even a comma. I want all me commas where they are! Otherwise the voice of the child will be lost. This is the way she spoke, I wrote down every word. So, I'm not having the integrity of my work corrupted,' I said, listening to his sharp intake of breath. I knew he was impressed at how professional I was. Yeah! That idea, 'integrity corrupted', just came at me out of the blue. I must have heard that somewhere. Jaysus, I'm really getting inta the swing of this!

I waited, listening to the silence. The only thing to be heard was the sighing. Then, another hour and we were sorted.

'Right! Are you agreed on that, Martha?'

'Definitely,' I said, nodding my head, forgetting he couldn't see it. Right! I thought, now to get down to the business of this editing.

'Well, that's it, Martha. The editing is over, now it goes off to the printers.'

'So, that's it,' I said quietly, taking in a big sigh, listening to her do the same. A companionable silence sat between us as we thought about that, letting it sink in.

'Thank you, I know it wasn't easy for you,' I said, thinking she should get a medal for her patience with me. The poor girl had a very rocky road, trying to prise even the smallest changes outa me. But we made very little change if any. She simply ran her eagle eye over the script, very minutely and painstakingly, making sure everything was as it should be. Oh, but she is good, no doubt about that. She certainly knows her job! God knows what would have happened if I was with someone less experienced.

'Right, that's a huge relief getting that done. Thanks for everything. Take care,' I said.

'Thank you, Martha. It certainly was interesting for me,' she said, sounding almost demented with the happiness at getting rid of me! I could hear it with her sighs, sounding like someone had just told her she was not going to get another battering. Then her voice really lifted with a chirpy sound, getting ready to erupt in a burst of victory.

She had done it! Survived my manuscript to produce the book!

'Good luck, Martha!'

'Thank you,' I said, slowly putting down the phone.

It's over, Martha, I thought. Now it's in the lap of the gods. Whatever happens now, it's out of my hands. I'm at the mercy of the world and his wife. I shook my head, giving a little shiver. Oh, well, you've faced worse! What will be, will be!

I listened as the publisher said the book '*Ma, He Sold Me for a Few Cigarettes* is still doing brilliantly, Martha! It went straight into number one in the bestselling list and it's still up there months later. It's flying off the shelves. The readers love it! Did you see the rave reviews it got? You must be delighted!'

'Yes, I am,' I said, still feeling numb, not able to take it in. 'Yes, I'm delighted, thrilled. I can't believe it! Isn't it great?' I said, wanting them to try to explain how that could have happened. Then there was silence, and I knew something was coming.

'Listen, Martha, we are inundated with phone calls from readers wanting to know when the next book is out. Martha, would you consider writing a sequel? Everyone wants to know what happened next in your story!'

I listened quietly, feeling completely shut down to that idea. 'No,' I said, 'I'm sorry but that was never intended to be a book. That's it, I'm afraid. Sorry,' I half-laughed, 'but, no, I won't be writing another book. That's it for me. I never intended to become an author. I'm not a writer. So, I'm afraid that's the end of it. I don't want to say any more about my life. But thank you for asking me.'

'OK, Martha, I just thought we should ask. We'll be in touch.'

'Thank you and thanks for passing on the great news,' I said, thinking, as I lowered the phone into its cradle, I was right about him. That publisher is one of the best. I know he's disappointed, but he would never push. He even goes out of his way to make things easy for everyone. No, I can't say a bad word against him.

I stood still, looking around the kitchen, trying to take in the news. People like it, I thought, feeling a quiet sense of deep satisfaction. I have achieved what I set out to do. I have left an account of my life as I lived it through the back streets of 1950s Dublin. Now there is an authentic record lived and shown through the eyes of a little girl. It is out there now, and anyone who wants to know what it was really like can walk with that child and experience life with her as she lives it in the raw.

Good, well done, Martha! I sighed contentedly as a great feeling of stillness came over me, settling into a wonderful sense of peace spreading itself all through me. Yeah, I feel very peaceful. I'm at peace with myself. Now it's all over I can move on, knowing I have left something of myself behind.

Then I came out of my daze and looked up at the clock. Right, time to get moving. The kids will be home from school soon wanting a bit of dinner on the table. OK, what's first? What are we having? Chicken – better bung that in the oven and wash the spinach, then roast a few potatoes. I can mash the rest.

I bent down quickly to grab a few potatoes out of the wicker basket under the work table, then I heard a squeal and felt me foot standing on something soft. Jaysus! I tried to lift myself off it and nearly toppled back, breaking me neck.

'Minnie!' I screamed, seeing her come out from behind me. 'You bloody eegit. You nearly got me killed!' I shouted, seeing her take off, giving a dirty look back, hobbling on three legs trying to make it to her basket. 'Oh! You're such an eegit,' I moaned, rushing down to take a look at her paw. 'Come here! What happened your poor little paw?' I said, lifting it up as she started moaning and crying, then I heard us getting a lovely aria going, with her keens higher and my moans lower.

'Oh, poor you, ye little gobshite! What were you doing anyway, sticking your nose into the vegetables? You don't even like them!' I whined, as her whines got louder.

'Right! I said, standing up. 'I think you need something nice to make that better. What about a biccie?' I opened the larder, taking out a big packet of digestive biscuits, then looked, seeing a blur of fluff as she was up and over so fast I barely got time to take the next breath. 'Jaysus, Minnie! You're a great Abbey actor! I should put you on the stage,' I snorted, seeing her take the biscuit between her pressed lips and gingerly carry it back to her basket, with not a bother on the leg.

'Ahh! You're better already, Minnie,' I said, seeing her turn around and drop it in the basket, then turn back to give me another dose of whines.

'No! Forget it, Minnie. That's yer lot!' I snorted. 'Now don't push your luck.'

She gave me another dirty look and lifted up the biscuit, starting to make short work of it.

Jaysus! That dog is worse than a child, I thought, rushing back to get on with me business.

I walked through the shopping centre, then rambled into the bookshop. Oh! I thought, seeing a line of my books all standing to attention up on the shop's bestselling list. It was number one! I stared – not able to take it in. That's my book! I thought, looking around seeing shelf after shelf of books, with some of the big-name authors, and mine was in the place of honour. How did that happen? I can't understand it! Jesus! It's impossible, I thought, shaking my head, not able to get it through to me.

A woman with grey hair tied up in a bun and a grey wrinkled face that looked like it needed a bit of sunshine and a dab of Polyfilla saw me looking up at my book.

'Oh! She's very popular,' the woman said, smiling at me.

'Really?' I said, wanting to hear more.

'Oh, yes, everyone is talking about it. It's a marvellous seller.'

'Gosh, isn't that great?' I said. 'What's it about?'

'Oh, it's about a young child growing up in terrible poverty,' she said, shaking her head with disgust.

'Oh, right!' I said, hoping she wouldn't expect me now to buy it after all the attention she gave me.

'Do you know,' she said, 'I believe the author is local.'

'Is she?' I roared, wondering how she got wind of that.

'Oh, yes, and of course we like to encourage our local authors.'

'Oh! Do you have many?' I said.

'Oh, indeed, yes, we do. We are famous for it!'

'Right, thank you very much,' I said, making me way out the door before I heard any more bad news. Jesus! Talk about Dublin being a village! Fuck! I wonder how they found out I live around here? Anyway, thank God they don't know me to see, but someone does!

I was just heading out of the shopping centre and made it into the car park when I heard a roar. 'Martha! Martha!'

I looked around wondering who was calling me, then I saw a woman waving at me like mad. It was one of the parents from the children's school. I wonder what she wants? I thought, seeing her rushing herself like mad wanting to talk to me. We don't have much to say to each other normally. I find her manner a bit too abrupt, so I give her a wide berth.

'Martha, I read your book!' She flew at me, coming to a skidding stop, breathing right down me neck with a big smile plastered on her face.

'You did?' I said, feeling myself turn all colours. 'Oh, great, thanks!' I said, turning and making for my car.

'No, wait! Hang on. I want to talk to you,' she said, grabbing hold of my arm, not wanting me to escape.

I couldn't take in what was happening; I had gone into shock. How did she know it was me? Jaysus! I don't give a fiddler's fart what they say about me – I would soon put them in their place. But the poor kids! They could get an awful time with all the other kids repeating what their parents said.

'I saw the children's names. You dedicated the book to them,' she said, beaming at me.

Oh, you dirty, thundering, stupid fuckin gobshite of a complete eegit, Martha! You bloody moron! I felt like crying with how thick I was.

'The book was brilliant. Oh! I couldn't get over how good it was. You are brilliant,' she said. 'Look! I have to give you a hug! I've been dying to meet you. That's all I wanted to do since I knew it was you. Come here!' she said, lunging at me. Then suddenly I was swallowed up and folded into a massive soft mound of flesh. She's a lovely big woman. She looks like Diana Dors, the big blonde bombshell actress. But she's dead now! I thought, wondering if it wouldn't have been a good idea for me to do the same before I ever had my name plastered all over a bookshop.

Then I came back to me senses, realising I was getting smothered in a delicious smell of Miss Dior perfume. Then she pushed me back, still holding on to me, and said, looking straight into my eyes, with hers shining in her head, 'Oh, you don't know how I've wanted to do that.' Then she leaned into me, whispering, 'I went through a terrible time, and as I was reading your book, well, you have no idea how much you helped me. I realised we do survive. Life can throw the worst at you, but it need not break you! Thank you for that, Martha,' she said, letting her eyes swim with tears. Then she smiled, trying to block them, saying, 'All my sisters are reading the book now, and my daughter. I made her read it.'

My heart was swelling with her goodness and the fact she saw the book for what it was. A life just lived – not something to be used against me, but something that would give people a little glimpse into a way of life now long dead and gone. I felt very humbled that I had the bad judgement to underestimate this woman's decent character. We stood talking while she told me some of what she had been going through. It was so terribly sad. You never know what goes on behind the front people put on. She is wealthy, with beautiful children, but she carried a terrible weight. Only now was she getting back on her feet because time had moved on and things were sorting themselves out. At last, life had finally given her a break and she could lift her head now and see the sunshine.

I lifted my head, looking into her face, seeing the honest goodness coming through in a big smile as she stared back at me, looking like I was someone worth knowing. We were equal; we both shared a common bond of pain and suffering. My face lit up as a surge of relief and happiness flew through me. I'm free! It's OK. I haven't done the wrong thing; everything will be grand.

'Listen, Penelope,' I said, putting my hand on her shoulder. 'You have no idea how you have just helped me,' I whispered. 'Thanks for that. Thank you for your goodness in letting me know. Yes, it really helped me,' I said, nodding my head, thinking about it. 'Bye, Penelope. It was lovely talking to you. Take care.'

'Oh! By the way, Martha! Ursula gave her copy of the book to your daughter. She wanted you to sign it. Did she give it to you?'

'Eh, no, but I'll be delighted. I'll take a look in her schoolbag. That child can be very scattered. See you again, Penelope. Bye!' Then I turned, heading off to make my way across the car park, wondering what happened to that child's book. I hope Madam didn't leave it down somewhere and walk off without it.

I got into the car and drove out of the car park heading for home. Suddenly, without warning, a gush of hot tears rolled down my cheeks. I wiped them away with the sleeve of my jumper, trying to see out through a mist of blurring tears flooding my eyes, blinding me. I blinked hard, staring ahead, then whispered, not able to get over it, 'People do care, they really do care. You can never underestimate the kindness of people when you get up close. My God, Martha, you are still learning. People are inherently full of goodness, and goodness can move mountains.'

I opened my shiny new laptop and stared at the reams of words now on a document. So, that's that finished! I thought, staring at it, thinking I had continued to write. It was talking to Penelope gave me that courage. I had now seen the world through her eyes. It told me there is room for everyone, even a little street kid. But as with the first book, I did not do it for the world; it was only for myself. The child in me still had a lot to say, so I allowed her to continue.

Yes, but now I have finished. This is as far as I want to allow her to go. It really is taking a lot out of me. I have to live it all over again, day by day, minute by minute, sitting inside her soul, becoming her again while she continues her journey through life. But now it's enough. I am exhausted. 'I'm worn out,' I sighed, feeling relieved that it's over. But it will be a long time before I can shift her out of my head and heart. She is becoming more powerful, more alive the longer I stay with her. It certainly helps me to grow – become more accepting of myself and who I really am. But the price is high on my health and I wonder in the long haul is it really worth that gain? 'Only time will tell,' I sighed heavily, feeling I need a good rest.

Rest? What a laugh! Two hopes, Martha – Bob Hope and no hope! I thought, looking out to see what Minnie is shouting about. Oh, bloody hell. She's managed to bully herself a biscuit out of next door, I thought, seeing the old lady leaning over the wall and shovelling them into her. The poor old woman is duty-bound now to share her eleven o'clock tea break with Minnie, otherwise the poor old soul won't get any peace sitting in that deckchair trying to get herself an airing.

'That bloody dog would buy and sell you,' I snorted, thinking she's sharper than the two kids put together. Those two haven't a blade of sense between them; they never stop killing each other. Minnie is blind, bothered and bewildered wondering which one to sink her teeth into and drag away by the knickers! She loves keeping law and order. I know she is only trying to copy me. Ah, gawd, she's lovely. Yeah, I really do have a great life. I'm blessed! Sure, isn't that rest!

I picked up the phone, asking to speak to the publisher.

'Hello, Martha! How are you?'

'Great! Listen, I have a finished manuscript. It's a sequel to the first book.'

'Wonderful!' he said, sounding delighted. 'What is the title, Martha?'

'"Ma, I'm Gettin Meself a New Mammy." Do you want to take a look at it?'

'Yes, that would be great. Can you send it to me, Martha?'

'Yeah! How will I send it?'

'By email. I will get someone to phone you straight away; they can guide you through it. OK, Martha, great to talk to you. I will be in touch soon.'

33

I headed for home, then stopped the car when I neared, looking around for a 'little brown man' – the ticket parking fella in his shite-brown uniform. Risk it? Yeah, go on.

I dived across the road and went tearing into the travel agent's, seeing there was one fella ahead of me discussing his holiday. Only problem was, he couldn't make up his bleedin mind. OK! I thought, making a snap decision and appearing at his elbow.

'Excuse me, would you mind awfulley,' I whispered in me best 'Missus Bucket' accent, 'if I may just ask a question to this nice lady here?' I beamed, looking up into the pair of china-blue eyes staring back, then shook me head mouthing, 'No?'

The eyebrows arched, making it to the ceiling. The nose pinched and the jowls sank, finally coming to rest before they hit the floor. You could hear a pin drop. 'Really!' he puffed, giving a practised sniff reserved for riff-raff like me, then turned the head, closing the eyes, waiting for the aul one to sort me out for being so rude.

'Goodness!' I shivered, feeling terribly rude. They're very delusional around here about their 'status'. You won't get any real Dubliners living here. Over this side of the river they're all a shower of culchies thinking they're now aristocrats, never mind true-blue Dubs! They write back to the bog, saying, 'We made it, Mammy! We're now living in them big houses dash once belonged chew dhe English!!' Well, that's what the mammies will say when they're bragging to the neighbours after Mass on Sunday!

Well! That's why I've pushed me way in and I'm now living right smack in the middle of them. I'm making a stand for the Dubliners, right on me own patch of grass. I was thinking of getting a flag and sticking it on the roof! Pity I didn't get the young fella to learn the bagpipes. Then, at the closing of the day, I could lower the flag while he plays 'Molly Malone in them fair streets a Dublin'.

I stood watching him still trying to turn the face inside out, but then got a better look when he finally straightened it out. Not bad looking, I thought, if you're desperate enough to put up with the ego. That fella loves himself, I sniffed. Anyway! He's too young for me. I prefer them when they've matured like old wine. There's many a sweet tune to be played on an old fiddle, I consoled meself. Jaysus, fuckin time is a bitch! It catches up with you to hand you old age, and just when the fun was starting . . . Now you have to go home early – you need your bed. Not to mention the goings-on wanting to look beautiful! That caper can take up to ten hours trying to get yourself ready, when once it only took ten minutes!

'Oh, God,' I puffed, feeling the guts sinking out of me with the melancholy of old age striking at me again. I watched your man's hair stand up from me blowing the air then seeing him grab his stuff, moving himself further down the counter.

'Yes! Would you mind waiting!' screamed the dyed redhead, looking about forty but trying to pass herself off as twenty. I leaned in for a better look. Yeah, she's hiding the wrinkles and bags under the eyes with a shovelful of pancake make-up.

'I am with this customer!' she snorted, going back to the fascinating fella with the ready tan, the big wallet and the St Laurent shiny suit – and he looked like he didn't have a ball and chain in tow. No wife, girlfriend or clinging mother to be seen on the horizon. He wanted a holiday for one.

Fuck this! I yanked the door open, flying me head up and down the road, looking for the shite-brown-coloured uniform, then peeled me eyes back to the car. No. No ticket yet.

'Listen, I have my mother in the car and I need to get her across the road to the hospital. She's waving over at me. I think she's having a chest attack . . . pain! Heart attack . . . Well, it may be serious. I offered to take her earlier to the hospital when she complained about the pain, but she refused to go,' I said sadly. 'She won't go in because she's worried about the cats. Six a them we have – all moggies! An a canary! He's called Johnny!' I said, half-smiling then looking very worried, with my face creasing and me head shaking.

I got nowhere. They just stared with the mouths open, then dropping the eyes to see any sign of what planet I might a come from. Then she sniffed, dropped her eyes back on the brochure, staring, then the mind was made up and she got back to business. He dropped the head, snapping it down with her.

'Now! I would recommend the Bahamas,' she whispered, sounding like a snake hissing, thinking she sounded sexy. 'Definitely!' she pouted, lifting the pointed finger to wave it at yer man. 'It's ideal! Made for a man of your calibre. Very sophisticated! Full of executive high flyers like yourself!'

He nodded like mad, rattling the head off himself agreeing with every word she said. Then she moved closer, pushing the brochure with her. He moved the head in for a better look, nearly tipping his chin on the desk while she rested her dyed hair – looking more like a blonde, dried-up dead bush! – letting it nestle close to his newly styled cut and blow-dry.

I stood sniffing, sighing and snorting, fretting and keening, then clamping and blowing the mouth off meself with the eyeballs boring holes in them. No good! The bleedin gobshites are not taking a blind bit of notice, I keened under me breath, nearly crying with the rage on me. Oh, bloody hell! I'm going to end up with a five-pound parking ticket!

I put my hand on me chest, hoping it might worry them I'm having a heart attack meself, then plunged the neck back out the door, swinging the head, with the eyeballs turning left to right. I was just in time to spot Adolf making his way slowly from the top of the road, easing his head in to squint at every car, checking to see if they had the car tax. Oh, holy Jesus! He's coming!

'Look, I better go!' I squealed, sounding like me arse was on fire. The head was out lunging for the door, but then me arse turned, heading straight back for the desk. I was now ready to lose the rag.

'Would you ever please just grab that ticket you have waiting for me? Martha Long is the name. I booked it by phone – one way to London travelling in two days' time.'

She stared at me, trying to digest that mouthful, but didn't stir to shift herself.

'It's serious! Adolf is making his way down the road and the ma is having apoplexy waving at me to hurry! For gawd's sake, you'll be the death of her! She's a ninety-seven-year-old woman!' I screamed, strangling meself, with the face turning blue and the eyeballs seeing stars.

'Give her the ticket. Sort the lady out first,' he snapped, shaking himself, lifting the neck.

I smiled. They were all now going into emergency mode. 'Thanks! Oh, you're a pal,' I snapped, slapping the money on the counter and grabbing up the wallet with the ticket, then taking off out the door with the arms waving, the feet skidding and the legs flying across the road.

I looked back as I dived into the car, seeing them cheek to jowl staring at the empty car, looking for the mammy. I gave a big cheery wave and a thumbs-up, then looked up to see little Adolf gamely making his way down to me. He was looking all the business with the hat wobbling on his head and the little legs buckling under him. His eyes were now locked on me, desperate to grab hold. I roared up the engine, lashing away the car, then tore to a stop right beside him on the double yellow line, pulling down the window. His chin wobbled and the hat shook as he swivelled to take me in.

'Ye're lookin very prosperous,' I grinned, pointing at the belly bursting out of the jacket. 'You should take it easy. You'll have a heart attack one of these days, Adolf! Then the missus won't have to be creeping around behind your back with the milkman,' I said, lowering my voice to a confidential whisper.

'What? The impudence! I'm not standing for this! That's it! I'm givin you a ticket,' he roared, shifting fast to get in front and take down my registration.

'Yeah! An I'm going to shove a red-hot poker up your arse, Adolf!' I snorted.

'That's it! I'm getting the guards for you. You're now after breaking a very serious law, threatening me! I have witnesses!' he screamed, looking around at a pensioner holding the lead of a geriatric mutt as it stopped for a piss, then sniffed. Now satisfied, it lifted the head, staring into the distance, then got moving and creaked off.

We watched as the pensioner suddenly came to life and shuffled after it, wanting to leave Adolf and the madness behind. Adolf watched them slowly make their way in the distance, then he whipped back on me.

'You stay right there! I'm making a citizen's arrest!' he croaked, letting out a tortured scream, waving the fist, shouting, 'POLICE! Get the guards!'

Fuck! I spun me head around seeing if there was a blue bottle galvanised into action? No, no sign of a copper beetling down the road with the flat feet hammering the footpath, book at the ready to sort me out. No! Nothing! Just a few heads turning to see what the fuss was about, saw it was only Adolf and kept moving. He's the man everyone loves to hate.

'Tut-tut! The heart! The heart,' I said slowly, really tormenting him now. 'Think of the wife, Adolf,' I warned, then took off in a puff of smoke, screaming up the road, melting tar.

'Home,' I breathed, walking back into the silent house. I stopped in the hall to throw down my bag, leaving the keys sitting on the table.

I lifted my shoulders, taking in a deep breath, feeling a tingle of excitement running through me. Right, better keep moving, things to do. First things first, get that phone call made. 'Holiday time! Nothing to do and all day to do it,' I sang, rushing for the phone. I waited, hearing it ring out, sounding like it is shrilling to an empty house. Nope! Not there, I thought, just about to hang up.

'Hello!' a voice boomed. My heart leapt, remembering the voice that gave so much pleasure, then quivered with remembered pain. Fuck! I am just like Pavlov's dog.

'Well, hello there,' I said sexily, hearing the ghost of a younger self suddenly spring to life. I clung to it momentarily, letting the bittersweet feelings wash over me, then reined them in as disgust poured out. That's it! Now delusional, I'm seeing a young Ralph.

'Martha?'

'Who else? Brigitte Bardot? I think you would have to dig her up!'

'No, you will do me nicely,' he said quietly, dropping his voice. 'How are you, my love? I was just this minute thinking of you. I was about to telephone. What is happening with you? All set for your break?'

'Oh, yes, happy days!'

'So, what are the arrangements, Martha? When shall I see you? Tomorrow night, I hope!'

'Don't be silly, Ralph! I'm a busy woman.'

'No! This is impossible. I do not see enough of you. I miss you, darling,' he whined, lowering his voice like he was in pain.

'Well, I will be in London on Friday, stay the week there with friends, then buy the plane ticket and travel over to you in France, arriving on the following Monday. I should get there sometime in the evening. How about that?'

'Oh, really, Martha, must you? I don't want to share you. As it is, we don't see enough of each other. You abandon me for too long,' he moaned, trying to make it into a joke.

Ah, here! Fuck this, I thought, getting a sudden rush of annoyance heating up the chest. 'Well! You live there and I have my commitments here. Commitments being the operative word, Ralph dear, as you once kept telling me.' I sniffed long and slowly, showing no mercy at the lonely cry tearing out of him, then suddenly getting a lovely sense of satisfaction out of that. Hmm, nothing like having the boot on the other foot. For the first time in his life it's hitting him what it feels like to be second best.

The phone went silent while he worked his head around that one. I listened, hearing the deep sighs of pity for himself, then the quick breaths as the brain suddenly came up with the idea I might not turn up at all.

'Yes,' he said slowly, speaking quietly like he was still thinking.

'Come on, Ralph! Say something or I'm going. I need to get moving. I have things to do,' I said, getting irritated at hearing nothing but the heavy breathing out of him. Now he's retired, he has all the time in the world to do nothing but take life easy.

'Too late have I loved thee,' he suddenly breathed heavily, sounding like it was a last gasp. 'We should have married. I should have married you!' he suddenly said, coming to life.

I listened, thinking about that, as a cold anger started to turn my blood to ice. All them years of emptiness, heartache, longing and loss. Because of him, twice I ran panicked. First time into that brick wall Ulick, knocking myself senseless with the shock of finding myself trapped, then stumbling out the other end bruised and battered. The second time I thought I had more sense. But only enough to get out of that mess and use the anger wisely. I took on fighting the world and walked away with my winning share. Oh, by hell did I just! Oh, yes! Now I am on equal terms with the best of them. Free, independent, no Jackser, no Ralph digging a hole in my heart. I made my own way and I am sitting on top of the world. My children are now ready to face out into a different world. It won't be as I once did, because they will be equipped.

'The world is ruled by law, kids. It dictates our every breathing moment,' I told them. 'Learn what it's about and be nobody's fool! Look down on no one and look up to nobody. Follow your gut feeling, trust your instincts and if something feels wrong, then it is! There is no need to search the world for answers. It is blind because it sees only what it wants and deaf because it listens only to what it wants to hear. In you lies truth, love, peace and the beauty that you are your own unique self. Have the will and you can move mountains. You carry all that power inside you. Just listen and you will hear it, be still and you will feel it. That is what I learned, making my way through the world.'

I wonder do they hear me, those children of mine, never mind even listen. Oh, well, they will find their own path. Youth is not wasted on the young. They need it to keep them going because they are so bloody daft. Oh, what fun it is to be young! But they can keep it. Once was enough for me!

Already I have done myself a big favour by letting go of the hidden pain. Now the world and his wife knows who I really was. I am free . . . Almost! Because here we go again. Ralph! The man who has wafted through life like a pharaoh on his throne – always, but always, the world thrown at his feet. The insensitive bastard – did he ever really understand the pain he cost me? Now he is old, left out to graze, and is sad and lonely – it is now he wants me, only now. He's had it all, now he wants the rest – a woman to cosset him when he has nothing better to do. The arrogant swine! It takes my breath away. Right, Ralph, two can play that game. Let's see where it goes.

'Ralph! Are you telling me now you never really loved me? It's only now dawning on you that you do and should have married me?'

'No, of course not. I have always loved you, but I do regret not marrying you.'

'Oh, right,' I said, shaking my head slowly, not doubting a word of the regret bit.

He said nothing while my brain ticked away, letting this bit of information slowly warm my belly. Oh, am I going to enjoy this!

Suddenly he interrupted, steaming into my thoughts, wanting to get in and spill his guts while the going was good.

'We could still be married!' he whispered, holding his breath in hope, chancing his fucking arm.

'Are you asking me to marry you?' I said quietly.

'Yes, my love. I want that more than anything,' he said, sounding like what God must have to his apostles when handing out the ten commandments. I could hear the sacred, solemn and commanding gravitas as he intoned this decision. Then he took in a sharp breath, waiting, holding it like his life depended on it.

'So ask me!' I said, sensing my time has come to clear my path strewn with a rubble of pain all thrown there by Ralph. A lifetime of loneliness, longing, hoping and waiting. Then a nothingness – just an empty heart rattling with echoes of the yesterdays' fading hopes and dying dreams. But it didn't kill me. It filled me with the wisdom of age as we look less for ourselves and more out for others. For me, it was my little ones!

'Really! Oh, my darling! You would like me to propose to you?' he said, sounding like he was flying to the moon.

'Yes!' I said quietly, nodding my head solemnly, feeling like the astronaut flying him there. I'm all command and fully in control.

'Oh, darling, would you really become my wife? I do so want to be your husband,' he laughed, letting his voice rise with the excitement.

I took in a deep breath. 'No, Ralph! Definitely not! First there's the little matter of "geriatric droop" and "little" is the operative word in this matter . . .'

'WHAT?!' he shouted. 'That is balderdash! Just you . . .'

'Don't interrupt, Ralph! I'm not finished!' I ordered.

'Very well! Carry on!' he commanded, now sounding cold, shock and disappointment suddenly replacing his joy.

I breathed in slowly and heavily, letting it out in a controlled nice and easy air of no hurry on me, then continued.

'Now, while you are fast galloping into your twilight years, I am a woman in my prime. I am still living in hopes of abandoning myself to some stunning stud who will convince me to throw away my vow of perpetual virginity! And . . .'

'Oh, really, Martha! What are you bloody on about? Of course I am still virile . . .'

'WE WOULD SPEND A BLEEDIN FORTUNE ON VIAGRA!

And that's only for a start,' I screamed, letting fly the rage erupting like a volcano.

Wait! That's no good. Forget that, Martha. Cool down. Vengeance, when a dish eaten cold, should be savoured slowly – you waited long enough for it! You want him to get the message, feel what you once felt. Bastard – even now he's still at it. The ego of him! He's now offering me the scrapings from the bottom of the pot! I snorted, letting my chest heave up and down, feeling the rage blinding me with red spots sparking in front of my eyeballs. I'm running away with myself again! It's too much. I have to get the boot in!

Enough, Martha, I told meself quietly. For fuck sake, calm down! Jaysus, I must have burst a blood vessel.

'Darling, please . . .'

'Don't darling me, Ralph Fitzgerald! You are only asking me now to marry you because you want me to push you around in your bleedin wheelchair,' I hissed. Then paused as a thought suddenly struck me. Hang on – there could be something in this! He's rich! Very rich . . . I was now getting the picture. All that money – isn't it better to be an old man's darling than a young man's slave? Definitely! Oh, definitely, indeed it is. Right! Now in for the kill.

'Ralph,' I croaked, hearing it come out in a strangled gasp now I was panting from excitement – it was all mixing with the anger.

'Ralph,' I coughed, hearing my voice mellow down into a sexy husk, letting a huge grin spread across my face. Softly softly catchee monkey! Better it come late than never.

'Yes, darling?' he sighed, sounding relieved I had calmed down.

I paused, trying to work out the best way of saying it.

'Go on, darling. What is it, my love?' he said, trying to coax me.

'Eh!' Cough. I was now sounding like the ma. 'What would we do for money? I mean, where would we live? We would have to sell your house in France. Or . . . keep it for the weekends? Or, wait, keep my house for the weekends? And, eh . . .'

'I do not need a wheelchair!' he barked. 'Nor do I yet need the aid of Viagra,' he mumbled, giving a half-laugh.

'Oh, if you say so, Ralph, I would well believe you!' I grinned happily, then settled to go straight in for the jugular. 'But now, more important pressing matters to discuss, Ralph. What about your money? Would

I get to inherit it all? Your estate, your entire assets clear and without impediment?'

The air suddenly changed, charged, then surged with exploding atoms as I listened, hearing it crackling through the silence. Then there was a slow deep breath.

'Martha, my wife would be well provided for! Yes, of course, she would inherit my estate. But I do see now where you are coming from,' he snapped coldly. 'I . . . this is so unworthy!'

Then silence. I waited, but everything had suddenly gone quiet.

I listened, now hearing only the dialling tone. I wonder were we cut off? 'Hello!' I shook the phone, rattling it, wondering what was happening. I looked, seeing it was still plugged into the socket. No, I hadn't pulled it out. Then it hit me – the fucker! He hung up on me. I stared at the phone with my mouth hanging open, then dropped it gently back into its cradle, still staring, still caught in the moment when I felt a sudden rush erupting. It screamed out of me, laughing. I doubled up, roaring the head off meself. Jaysus! You old fool. I don't need you or your money! Shows how much the little you know about me! No, Doctor . . . Father Ralph Fitzgerald, that road is closed long ago with no way back.

Oh, Ralph Fitzgerald, you never did love me then, I thought sadly, and you don't love me now. You just need me. 'No,' I muttered quietly, 'my love once given is for ever. I have always loved you, Ralph, and deep down I always will. But I wouldn't sell my soul to the devil and let you win! Because what is left of my life is worth more than you now, and all your money, can give me.'

For some reason, tears were streaming down my face. I was crying for all the tears shed for the loss of a love that never really existed. I blew my nose and wiped them away, then grabbed my coat and bag, heading out for the evening. Right, dinner with Yvonne then pack later. Celebration time – holidays! I told myself, lifting my shoulders and straightening myself to make the picture of Ralph in his loneliness disappear. It's funny, but this is not the outcome I expected.

'Bye, Ralphie,' I whispered, 'pity you didn't tune in earlier when I recently landed myself back into your life, then. You would have seen I had a hidden agenda. Oh, yes! Vengeance is indeed a dish best eaten cold.'

Or is it? I don't feel triumphant with victory, just a little diminished

– hollow. Yet, you caused me so much pain and sadness, I knew this day would come. We have spent a lifetime weaving our way in and out of each other's lives – embracing like two doomed lovers, then fleeing into the night. For me, racing from an agony of demons and a sense of loss so great it plunged me thundering back into a pitch-black darkness of stormy seas, I have been lashed, battered and thrown. But always in my heart I knew I would ride it out. There is a higher power and I prayed it would take me to sanctuary and land me down in a safe port. I was right to believe, because I am there now.

Yes, it was as if our life played out on the open seas. One with all the majesty of a great ocean liner; the other, a small rust bucket. You stopped to offer assistance, comfort and a few words of kindness but then sailed off into the sunset, leaving me clinging to a raft. Now more forlorn and drifting directionless, I was heading deeper into very dangerous waters. All I could do was cling on as the vast ocean sea swept me up and hurtled me down, dragging me all the way into a darkness, a nothingness, with a treacherous sea of murderous loneliness. Oh, it nearly killed me. I almost drowned.

Would I have been better off if our paths hadn't crossed on that dark fateful winter night so very long ago? I only know we met again and this time we were almost equal. It was full of promise, but yet again he took sail, leaving me to face into the wind and take more chances. Too late I saw the dark menacing clouds descending over my head. That was only when I was in the thick of it. Nothing for it but to battle on, the future promising even more vicious and treacherous snares. I was to meet unfettered madness revelling in a pure form of evil so villainous it made even Jackser look innocent. It was all waiting for me, but on and on I ploughed, vowing never to look back.

Not until now, when we have met again. Only this time he is shipwrecked, stranded on a lonely island of old age with no way off. It is he who now watches forlornly as I sail away in all my majesty, heading for the sunset. So be it! This is the course he set himself all those long years ago. The march of time has finally caught up with him and now he knows what it feels like to bleed from the raw pain of loneliness just as I once did. I only hope his God is merciful, as mine was to me.

34

I stared at the manuscript, looking at the lines of words filling up the white spaces that made up a document. For now they were nothing, just letters sitting there staring back at me that would mean nothing to no one if left alone. All the huff and puff, the blood, sweat and tears, the agony and the ecstasy that has poured into the writing of these words means nothing while they just sit there. But it has been my life, my guts, my soul. I feel emptied now. No, I don't want to part with this. Once I hand this over, it feels like I will be giving my soul to the world and the devil to do with me what they will.

'Oh, just think about it, Martha,' I muttered, sighing long and hard, feeling very weary as I closed the laptop on the last book in the 'Ma' series – *Ma, Jackser's Dyin Alone.* 'Yes, the very last one,' I sighed. 'Seven books in all. Now it really is over,' I muttered, feeling my heart plunge to sit in my belly. I'm not sending this to the publishers and I don't know why. But maybe I'm just tired after coming to the end of a long and painful aul journey. I have been writing non-stop since the few years after Jackser died. I forgave him and that opened the door to setting me free. But how could I be free when I didn't know who I was? I had discovered bits of me when sitting at Jackser's bedside – it was during the last days of his life when he lay dying. So, there was nothing for it now but to go back and find the rest.

It was the real Martha Long, 'the little one', who had forgiven Jackser, but I had left her behind because she wasn't good enough for me. Now I needed to find her and ask forgiveness. Oh, the road was hard and sometimes hell with the devil on my back, but each book was a landmark stripping away the masks. Now I'm sitting gaping, staring inside myself, I feel naked and exposed, left bare without any masks to hide behind. Jesus, I'm looking at myself as I truly am! Do

I really want to cover up again? Is that what this is about, what is really wrong with me? No! I wouldn't want to go back to being a shadow, a woman wafting through life like the world was her stage. She was hollow, because no one could get close. She could be whatever you wanted her to be; she had a mask for every occasion. The isolation was so lonely sometimes I felt like I could be from another planet. Nobody on this earth knew the real me; I didn't even know myself.

'Ready, Mum! WE HAVE TO LEAVE! HURRY!'

I lifted my head, letting it shoot from my chest as the door blew open bringing a sudden explosion of noise ripping through my skull, wind blowing the breath out of me and the nostrils flaring in a puff of perfume that threatened to suffocate me.

'TAKE IT EASY!' I squealed, getting a fright from the young walking dynamo of energy with the voice loud enough to wake the dead, never mind wake me from my melancholic musings about wanting to put myself back into a private place where no one could get their hands on me.

'What are you doing, Mum?' my daughter asked absent-mindedly, as she examined herself in the mirror over the fireplace.

I eyed her sourly, wondering why she asked the bloody question if she can't even bother to look at me. W.C. Fields was right – anyone who can't stand dogs and kids can't be all that bad. Right! Let's see what she thinks.

'Oh! Well, I'll tell you if you're interested. Do you want to hear?'

'Of course I do, Mum!' she said, outraged at the idea I would even think she wasn't fascinated by my daily doings.

'I'm writing about my life,' I said, giving another look to see if she was still interested.

'Hurry, Mum! Tell me! I have to go!'

'OK,' I said, quickly taking a sharp intake of breath. 'I have just been writing about my life growing up in a harem, then how I ran me own brothel. Now I do the odd few killings as a hit woman,' I muttered. 'Teenagers are my speciality. You would be surprised at how many mothers want to choke them but can't bring themself to do it!' I said conversationally, nodding my head gently.

'Oh! Great!' she sang, slapping her lips together, checking to see if her lipstick was looking good, then leaning in closer to examine her bright green eyes, looking even brighter now with the help of something to lift and dazzle, blinding you with the beauty.

'We're off! Hurry, Mum! We don't want to miss our flights!' she suddenly roared, managing to tear herself away from such beauty and finally rest her eyes on me without seeing a thing. Her mind was now on more important things. Holidays, freedom without me, Attila the hen, roping her in and keeping her in line. I didn't shift meself. I sat frozen with the chin resting on the hands, staring, waiting to get her full attention.

'What? What's wrong?' she puffed, widening the big eyes and flicking back the long silk tresses to get a better look at me.

'Did you hear even one word I said?' I sniffed, feeling very sorry and fed up they had never bothered to ask about my writing. All that slaving over a hot laptop.

'You two are spoilt!' is all I could get out before turning my head away and giving up. She stared down at the laptop now closed as I muttered, 'I have just finished the last book. That's it! My journey ends there,' I said, wondering why I felt so empty and vulnerable.

There was silence as she stared at me, now really listening, hearing what I was saying. 'Mum,' she whispered, 'when we read your first book, we were shocked. We couldn't read any more,' she said quietly, sitting down and putting her arm around me. 'We still can't understand how you did it all, even though we saw you do it. Everything you touch turns to gold. You really are extraordinary, Mum! Even for someone who has had every advantage your life would have been a brilliant success. But you did it all without any help. You came from nothing, Mum! You didn't even go to school! It really is astonishing how much you have achieved. Now, to crown it all, you have written all those books,' she said, dropping her eyes, thinking about it.

I said nothing, just listened. Then I sighed, wanting her to understand something very important.

'Listen to me, pet. I hope I have given you something more important than just a comfortable life. You are at the end of your childhood. Your school days are now behind you. Soon you and your brother will be going to university. You earned a place at a top college and that's a huge achievement. It rivals anything the best of the best has to offer.

They accepted you because you are among the cream of the crop, the next batch of movers and shakers. This is it – your time has come. Now you are going to take your first step as an adult building your own life. I only hope I have given you enough goodness, nourished you with enough care and love to cope with whatever the world throws at you. These people will have different values. They will use you, chew you up and spit you out if you let them. They are used to the best money can buy. The excitement of drugs, sex, drink – they will have and want it all. So stand back, don't get too close until you see what you are dealing with. Happiness not earned is not worth having. You can't be happy at the expense of someone else's misery. I hope now you have learned to tell the difference and be guided by that. Hold your head up, look the world straight in the eye and say, "Here I am, this is me – take me or leave me!"'

'Mum, there is no need to worry about us. You just take care of yourself now. Because we worry about you. We know you had to fight hard, but it won't be like that for us. We had a very comfortable upbringing and you gave us that. You even managed to be at home waiting with our dinner on the table when we came in from school. A lot of families with even two parents find that difficult, because it's not easy. We want to make you proud of us because we are very proud of you, Mum,' she said softly, looking straight into my eyes. Then she let go and looked at me, nodding her head gently, saying, 'We will make you proud.'

I stared back at her, seeing what a lovely young woman she is. Yes, I thought, letting my mind wander back into the distance. These two were such a gift. When I was in my darkest hour, all I had to do was hang on. It was all just waiting for me around the next corner.

Come on, Martha! Don't be afraid. It won't bite you! Accept it – SUCCESS! I found myself at last. I have come home. I am comfortable in my own skin. I am the raw and unvarnished, the real Martha Long! Yeah, life is a bowl of cherries! You were right about that one, Martha. But wrong about 'Laugh and the world will laugh with you; cry and you cry alone'. Well, I don't have to cry alone. The world out there has cried with me. God, it's packed with people just like me! All wanting to just fit in and say 'I'm home', then feel the cares of the world slip away as you feel safe and warm.

ENVOI

To all my readers, without whom these books would not see the light of day. My journey wobbling along a sometimes treacherous and merciless path of life would now be just fading private memories when I hurtle down the other side of the mountain, heading towards the last days of my end. Now, because of you, I will not be planted, taking with me the memories of a life once lived.

For that, dear readers, I thank you.

Also, not since my lonely journey recording my very early years in *Ma, He Sold Me for a Few Cigarettes* have I ever again felt that loneliness when I sat to put pen to paper and continue that journey. From then on, I felt the spirit of your goodness leaning over my shoulder. It was your kindness, your good wishes, your total acceptance and understanding of me as just one person sharing my life with you. You appreciated it; you even said it helped you. What more could I ask for?

I kept going because you were willing to listen. It has been worth every nightmare come back to haunt me. I have laughed, cried and dripped snots, but I kept going, knowing you were waiting. You cared, so my life did matter. You made me somebody! You are somebody to me.

You are the little girl who lost her mother through cancer. Thank you, darling, for telling me I helped you get out of bed and face the day. Keep going, little one. You have a whole lifetime ahead of you, sweetheart, just as I once did.

You are the lonely mother, faced with bringing a child up alone.

You are the tortured soul isolated from the world, suffering from deep depression. It may even bring you to the edge, as it did me. But life is just around the next corner – only don't let go! Just hang on. It's coming!

You are the eighty-year-old grandmother now living in a faraway land, forced to carry the dreadful secret of the monster's shame who robbed you of your childhood. It is only now you whisper it, as you write to me of your pain.

So, for all of you – you matter to me. We have helped each other along the way. What more do we need but just to know we are not alone? You gave me that.

I say this to you quietly, because it comes from very deep in my heart:

Thank you. I wish you all peace and contentment.

THE END